Advanced JavaServer Pages™

DAVID M. GEARY

Prentice Hall PTR, Upper Saddle River, NJ 07458
www.phptr.com

Sun Microsystems Press
A Prentice Hall Title

Editorial/Production Supervision: *Patti Guerrieri*
Acquisitions Editor: *Gregory G. Doench*
Editorial Assistant: *Brandt Kenna*
Marketing Manager: *Debby vanDijk*
Manufacturing Manager: *Maura Zaldivar*
Cover Design Director: *Jerry Votta*
Cover Designer: *Anthony Gemmellaro*
Art Director: *Gail Cocker-Bogusz*
Series Design: *Meg VanArsdale*

Sun Microsystems Press
Marketing Manager: *Michael Llwyd Alread*
Publisher: *Rachel Borden*

© 2001 Sun Microsystems, Inc.—
Published by Prentice Hall PTR
Prentice-Hall , Inc.
Upper Saddle River, NJ 07458

Printed in the United States of America

10 9 8 7 6 5 4 3 2 1

ISBN 0-13-030704-1

Sun Microsystems Press

A Prentice Hall Title

For Anjin, Mariko, and Kiku

Contents

Preface

Shortly after the Swing volume of *Graphic Java* was published in March 1999, I became aware of the mass exodus from client-side Java to server-side Java. Because I make a living writing books, I took that exodus very seriously, so I began exploring server-side Java in search of a technology that would be appropriate for my next book. At first, I was enamored with XML, XSLT, and Java, and I spent a good deal of time experimenting with those technologies. But as exciting as those technologies are, it seemed to me that they were on the periphery of developing web applications, and I wanted something that was directly involved in the creation of web applications. Then I discovered servlets.

To be honest, I wasn't too excited about servlets. Were software developers really going to create user interfaces by generating HTML with print statements from the guts of some servlet? I knew of at least one software developer that was not. Since 1984, I've had the good fortune to develop software by using a number of object-oriented languages and very cool user interface toolkits. I've developed applications in Smalltalk, Eiffel, and NeXTSTEP, and it seemed to me that developing applications with HTML—especially HTML manually generated from servlets—was akin to trading in a Ferrari for a Yugo. Then I discovered JSP.

Although back in 1999 JSP was in its infancy, it was easy to see its potential. Here was a way to mix Java with HTML, which opened the door to all kinds of interesting possibilities. And in the Future Directions section of the JSP 1.0 specification, I saw something that really caught my eye: *A portable tag extension mechanism is being considered for the JSP 1.1 specification. This mechanism permits the description of tags that can be used from any JSP page.* Wow. With custom tags you could encapsulate Java code, which would essentially allow you to create custom components, in the form of tags, that could be used in conjunction with HTML. From then on, I knew that my next book would be about JSP.

So I started to write an introductory JSP book, and I actually wrote the first chapter of that book before I realized two things. First, there was going to be a glut of introductory JSP books, and I did not want to compete against all of those books. Second, and most important, that first chapter was boring, and I hate to read boring books, let alone write them. So, I decided to write this book instead.

What This Book Is About

As its name suggests, this book is an advanced treatment of JavaServer Pages. The central theme of this book is the design and implementation of flexible, extensible, and maintainable applications with beans, servlets, and JSP.

This book begins where most introductory JSP books leave off, by showing you how to implement JSP custom tags. The ability to create custom tags is arguably JSP's greatest strength because it allows software developers and page authors to work in parallel with few dependencies. Subsequent chapters cover HTML forms, JSP templates, Model 1 and Model 2 architectures, a simple Model 2 framework, handling events, internationalization, security, databases, and XML. This book concludes with a comprehensive case study that shows how to use the techniques discussed in this book to develop a nontrivial web application.

The Servlet and JSP APIs This Book Depends Upon

The code in this book depends upon the Servlet 2.2 and JSP 1.1 specifications. Although the Servlet 2.3 and JSP 1.2 specifications were first released in draft form in November 2000, as this book went to press they were still in a state of flux. Because servlet filters are arguably the most important addition to the Servlet 2.3 specification, that topic is covered in "Servlet Filters" on page 470; however, you should be aware that the code in that appendix is very likely to change by the time you read this.

How This Book's Code Was Tested

I tested all of the code in this book with Tomcat 3.2.1. If a code example from this book does not work correctly with Tomcat 3.2.1, such as the example in "Digest Authentication" on page 259, that fact is pointed out in the book's text.

Because Tomcat is the reference implementation for the Servlet and JSP specifications, all of the code in this book should work with any servlet container that conforms to the Servlet 2.2 and JSP 1.1 (or higher) specifications. If an example from this book does not work with your servlet container, it is most likely a bug in that servlet container.

I also tested all of the code in this book against Resin 1.2, which is an excellent servlet container available from `http://www.caucho.com`. As a general rule, it is beneficial to test your code against more than one servlet container to ensure correctness and portability.

This Book's Audience

This book was written for Java developers with a basic understanding of servlets and JSP. For most Java developers, this should be their second book that covers servlets and JSP. If you are new to servlets and JSP, I recommend the following books for your first book on those topics:

- *Core Servlets and JSP* by Marty Hall, Sun Microsystems Press

- *Java Servlet Programming* by Jason Hunter, O'Reilly

- *Web Development with JavaServer Pages* by Fields and Kolb, Manning

It also won't hurt to have a basic understanding of design patterns and the Unified Modeling Language (UML). This book demonstrates how to implement a number of design patterns in JSP-based web applications and uses UML class and sequence diagrams to show how classes are related and how they interact, respectively. See page 181 for a list of resources on design patterns and UML.

This book was *not* written for page authors. If you are a page author with no Java experience, you will be better served by one of the books listed above.

How This Book Was Written

Designing object-oriented software is very much an iterative process. You start with a few classes and build on them, all the while iterating over classes, both old and new, as you integrate them to build an ever-evolving system. In object-oriented parlance, that process is known as refactoring.

After working for 15 years as a software engineer, I tend to write books the way I write software. Each of this book's chapters started out in humble fashion. And each chapter was subsequently refactored into the final product that you hold in your hands.

You can get a glimpse into this process by looking at a JavaWorld article that I wrote about JSP templates.[1] That article is the first cut of this book's Templates chapter, so you can see where the process started for that chapter and where it ended; both the chapter and the code that it discusses underwent much refactoring.

How To Use This Book

This book is not a novel, so I don't expect anyone to sit down and read it cover to cover. Because most readers will read chapters out of order in a random fashion, nearly every chapter in the book can stand on its own. There is one exception to that rule. Chapter 6, which discusses a simple Model 2 framework, depends on Chapter 5, which introduces the Model 2 architecture. Chapter 6 retrofits an example from Chapter 5; therefore, Chapter 5 is a prerequisite for Chapter 6.

The last chapter in this book is a comprehensive case study that employs the techniques discussed throughout this book to implement a nontrivial web application. You can read (or most likely, skim) that chapter first to get a feel for those techniques, or you can read it last to see how to integrate those techniques. Or you can do both.

---

1. See `http://developer.java.sun.com/developer/technical Articles/javaserverpages/jsp_templates`.

This Book's Custom Tag Libraries

This book discusses the implementation of approximately 50 JSP custom tags, ranging from internationalization tags to tags that use XML's Document Object Model to parse XML. There are no legal restrictions whatsoever on those tags, so you are free to use those tags in any manner you deem appropriate. See "This Book's Code" on page xvii to see how you can download those tags.

This book's custom tags serve two purposes. First, they illustrate how you can implement your own custom tags. Second, they serve to reinforce the concepts discussed throughout this book. But those custom tags are not the focus of this book; rather, it's the concepts that those tags embody that are important. For example, if you look at the internationalization chapter, you will see that most of that chapter is dedicated to internationalizing text, numbers, dates, and currency in a JSP-based web application. The last few pages of that chapter show how to implement two custom tags that perform internationalization. But it's the internationalization concepts, and not the custom tags, that take center stage in that chapter.

This Book's Code

You can download all of the code from this book, including the book's custom tag libraries, from the following URL: http://www.phptr.com/advjsp.

Conventions Used in This Book

Table P-1 shows the coding conventions used in this book.

Table P-1 Coding Conventions

Convention	Example
Class names have initial capital letters.	`public class ClassName`
Method names have initial lower case, and the rest of the words have an initial capital letter.	`getLength`
Variable names have initial lower case, and the rest of the words have an initial capital letter.	`private int length` `private int bufferLength`

Note that, for the most part, methods are referred to without their arguments; however, arguments are included when the discussion warrants them.

Table P-2 shows the typographic conventions used in this book.

Table P-2 Typographic Conventions

Typeface or Symbol	Description
courier	Indicates a command, file name, class name, method, argument, Java keyword, HTML tag, file content, code excerpt, or URL.
bold courier	Indicates a sample command-line entry.
italics	Indicates definitions, emphasis, a book title, or a variable that should be replaced with a valid value.

Acknowledgments

Although my name is on the cover, many people have made contributions to this book. First, I would like to thank my reviewers, who provided me with a great deal of valuable feedback.

Craig McClanahan, who is the lead developer for Tomcat and the Apache Struts JSP application framework, offered many insights into servlets and JSP that only someone with his level of expertise could have provided.

Scott Ferguson, the developer of the Resin servlet container, provided excellent review comments and, much to my surprise, also offered good advice on writing. Not only are technical details in the book more accurate because of his comments, but this book also provides more motivation for readers and presents topics in a more logical sequence because of Scott's review comments.

Larry Cable, who coauthored the original JSP specification, was also instrumental in making this book more robust; for example, the detailed discussion of custom tag body content in the Custom Tag Advanced Topics chapter would not be in this book if it were not for one of Larry's many excellent suggestions.

Rob Gordon, with whom I had the pleasure of working when I was an employee at Sun Microsystems, also provided many insightful review comments that only someone with his level of expertise in writing, Java, and object-oriented software development could provide.

Besides my reviewers, I would also like to thank the folks on the Struts mailing list who provided excellent feedback on the JSP templates custom tag library that I contributed to Struts. With their feedback, I was able to vastly improve that tag library, which is discussed at length in this book's Templates chapter. Cedric Dumoulin deserves special mention for his ideas on extending that original tag library to include component capabilities.

I would also like to thank Yun Sang Jung and Chen Jia Ping, who translated English properties files to Korean and Chinese, respectively, for the I18N and Case Study chapters.

Rational Rose Software provided me with a copy of Rational Rose for Java, which was used for all of the UML diagrams in this book.

Mary Lou Nohr, who has been my editor since the first edition of *Graphic Java* way back in 1996, once again did a masterful job of making substantial improvements to my writing.

Greg Doench, from Prentice Hall, and Rachel Borden, from Sun Microsystems Press, also deserve mention for having faith in me and for helping to pull this book together. Patti Guerrieri from Prentice Hall, who is always a pleasure to work with, did a great job of taking my final manuscript and polishing it into this book.

Finally, as always, I would like to thank Lesa and Ashley Anna Geary. Without their patience and understanding, I would never have been able to get this book out the door. A final tip of the hat to Blazey who has been my constant companion while writing this book.

Advanced JavaServer Pages™

CUSTOM TAG
FUNDAMENTALS

Topics in this Chapter

Chapter 1

XML is a hot technology, in no small part because it's a simple metalanguage used to create tags. XML tags represent data specific to a particular domain; for example, the following XML fragment represents a CD collection:

```
<cd_collection>
  <cd>
    <artist>Radiohead</artist>
    <title>OK Computer</title>
    <price>$14.99</price>
  </cd>
  ...
</cd_collection>
```

Like XML, JSP can be used to create tags; however, whereas XML tags represent *data*, JSP custom tags represent *functionality* specific to a particular domain.[1] For example, the JSP fragment listed in Example 1-1 uses custom tags to display a table from a database:

---

1. The term *custom tag* differentiates between built-in tags and user-implemented (custom) tags. XML has no built-in tags, so there is no need to differentiate.

Example 1-1   Database Access with Custom Tags

```
<html><title>Database Example</title>
<head>
    <%@ taglib uri='/WEB-INF/tlds/database.tld' prefix='database'%>
</head>
<body>

<database:connect database='F:/databases/sunpress'>
   <database:query>
      SELECT * FROM Customers, Orders
   </database:query>

   <table border='2' cellpadding='5'>
      <database:columnNames columnName='column_name'>
         <th><%= column_name %></th>
      </database:columnNames>

      <database:rows><tr>
         <tr><database:columns columnValue='column_value'>
            <td><%= column_value %></td>
         </database:columns></tr>
      </database:rows>
   </table>
</database:connect>

</body>
</html>
```

Example 1-1 creates an HTML table with a mixture of HTML and JSP custom tags. The connect tag makes a database connection, the query tag performs a database query, and rows, columns, and columnNames iterate over the query results.

JSP custom tags can be quite sophisticated, as Example 1-1 illustrates. The query tag interprets its body content as SQL, and the connection and query tags collaborate with other tags in the page. The columns and columnNames tags iterate over the query result and create scripting variables named by the JSP developer. In the code fragment listed in Example 1-1, those names are column_name and column_value.

Custom tags have an impressive list of features; they can:

- Have a body or be empty
- Be nested arbitrarily deep within other custom tags
- Manipulate flow of control; for example, if statement and iteration

- Manipulate the contents of their bodies; for example, filtering and editing
- Collaborate with other tags on a page
- Access page information (request, response, session, etc.)
- Create scripting variables

JSP custom tags conform to the XML specification, so they are, in fact, XML tags. This is significant because it means that JSP custom tags can be manipulated in XML and HTML tools.

All of the custom tags in Example 1-1 have start and end tags with body content in between. Custom tags can also be empty, where the start and end tags are combined, like this:

```
<prefix:someTag/>
```

All JSP custom tags are grouped into libraries. Custom tags are distinguished by a prefix associated with their library, which allows tags of the same name from different libraries to be used together.

As of the JSP 1.1 specification, an initiative is underway to specify a standard tag library in a future version of the specification.[2] That tag library will include tags for database access and a number of other useful utility tags.

JSP Tip

Custom Tags Are JSP's Most Powerful Feature

Custom tags afford software developers and page authors the freedom to work independently. Page authors can concentrate on using sets of tags, such as HTML, XML, or JSP to create web sites. Software developers can concentrate on implementing low-level functionality, such as internationalization or database access, which is subsequently made available to page authors in the form of custom tags.

Using Custom Tags—The JSP File

Figure 1-1 shows a JSP page that uses the simplest of custom tags—one that has no attributes and no body. The tag is a hit counter that keeps track of the number of times a JSP page has been accessed.

---

2.   The initiative is a Java Specification Request (JSR)—see http://java.sun.com.

Advanced JavaServer Pages

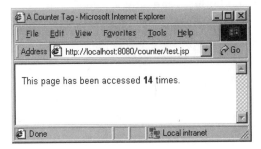

Figure 1-1 A Counter Tag

The JSP page shown in Figure 1-1 is listed in Example 1-2.a.

Example 1-2.a /test.jsp

```
<html><head><title>A Counter Tag</title></head>
<body>

<%@ taglib uri='/WEB-INF/tlds/counter.tld' prefix='util' %>

This page has been accessed <b><util:counter/></b> times.

</body></html>
```

Example 1-2.a includes a `taglib` directive specifying a URI that defines the library and its tags. That URI points to a tag library descriptor (TLD), thus the `tld` extension in `counter.tld`. The `taglib` directive also requires a `prefix` attribute that specifies the prefix used to access the library's tags; in Example 1-2.a, that prefix is `util`, so the counter tag is accessed with `<util:counter/>`.

The TLD in Example 1-2.a is located in `WEB-INF/tlds`. Locating the TLD there is not required but is recommended practice.

Defining Custom Tags—The TLD

A tag library descriptor is an XML document that defines a tag library and its tags. Example 1-2.b lists the TLD for the tag used in Example 1-2.a.

Example 1-2.b /WEB-INF/tlds/counter.tld

```
<?xml version="1.0" encoding="ISO-8859-1" ?>
<!DOCTYPE taglib PUBLIC
  "-//Sun Microsystems, Inc.//DTD JSP Tag Library 1.1//EN"
  "http://java.sun.com/j2ee/dtds/web-jsptaglibrary_1_1.dtd">
```

```
<taglib>
      <tlibversion>1.0</tlibversion>
      <jspversion>1.1</jspversion>
      <shortname>Sun Microsystems Press Tag Library</shortname>
      <info>This tag library has a single counter tag</info>

      <tag>
          <name>counter</name>
          <tagclass>tags.CounterTag</tagclass>
          <bodycontent>empty</bodycontent>
      </tag>
</taglib>
```

The first line of the file identifies it as an XML document. The second line further identifies the document type as taglib and supplies a URL to a document type definition (DTD) that defines the structure of taglib documents. That DTD is used by servlet containers to validate the document.

Tag libraries are defined with <taglib>. In Example 1-2.b, the tag library's version is specified as 1.0, and the library must be used with a JSP implementation that conforms to the 1.1 version (or later) of the JSP specification.

A short name is specified for the tag library listed in Example 1-2.b, in addition to some information about the library. Those values are typically used by page authoring tools.

Tags are defined with <tag>, which has two mandatory elements: the tag's <name> and its <tagclass>. The latter specifies the Java class that implements the tag's functionality. Those types of classes are known as tag handlers.

The counter tag's body content is specified as empty, meaning that it's illegal for counter tags to have a body.

Both <taglib> and <tag> have more elements than the ones used above. See "<taglib> and <tag>" on page 11 for more information on those tags and their elements.

Implementing Custom Tags—Tag Handlers

Tag handlers implement the Tag interface from javax.servlet.jsp.tagext. That interface defines six methods; the three that are most often used are listed below:[3]

---

3.   See "The Tag Interface" on page 25 for more information on the Tag interface.

```
int doStartTag() throws JspException
int doEndTag() throws JspException
void release()
```

Servlet containers invoke the `Tag` methods listed above in the order they are listed. The `doStartTag` and `doEndTag` methods are invoked at the start and end, respectively, of a tag. Both methods return `integer` constants defined in the `Tag` interface, specifying how the servlet container should proceed when the methods return.

The servlet container invokes the `release` method after calling `doEndTag`. The `release` method should release any resources the tag handler maintains.

Let's see how the counter tag's handler, listed in Example 1-2.c, implements the `Tag` methods listed above.

Example 1-2.c   /WEB-INF/classes/tags/CounterTag.java

```java
package tags;

import java.io.File;
import java.io.FileReader;
import java.io.FileWriter;
import java.io.IOException;

import javax.servlet.jsp.JspException;
import javax.servlet.jsp.tagext.TagSupport;
import javax.servlet.http.HttpServletRequest;

public class CounterTag extends TagSupport {
   private int count = 0;
   private File file = null;

   public int doStartTag() throws JspException {
      try {
         checkFile();
         readCount();
         pageContext.getOut().print(++count);
      }
      catch(java.io.IOException ex) {
         throw new JspException(ex.getMessage());
      }
      return SKIP_BODY;
   }
   public int doEndTag() throws JspException {
      saveCount();
      return EVAL_PAGE;
   }
```

```java
    private void checkFile() throws JspException, IOException {
        if(file == null) {
            file = new File(getCounterFilename());
            count = 0;
        }
        if(!file.exists()) {
            file.createNewFile();
            saveCount();
        }
    }
    private String getCounterFilename() {
        HttpServletRequest req = (HttpServletRequest)pageContext.
                                                     getRequest();
        String servletPath = req.getServletPath();
        String    realPath = pageContext.getServletContext().
                                 getRealPath(servletPath);

        return realPath + ".counter";
    }
    private void saveCount() throws JspException {
        try {
            FileWriter writer = new FileWriter(file);
            writer.write(count);
            writer.close();
        }
        catch(Exception ex) {
            throw new JspException(ex.getMessage());
        }
    }
    private void readCount() throws JspException {
        try {
            FileReader reader = new FileReader(file);
            count = reader.read();
            reader.close();
        }
        catch(Exception ex) {
            throw new JspException(ex.getMessage());
        }
    }
}
}
```

The tag handler listed above keeps track of the number of times that a tag—and therefore that tag's JSP page—has been accessed, by storing a count in a file. That file has the same name as its corresponding JSP page, with a `.counter` suffix; for example, if the file `/index.jsp` used a counter tag, a corresponding `/index.jsp.counter` file would contain a count of how many times `/index.jsp` had been accessed.

Like many tag handlers, `tags.CounterTag` extends `TagSupport`, an implementation of the `Tag` interface that provides a number of utility methods. `TagSupport` is discussed in more detail in "The TagSupport Class: Ancestors, Values, and IDs" on page 26.

The `CounterTag.doStartTag` method prints the count by using its `pageContext`[4] to access the implicit `out` object and returns `SKIP_BODY` to indicate that the tag's body, if present, should be ignored. The servlet container subsequently invokes `CounterTag.doEndTag`, which returns `EVAL_PAGE`. That constant directs the servlet container to evaluate the rest of the page following the end tag.

The `CounterTag` class does not implement a `release` method because neither of its two member variables—`count` and `file`—need to be reset for counter tags to be reused. That's because the `count` and `file` member variables are reset every time `doStartTag` is called.

Specifying the TLD in WEB-INF/web.xml

The JSP file in Example 1-2.a on page 6 uses the `taglib` directive to directly access a tag library descriptor. The `taglib` directive can also indirectly specify a TLD by referencing another `taglib` in the web application's deployment descriptor. For example, the `taglib` directive in Example 1-2.a could be specified as follows:

```
// in a JSP file ...

<%@ taglib uri='counters' prefix='util' %>
```

A second `taglib` directive in the web application's deployment descriptor specifies the actual location of the TLD for a tag library identified by a URI of `counters`:

```
// in web.xml ...

<taglib>
    <taglib-uri>counters</taglib-uri>
    <taglib-location>/WEB-INF/tlds/counter.tld</taglib-location>
</taglib>
```

---

4.   `pageContext` is a `protected` member of the `TagSupport` class.

Indirectly specifying a TLD affords more flexibility because the TLD can be moved without modification to the JSP file; therefore, indirect specification is preferred for deployment. Directly specifying a TLD is simpler and is usually preferred during development.

JSP Tip

Creating Simple Custom Tags

Implementing custom tags is straightforward in general and is quite simple for tags that do not have attributes or manipulate their bodies. Here are the steps required for creating simple custom tags:

- Add a `taglib` directive to JSP files that use the tags.
- Create a tag library descriptor (`.tld`) describing the tags.
- Implement a tag handler that extends `TagSupport` and overrides `doStartTag()` or `doEndTag()`.

\<taglib\> and \<tag\>

This section summarizes the elements for `<taglib>` and `<tag>` in a tag library descriptor (TLD).[5] See Example 1-2.b on page 6 for an example of how you use those tags. Table 1-1 lists the elements associated with the `<taglib>` tag.

Table 1-1 \<taglib\> Elements (listed in order of appearance)

Element	Type[1]	Description
tlibversion	1	The version of the tag library
jspversion	?	The version of the JSP specification the library depends on; <u>default</u> is JSP 1.1
shortname	1	Used by JSP page authoring tools for identifying the library
uri	?	A URI that uniquely identifies the library
info	?	A description of how the tag library is used
tag	+	The tags contained in the library

1. 1 = one, required... ? = one, optional...   + = one or more...

5.   According to JSP1.1.

Tags are defined with `<tag>`; for example, in Example 1-2.b on page 6, the specifics of the `counter` tag—its name, tag class, body content type, and information about the tag—are defined. Table 1-2 describes the elements associated with `<tag>`.

Table 1-2 `<tag>` Elements (listed in order of appearance)

Element	Type[1]	Description
`name`	1	The name comes after the tag prefix, as in: *<prefix:name ...>*
`tagclass`	1	The tag handler's class; tags must implement the `Tag` interface
`teiclass`	?	The class that defines scripting variables for a tag
`bodycontent`	?	A description of body content as one of: • Tag dependent (tag evaluates body content) • JSP (default) (servlet container evaluates body content) • Empty (body must be empty)
`info`	?	Information about the tag
`attribute`	*	A tag attribute; see "<attribute> Elements" on page 18

    1. 1 = one, required... ? = one, optional...   * = zero or more...

Tag attributes are specified with the `attribute` element, which is further discussed in "Tags with Attributes" on page 14.

The `bodycontent` attribute influences how a tag's body content is handled by servlet containers. The default value is `JSP`, which causes servlet containers to evaluate the body of the tag. If `tagdependent` is specified for `bodycontent`, the tag's body is not evaluated by the servlet container; that evaluation is left up to the tag handler. An `empty` value means that it's illegal for a tag to have a body.

The Tag Life Cycle

Tag handlers are software components that are plugged into a servlet container. Servlet containers create tag handlers, initialize them, and call `doStartTag`, `doEndTag`, and `release`, in that order. For simple tags, initialization consists of setting the tag's page context and parent. Once a tag handler's `release` method has been invoked, that handler may be made available for reuse.

Figure 1-2 shows an interaction diagram for the counter tag discussed throughout this chapter.

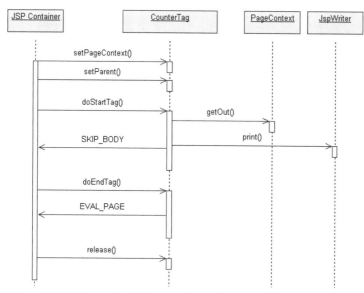

Figure 1-2 Interaction Diagram for a Counter Tag

Figure 1-2 is typical of simple tags without bodies or attributes. The servlet container invokes doStartTag, and the tag reacts in some manner, subsequently returning SKIP_BODY to indicate that the body of the tag, if present, should not be processed.

Nearly all tags return EVAL_PAGE from doEndTag, so the servlet container processes the rest of the JSP page. After doEndTag, the servlet container calls the tag's release method, where resources, such as database connections, are released and class member variables are reset.

More complex tags have more complicated interaction diagrams. For example, tag handlers that manipulate their bodies have additional methods that are invoked by the servlet container. Interaction diagrams for a tag with an attribute, and a tag that iterates over its body content are shown in Figure 1-5 on page 19 and Figure 2-2 on page 40, respectively.

Thread Safety

Regarding the lifetime of Tag instances, the JSP 1.1 specification states:

At execution time the implementation of a JSP page will use an available Tag *instance ... that is not being used .... Afterward, it will release the instance and make it available for further use.*

The specification's intent is clear: tags are used by one thread at a time. Single-threaded tag access means that tag handlers don't have to guard class members against multithreaded access. Of course, tag handlers must be careful with other thread-sensitive data, such as session or application attributes.

Because servlet containers can reuse tag handlers, you must be diligent about implementing the `release` method and careful about instantiating resources in doStartTag; for example, this tag handler should work as expected—

```
public class TagHandler extends TagSupport {
   private Hashtable hashtable;
   ...
   public int doStartTag() throws JspException {
      hashtable = new Hashtable();
      ...
   }
   public void release() {
      hashtable = null;
   }
   ...
}
```

—but this tag handler is likely to cause a null pointer exception if it's reused:

```
public class TagHandler extends TagSupport {
   private Hashtable hashtable;
   ...
   public TagHandler() {
      hashtable = new Hashtable();
      ...
   }
   public void release() {
      hashtable = null;
   }
   ...
}
```

Tags with Attributes

Custom tags can have any number of attributes—required or optional—specified as *attr=quoted value,* where *attr* is the attribute name and *quoted value* is the attribute's value. Here's a tag with a single attribute:

```
<util:iterate times='4'>
```

Attributes can be specified with request time attribute values, like this:

```
<util:iterate collection='<%= aCollection %>'>
```

The fragment above sets the `collection` attribute to a variable that represents a collection.

Adding an attribute to a tag is a three-step process, outlined below.

1. Add the attribute, where applicable, to existing tags in JSP files.
2. Add an attribute tag to the TLD.
3. Implement a `setAttr`[6] method in the tag handler.

It's also common to implement a getter method in the tag handler; that way, nested tags have access to properties.

The preceding steps are illustrated below with a simple but useful custom tag that has a single attribute. First, we'll take a look at the motivation for the tag, followed by a discussion of its implementation.

It's often desirable for textfields to retain their values when a form is redisplayed. For example, Figure 1-3 shows a registration page that is redisplayed if it's not filled out correctly. The left picture shows the incomplete registration, and the right picture shows the response, which redisplays the registration form with a message. The fields in the form retain their values so that users are not unduly punished by having to retype them.

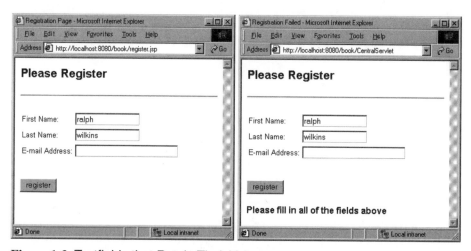

Figure 1-3 Textfields that Retain Their Values

Your first attempt to retain textfield values might be something like this:

---

6.   Substitute JavaBeans-compliant attribute name for `Attr`.

```
<input type='text' size=15 name='firstName'
        value='<%= request.getParameter("firstName")%>'>
```

The `value` attribute of the HTML `input` tag is set to the request parameter corresponding to the textfield's value. Thus, if the page shown in Figure 1-3 is redisplayed with the original request parameters, the fields will retain their values.

There is one drawback to this implementation, as illustrated by Figure 1-4. If no request parameters correspond to the field names, as is the case when the form is initially displayed, `ServletRequest.getParameter` returns `null`, which is displayed in the fields.

Figure 1-4 Drawback to Using
`request.getParameter` Directly

One solution to this problem is to implement a custom tag that returns a request parameter's value if the parameter exists, and an empty string otherwise. Example 1-3.a illustrates the use of such a tag with a partial listing of the JSP page shown in Figure 1-3. The `requestParameter` tag has a single required attribute corresponding to the name of the request parameter.

Example 1-3.a /register.jsp

```
<%@ taglib uri='WEB-INF/tlds/html.tld' prefix='html'%>
...
<table>
    <tr>
      <td> First Name: </td>
      <td><input type='text' size=15 name='firstName'
           value='<html:requestParameter property="firstName"/>'>
      </td>
    </tr>
    <tr>
      <td> Last Name: </td>
      <td><input type='text' size=15 name='lastName'
           value='<html:requestParameter property="lastName"/>'>
         </td>
    </tr>
    <tr>
      <td> E-mail Address: </td>
      <td><input type='text' size=25 name='emailAddress'
           value='<html:requestParameter
                  property="emailAddress"/>'>
      </td>
    </tr>
   </table>
 ...
```

Tag attributes are declared in the tag library descriptor. Example 1-3.b lists the TLD for the tag library containing the requestParameter tag.

Example 1-3.b /WEB-INF/tlds/html.tld

```
...
<taglib>
    ...
    <tag>
        <name>requestParameter</name>
        <tagclass>tags.GetRequestParameterTag</tagclass>
        <bodycontent>empty</bodycontent>

        <attribute>
            <name>property</name>
            <required>true</required>
            <rtexprvalue>true</rtexprvalue>
        </attribute>
    </tag>
</taglib>
```

The `property` attribute is required and can be specified with a request time attribute value. Valid elements for the `attribute` tag are listed in Table 1-3.[7]

Table 1-3 <attribute> Elements

Element	Type[1]	Description
name	1	The attribute's name
required	?	If true, the attribute must be specified
rtexprvalue	?	If true, the attribute can be specified with a JSP request time attribute value

1. 1 = one, required... ? = one, optional...

The tag handler for the `requestParameter` tag is listed in Example 1-3.c.

Example 1-3.c /WEB-INF/classes/tags/GetRequestParameterTag.java

```java
package tags;

import javax.servlet.ServletRequest;
import javax.servlet.jsp.JspException;
import javax.servlet.jsp.tagext.TagSupport;

public class GetRequestParameterTag extends TagSupport {
   private String property;

   public void setProperty(String property) {
      this.property = property;
   }
   public int doStartTag() throws JspException {
      ServletRequest req = pageContext.getRequest();
      String value = req.getParameter(property);

      try {
         pageContext.getOut().print(value == null ? "" : value);
      }
      catch(java.io.IOException ex) {
         throw new JspException(ex.getMessage());
      }
      return SKIP_BODY;
   }
}
```

7.   The elements are valid according to the JSP 1.1 specification.

Tag handlers
for each of '
are typica'
are guar'
called.

The (
pr¢
G∈
r

'he JavaBeans API
ε values, which
setter methods
∠Tag method is

ethod for the
rivate member of the
ısed in the doStartTag

uence of events that occurs

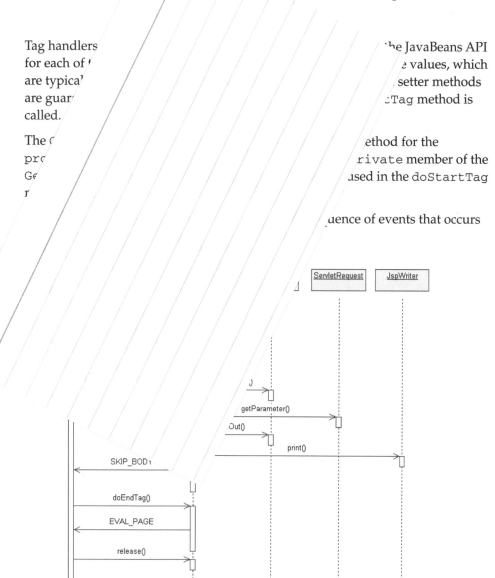

Figure 1-5 Interaction Diagram for the GetRequestParameterTag

JSP Tip

Tag Attributes and Tag Handler Properties

For every attribute defined for a custom tag, there must be a corresponding JavaBeans property in the tag handler class. The tag handler must also provide a setter method for the property, which is guaranteed to be invoked before the tag handler's doStartTag method is called. Because of this sequence of method calls, the doStartTag method always has access to tag attribute values.

Accessing Page Information

Custom tags often need access to information about their page, perhaps to examine request parameters or to retrieve an object from a particular scope. Page information is made available to tags with the pageContext, an instance of PageContext, that is a protected member of the TagSupport class.

The PageContext class provides a set of utility methods that falls into the following categories:[8]

- Accessing attributes in page scope
- Accessing attributes in a specified scope
- Forwarding and including
- Servlet container methods

All but the last category listed above are useful to custom tag implementers. For example, a custom tag could access an object in page scope like this:

```
public class SomeTag extends TagSupport {
    public int doStartTag() throws JspException {
        User user = (User)pageContext.getAttribute("user");
        ....
    }
}
```

A tag could also access an object from a specific scope:

```
User user = (User)pageContext.getAttribute("user",
                                PageContext.SESSION_SCOPE);
```

---

8. See Figure 1-6 on page 24 for more on the PageContext class.

The `PageContext.getAttribute` method returns an `Object` reference, given a name and a scope. The valid scopes are: `PAGE_SCOPE`, `REQUEST_SCOPE`, `SESSION_SCOPE`, and `APPLICATION_SCOPE`, all of which are defined in the `PageContext` class.

The `pageContext` can also be used to access request information, such as a request's locale, as follows:

```
public class SomeTag extends TagSupport {
    public int doStartTag() throws JspException {
        ServletRequest request = pageContext.getRequest();
        Locale locale = request.getLocale();
        ...
    }
}
```

Table 1-4 lists `PageContext` methods that are useful to custom tag implementers.

Table 1-4 PageContext Methods for Custom Tag Implementers

Methods	Description
`Object findAttribute(String)`	Searches page, request, session, and application scopes for an attribute
`Object getAttribute(String)`	Returns an object from page scope, or null if the object is not found
`void setAttribute(String, Object)`	Stores an object in page scope
`void removeAttribute(String)`	Removes an object from page scope
`JspWriter getOut()`	Returns the JspWriter that tags use to produce output
`ServletRequest getRequest()`	Returns the request object
`ServletResponse getResponse()`	Returns the response object
`ServletContext getServletContext()`	Returns the application object
`HttpSession getSession()`	Returns the session object
`void forward(String path)`	Forwards requests to a relative path
`void include(String path)`	Includes an HTML or JSP file, given a relative path

`setAttribute`, `getAttribute`, and `removeAttribute` are all overloaded with methods that take an additional `integer` value. That `integer` value represents scope, allowing attributes to be stored in different scopes. Methods that do not specify a scope operate on attributes in page scope.

The `PageContext` class also provides access to implicit variables from the tag's page, such as `out`, `session`, etc. `PageContext.getOut` is one of the most heavily used methods, especially by tags that filter or edit body content.

It's a simple matter to forward to, or include, a Web component such as a servlet or JSP page from within a custom tag. The `PageContext` `forward` and `include` methods are passed a string representing the relative path of the resource.

As of the JSP 1.1 specification, it is illegal to include a resource from within a body tag handler. This restriction is due to underlying servlet semantics regarding buffering; it should be remedied in the JSP 1.2 specification.

Error Handling

Tag handlers must be able to react to exceptional conditions; for example, a tag handler may choose to throw an exception if a tag attribute is specified with an illegal value.

Exceptions, in the form of `JspExceptions`, can be thrown by tag handlers. Those exceptions are handled by displaying the error page associated with the page in which the tag resides. For example, the JSP code fragment listed below specifies a tag library and an error page.

```
...
<%@ taglib uri='util.tld' prefix='util'%>
<%@ page errorPage='error.jsp' %>
...
```

A hypothetical tag handler for the JSP code fragment listed above might look like this:

```
import javax.servlet.jsp.JspException;
import javax.servlet.jsp.tagext.TagSupport;

public class SomeTagHandler extends TagSupport {
    private boolean someCondition;
    ...
    public int doStartTag() throws JspException {
        ...
        if(someCondition == false)
            throw new JspException("informative message");
        ...
    }
}
```

The `error.jsp` page referenced above is invoked as a result of the exception thrown by the `SomeTagHandler.doStartTag` method.

The Tag Package

The `javax.servlet.jsp.tagext` package provides interfaces and classes needed to implement custom tags, in addition to a number of classes that maintain information about tag libraries. The former, which is of interest to custom tag implementers, is the focus of this section.

The class diagram in Figure 1-6 depicts the classes and interfaces involved in the implementation of custom tags.

All tag handlers must implement the `Tag` interface, and nearly all do so by extending either `TagSupport` or `BodyTagSupport` (or some subclass thereof).

From their names, it might appear as though `BodyTagSupport` is for tags that have a body, and `TagSupport` is for tags that do not; however, that is not the case. Both kinds of tags can have a body, but `TagSupport` extensions are restricted to ignoring body content or passing it through unchanged. Extensions of `BodyTagSupport`, on the other hand, can manipulate their body content in any fashion.

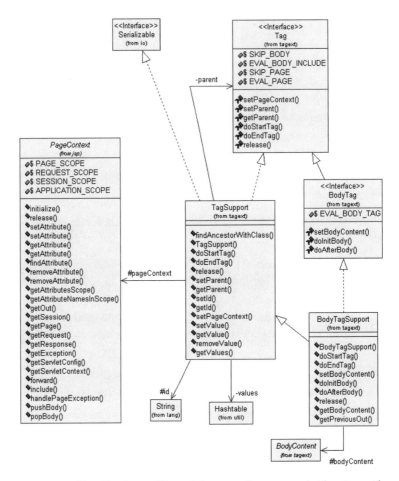

Figure 1-6 Tag Package Class Diagram (javax.servlet.jsp.tagext)

Tags have access to page information, including the implicit JSP objects, through a page context that is associated with every tag. As can be seen from Figure 1-6, the `PageContext` class provides a wealth of information about the page in which a tag resides.

The Tag Interface

The Tag interface defines fundamental tag capabilities; its methods are listed below:

```
void setPageContext(PageContext)
void setParent(Tag)
int doStartTag() throws JspException
int doEndTag() throws JspException
void release()

Tag getParent()
```

The methods in the first group listed above are listed in the order in which they are invoked. When a start tag is encountered, the servlet container calls setPageContext and setParent, in that order. doStartTag is called next, followed by a call to doEndTag at the corresponding end tag.[9] The doEndTag method is followed by a call to the tag's release method, which will release tag handler resources.

Both doStartTag and doEndTag return integer values that determine the course of action taken by the servlet container when the methods return. Table 1-5 lists valid return values and their meanings.

Table 1-5 Return Values for `Tag.doStartTag` and `Tag.doEndTag`

Method	Valid Return Values
doStartTag()	SKIP_BODY: do not process body EVAL_BODY_INCLUDE: pass through body content unchanged
doEndTag()	SKIP_PAGE: do not process the page beyond the end tag EVAL_PAGE: process the page after the end tag

All tags have a parent tag, which is null for top-level tags and is the innermost containing tag for nested tags. For example, in the following JSP fragment, the inbetween tag is the parent of the innermost tag, and the outermost tag is the parent of the inbetween tag.

```
<example:outermost>
    <example:inbetween>
        <example:innermost>
        ...
        </example:innermost>
    <example:inbetween>
</example:outermost>
```

9.   If a tag is empty, doEndTag is called immediately after doStartTag.

All tags enclosing other tags are referred to as ancestors of the enclosed tags, so in the listing above, the `inbetween` and `outermost` tags are ancestors of the `innermost` tag.

The `Tag` interface provides access to a tag's parent, but the setter methods for the parent and page context are meant for servlet container implementers and normally should not be invoked by JSP developers.

Developers rarely implement the `Tag` interface directly because it is much more convenient to extend `TagSupport` or `BodyTagSupport`. See "Body Tag Handlers" on page 34 for a discussion of tags that extend `BodyTagSupport`.

The TagSupport Class: Ancestors, Values, and IDs

Tags that do not manipulate body content or flow control typically extend the `TagSupport` class, which in turn implements the `Tag` interface. `TagSupport` provides the following functionality:

- Locate a tag's ancestors
- Access a tag's ID
- Store and retrieve named values

By default, `TagSupport` extensions ignore their body content and process the JSP page following their end tag. They accomplish this by returning `SKIP_BODY` from `doStartTag` and `EVAL_PAGE` from `doEndTag`.

The `TagSupport` methods are listed below:

```
// TagSupport implements the Tag interface and adds the following
// methods:

protected String id;
protected PageContext pageContext;

static Tag findAncestorWithClass(Tag, Class)

Object getValue(String key)
void setValue(String key, Object value)
void removeValue(String key)
Enumeration getValues()

String getId()
void setId()
```

`TagSupport` extensions have access to two `protected` variables: the tag's ID, and the page context.

The findAncestorWithClass method locates a tag's ancestor of a specified Java class. That static method is passed the tag where the search originates and the ancestor's class. See "Locating Ancestor Tags" on page 57 for an example of accessing an ancestor tag.

The third group of TagSupport methods listed above provide access to a tag's values, which are key/value pairs where the key is a string and the value can be any object.

JSP Tip

Most Custom Tags Extend TagSupport or BodyTagSupport

The TagSupport and BodyTagSupport classes provide enough basic functionality that they are almost always extended instead of implementing the Tag and BodyTag interfaces directly.

Because Java does not support multiple inheritance, existing classes don't have the option to extend TagSupport or BodyTagSupport. Those classes are good candidates to implement Tag or BodyTag directly. In practice, such classes are rare.

Tags with Bodies

Any tag can have a body, but only tag handlers that implement the BodyTag interface—hereafter known as body tag handlers—can manipulate their body content.[10]

Tag handlers that do not implement BodyTag are restricted to either ignoring their body content or passing it through unchanged. The JSP page shown on the right in Figure 1-7 contains a simple tag that displays its body content if the login is successful and the user's role is recognized as 'user'. Otherwise, the tag's body content is ignored.

---

10. Tags that specify empty for their body content cannot have a body.

Figure 1-7 An Authentication Tag

The example shown in Figure 1-7 consists of a login page with a form that forwards to a welcome page—welcome.jsp—if the login is valid.[11] That welcome page, which is listed in Example 1-4.a, uses an authenticate tag, which passes its body through unchanged if the user's role is 'user'.

Example 1-4.a /welcome.jsp

```
<html><head><title>Welcome</title></head>
<body>

<%@ taglib uri='/WEB-INF/tlds/authenticate.tld'
        prefix='security'%>

<h3>Welcome <%= request.getUserPrincipal() %></h3>

<security:authenticate role='user'>
  You are a user
</security:authenticate>

</body></html>
```

The tag handler for the authenticate tag is listed in Example 1-4.b.

Example 1-4.b /WEB-INF/classes/tags/AuthenticateTag.java

```
package tags;

import javax.servlet.http.HttpServletRequest;
```

---

11. Actually, the servlet container invokes welcome.jsp; see "Security" on page 250 for more information concerning login and security in general.

```java
import javax.servlet.jsp.JspException;
import javax.servlet.jsp.tagext.TagSupport;

public class AuthenticateTag extends TagSupport {
   private String role = null;

   public void setRole(String role) {
      this.role = role;
   }
   public int doStartTag() throws JspException {
      HttpServletRequest request = (HttpServletRequest)
                                     pageContext.getRequest();
      if(request.isUserInRole(role)) {
         return EVAL_BODY_INCLUDE;
      }
      return SKIP_BODY;
   }
   public int doEndTag() throws JspException {
      return EVAL_PAGE;
   }
}
```

AuthenticateTag extends TagSupport and supports a single property
corresponding to the role attribute in the authenticate tag.

If the user's role is 'user', doStartTag returns EVAL_BODY_INCLUDE, and the
body of the tag is included. If the user's role is not 'user', the method returns
SKIP_BODY and the body content is ignored.

JSP Tip

Including Body Content

Custom tags that do not implement the BodyTag interface can pass through
body content unchanged by returning EVAL_BODY_INCLUDE from doStartTag.
If tags need to manipulate the content of their bodies, they must implement the
BodyTag interface, as discussed in "Body Tag Handlers" on page 34.

Conclusion

Custom tag libraries are JSP's greatest strength, as will become more apparent as
JSP matures and its acceptance grows. Custom tags make JSP easier to use and,
therefore, available to a wider audience. As of this writing, a number of custom
tag library initiatives were underway.

The standard tag library, which will become part of a future JSP specification, will have a profound effect on JSP's usability. By providing tags for commonplace functions such as iteration and database access, the standard tag library will broaden JSP's appeal.

Many custom tags are simple tags with limited attributes that do not process their body content. Along with an introduction to the JSP tag package, simple tags were the focus of this chapter. The next chapter discusses more sophisticated aspects of custom tags, including tags that process the contents of their bodies in some fashion.

CUSTOM TAG ADVANCED CONCEPTS

Chapter 2

Sophisticated custom tags often manipulate their body content; for example, a custom tag could wrap its body content in an HTML SELECT tag, so that tag might be used like this—

```
<html:links name='api'>
  <option value='Servlets'>servlets</option>
  ...
</html:links>
```

—and end up producing HTML like this:

```
<select name='api' onChange='this.form.submit()'>
  <option value='Servlets'>servlets</option>
  ...
</select>
```

Besides manipulating body content, many custom tags make beans or scripting variables available to their JSP pages. It's a bit more work for tag handlers to create scripting variables, but the simplification of the tag's JSP page is usually worth the effort. Consider an iterate tag that makes the current item in a collection available as a bean:

```
<smp:iterate collection='<%= vector %>'>
  <jsp:useBean id='item' scope='page' class='java.lang.String'/>
    Item: <%= item %><br>
</smp:iterate>
```

versus a scripting variable:

```
<smp:iterate collection='<%= vector %>'>
   Item: <%= item %><br>
</smp:iterate>
```

Both implementations of the `iterate` tag listed above are discussed in "Iteration" on page 36 and "Scripting Variables" on page 41.

This chapter begins with a discussion of custom tags that can iterate and manipulate their body content. Tags that make beans and scripting variables available to their JSP pages are the next topic of discussion, followed by an in-depth look at how body content works. This chapter concludes with a discussion of nested tags, including locating ancestor tags and sharing data between tags.

Body Tag Handlers

Body tag handlers, meaning tags that implement the `BodyTag` interface, have two abilities that other tag handlers lack:

- They can iterate (see "Iteration" on page 36)
- They can manipulate their body content (see "Body Content" on page 46)

The BodyTag Interface

The `BodyTag` interface extends `Tag` and defines the methods listed below.

```
// BodyTag extends the Tag interface, and adds these methods:

void doInitBody()
int doAfterBody()

void setBodyContent(BodyContent)
```

The methods defined by the `BodyTag` interface are the foundation for custom tag iteration and body content manipulation. Servlet containers invoke those methods like this:

```
// A servlet container invokes BodyTag methods like this:

if(tag.doStartTag() == EVAL_BODY_TAG) {
   tag.setBodyContent(bodyContent);
   ...
   tag.doInitBody();
   do {
      // evaluate body content
   }
   while(tag.doAfterBody() == EVAL_BODY_TAG);
}
```

`doInitBody` is invoked exactly once, whereas `doAfterBody` can be invoked repeatedly. Thus, custom tags can iterate; for example, here's a tag that loops five times:

```
<util:loop from='1' to='5'>
   ...
<util:loop>
```

The `loop` tag could access the `from` and `to` attributes in `doInitBody` to set up a loop. That tag's `doAfterBody` method would repeatedly return `EVAL_BODY_TAG` until the loop is finished and `SKIP_BODY` is returned.

Both `doInitBody` and `doAfterBody` have access to a tag's body content, but `doInitBody` is called before that body content has been evaluated for the first time; see "Body Content" on page 46 for more information about evaluating body content.

Table 2-1 lists the valid return values for `BodyTag` methods that influence flow of control.

Table 2-1 BodyTag Method Return Values

Method	Valid Return Values
`doStartTag()`	EVAL_BODY_TAG: evaluate body content and store the result in a BodyContent object SKIP_BODY: do not evaluate body
`doAfterTag()`	EVAL_BODY_TAG: reevaluate body content SKIP_BODY: do not reevaluate body content
`doEndTag()`	EVAL_PAGE: process the page after the end tag SKIP_PAGE: do not process the page beyond the end tag

The BodyTagSupport Class

Nearly all body tag handlers extend the `BodyTagSupport` class—an implementation of `BodyTag`—instead of directly implementing the `BodyTag` interface. `BodyTagSupport` is popular because it provides default implementations of both `TagSupport` and `BodyTag` by extending the former and implementing the latter.

`BodyTagSupport` defines the methods listed below.

```
// BodyTagSupport extends TagSupport and
// implements BodyTag. It adds the following methods:

BodyContent getBodyContent()
JspWriter getPreviousOut()
```

BodyTagSupport adds the two methods listed above to those inherited from BodyTag and TagSupport. The getBodyContent method returns a tag's body content, and the getPreviousOut method returns a writer associated with the tag's enclosing tag, or the out implicit variable if the tag is a top-level tag. See "Understanding How Body Content Works" on page 48 for more information about those two methods.

By default, BodyTagSupport extensions evaluate their body once. That is evidenced by the default return values for the BodyTagSupport methods, listed in Table 2-2.

Table 2-2 Default BodyTagSupport Behavior

Method	Returns
doStartTag()	EVAL_BODY_TAG: evaluate body
doAfterTag()	SKIP_BODY: do not repeat evaluation
doEndTag()	EVAL_PAGE: evaluate the rest of the page

Iteration

Body tag handlers have a built-in do-while loop that lets them iterate, as discussed in "The BodyTag Interface" on page 34; for example, the JSP page shown in Figure 2-1 features a custom tag that iterates over the contents of a Java collection.

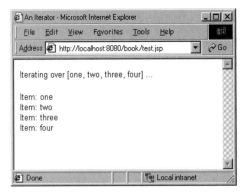

Figure 2-1 An Iterator Tag

The JSP page shown in Figure 2-1 is listed in Example 2-1.a.

Example 2-1.a /test.jsp

```
<html><head><title>An Iterator</title></head>
<%@ taglib uri='/WEB-INF/tlds/iterator.tld' prefix='it' %>
<body>

<% java.util.Vector vector = new java.util.Vector();
    vector.addElement("one");   vector.addElement("two");
    vector.addElement("three"); vector.addElement("four");
%>

Iterating over <%= vector %> ...<p>

<it:iterate collection='<%= vector %>'>
   <jsp:useBean id='item' scope='page' class='java.lang.String'/>
   Item: <%= item %><br>
</it:iterate>

</p>
</body>
</html>
```

In Example 2-1.a, vector of strings is specified as the iterate tag's collection
attribute. That iterate tag iterates over those strings and stores the current
string in page scope. In the code fragment listed above, the body of that iterate
tag uses <jsp:useBean> to retrieve that string from page scope, and a JSP
expression displays it.

Example 2-1.b lists the tag handler for the iterate tag.

Example 2-1.b /WEB-INF/classes/tags/IteratorTag.java

```
package tags;

import java.util.Collection;
import java.util.Iterator;

import javax.servlet.jsp.JspException;
import javax.servlet.jsp.tagext.BodyTagSupport;

public class IteratorTag extends BodyTagSupport {
   private Collection collection;
   private Iterator iterator;

   public void setCollection(Collection collection) {
      this.collection = collection;
   }
```

```
public int doStartTag() throws JspException {
    return collection.size() > 0 ? EVAL_BODY_TAG : SKIP_BODY;
}
public void doInitBody() throws JspException {
    iterator = collection.iterator();
    pageContext.setAttribute("item", iterator.next());
}
public int doAfterBody() throws JspException {
    if(iterator.hasNext()) {
        pageContext.setAttribute("item", iterator.next());
        return EVAL_BODY_TAG;
    }
    else {
        try {
            getBodyContent().writeOut(getPreviousOut());
        }
        catch(java.io.IOException e) {
            throw new JspException(e.getMessage());
        }
        return SKIP_BODY;
    }
}
}
```

Example 2-1.b lists the `IteratorTag` methods in the order they are invoked. The servlet container calls the `setCollection` method first and passes it the value of the tag's `collection` attribute.

Next, the servlet container calls `doStartTag`, which returns `EVAL_BODY_TAG` only if there are items in the collection. If there are no items, `doStartTag` returns `SKIP_BODY` and the servlet container will not invoke `doInitBody` or `doAfterBody`.

If the collection has items, the servlet container calls `doInitBody`, which obtains an iterator from the collection, retrieves the collection's first item, and stores it in page scope under the name "`item`".

After the body is initialized and the tag's body content has been evaluated, doAfterBody is invoked. If the collection has more items, doAfterBody retrieves the next item and stores it in page scope. Subsequently, doAfterBody returns EVAL_BODY_TAG, forcing a reevaluation of the tag's body content. If there are no more items in the collection, body content is written out, SKIP_BODY is returned, and the iteration terminates.

The iterate tag handler does not implement a release method because that class does not contain any information that needs to be reset in order for an iterate tag to be reused.

At first glance, it may seem rather curious that the iterate tag writes its body content to something known as the *previous out*. You may also wonder why that body content is written out in doAfterBody instead of doEndTag. Both of those questions are answered in "Understanding How Body Content Works" on page 48.

Figure 2-2 shows a interaction diagram for the IteratorTag class listed in Example 2-1.b. Each item in the collection is stored in page scope by the tag handler, like this:

```
pageContext.setAttribute("item", iterator.next());
```

Those items are subsequently retrieved in the JSP page with <jsp:useBean>, like this:

```
<jsp:useBean id='item' scope='page' class='java.lang.String'>
```

Notice that the key specified in setAttribute—"item"—must match the id attribute in the useBean tag and the scopes must also be the same.

You can eliminate those dependencies by making items available as scripting variables. In that case, there is no need for <jsp:useBean>. Just such an implementation of the IteratorTag class is discussed in "Scripting Variables" on page 41.

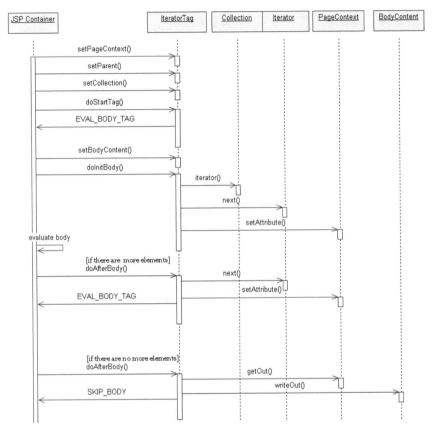

Figure 2-2 `IteratorTag` Interaction Diagram

JSP Tip

Body Tags Handlers Cannot Automatically *Include* Their Bodies

Tag handlers that do not implement the BodyTag interface can return EVAL_BODY_INCLUDE from doStartTag to alert the JSP container to pass their body content through unchanged.

However, by implementing the BodyTag interface, a tag handler is indicating that it—not the JSP container—is responsible for its body content. Therefore, it is illegal for body tag handlers to return EVAL_BODY_INCLUDE from doStartTag; instead, body tag handlers must manually pass through their body content, as illustrated in Example 2-1.b.

Scripting Variables

It's not uncommon for custom tags to make objects available to their JSP page. For example, the `iterate` tag discussed in "Iteration" on page 36 provides access to items in a collection.

It's often more convenient for custom tags to make objects available as scripting variables rather than simply making beans available. For example, consider the JSP file listed in Example 2-2.a, which uses an `iterate` tag that makes the current item in a collection available as a scripting variable.

Example 2-2.a /test.jsp

```
<html><head><title>Scripting Variable Example</title></head>

<%@ taglib uri='iterator.tld' prefix='it' %>

<% java.util.Vector vector = new java.util.Vector();
   vector.addElement("one");   vector.addElement("two");
   vector.addElement("three"); vector.addElement("four");
%>

Iterating over <%=vector %> ...<p>

<it:iterate collection='<%= vector %>'>
   item <%= item %><br>
</it:iterate>

</p></body>
</html>
```

The result of Example 2-2.a is exactly the same as that shown in Figure 2-1 on page 36.

If you contrast Example 2-2.a with Example 2-1.a on page 37, you can see that scripting variables eliminate the need for `<jsp:useBean>`, which results in two benefits: the JSP code is simpler and the bean's scope does not need to be specified.

As evidenced by Example 2-2.a, using scripting variables is straightforward. Implementing a custom tag that creates scripting variables is a three-step process:

1. Implement the tag handler that stores one or more objects in page scope.
2. Implement an extension of `TagExtraInfo` that specifies properties associated with the scripting variable(s).
3. Modify the TLD to declare the instance of `TagExtraInfo` from step 2.

The steps outlined above are discussed below for the iterate tag used in Example 2-2.a on page 41.

Storing Beans in Page Scope

The tag handler for the iterate tag listed above is identical to the IterateTag class listed in "/WEB-INF/classes/tags/IteratorTag.java" on page 37. That's because step 1 above is the same as the only step required for making a bean available to a JSP page: Storing that bean in page scope. That's why the IteratorTag class from "/WEB-INF/classes/tags/IteratorTag.java" on page 37 can be used here.

Specifying Scripting Variable Information

JSP containers need to know a scripting variable's name, its type, whether the variable already exists or needs to be created, and the scope of the variable's lifetime. That information is encapsulated in an object—known as a *tag extra info*. Those objects extend TagExtraInfo from the javax.servlet.jsp.tagext package.

Example 2-2.b lists the IteratorTagInfo class for the iterator tag used in Example 2-2.a on page 41.

Example 2-2.b   /WEB-INF/classes/tags/IteratorTagInfo.java

```
package tags;

import javax.servlet.jsp.tagext.TagData;
import javax.servlet.jsp.tagext.TagExtraInfo;
import javax.servlet.jsp.tagext.VariableInfo;

public class IteratorTagInfo extends TagExtraInfo {
   public VariableInfo[] getVariableInfo(TagData data) {
      return new VariableInfo[] {
         new VariableInfo(data.getId(), // scripting var's name
               "java.lang.Object", // variable's type
               true, // whether variable is created
               VariableInfo.NESTED) // scope
      };
   }
}
```

The getVariableInfo method returns an array of VariableInfo objects, each of which represents a scripting variable. In Example 2-2.b the getVariableInfo method returns an array with a single instance of VariableInfo representing the item scripting variable used in Example 2-2.a.

Three VariableInfo constants specify a scripting variable's scope:

- VariableInfo.AT_BEGIN
- VariableInfo.NESTED
- VariableInfo.AT_END

AT_BEGIN and AT_END specify scopes from the start tag or end tag, respectively, to the end of the page. NESTED scope is between the start and end tags.

Associating a Tag Handler and Scripting Variables

The final step in creating scripting variables is associating a tag handler with its tag extra info. That association is made in a tag library descriptor. The TLD for the iterate tag is listed in Example 2-2.c.

Example 2-2.c /WEB-INF/tlds/iterator.tld

```
<taglib>
   <tag>
      <name>iterate</name>
      <tagclass>tags.IteratorTag</tagclass>
      <teiclass>tags.IteratorTagInfo</teiclass>
      <bodycontent>JSP</bodycontent>
      <attribute>
         <name>collection</name>
         <required>true</required>
         <rtexprvalue>true</rtexprvalue>
      </attribute>
      <info>Iterates over a collection</info>
   </tag>
</taglib>
```

The TLD listed in Example 2-2.c specifies the tag extra info class with the <teiclass> element of the taglib tag.

JSP Tip

Scripting Variables Are Preferable to Beans

Custom tags can grant JSP pages access to beans simply by storing beans in the page context. With a little more effort, custom tags can make scripting variables available to a JSP page.

Because JSP pages can access scripting variables directly, using scripting variables is preferable to accessing beans with the <jsp:useBean> action.

Using Custom Tag IDs

Scripting variables, as opposed to beans, reduce dependences between custom tags and the JSP pages that use them, as discussed in "Scripting Variables" on page 41. But if you look closely at the example in that section, you will see that that example's JSP page has to know the name of the scripting variable that it uses—here is the pertinent code from that JSP page:

```
...
<it:iterate collection='<%= vector %>'>
   item <%= item %><br>
</it:iterate>
...
```

In the preceding code fragment, the scripting variable is referred to as item. That name comes from the tag extra info, as you can see from the code fragment listed below.

```
...
public VariableInfo[] getVariableInfo(TagData data) {
   return new VariableInfo[] {
      new VariableInfo("item", "java.lang.Object",
                       true,  VariableInfo.NESTED)
   };
}
...
```

Because JSP pages must refer to scripting variables by name, the dependency illustrated above will always exist. But you can negate that dependency by letting JSP pages specify scripting variable names with a tag's id attribute; for example, the iterate tag discussed above could require an id attribute that it uses to name its scripting variable. That tag would be used like this:

```
...
<it:iterate id='anItem' collection='<%= vector %>'>
    item <%= anItem %><br>
</it:iterate>
...
```

In the preceding code fragment, the JSP page chooses anItem for the scripting variable's name, but it's free to choose any name. The price a custom tag developer has to pay for this useful functionality is minimal. First, an id attribute is specified in the tag library descriptor, like this:

```
<taglib>
    <tag>
        <name>iterate</name>
        <tagclass>tags.IteratorTag</tagclass>
        <teiclass>tags.IteratorTagInfo</teiclass>
        <bodycontent>JSP</bodycontent>
        <attribute>
            <name>id</name>
            <required>true</required>
            <rtexprvalue>true</rtexprvalue>
        </attribute>
        <attribute>
            <name>collection</name>
            <required>true</required>
            <rtexprvalue>true</rtexprvalue>
        </attribute>
        <info>Iterates over a collection</info>
    </tag>
</taglib>
```

Then the tag extra info is modified to use the value of the id attribute, as shown below for the iterate tag discussed above.

```
public class IteratorTagInfo extends TagExtraInfo {
    public VariableInfo[] getVariableInfo(TagData data) {
        return new VariableInfo[] {
            new VariableInfo(data.getId(), // scripting var's name
                "java.lang.Object", // variable's type
                true, // whether variable is created
                VariableInfo.NESTED) // scope
        };
    }
}
```

That's all there is to naming scripting variables according to a tag's id attribute. Tag handlers that extend TagSupport or BodyTagSupport do not have to do anything special to support this feature because the TagSupport class maintains an id attribute and provides a setId method.

Body Content

It's often necessary for custom tags to manipulate their body content; for example, a database query tag might interpret its body content as SQL. Tag handlers that extend the BodyTag interface have access to their tag's body content, as illustrated by the JSP page shown in Figure 2-3.

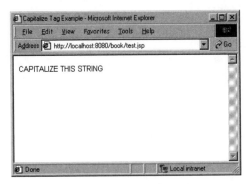

Figure 2-3 Manipulating Body Content
with a Custom Tag

The JSP page shown in Figure 2-3 uses a capitalize custom tag that capitalizes its body content. That tag, which is listed in Example 2-3.a, subsequently prints the capitalized content to the servlet response stream.

Example 2-3.a /test.jsp

```
<html><head><title>Capitalize Tag Example</title></head>

<%@ taglib uri='example' prefix='example' %>

<example:capitalize>
   capitalize this string
</example:capitalize>

</body>
</html>
```

The tag handler for the capitalize tag is listed in Example 2-3.b.

Example 2-3.b   /WEB-INF/classes/tags/CapitalizeTag.java

```
package tags;

import javax.servlet.jsp.JspException;
import javax.servlet.jsp.tagext.BodyTagSupport;

public class CapitalizeTag extends BodyTagSupport {
    public int doAfterBody() throws JspException {
        try {
            String content = bodyContent.getString();
            String   upper = content.toUpperCase();

            bodyContent.clearBody();
            bodyContent.print(upper);
            bodyContent.writeOut(getPreviousOut());
        }
        catch(java.io.IOException e) {
            throw new JspException(e.getMessage());
        }
        return SKIP_BODY;
    }
}
```

The tag handler listed above overrides doAfterBody and uses the
bodyContent member defined in BodyTagSupport to obtain the tag's body
content as a string. That content is converted to upper case and the tag's body
content is cleared. Subsequently, the doAfterBody method prints the uppercase
version of the content back into the body content and writes that content to the
response stream.

Like the iterate tag handler listed in Example 2-1.b on page 37, the
capitalize tag handler listed above writes its body content to the previous out.
See "Understanding How Body Content Works" on page 48 for more information
about writing to the previous out.

In addition to making body content available to tag handlers, servlet containers
also evaluate body content before it is made available to a tag handler. For
example, the following use of the capitalize tag will result in the same output
as shown in Figure 2-3 on page 46, because the JSP expression in the tag's body
content is evaluated and the result of that evaluation—the string "capitalize
this string"—is made available to the tag handler.

```
<example:capitalize>
  <%= "capitalize this string" %>
</example:capitalize>
```

The preceding code fragment will produce the same output shown in Figure 2-3 as long as JSP, which is the default value, is specified for the tag's body content in the tag library descriptor, as follows.

```
...
<tag>
   <name>capitalize</name>
   <tagclass>tags.CapitalizeTag</tagclass>
   <bodycontent>JSP</bodycontent>
</tag>
...
```

Sometimes, you don't want a tag's body content to be evaluated; for example, you wouldn't want SQL in the body of a database query tag to be evaluated as JSP. For those tags, you can specify tagdependent for the tag's body content in the tag library descriptor, like this:

```
...
<tag>
   <name>capitalize</name>
   <tagclass>tags.CapitalizeTag</tagclass>
   <bodycontent>tagdependent</bodycontent>
</tag>
...
```

Understanding How Body Content Works

If you want to implement custom tags that manipulate their body content, such as the capitalize and iterate tags discussed in "Body Content" on page 46 and "Iteration" on page 36, respectively, you must understand exactly what body content is and how it's handled by your servlet container. This section begins with a discussion of the former followed by a discussion of the latter.

Body content, represented by the BodyContent class, is a buffered writer that contains a tag's evaluated body content. You can use that buffer to manipulate a tag's body content in any fashion. Figure 2-4 shows a BodyContent class diagram.

The BodyContent class extends JspWriter, which not coincidentally, is the type of the implicit out variable. Normally, in a JSP page, when you write to the implicit out variable, the output goes to the response stream. In a custom tag, output goes to a BodyContent instance.

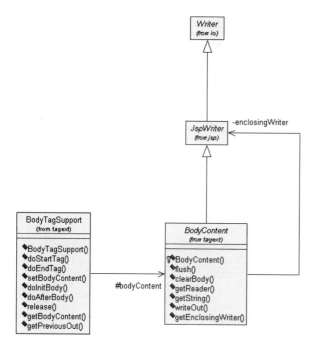

Figure 2-4 `BodyContent` Class Diagram

Servlet containers maintain a stack of `BodyContent` objects so that a nested tag does not overwrite the body content of one of its ancestor tags. Every `BodyContent` object maintains a reference to the buffered writer—either a body content or the implicit `out` variable—underneath it on that stack. That writer is known as the *previous out*, or the *enclosing writer*, and is available through `BodyContent.getEnclosingWriter` or `BodyTagSupport.getPreviousOut`.

It's important to know how that stack of `BodyContent` objects is maintained by your servlet container. Without that understanding, it's difficult to know what JSP writer to use after you have modified a tag's body content, or even what methods from `BodyTagSupport` to override. A simple JSP page, listed in Example 2-4.a, and a simple custom tag illustrate how servlet containers handle body content.

Example 2-4.a   /test.jsp

```
<html><head><title>Body Content</title></head>

<%@ taglib uri='body' prefix='body' %>

<body:printBody>
   BODY 1<br>

   <body:printBody>
      BODY 2<br>
   </body:printBody>

</body:printBody>

</body>
</html>
```

The JSP page listed above uses nested `printBody` tags to produce the output shown in Figure 2-5.

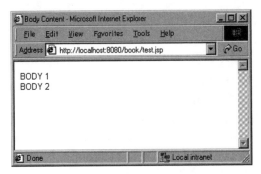

Figure 2-5 Manipulating Body Content

As you can see from Figure 2-5, those `printBody` tags, as their name implies, print their body content. The tag handler for the `printBody` tag is listed in Example 2-4.b.

Example 2-4.b /WEB-INF/classes/tags/PrintBodyTag.java

```
package tags;

import javax.servlet.jsp.JspException;
import javax.servlet.jsp.tagext.BodyTagSupport;

public class PrintBodyTag extends BodyTagSupport {
```

```
public int doAfterBody() throws JspException {
   try {
      getBodyContent().writeOut(getPreviousOut());
   }
   catch(java.io.IOException e) {
      throw new JspException(e.getMessage());
   }
   return SKIP_BODY;
}
```

You won't find a much simpler tag handler than the preceding one, but nonetheless, it can be difficult to understand because it writes to the previous out. To understand what the previous out is and why it's written to, let's look at the JSP page listed in Example 2-4.a on page 50 from the servlet container's perspective:

```
1
<body:printBody> <%-- pageContext.pushBody()* --%>
   2
   BODY 1<br>

   <body:printBody> <%-- pageContext.pushBody()* --%>
      3
      BODY 2<br>
   </body:printBody> <%-- pageContext.popBody()** --%>
   2
</body:printBody> <%-- pageContext.popBody()** --%>
1

 * Called by the servlet container after it calls doStartTag()
** Called by the servlet container after it calls doAfterTag() and
   before doEndTag()
```

Before the outer `printBody` tag is entered in the listing above, the JSP implicit `out` variable points to a `JspWriter` that writes to the response stream. That state, depicted by the numeral 1 in the code fragment listed above, is also illustrated in Figure 2-6, which depicts the three states referenced above. In Figure 2-6, the two `printBody` tags are referred to as the outer and inner tags.

Just after the servlet container calls `doStartTag` for the outer `printBody` tag, it redirects the implicit `out` variable to a `BodyContent` instance. That body content maintains a reference—known as the previous out—to the `JspWriter` that writes to the response stream. This effectively creates a stack of writers, as shown in the depiction of state #2 in Figure 2-6. This process of pushing a body content on the stack is implemented by the page context in `PageContext.pushBody`. That method is called by the servlet container just after it calls `doStartTag` for the outer `printBody` tag.

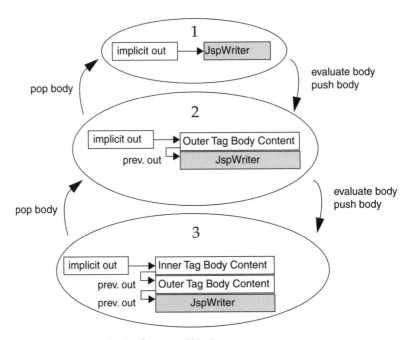

Figure 2-6 How Body Content Works

The servlet container calls `PageContext.pushBody` again after it enters the inner `printBody` tag. Now the body content stack contains the inner tag's body content, the outer tag's body content, and the JSP writer that writes to the response stream, in that order from top to bottom, as shown in state #3 in Figure 2-6. Notice that the previous out for the inner tag's body content is the outer tag's body content. The previous out for the outer tag's body content is the JSP writer that writes to the response stream.

The servlet container calls `PageContext.popBody` after the inner `printBody` tag's `doAfterBody` method has been called and before its `doEndTag` method is invoked. That `popBody` method pops the current body content off the stack, resulting in state #2 as shown in Figure 2-6.

Because the servlet container invokes `PageContext.popBody` between calls to the tag's `doAfterBody` and `doEndTag` methods, the body content stack is in state #3 in the inner `printBody` tag's `doAfterBody` method but is in state #2 in that tag's `doEndTag` method. If you are not aware of this fact, it can be difficult to manipulate body content as you would like.

Finally, the servlet container calls `PageContext.popBody` after it calls `doAfterBody` for the outer tag.

Now it's apparent why `PrintBodyTag.doAfterBody` prints its body content to the previous out. Because that tag's body content is still on the stack when `doAfterBody` is called, that tag writes to the previous out. The inner `printBody` tag in Example 2-4.a on page 50 writes to the outer `printBody`'s body content. The outer `printBody` content writes that content and its own to the JSP writer that writes to the response stream. If `PrintBodyTag.doAfterBody` wrote its body content to the implicit `out` variable, it would just be overwriting its own body content, which is discarded when it's popped off the stack.

You may wonder why the `PrintBodyTag` doesn't override `doEndTag` so that it can write to the implicit `out` variable. By the time `doEndTag` is called, the tag's body content has been popped off the stack, and that method could just write to the implicit `out` variable, which points to the enclosing tag's body content. Most of the time, that approach will work; however, the JSP 1.1 specification states that after a body content has been popped off the stack, it is available for reuse. Because of that condition, it is unsafe to access body content in a tag handler's `doEndTag` method.

JSP Tip

Don't Access Body Content in doEndTag()

By the time a servlet container calls a tag handler's doEndTag method, that servlet container may have reused that tag's body content, as allowed by the JSP 1.1 specification. Tags that access their body content in doEndTag risk accessing another tag's body content, or perhaps null values, and that results in undefined behavior.

Instead of accessing body content in doEndTag, tag handlers should place that functionality in doAfterBody, which is called before the servlet container makes a tag's body content available for reuse.

Generating JavaScript

This section discusses a custom tag that wraps its body content in an HTML tag and subsequently appends JavaScript to that body content. The ability for custom tags to generate JavaScript is a powerful combination of client- and server-side technologies.

Figure 2-7 shows a JSP page with a custom tag that manipulates its body content by wrapping it in an HTML SELECT tag. The custom tag generates the SELECT tag in addition to JavaScript that submits the list's form when an option is selected. This type of list is handy for providing a set of links that are activated when selected.

The left picture in Figure 2-7 shows an option being selected, and the right picture shows the result of that selection: the JSP page specified as the action for the list's form is displayed.

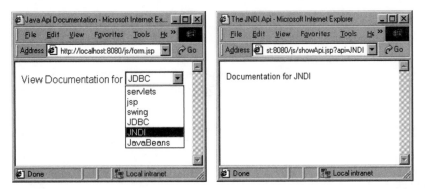

Figure 2-7 A Links Tag

The JSP page used in Figure 2-7 is listed in Example 2-5.a.

Example 2-5.a /test.jsp

```
<html><title>Java Api Documentation</title>
<body>

<%@ taglib uri='html' prefix='html' %>

<form action='showApi.jsp'>
   <font size='4'> View Documentation for</font>
      <html:links name='api'>
         <option value='Servlets'>servlets</option>
         <option value='JSP'>jsp</option>
```

```
        <option value='Swing'>swing</option>
        <option value='JDBC'>JDBC</option>
        <option value='JNDI'>JNDI</option>
        <option value='JavaBeans'>JavaBeans</option>
      </html:links>
  </form>

  </body>
  </html>
```

The links tag is used like the HTML select tag, with HTML option tags for its body content. The action for the tag's form in Example 2-5.a is specified as showApi.jsp, which is listed in Example 2-5.b.

Example 2-5.b /showApi.jsp

```
<html><title>The <%= request.getParameter("api") %> Api</title>
<body>
    Documentation for <%= request.getParameter("api") %>
</body>
</html>
```

showApi.jsp exists merely to illustrate its ability to find out which option was selected. A nontrivial implementation would have different content depending on the api selected. The real action, as far as custom tags are concerned, takes place in the tag handler, listed in Example 2-5.c.

Example 2-5.c /WEB-INF/classes/tags/LinksTag.java

```
package tags;

import javax.servlet.jsp.JspException;
import javax.servlet.jsp.tagext.BodyContent;
import javax.servlet.jsp.tagext.BodyTagSupport;

public class LinksTag extends BodyTagSupport {
   private String name;
   private StringBuffer buffer;

   public void setName(String name) {
      this.name = name;
   }
   public int doAfterBody() throws JspException {
      try {
         String body = bodyContent.getString();
         bodyContent.clearBody();

         buffer = new StringBuffer(
```

```
                        "<select name='" + name + "'  " +
                           "onChange='this.form.submit()'>" +
                           body + "</select>");

        bodyContent.print(buffer.toString());
        bodyContent.writeOut(getPreviousOut());
      }
      catch(java.io.IOException ex) {
        throw new JspException(ex.getMessage());
      }
      return SKIP_BODY;
   }
 }
```

The links tag, like the HTML select tag, has a name attribute,[1] and as required, the LinksTag class has a corresponding property that complies with the JavaBeans API.

The doAfterBody method obtains a reference to the tag's body content as a string with the BodyContent.getString method. The body content is then cleared, and a string buffer is constructed with the body content bracketed by a select tag. Finally, the contents of the buffer is printed to the body content, which is subsequently written to the tag's enclosing writer. Here's what the generated select tag looks like:

```
<select name='api' onChange='this.form.submit()'>
   <option value='Servlets'>servlets</option>
   <option value='JSP'>jsp</option>
   <option value='Swing'>swing</option>
   <option value='JDBC'>JDBC</option>
   <option value='JNDI'>JNDI</option>
   <option value='JavaBeans'>JavaBeans</option>
</select>
```

The select tag is generated with an onChange attribute specifying a snippet of JavaScript—this.form.submit()—that submits the form whenever one of the list's options is selected.

In addition to manipulating body content, this example also illustrates how JSP and JavaScript can be used together. JSP and JavaScript are a powerful combination of client- and server-side technologies for creating flexible and complex web applications. Custom tags can encapsulate JSP and JavaScript functionality in a format familiar to web page authors.

---

1.   Unlike select, links does not have size and multiple attributes.

Nested Tags

Top-level tags can communicate by storing objects in a particular scope through the page context, as outlined above. Nested tags can do the same, but they can also communicate directly with the `static findAncestorWithClass(Tag, Class)` method from `TagSupport`.

Locating Ancestor Tags

Although `findAncestorWithClass` is a `static` method—callable without a tag instance—it is usually invoked from within a tag handler method. In that case, the tag passed to `findAncestorWithClass` is the tag that invokes the method and is specified as `this`, as follows:

```
// in some TagSupport extension ...

public int doStartTag() throws JspException {
    try {
        // find an ancestor of this class
        Class klass = com.companyname.TagName".class;
        Tag ancestor = findAncestorWithClass(this, klass);
    }
    catch(ClassNotFoundException ex) {
        throw new JspException(ex.getMessage());
    }
}
```

Almost invariably, the ancestor itself is an extension of `TagSupport`. Because `findAncestorWithClass` returns a reference to a `Tag` instance, it is necessary to cast the reference to `TagSupport` in order to access its `TagSupport` functionality.

One other thing: `findAncestorWithClass` must be passed a reference to a `Class`. Typically, the *name* of the ancestor class is known, but there's not a reference to the corresponding *class* available, so one has to be manufactured for the occasion.

A short but handy method meant for `TagSupport` extensions is listed below; it addresses all of the issues discussed above. The method returns a reference to a `TagSupport` ancestor given the ancestor's class name.

```
// A method for TagSupport extensions that simplifies
// ancestor access

private TagSupport getAncestor(String className)
                        throws JspException {
```

```
Class klass = null; // can't name variable class
try {
    klass = Class.forName(className);
}
catch(ClassNotFoundException ex) {
    throw new JspException(ex.getMessage());
}
return (TagSupport)findAncestorWithClass(this, klass);
}
```

Sharing Data

The ability for a tag to locate ancestor tags, combined with the ability to store named values in a tag, means that tags can directly share information with their ancestors. For example, consider the following JSP fragment where the ancestor tag sets a value that is retrieved by the offspring tag.

```
<smp:ancestor>
    <smp:offspring/>
</smp:ancestor>
```

The ancestor tag sets the value of "name" to "value" in its doStartTag method, as follows:

```
package tags;

public class AncestorTag extends TagSupport {
    public int doStartTag() throws JspException {
        setValue("name", // must be a string
                 "value"); // can be any object

        return EVAL_BODY_INCLUDE;
    }
    ...
}
```

Ancestor.doStartTag returns EVAL_BODY_INCLUDE, instructing the JSP container to pass body content through unchanged. That body content, of course, is the offspring tag, whose tag handler is implemented like this:

```
public class OffspringTag extends TagSupport {
    public int doStartTag() throws JspException {
        AncestorTag ancestor = null;

        try {
            ancestor = (AncestorTag)findAncestorWithClass(this,
                               tags.AncestorTag.class);
```

```
        pageContext.getOut().println(
                        ancestor.getValue("name"));
      }
      catch(Exception ex) {
          throw new JspException(ex.getMessage());
      }
      return EVAL_BODY_INCLUDE;
   }
 }
```

OffSpringTag.doStartTag calls findAncestorWithClass to locate the nearest ancestor of class tags.AncestorTag.
TagSupport.getValue("name") returns the value—"value"—that is subsequently printed to the out implicit variable.

Conclusion

Approximately 30% of the JSP 1.1 specification is devoted to custom tags. Obviously, the specification's authors regarded custom tags as one of JSP's greatest assets. This chapter should reinforce that perception by providing an overview of more sophisticated custom tag capabilities.

In addition to this chapter and the last, a number of other custom tags are explored elsewhere in this book. Those tags constitute a modest tag library, and you can use that tag library anyway you'd like.

HTML FORMS

Topics in this Chapter

Chapter 3

HTML forms are to web applications what user interface frameworks, such as Swing and the AWT, are to traditional software. Instead of working with a user interface toolkit, page authors use forms to construct user interfaces.

The JSP specification does not directly include support for forms; however, you can easily use `jsp:useBean` to store form values in beans. Storing the state of an object (in this case, a form element) in another object (a bean) is an example of the Memento design pattern.

This chapter begins with a discussion of encapsulating form state in beans. Next, both client-side and server-side validation are explored, followed by an examination of a beans form framework and a custom tag that extends the HTML `form` tag.

Forms with Beans

Using beans to capture state is the preferred method for handling forms: JSP pages have easy access to beans and you can easily restore a form's values with those beans.

Transmission of Form Data

When a user submits a form, the browser sends a string to the URL specified by the form's action.[1] That string contains element names and values, and is encoded like this: *name1=value1&name2=value2&...&nameN=valueN*. For example, for a form with a single name textfield with the value Jon, the string would be: "name=Jon"; for a name and phone number: "name=Jon&phone=555-1212".

You can access forms in servlets and JSP pages with the request object; for example, a JSP page could print a textfield's value like this:

```
<%= request.getParameter("name") %>
```

Alternatively, you can set all of a form's values in a corresponding bean:

```
<jsp:useBean id='form' class='beans.Form' scope='request'>
    <jsp:setProperty name='form' property='*'/>
</jsp:useBean>
```

When you specify '*' for jsp:setProperty, as in the preceding code fragment, Java reflection is used to set bean properties that correspond to request parameters; for example, a bean's setName method would be invoked in response to a name parameter.

The two sections that follow illustrate how you can use jsp:useBean to store the state of a form in a single bean. "Server-side Validation with Servlets and JSP Pages" on page 75 discusses further encapsulating state in separate beans for each element, which is a more complicated, but more reusable, solution.

JSP Tip

Forms, Beans, and the Memento Pattern

The Memento design pattern stores an object's state externally so that state can be restored. You can implement the Memento design pattern for HTML forms by storing the state of a form in one or more beans.

Textfields, Text Areas, and Radio Buttons

Textfields, text areas, and radio buttons are grouped in this section because they all generate a single request parameter when their form is submitted. See "Checkboxes and Options" on page 65 for a discussion about elements that can generate multiple request parameters.

---

1.   If the action attribute is omitted, the page is reloaded.

The JSP page shown in Figure 3-1 contains a form with a textfield, radio buttons, and a text area. The form does not specify an action, so the JSP page is redisplayed when the form is submitted. The left picture in Figure 3-1 shows the page after the form has been filled out but before it has been submitted. The right picture shows the page after the form has been submitted.

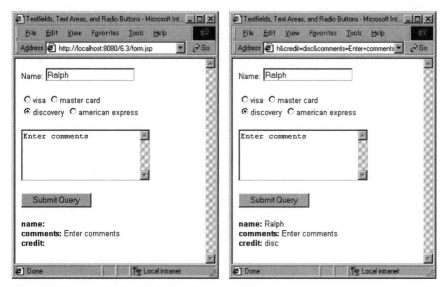

Figure 3-1 Saving Form Values in a Bean

When the form in Figure 3-1 is redisplayed, the form's elements retain their values with state stored in a bean. The JSP page shown in Figure 3-1 is listed in Example 3-1.a.

Example 3-1.a /form.jsp

```
<html><title>Textfields, Text Areas, and Radio Buttons</title>
<body>

<jsp:useBean id='form' class='beans.Form' scope='request'>
   <jsp:setProperty name='form' property='*'/>
</jsp:useBean>

<form>
   Name:<input type='text' name='name'
            value='<%=form.getName()%>' /><p>

   <input type='radio' name='credit' value='visa'
```

```
<%= form.creditSelectionAttr ("visa") %>>visa

<input type='radio' name='credit' value='mc'
<%= form.creditSelectionAttr ("mc") %>>master card<br>

<input type='radio' name='credit' value='disc'
<%= form.creditSelectionAttr ("disc") %>>discovery

<input type='radio' name='credit' value='amex'
<%= form.creditSelectionAttr ("amex") %>>american express

</p><p><textarea name='comments' cols='25'
           rows='5'><%= form.getComments() %></textarea>

</p><p><input type='submit'/></p>
</form>

<%@ include file='showForm.jsp' %>

</body></html>
```

Every time the page listed in Example 3-1.a is accessed, a bean of type beans.Form is created and stored in request scope. The jsp:setProperty action sets the bean's properties according to the request parameters. That bean is subsequently used to retrieve the name request parameter, in addition to selecting a radio button.

The JSP page listed in Example 3-1.a includes another JSP page— showForm.jsp—that also uses the form bean to display the values of the textfield, text area, and the selected radio button. showForm.jsp is listed in Example 3-1.b.

Example 3-1.b /showForm.jsp

```
<b>name:      </b> <%= form.getName()     %><br>
<b>comments: </b> <%= form.getComments() %><br>
<b>credit:    </b> <%= form.getCredit()   %></p>
```

showForm.jsp has access to the form bean because it is included in form.jsp with the include *directive*, which includes showForm.jsp at *compile* time. If the JSP include *action* were used in Example 3-1.a, showForm.jsp would be evaluated on its own at ***runtime***. That would result in a runtime error because the form variable would be undefined in showForm.jsp.

Example 3-1.c lists the bean created by the JSP page listed in Example 3-1.a.

Example 3-1.c WEB-INF/classes/beans/Form.java

```java
package beans;

public class Form {
    String name, comments = "Enter comments", credit;

    public void setName(String s) { name = s; }
    public String getName() { return name != null ? name : ""; }

    public void setComments(String s) { this.comments = s; }
    public String getComments() { return comments; }

    public void setCredit(String s) { credit = s; }
    public String getCredit() {
        return credit != null ? credit : "";
    }

    public String creditSelectionAttr(String creditName) {
        if(credit != null) {
            return credit.equals(creditName) ? "checked" : "";
        }
        return "";
    }
}
```

The Form bean listed above has accessor methods that comply with the JavaBeans specification for the form's textfield (name), text area (comments), and radio buttons (credit). The most noteworthy aspect of the Form bean is that it encapsulates the code for accessing form values—including working around null values—instead of embedding that code within a JSP page. Keeping code out of JSP pages makes them more readable and easier to maintain.

Checkboxes and Options

Lists are created with HTML select and option tags, like this:

```html
<select name='years' size='5' multiple>
    <option value='2000'>2000</option>
    <option value='2001'>2001</option>
    <option value='2002'>2002</option>
    ... more options ...
</select>
```

If 2000, 2001, and 2002 were selected from the list, the following string would be passed to the form's action: "... years=2000&years=2001&years=2002 ...". Because there are multiple occurrences of the `years` parameter, JSP pages would access parameter values like this:

```
<% String[] value= request.getParameterValues("years") %>
```

As you can see from the code fragment listed above, a list of options generates an array of strings, unlike elements such as textfields and text areas, which generate a single string.

Checkboxes, like options, can generate multiple values when a group of checkboxes is given the same name, which is typical. Let's discuss how you can handle those values.

Figure 3-2 shows a JSP page with a form containing checkboxes and options. As was the case for Figure 3-1 on page 63, the form shown in Figure 3-2 does not specify an action and therefore the page is redisplayed when the form is submitted. The left picture shows the page before the form is submitted, and the right picture shows the page after submission.

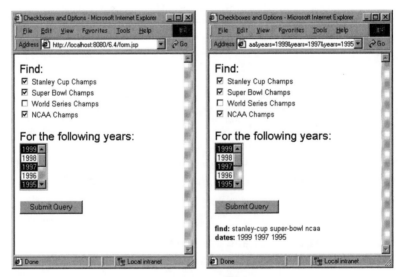

Figure 3-2 Beans for Checkboxes and Options

The JSP page shown in Figure 3-2 is listed in Example 3-2.a.

Example 3-2.a   /form.jsp

```
<html><title>Checkboxes and Options</title>
<body>

<jsp:useBean id='form' class='beans.Form' scope='request'>
  <jsp:setProperty name='form' property='*'/>
</jsp:useBean>

<form>
 <font size='5'>Find:</font><br>
   <input type='checkbox' name='categories' value='stanley-cup'
      <%= form.categorySelectionAttr("stanley-cup") %>>
      Stanley Cup Champs<br>

   <input type='checkbox' name='categories' value='super-bowl'
       <%= form.categorySelectionAttr("super-bowl") %>>
      Super Bowl Champs<br>

   <input type='checkbox' name='categories' value='world-series'
       <%= form.categorySelectionAttr("world-series") %>>
      World Series Champs<br>

   <input type='checkbox' name='categories' value='ncaa'
      <%= form.categorySelectionAttr("ncaa") %>>
      NCAA Champs<br>

   <p><font size='5'>For the following years:</font><br>

   <select name='years' size='5' multiple>
<%     for(int year=1999; year > 1989; --year) { %>
          <option value='<%= year %>'
          <%= form.yearSelectionAttr(Integer.toString(year)) %>>
          <%=year%></option>
<%     }     %>
   </select>

   </p><p><input type='submit'/></p>
</form>

<%@ include file='showForm.jsp' %>

</body></html>
```

Like the JSP page listed in Example 3-1.a on page 63, the page listed in Example 3-2.a creates a bean of type beans . Form and initializes it according to the request parameters. That bean is subsequently used to restore the state of the checkboxes and options.

Also, like the JSP page listed in Example 3-1.a on page 63, the page listed in Example 3-2.a includes another JSP page that displays form values. That page is listed in Example 3-2.b.

Example 3-2.b /showForm.jsp

```
<% if(form.getCategories() != null) { %>
    <b>find:</b>
<%      String[] strings = form.getCategories();
        for(int i=0; i < strings.length; ++i) { %>
          <%= strings[i] %>
<%      }
    }
    if(form.getYears() != null) { %>
        <br><b>dates:</b>
<%      String[] strings = form.getYears();
        for(int i=0; i < strings.length; ++i) { %>
          <%= strings[i] %>
<%      }
    }
%>
```

The JSP page listed above displays the selected categories and years. Example 3-2.c lists the bean used in Example 3-2.a and Example 3-2.b.

Example 3-2.c /WEB-INF/classes/beans/Form.java

```
package beans;

public class Form {
   String[] years, categories;

   public String[] getCategories() { return categories; }
   public void setCategories(String[] categories) {
      this.categories = categories;
   }
   public String categorySelectionAttr(String category) {
      if(categories != null) {
         for(int i=0; i < categories.length; ++i) {
            if(categories[i].equals(category))
               return "checked";
         }
      }
      return "";
   }
```

```
public String[] getYears() { return years; }
public void setYears(String[] years) { this.years = years; }

public String yearSelectionAttr(String year) {
    if(years != null) {
        for(int i=0; i < years.length; ++i) {
            if(years[i].equals(year))
                return "selected";
        }
    }
    return "";
}
}
```

Like the bean listed in Example 3-1.c on page 65, the bean listed above provides JavaBeans-compliant accessories for form elements. Unlike the bean listed in Example 3-1.c, the bean listed in Example 3-2.c deals in arrays because request parameters for checkboxes and options are represented by arrays of strings.

Because checkboxes are selected with a "checked" attribute and options are selected with a "selected" attribute, the methods categorySelectionAttr and yearSelectionAttr return "checked" and "selected", respectively, when a checkbox or option is selected.

Validation

Validation is often required for HTML forms and can be performed client-side—typically with JavaScript—or server-side, with JSP pages or servlets.

Because client-side validation is performed on the client, feedback is much faster than for server-side validation, which requires a round trip to the server. On the other hand, server-side validation is more dependable because users can disable JavaScript, rendering client-side validation useless.

If client-side validation is faster but server-side validation is more dependable, which one should be used? For robustness, the answer has to be both, with server-side validation duplicating the efforts of the client.

Client-side Validation with JavaScript

Although it is has nothing to do with JSP, client-side validation is frequently employed for HTML forms and therefore is briefly discussed in this section.

Advanced JavaServer Pages

Figure 3-3 shows a JSP page that has a simple form with textfields for a name and an e-mail address. That JSP page contains JavaScript to validate that all of the fields are filled in and that the e-mail address contains '@' and ends in either .com or .edu.

The left picture in Figure 3-3 shows the form partially filled in, and the right picture shows the result of submitting a partially filled in form.

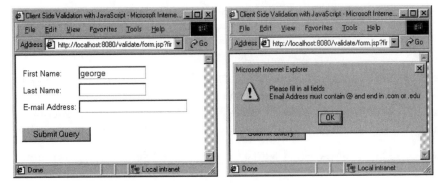

Figure 3-3 Using JavaScript for Client-side Validation

The JSP page shown in Figure 3-3 is listed in Example 3-3.

Example 3-3 /form.jsp

```
<html><head>
   <title>Client Side Validation with JavaScript</title>
</head>

<body>
<jsp:useBean id='form' scope='request' class='beans.Form'>
   <jsp:setProperty name='form' property='*'/>
</jsp:useBean>

<form name='simpleForm' onSubmit='return validate()'>
<table><tr>
   <td>First Name:</td>
   <td><input type='text' size=15 name='firstName'
        value='<%= form.getFirstName() %>'/></td></tr><tr>

   <td>Last Name:</td>
   <td><input type='text' size=15 name='lastName'
        value='<%= form.getLastName() %>'/></td></tr><tr>
```

```
    <td>E-mail Address:</td>
    <td><input type='text' size=25 name='emailAddress'
         value='<%= form.getEmailAddress() %>'/></td></tr>
    </table>
    <p><input type='submit'/></p>
</form>

<script language='JavaScript'>
    function validate() {
        var firstName = simpleForm.firstName.value,
             lastName = simpleForm.lastName.value,
          emailAddress = simpleForm.emailAddress.value,
              errorMsg = "",
         errorDetected = false;

        if(firstName == "" || lastName == "" || emailAddress == ""){
           errorMsg += "Please fill in all fields";
           errorDetected = true;
        }
        if(!isEmailAddressValid(emailAddress)) {
            if(errorMsg.length > 0)
               errorMsg += "\n";

            errorMsg += "Email Address must contain @ and " +
                        "end in .com or .edu";
            errorDetected = true;
        }
        if(errorDetected)
           alert(errorMsg);

        return !errorDetected;
    }
    function isEmailAddressValid(s) {
        var atSign = new RegExp(".*(@).*"),
            dotEdu = new RegExp(".edu$"),
            dotCom = new RegExp(".com$");

        return atSign.test(s) && (dotCom.test(s) || dotEdu.test(s));
    }
</script>
</body></html>
```

The form's onSubmit attribute is set to 'return validate()', which causes
the JavaScript validate function to be invoked when the form is submitted. If
validate returns true, the form is submitted; otherwise, the submission is
canceled and an error dialog is shown.

Like the examples discussed in "Forms with Beans" on page 61, the JSP page shown in Figure 3-3 uses a bean for retaining form values. Because that bean is not germane to this discussion and because similar beans have been previously discussed, that bean is not listed here.[2]

The JSP page listed in Example 3-3 is an example of using JSP and JavaScript together. Because JSP containers pass through template text unchanged, JavaScript can be included in a JSP page exactly as it would in an HTML file.

Server-side Validation with JSP

Server-side validation can be performed with JSP pages or servlets. This section discusses the former, and "Server-side Validation with Servlets" on page 73 discusses the latter.

Figure 3-4 shows a JSP page that contains a form identical to the one shown in Figure 3-3. The left picture in Figure 3-4 shows the form before it is submitted, and the right picture shows the results of the submission.

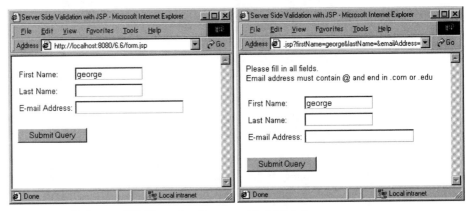

Figure 3-4 Using a JSP Page for Server-side Validation

The code for the JSP page shown in Figure 3-4 is identical to the listing in Example 3-3 on page 70, except that it has no JavaScript code and its form's action is set to `validate.jsp`, as listed below.

```
...
<form name='simpleForm' action='validate.jsp'/>
    ...
</form>
...
```

---

2. The bean is included in the book's code, which you can download from
    `http://www.phptr.com/advjsp`.

When that form is submitted, `validate.jsp`, which is listed in Example 3-4, is invoked.

Example 3-4   /validate.jsp

```
<% String first = request.getParameter("firstName");
   String  last = request.getParameter("lastName");
   String email = request.getParameter("emailAddress");
   String errorMsg = "";
   boolean errorDetected = false;

   if(first.equals("") || last.equals("") || email.equals("")) {
      errorMsg += "Please fill in all fields.";
      errorDetected = true;
   }
   if(email.indexOf("@") == -1 ||
      (!email.endsWith(".com") && !email.endsWith(".edu"))) {
      if(errorMsg.length() > 0)
         errorMsg += "<br>";

      errorMsg += "Email address must contain @ and " +
                  "end in .com or .edu";
      errorDetected = true;
   }
   if(errorDetected) { %>
      <%= errorMsg %>
      <jsp:include page='form.jsp' flush='true'/>
<%    } else { %>
      <jsp:forward page='registrationComplete.jsp'/>
<% } %>
```

The JSP page listed above obtains form values from the request and validates according to the same criteria used by the JavaScript code listed in Example 3-3 on page 70. If the form values are valid, the JSP page listed above forwards to `registrationComplete.jsp`; otherwise, it prints an error message and includes the original form.

Server-side Validation with Servlets

Server-side validation can be performed with a servlet instead of a JSP page. The only difference, as far as the JSP page containing the form is concerned, is the action associated with the form. The JSP fragment listed below specifies the action for the form shown in Figure 3-4 on page 72 as `ValidationServlet`.

```
...
<form name='simpleForm' action='ValidationServlet'/>
     ...
</form>
...
```

The servlet referred to above is listed in Example 3-5.

Example 3-5 /WEB-INF/classes/ValidationServlet.java

```java
import java.io.IOException;

import javax.servlet.RequestDispatcher;
import javax.servlet.ServletException;
import javax.servlet.http.HttpServletRequest;
import javax.servlet.http.HttpServletResponse;
import javax.servlet.http.HttpServlet;

public class ValidationServlet extends HttpServlet {
   public void service(HttpServletRequest req,
                        HttpServletResponse res)
                  throws IOException, ServletException {
      String first = req.getParameter("firstName"),
             last = req.getParameter("lastName"),
             email = req.getParameter("emailAddress"),
          errorMsg = "", nextStop = "/registrationComplete.jsp";

      boolean errorDetected = false;

      if(first.equals("") || last.equals("") ||
                         email.equals("")) {
         errorMsg += "Please fill in all fields.";
         errorDetected = true;
      }
      if(email.indexOf("@") == -1 ||
        (!email.endsWith(".com") && !email.endsWith(".edu"))) {
         if(errorMsg.length() > 0)
            errorMsg += "<br>";

         errorMsg += "Email address must contain @ and " +
                     "end in .com or .edu";
         errorDetected = true;
      }
      if(errorDetected) {
         res.getWriter().print(errorMsg);
         nextStop = "/form.jsp";
      }
      RequestDispatcher rd;
```

```
    rd = getServletContext().getRequestDispatcher(nextStop);

    if(nextStop.equals("/form.jsp"))
       rd.include(req, res);
    else
       rd.forward(req, res);
  }
}
```

The servlet listed in Example 3-5 is functionally identical to the JSP page listed in Example 3-4 on page 73. All other things being equal, it is recommended that validation is handled by servlets or beans, to keep that code out of JSP pages. See "Validation" on page 88 for more information concerning the use of servlets vs. JSP pages for validation.

JSP Tip

Implement Client-side and Server-side Validation

Robust web applications should implement both client-side and server-side validation. Server-side validation should be implemented to provide redundant checking[1] because there are no guarantees that JavaScript will be enabled in a user's browser.

Implementing both client-side and server-side validation provides immediate feedback when JavaScript is enabled and offers a safety net of redundant checking when JavaScript is disabled.

1. Redundant checking is common in both software and natural systems.

Server-side Validation with Servlets and JSP Pages

The previous two sections explored server-side validation with either servlets or JSP pages. Neither of those solutions is ideal because either the validation servlet produces HTML, or the validation JSP page performs the validation. Because servlets are controllers and JSP pages are views, servlets should not display content and JSP pages should not contain business logic.

A better solution is to use a servlet and a JSP page for validation, with that servlet performing the validation logic and that JSP page displaying validation error messages.

It's easy to modify the servlet listed in Example 3-5 on page 74 to store its error message in request scope, instead of printing it. A partial listing of that updated servlet is listed below.

```
public class ValidationServlet extends HttpServlet {
   public void service(HttpServletRequest req,
                       HttpServletResponse res)
                          throws IOException, ServletException {
      String first = req.getParameter("firstName"),
              last = req.getParameter("lastName"),
             email = req.getParameter("emailAddress"),
          errorMsg = "", nextStop = "/registrationComplete.jsp";

      boolean errorDetected = false;

      ...
      if(errorDetected) {
         req.setAttribute("validate-error", errorMsg);
         nextStop = "/form.jsp";
      }
      ...
   }
   ...
}
```

Because the validation servlet stores an error message in request scope, a JSP page can access that error message with a scriptlet, like this:

```
<html><head><title>Server Side Validation</title>
   <%@ taglib uri='validate' prefix='validate' %>
</head>

<body>
<% String errorMsg = (String)request.getAttribute(
                                    "validate-error");

   if(errorMsg != null) { %>
   <%= errorMsg %>
<% } %>

<p>
<form name='simpleForm' action='ValidationServlet'/>
   ...
</form>
</p>
</body></html>
```

If you want to purge the JSP page listed above of its scriptlet, you could implement a custom tag that shows the validation error. That custom tag would be used like this:

```
<html><head><title>Server Side Validation</title>
   <%@ taglib uri='validate' prefix='validate' %>
</head>

<body>
<validate:showValidateError/>
<p>
<form name='simpleForm' action='ValidationServlet'/>
   ...
</form>
</p>
</body></html>
```

The custom tag shown in the code fragment listed above is listed in Example 3-6.

Example 3-6   /WEB-INF/classes/tags/ShowValidateErrorTag.java

```
package tags;

import javax.servlet.jsp.JspException;
import javax.servlet.jsp.tagext.TagSupport;

public class ShowValidateErrorTag extends TagSupport {
    public int doEndTag() throws JspException {
        String msg = (String)pageContext.getRequest().
                            getAttribute("validate-error");
        if(msg != null) {
            try {
                pageContext.getOut().print(msg);
            }
            catch(java.io.IOException ex) {
                throw new JspException(ex.getMessage());
            }
        }
        return EVAL_PAGE;
    }
}
```

A Form Framework

Let's briefly revisit the use of beans to encapsulate the state of form elements, as outlined in "Forms with Beans" on page 61. Typically, a JSP page containing a form creates a bean somewhere near the top of the page, like this:

```
<jsp:useBean id='form' class='beans.Form' scope='request'>
     <jsp:setProperty name='form' property='*'/>
</jsp:useBean>
```

If you specify '*' for the `property` attribute of the `jsp:setProperty` tag, the JSP container uses Java reflection to set the bean's properties from request parameters. For example, for a request parameter named `category`, the JSP container will look for a bean method named `setCategory`. If the method exists, the JSP container will invoke it with the value of the `category` request parameter. This same algorithm is applied to all request parameters.

Using Java reflection is a slick way to impart request parameter values to a bean, but it has a drawback: distinct JavaBeans classes must be implemented for every form, assuming different forms provide different names for their elements, which is nearly always the case.

Because different classes are implemented for each form, nearly identical code will be duplicated among the beans. For example, consider the following code fragment taken from Example 3-2.c on page 68:

```
...
private String[] categories;
...
public String categorySelectionAttr(String category) {
    if(categories != null) {
        for(int i=0; i < categories.length; ++i) {
            if(categories[i].equals(category))
                return "checked";
        }
    }
    return "";
}
...
```

The `categorySelectionAttr` method listed above determines whether a checkbox named `category` is selected and returns an appropriate string—`"checked"` or an empty string—that can be used as an attribute for the HTML input tag. Other beans implement nearly identical methods for checkboxes in other forms; for example, for a set of checkboxes named `grocery`, a form bean might implement the following method, which is nearly identical to the code fragment listed above:

```
...
private String[] groceries;
...
public String grocerySelectionAttr(String grocery) {
    if(categories != null) {
        for(int i=0; i < groceries.length; ++i) {
            if(groceries[i].equals(grocery))
                return "checked";
```

```
            }
        }
    return "";
}
...
```

Implementing nearly identical methods among different beans is tedious and error prone. One way to reduce the amount of code that must be duplicated is to use the façade design pattern.

Façade Design Pattern for HTML Forms

A *façade object* "provides a single, simplified interface to the more *general facilities* of a subsystem".[3] In the case of HTML forms, the façade design pattern can be implemented as illustrated in Figure 3-5.

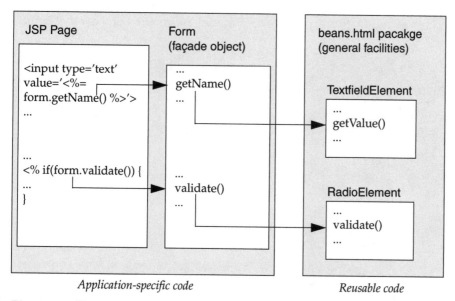

Figure 3-5 The Façade Design Pattern for Handling Forms

The façade object is a form bean, and the "general facilities"—classes in the beans.html package—represent code common to form elements. The general facilities in Figure 3-5 constitute reusable code; that reuse is the major benefit of using the façade pattern for handling forms.

---

3.   From Gamma, Helm, Johnson, Vlissides, *Design Patterns*. Addison-Wesley, 1995.

Webster's defines façade as a false, superficial, or artificial appearance or effect. That's an apt description of the form bean in Figure 3-5, which simply delegates functionality to more general facilities. For example, for the categorySelectionAttr method, discussed in "Server-side Validation with Servlets and JSP Pages" on page 75, a form bean might look something like this:

```java
public class Form {
   CheckboxElement categories = new CheckboxElement();
   ...
   public String categorySelectionAttr() {
      return categories.selectionAttr(category);
   }
   ...
}
```

In the code fragment listed above, Form.categorySelectionAttr returns a string that is used as a checkbox selection attribute for an HTML input tag; see "Checkboxes and Options" on page 65 for more information on how that method is used.

The CheckboxElement used by the Form bean would look like this:

```java
public class CheckboxElement {
   private String[] items;
   ...
   public String selectionAttr(String item) {
      if(items != null) {
         for(int i=0; i < items.length; ++i) {
            if(items[i].equals(item))
               return "checked";
         }
      }
      return "";
   }
   ...
}
```

Using the façade pattern greatly reduces the amount of code that must be implemented for handling forms because the code that determines whether a checkbox is selected is encapsulated in a reusable class.

You can implement classes similar to CheckboxElement for other types of HTML form elements, such as text areas, radio buttons, options, etc. A framework of such classes is discussed in the next section.

The Framework

A form framework can greatly simplify storing form state, as discussed in "Façade Design Pattern for HTML Forms" on page 79. There are many ways to implement such a framework; this section discusses one way. First, we discuss the use of the framework, followed by an examination of its implementation.

Figure 3-6 shows a JSP page containing a form with a number of elements. The form does not specify an action, so the same page is redisplayed when the form is submitted. When the form is redisplayed, all of the values previously entered are retained.

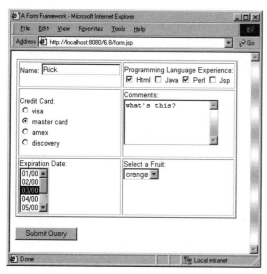

Figure 3-6 Using the Form Framework

The JSP page shown in Figure 3-6 is rather lengthy, so a truncated version of the page, listing one of each element, is listed in Example 3-7.a.

Example 3-7.a /form.jsp (truncated listing)

```
...
<jsp:useBean id='form' class='beans.Form' scope='request'>
   <jsp:setProperty name='form' property='*' />
</jsp:useBean>

<form>
...
```

```
<%-- Textfield --%>
Name: <input type='text' name='name'
             value='<%= form.getName() %>'/>
...
<%-- Checkboxes --%>
Programming Language Experience:<br>
<input type='checkbox' name='languages' value='html'
     <%= form.languageSelectionAttr("html") %> /> Html
...
<%-- Radio Buttons --%>
Credit Card:<br>
   <input type='radio' name='credit' value='visa'
      <%= form.creditSelectionAttr("visa") %>>
            visa</input type='radio'><br>
   ...
<%-- Text Area --%>
Comments:<br>
<textarea name='comments' cols='20' rows='5'>
   <%= form.getComments() %></textarea><p>
...
<%-- List --%>
Expiration Date:<br>
<select name='expiration' size=5>
   <option <%= form.expirationSelectionAttr("01/00") %>
         value='01/00'>01/00</option>
   ...
</select>
<%-- Drop-down List --%>
...
Select a Fruit:<br>
<select name='fruit'>
   <option <%= form.fruitSelectionAttr("apple") %>
      value='apple'>apple</option>
   ...
</select>
...
<%-- Submit Button --%>
<p><input type='submit'/></p>
</form>
</body></html>
```

The JSP page listed above instantiates a bean of type beans.Form when the page is loaded and imparts request parameters to that bean, as described in "Server-side Validation with Servlets and JSP Pages" on page 75. That bean is subsequently used to set form values, as described in "Forms with Beans" on page 61.

The form bean used in Example 3-7.a is listed in Example 3-7.b.

Example 3-7.b /WEB-INF/classes/beans/Form.java

```java
package beans;

import beans.html.CheckboxElement;
import beans.html.OptionsElement;
import beans.html.RadioElement;
import beans.html.TextElement;
import beans.html.TextAreaElement;

public class Form {
    TextElement name = new TextElement();
    RadioElement credit = new RadioElement();
    TextAreaElement comments = new TextAreaElement();
    CheckboxElement languages = new CheckboxElement();
    OptionsElement expiration = new OptionsElement();
    OptionsElement fruit = new OptionsElement();

    public String getName() { return name.getValue(); }
    public void setName(String s) { name.setValue(s); }

    public String getComments() { return comments.getValue();}
    public void setComments(String s) { comments.setValue(s); }

    public String getCredit() { return credit.getValue(); }
    public void setCredit(String s) { credit.setValue(s); }

    public String[] getLanguages() { return languages.getValue(); }
    public void setLanguages(String[] s) { languages.setValue(s); }

    public String[] getFruit() {return fruit.getValue();}
    public void setFruit(String[] s) {fruit.setValue(s);}

    public String[] getExpiration() {return expiration.getValue();}
    public void setExpiration(String[] s) {expiration.setValue(s);}

    public String creditSelectionAttr(String s) {
        return credit.selectionAttr(s);
    }
    public String languageSelectionAttr(String s) {
        return languages.selectionAttr(s);
    }
    public String expirationSelectionAttr(String s) {
        return expiration.selectionAttr(s);
    }
    public String fruitSelectionAttr(String s) {
        return fruit.selectionAttr(s);
    }
}
```

The bean listed in Example 3-7.b uses a number of objects from a `beans.html` package, such as `TextElement`, `RadioElement`, etc. Although the listing is somewhat lengthy because of the number of elements in the form, using objects from the `beans.html` package greatly simplifies the bean's implementation. Compare the bean listed above to a bean—listed in "/WEB-INF/classes/beans/Form.java" on page 68—that represents a much simpler form, to see how programmers can simplify a bean's code by delegating functionality.

Because the bean listed in Example 3-7.b does not implement any functionality other than delegation to more general objects, it is a façade in the truest sense of the word. It is also interesting to note that code for a façade bean, such as the one listed in Example 3-7.b, could be generated by software that parses HTML.

The most interesting aspect of the JSP page shown in Figure 3-6 on page 81 is the design of the `beans.html` package. We begin our discussion of the `beans.html` package with the class diagram shown in Figure 3-7.

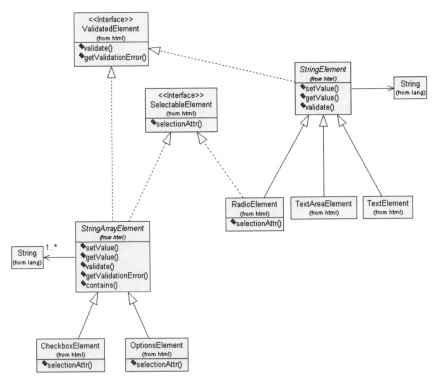

Figure 3-7 Class Diagram for the `beans.html` Package

From the point of view of the beans.html package, there are two types of form elements: those that generate a single request parameter—such as textfields, text areas, and radio buttons—and those that can generate multiple request parameters, such as checkboxes and options. Those types of elements are represented by two abstract classes—StringElement and StringArrayElement.

Because all of the classes representing form elements should provide methods for validation, both StringElement and StringArrayElement implement the ValidatedElement interface, which is listed in Example 3-7.c.

Example 3-7.c /WEB-INF/classes/beans/html/ValidatedElement.java

```
package beans.html;

public interface ValidatedElement {
   boolean validate();
   String getValidationError();
}
```

The ValidatedElement interface defines a validate method that indicates whether an element is valid. If validation fails—meaning validate returns false—the getValidationError method must return a string indicating why the element was invalid.

The StringElement class is listed in Example 3-7.d.

Example 3-7.d /WEB-INF/classes/beans/html/StringElement.java

```
package beans.html;

public class StringElement implements ValidatedElement {
   final protected String emptyString = "";
   private String value;

   public void setValue(String value) {
      this.value = value;
   }
   public String getValue() {
      return value != null ? value : emptyString;
   }
   public boolean validate() {
      return true;
   }
   public String getValidationError() {
      return emptyString;
   }
}
```

StringElement maintains a string that is accessed with getValue, which returns an empty string if a value has not been specified. Returning an empty string for unspecified values ensures that "null" will not be returned and subsequently displayed in a corresponding HTML element.

By default, StringElement extensions are always valid. It's up to StringElement subclasses to override validate and getValidationError. See "Validation" on page 88 for an example of how the two methods might be overridden.

The TextElement and TextAreaElement classes, listed below, are extensions of StringElement that provide no additional functionality. Those classes exist to increase code readability and to provide placeholders for future functionality.

```
public class TextElement extends StringElement {}
public class TextAreaElement extends StringElement {}
```

The StringArrayElement class, which is the superclass for CheckboxElement and OptionsElement, is listed in Example 3-7.e.

Example 3-7.e   /WEB-INF/classes/beans/html/StringArrayElement.java

```java
package beans.html;

public abstract class StringArrayElement
                implements SelectableElement, ValidatedElement {
   final String emptyString = "";
   private String[] value;

   public void setValue(String[] value) {
      this.value = value;
   }
   public String[] getValue() {
      return value != null ? value : new String[]{};
   }
   public boolean validate() {
      return true;
   }
   public String getValidationError() {
      return "";
   }
   public boolean contains(String s) {
      String[] strings = getValue();

      for(int i=0; i < strings.length; ++i) {
```

```
            if(strings[i].equals(s))
                return true;
        }
        return false;
    }
}
```

StringArrayElement is similar to StringElement, except its value is an array of strings.[4] Like StringElement, extensions of StringArrayElement are valid by default.

The contains method is a utility method used by StringArrayElement extensions to determine whether a checkbox or option is selected.

Selectable Elements

Checkboxes, radio buttons, and options typically exist in groups of like elements where one (in the case of radio buttons) or more (for checkboxes and options) elements can be selected. Those types of elements are represented in the form framework by the SelectableElement interface, which is listed in Example 3-7.f.

Example 3-7.f /WEB-INF/classes/beans/html/SelectableElement.java

```
package beans.html;

public interface SelectableElement {
    String selectionAttr(String s);
}
```

The RadioElement, CheckboxElement, and OptionsElement classes all implement the SelectableElement interface. Their selectionAttr methods return "checked", or "selected" depending upon whether an element with the specified name is selected. If an element is not selected, an empty string is returned. All three classes are listed below.

```
// emptyString is a protected member of StringElement

public class RadioElement extends StringElement
                                implements SelectableElement {
    public String selectionAttr(String value) {
        return getValue().equals(value) ? "checked" : emptyString;
    }
}
```

---

4.   See "Checkboxes and Options" on page 65.

```
public class CheckboxElement extends StringArrayElement {
   public String selectionAttr(String s) {
      return contains(s) ? "checked" : emptyString;
   }
}
public class OptionsElement extends StringArrayElement {
   public String selectionAttr(String s) {
      return contains(s) ? "selected" : emptyString;
   }
}
```

By default, all objects from the `beans.html` package are valid. Implementing validation constraints, which is the topic of the next section, involves extending `beans.html` classes and overriding the methods defined by the `ValidationElement` interface.

Validation

This section illustrates extending the framework discussed in "Server-side Validation with Servlets and JSP Pages" on page 75 by implementing validation for HTML elements.

The JSP page shown in Figure 3-8 validates its name and credit card. That page's form is valid if the name is filled in and does not contain spaces or digits and if a credit card is selected. The left picture in Figure 3-8 shows the form before an incomplete submission, and the right picture shows the result of that submission.

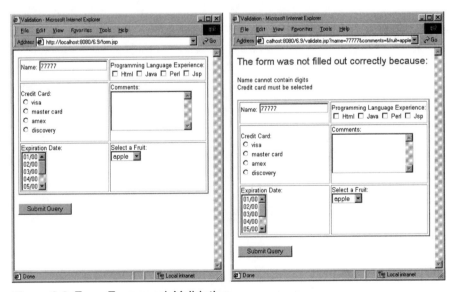

Figure 3-8 Form Framework Validation

Given the framework discussed in "Server-side Validation with Servlets and JSP Pages" on page 75, adding validation is a relatively simple task. First, you specify a JSP page that performs the validation as a form's action. That's what the JSP page shown in Figure 3-8 does, as listed below.

```
// omitted code can be found in Example 3-7.a on page 81
...
<form action='validate.jsp'>
...
```

The next step is implementing `validate.jsp`, which is listed in Example 3-8.a.

Example 3-8.a /validate.jsp

```
<jsp:useBean id='form' class='beans.Form' scope='request'>
   <jsp:setProperty name='form' property='*' />
</jsp:useBean>

<% String errorMsg = "";
   boolean errorDetected = false;

   if(!form.validate()) {
        errorMsg += form.getValidationError();
        errorDetected = true;
   }
   if(errorDetected) { %>
      <font color='red' size='5'>
      The form was not filled out correctly because:<p>
      </font><font size='3'>
      <%= errorMsg %></font></p>
      <jsp:include page='form.jsp' flush='true' />
<%   } else { %>
      <jsp:include page='registrationComplete.jsp' flush='true' />
<% } %>
```

`validate.jsp` creates a form bean and sets the bean's properties from `request` parameters. That bean is subsequently used to validate the form. If the form is invalid, an error message is obtained from the bean and displayed and the JSP page containing the form is included. If the form is valid, control is forwarded to another JSP page.

Because `validate.jsp` uses the `setProperty` tag, in this case it is more difficult to implement validation in a servlet. Servlets, unlike JSP pages, do not provide a mechanism that uses Java reflection to impart request parameters to a bean.

The form bean used in Example 3-8.a is listed in Example 3-8.b.

Example 3-8.b /WEB-INF/classes/beans/Form.java

```java
// omitted code can be found in Example 3-7.b on page 83
// package beans;

public class Form implements ValidatedElement {
    private CreditElement credit = new CreditElement();
    private NameElement     name = new NameElement();
    private String error;
    ...
    public boolean validate() {
        error = "";

        if(!name.validate()) {
            error += name.getValidationError();
        }
        if(!credit.validate()) {
            if(error.length() > 0)
                error += "<br>";

            error += credit.getValidationError();
        }
        return error == "";
    }
    public String getValidationError() {
        return error;
    }
    ...
}
```

The form bean listed in Example 3-8.b is identical to the form bean listed in
Example 3-7.b on page 83, except that instances of NameElement and
CreditElement are created instead of TextElement and CheckboxElement,
respectively. Also, the form bean is now a validated element; its validate
method validates the name and credit elements. If validation fails, an error
message is recorded and subsequently returned from getValidationError.

The NameElement and CreditElement classes are extensions of
TextElement and CheckboxElement, respectively, that override the methods
defined by the ValidatedElement interface. The CreditElement class is
listed in Example 3-8.c.

Example 3-8.c /WEB-INF/classes/beans/CreditElement.java

```
package beans.html;

public class CreditElement extends RadioElement {
   private String error;

   public boolean validate() {
      boolean valid = true;
      String  value = getValue();

      error = "";

      if(value == null || value.length() == 0) {
         valid = false;
         error = "Credit card must be selected";
      }
      return valid;
   }
   public String getValidationError() {
      return error;
   }
}
```

The validate method for CreditElement returns true if a radio button is selected, and returns false otherwise.

The NameElement class is listed in Example 3-8.d.

Example 3-8.d /WEB-INF/classes/beans/NameElement.java

```
package beans.html;

public class NameElement extends TextElement {
   private String error;

   public boolean validate() {
      boolean valid = true;
      String  value = getValue();

      error = "";

      if(value.length() == 0) {
         valid = false;
         error = "Name field must be filled in";
```

```
      }
      else {
         for(int i=0; i < value.length(); ++i) {
            char c = value.charAt(i);

            if(c == ' ' || (c > '0' && c < '9')) {
               valid = false;
               if(c == ' ')
                  error = "Name cannot contain spaces";
               else
                  error = "Name cannot contain digits";
            }
         }
      }
      return valid;
   }
   public String getValidationError() {
      return error;
   }
}
```

`NameElement.validate` returns `true` if the name has been filled in and does not contain spaces or digits.

As you can see, incorporating validation into the form framework is straightforward. Validation methods are added to the form bean, and element classes are extended to override the `validation` and `getValidationError` methods, according to individual validation criteria.

JSP Tip

Form-handling Code Reuse

The previous section, starting at "Server-side Validation with Servlets and JSP Pages" on page 75, discussed a form framework that can simplify handling forms with JSP. In all likelihood, you will implement your own framework or use someone else's, so it's the concepts behind the framework, not the framework itself, that are important to understand.

The major benefit of a form framework is code reuse, as illustrated in "The Façade Design Pattern for Handling Forms" on page 79. That reuse can also be attained by other means; for example, general form handling can be encapsulated in custom tags, which can obviate the need for a form framework.

Custom Tags

Wouldn't it be nice if HTML tags were extensible? If, for example, the select tag could be extended as a list of links? Although it's not possible to extend HTML tags directly, it is possible to implement JSP custom tags that provide such functionality; in fact, a select tag similar to the one described above is discussed in "Generating JavaScript" on page 54.

This section discusses the implementation of a custom tag that serves as a replacement for the HTML form tag with an additional focus attribute. That tag sets focus to a specified element in a form when that form is loaded. Example 3-9.a illustrates the use of that custom tag.

Example 3-9.a   Using the form Custom Tag

```
...
<%@ taglib uri='form.tld' prefix='html' %>
...
<%-- the name field receives focus when the form is loaded --%>
<html:form name='myForm' focus='name' method='post'>
     <%-- form elements from Example 3-7.a on page 81 --%>
     ...
</html:form>
...
```

The form listed in Example 3-9.a is identical to the form shown in Figure 3-8 on page 88, except the name textfield receives focus when the form is loaded. For the sake of brevity, the form elements are not listed in Example 3-9.a—see Example 3-7.a on page 81 for a partial listing of those elements.

The tag handler for the form tag is listed in Example 3-9.b.

Example 3-9.b   /WEB-INF/classes/tags/FormTag.java

```
package tags;

import javax.servlet.jsp.*;
import javax.servlet.jsp.tagext.*;

public class FormTag extends BodyTagSupport {
   public String method, name, focus;

   public void setName(String name) { this.name = name; }
   public void setMethod(String method) { this.method = method; }
   public void setFocus(String focus) { this.focus = focus; }
```

```
public int doEndTag() throws JspException {
    try {
        String body = bodyContent.getString();
        bodyContent.clearBody();

        StringBuffer buffer = new StringBuffer(
            "<form name='" + name + "' method='" + method + "'>"
            + body + "\n</form>\n" +
            "<script language='JavaScript'>\n" +
            "document." + name + "." + focus + ".focus()" +
            "\n</script>");

        bodyContent.print(buffer.toString());
        bodyContent.writeOut(pageContext.getOut());
    }
    catch(java.io.IOException ex) {
        throw new JspException(ex.getMessage());
    }
    return EVAL_PAGE;
    }
}
```

This section is not concerned with the specifics of implementing custom tags; see "Custom Tag Fundamentals" on page 2 and "Custom Tag Advanced Concepts" on page 32 for those specifics. What this section does illustrate is how to extend an HTML tag's capabilities with a custom tag.

The tag handler listed in Example 3-9.b generates an HTML form tag, passing through the method and name attributes. Note that other HTML form attributes are not accounted for in Example 3-9.b; most notably, the action tag is omitted. Those missing attributes are left out in the interests of brevity and readability, but it's a simple matter to add them in the same manner as the method and name attributes.

Setting focus is implemented with generated JavaScript. Custom tags that generate JavaScript are a powerful combination of client-side and server-side technology that can be used to implement functionality that would otherwise be difficult to achieve.

Conclusion

Two design patterns were applied to handling HTML forms in this chapter: Memento, for storing form state in Java beans, and façade, for encapsulating and simplifying access to reusable code. Those design patterns were implemented in a simple form framework that you may find useful as a basis for your own framework.

"Custom Tags" on page 93 discussed a simple custom tag that replaces the HTML form tag with the ability to set focus. If you're interested in implementing a set of HTML form replacement tags, "Custom Tags" on page 93 can get you started. On the other hand, a number of such initiatives are already under way; here are some URLs to investigate.

- Apache Struts:
  http://jakarta.apache.org/struts/index.html
- IN16 JSP Tag Library:
  http://sourceforge.net/projects/jsptags/
- Form Taglib:
  http://cupid.suninternet.com/~joeo/Form.html

TEMPLATES

Topics in this Chapter

- Encapsulating Layout
- Optional Content
- Role-based Content
- Defining Regions Separately
- Nesting Regions
- Extending Regions
- Combining Features
- Region Tag Implementations
- Conclusion

Chapter 4

Window toolkits typically provide three types of objects that greatly facilitate the implementation of flexible, extensible, and reusable applications: components, containers, and layout managers. Components are graphic objects such as buttons, menus, or lists, and containers are groups of components. Layout managers position and size a container's components.[1]

Components, containers, and layout managers are typically implemented with two design patterns: Composite and Strategy.[2] The Composite design pattern, used to implement components and containers, specifies that a container is a component, so you can place any component—even if it's a container—within any container. That handy feature lets you nest components as deeply as you want in a tree structure.

Layout managers are implemented with the Strategy pattern, which defines a family of algorithms and encapsulates each one. That makes layout algorithms interchangeable. Encapsulating layout also lets you modify layout algorithms without changing the containers that use them.

1. See Geary. *Graphic Java Volume 1: AWT*, Prentice Hall, 1998.
2. See Gamma, Helms, Johnson, Vlissides. *Design Patterns*, Addison-Wesley, 1994.

JSP does not provide anything analogous to components, containers, or layout managers. But JSP has two features—custom tags and the ability to include web components—that let you implement your own components, containers, and layout managers.[3] This chapter shows you how to do that so you can create web applications that are easy to maintain, extend, and reuse.

The components, containers, and layout managers discussed in this chapter are a little different from their window toolkit counterparts. To reflect that difference, they have different names:

- *Section*: An object that renders HTML or JSP in a page context
- *Region*: An object that contains sections
- *Template*: A JSP page that defines how regions and sections are laid out

Regions and templates are similar to containers and layout managers, respectively. Sections are different from components because they do not handle events; sections, however, are similar to components because they render content. That content is either an HTML file or a JSP page.

This chapter is divided into two parts. The first part, which begins with "Encapsulating Layout" below, shows you how to use a custom tag library to implement JSP pages with sections, regions, and templates. The second section, which starts at "Region Tag Implementations" on page 116, shows how those custom tags and their associated beans are implemented.

Note: The techniques discussed in this chapter represent an implementation of the J2EE Composite View pattern, which lets you compose a single view from multiple sub-views, using beans and JSP custom tags. You can read more about that design pattern and others in Core J2EE Patterns by Alur, Crupi, and Malks, published by Prentice Hall and Sun Microsystems Press.

Encapsulating Layout

Because layout typically undergoes many changes over the course of development, it's important to encapsulate that functionality so it can be modified with minimal impact to the rest of the application. In fact, layout managers are an example of one of the tenets of object-oriented design: *encapsulate the concept that varies*, which is also a fundamental theme for many design patterns.

---

3.   The term *web component* refers to a servlet, HTML file, or JSP page and is unrelated to the more general term *component* used in this chapter.

Most web pages contain multiple sections that display their own content; for example, Figure 4-1 shows a web page containing header, footer, sidebar, and main content sections.

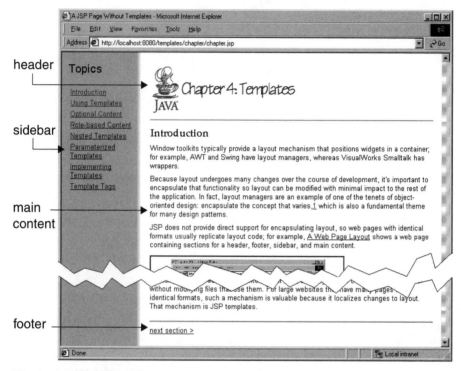

Figure 4-1 Web Page Layout

The layout of the page shown in Figure 4-1 can be implemented with HTML `table` tags, as listed in Example 4-1.

Example 4-1 Including Content

```
<html><head>
   <title>A JSP Page Without Templates</title>
</head>

<body background='graphics/blueAndWhiteBackground.gif'>

<table>
  <tr valign='top'>
    <td>
      <jsp:include page='sidebar.jsp' flush='true'/>
    </td>
```

```
<td>
  <table>
    <tr>
      <td>
        <jsp:include page='header.jsp' flush='true'/>
      </td>
    </tr>
    <tr>
      <td>
        <jsp:include page='introduction.jsp' flush='true'/>
      </td>
    </tr>
    <tr>
      <td>
        <jsp:include page='footer.jsp' flush='true'/>
      </td>
    </tr>
  </table>
</td>
</tr>
</table>

</body>
</html>
```

In the JSP page listed in Example 4-1, content is included with the `jsp:include` action, which allows us to vary the content of that page—by changing the included files—without modifying the page itself. But because layout is hardcoded in the page, layout changes will require modifications to that page. If a web site has multiple pages with identical formats, even simple layout changes will require modifications to all of those pages.

Besides *separating content* from the JSP pages that display it, as is the case for the JSP page listed in Example 4-1, we can also *separate layout* from JSP pages. That separation means we can change layout without modifying the JSP files that use it.

Sections, Regions, and Templates

To separate layout from JSP pages, we will use one of the oldest programming tricks in the book: indirection. We will split the single JSP page listed in Example 4-1—which includes content and performs layout—into two JSP pages: a region that defines content and a template that performs layout. That region is listed in Example 4-2.a.

Example 4-2.a A JSP Page That Defines a Region

```
<%@ taglib uri='regions' prefix='region' %>

<region:render template='/template.jsp'>
  <region:put section='title'  content='Templates' direct='true'/>
  <region:put section='header' content='/header.jsp' />
  <region:put section='sidebar' content='/sidebar.jsp' />
  <region:put section='content' content='/introduction.jsp'/>
  <region:put section='footer' content='/footer.jsp' />
</region:render>
```

The JSP page listed above uses custom tags to define and render a region. That region contains the four sections shown in Example 4-1 on page 99.

Every region is associated with a single template, which is specified with the template attribute of the region:render tag. The region:render start tag creates a region—see "The Beans" on page 116 for more about how regions are implemented—and places it in application scope.

The region:put tags store a name/value pair in the region created by the region:render start tag. Those name/value pairs represent section names and content; for example, for the region listed in Example 4-2.a, a header section is defined whose content is /header.jsp.

Finally, the region:render end tag includes the template defined by that tag's template attribute. The template included by the region defined in Example 4-2.a is listed in Example 4-2.b.

Example 4-2.b The Template Used by the Region Defined in Example 4-2.a

```
<%@ taglib uri='regions' prefix='region' %>

<html><head>
   <title><region:render section='title'/></title>
</head>

<body background='graphics/blueAndWhiteBackground.gif'>

<table>
  <tr valign='top'>
    <td>
      <region:render section='sidebar'/>
    </td>
    <td>
      <table>
        <tr>
```

```
            <td>
              <region:render section='header'/>
            </td>
          </tr>
          <tr>
            <td>
              <region:render section='content'/>
            </td>
          </tr>
          <tr>
            <td>
              <region:render section='footer'/>
            </td>
          </tr>
        </table>
      </td>
    </tr>
  </table>

  </body>
  </html>
```

Like all templates, the template listed in Example 4-2.b uses the `region:render` tag to render a region's sections. That tag accesses the region, stored in application scope, that included the template. From that region, the `region:render` tag obtains the name of the content associated with a section and includes it.[4]

A `direct` attribute can be specified for `region:render`; if that attribute is set to `true`, the content associated with that tag is not included by `region:render` but is printed directly to the implicit `out` variable. For example, in Example 4-2.a the `title` content—"Templates"—is used as the window title.

Web sites containing multiple pages with identical formats have one template, such as the one listed in Example 4-2.b, and many JSP pages, such as Example 4-2.a, that use the template. If the format is modified, *changes are restricted to the template.*

Another benefit of templates, and included content in general, is modular design. For example, the JSP file listed in Example 4-2.a ultimately includes `/header.jsp`, which is listed in Example 4-2.c.

---

4.   The `region:render` tag pulls double duty by rendering regions and sections.

Example 4-2.c /header.jsp

```
<table>
  <tr>
    <td><img src='graphics/java.gif'/></td>
    <td><img src='graphics/templates.gif'/></td>
  </tr>
</table>
<hr>
```

Because /header.jsp is included content, it does not have to be replicated among pages that display a header. Also, notice that /header.jsp does not contain the usual preamble of HTML tags, such as <html>, <head>, <body>, etc., that most JSP pages contain; those tags are supplied by the template that includes that JSP file. The /header.jsp file is simple and easy to maintain.

This section has illustrated the basic capabilities of two custom tags—region:render and region:put—from the regions custom tag library. That tag library provides other features, such as optional and role-based content, that are explored in the sections that follow.

JSP Tip

Use Templates to Implement Web Applications with Modular Components

The techniques discussed in this chapter—using sections, regions, and templates to implement web pages—lets you construct web applications with modular components.

Encapsulating content lets you modify that content without modifying JSP pages that display it. Similarly, encapsulating layout lets you modify the layout used by multiple JSP pages by changing a single template.

Optional Content

All content rendered by a template is optional, which makes a single template useful to many regions; for example, Figure 4-2 shows two regions that use the same template. The region on the left specifies content for all four of its sections: sidebar, header, content, and footer. The region on the right only specifies content for three of its regions: sidebar, header, and footer. As you can see from Figure 4-2, if a template cannot locate content for a given section, it merely ignores that section.

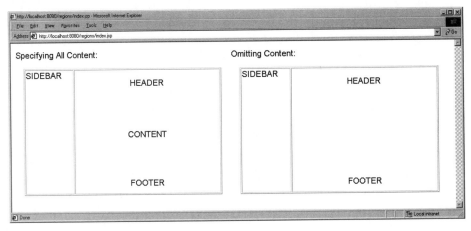

Figure 4-2 Optional Content

The JSP page shown in Figure 4-2 is listed in Example 4-3.a.

Example 4-3.a   Specifying a Region with Inline Content and Omitted Content

```
<%@ taglib uri='regions' prefix='region' %>

<table>
   <tr>
      <td valign='top'>
         <font size='5'>Specifying All Content:</font>
         <table cellspacing='20'>
            <tr>
               <td>
                  <%--all content is specified for this region--%>
                  <region:render template='hscf.jsp'>
                     <region:put section='header'
                                 content='/header.jsp'/>

                     <region:put section='sidebar'
                                 content='/sidebar.jsp'/>

                     <region:put section='content'
                                 content='/content.jsp'/>

                     <region:put section='footer'
                                 content='/footer.jsp'/>
                  </region:render>
               </td>
            </table>
         </td>
```

```
<td valign='top'>
    <font size='5'>Omitting Content:</font>
    <table cellspacing='20'>
        <tr>
            <td>
                <%--content is omitted for this region--%>
                <region:render template='hscf.jsp'>
                    <region:put section='header'
                                content='/header.jsp' />

                    <region:put section='sidebar'
                                content='/sidebar.jsp' />

                    <region:put section='footer'
                                content='/footer.jsp' />
                </region:render>
            </td>
        </tr>
    </table>
    </td>
</tr>
</table>
```

In the JSP page listed above, the JSP pages specified as section content are very simple; for example, /sidebar.jsp is listed below:

```
<font size='5'>SIDEBAR</font>
```

The other JSP pages specified as content in Example 4-3.a are identical to /sidebar.jsp, except for the text they display; for example, /header.jsp is:

```
<font size='5'>HEADER</font>
```

In a real application, the JSP pages specified as section content would display more meaningful content, but the simple JSP pages used in Example 4-3.a serve to illustrate the use of regions and templates, so they are used throughout this chapter.

The template used by the regions listed in Example 4-3.a—/hscf.jsp—is listed in Example 4-3.b.[5]

---

5.   hscf stands for **h**eader, **s**idebar, **c**ontent, and **f**ooter.

Example 4-3.b   /hscf.jsp: The Template Used in Example 4-3.a

```
<html><head>
   <%@ taglib uri='regions' prefix='region' %>
</head>

<table border='1' width='500'>
   <tr> <%-- Sidebar --%>
      <td valign='top' width='25%'>
         <region:render section='sidebar'/>
      </td>
      <td valign='top' align='center' width='*'>
         <table height='300'>
            <tr> <%-- Header --%>
               <td align='center' height='20%'>
                  <region:render section='header'/>
               </td>
            </tr> <%-- Main Content --%>
               <td align='center' height='*'>
                  <region:render section='content'/>
               </td>
            </tr> <%-- Footer --%>
               <td align='center' height='15%'>
                  <region:render section='footer'/>
               </td>
            </tr>
         </table>
      </td>
   </tr>
</table>

</body></html>
```

The template listed in Example 4-3.b, like the template listed in Example 4-2.b on page 101, uses HTML table tags to lay out its four sections.

For the sake of illustration, the template listed above specifies a border width of 1 for its outermost table. Normally, templates should not render anything except their sections.

Role-based Content

Web applications often discriminate content based on a user's role. For example, the two pages shown in Figure 4-3 are produced by the same JSP template, which includes the edit panel only if the user's role is curator.

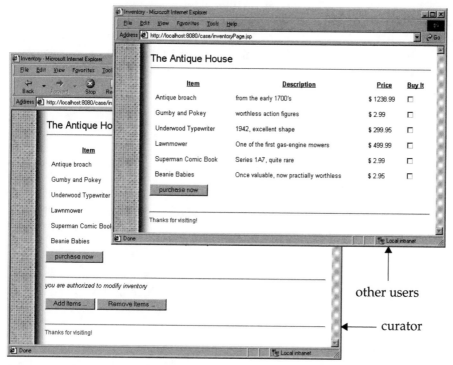

other users

curator

Figure 4-3 Role-based Content

Both of the JSP pages shown in Figure 4-3 use the same template, which is partially listed below.

```
<%@ taglib uri='regions.tld' prefix='region' %>
...
<table>
   ...
   <td><region:render section='editPanel' role='curator'/></td>
   ...
</table>
...
```

The `region:render` tag only renders a section's content if the user's role matches the `role` attribute. That `role` attribute is optional; if a role is not specified for a given section, that section, if it has content, is always rendered.

In the preceding code fragment, the template only renders the `editPanel` section if the user's role is `curator`. That means that every region that uses that template must abide by that restriction. Sometimes, you want individual regions to specify role-based content; to facilitate that intent, the `region:put` tag also has an optional role attribute. That attribute is used like this:

```
<region:render template='hscf.jsp'>
   ...
   <region:put section='header' content='/header.jsp'
               role='curator'/>
   ...
</region:render>
```

The `region:put` tag used in the code fragment above will only add the `header` section to the region created by the `region:render` start tag if the user's role is curator.

Defining Regions Separately

So far, all of the regions in this chapter have been defined and rendered in one place; for example, consider the JSP page shown in Figure 4-4.

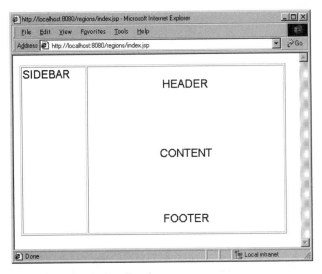

Figure 4-4 Defining Regions

The JSP page shown in Figure 4-4 can be created with a single region that has four sections. That region can be defined and rendered all at once, as listed in Example 4-4.

Example 4-4 Defining and Rendering a Region in One Place

```
<%@ taglib uri='regions' prefix='region' %>

<table>
    <tr>
        <td>
            <%--content for this region is specified inline--%>
            <region:render template='hscf.jsp'>
                <region:put section='header'  content='/header.jsp'/>
                <region:put section='sidebar' content='/sidebar.jsp'/>
                <region:put section='content' content='/content.jsp'/>
                <region:put section='footer'  content='/footer.jsp'/>
            </region:render>
        </td>
    </tr>
</table>
```

Instead of defining regions inline, as is the case for the region listed in Example 4-4, regions can be defined someplace other than where they are rendered; for example, Example 4-5.a shows how the JSP page shown in Figure 4-4 can be rendered from an existing region.

Example 4-5.a A JSP File That Uses an Existing Region

```
<%@ taglib uri='regions' prefix='region' %>

<%@ include file='/regionDefinitions.jsp' %>

<region:render region='SIDEBAR_REGION'/>
```

The JSP page listed in Example 4-5.a renders an existing region. That region—SIDEBAR_REGION—is defined in /regionDefinitions.jsp, which is included by the JSP page listed in Example 4-5.a. /regionDefinitions.jsp is listed in Example 4-5.b.

Example 4-5.b /regionDefinitions.jsp: Defining a Region

```
<%@ taglib uri='regions' prefix='region' %>

<region:define id='SIDEBAR_REGION' scope='application'
          template='hscf.jsp'>
    <region:put section='header'  content='/header.jsp'/>
    <region:put section='sidebar' content='/sidebar.jsp'/>
    <region:put section='content' content='/content.jsp'/>
    <region:put section='footer'  content='/footer.jsp'/>
</region:define>
```

The JSP page listed in Example 4-5.b uses the `region:define` tag to define a region named `SIDEBAR_REGION` that's stored in application scope. That region is created by the `region:define` start tag and its name and scope are specified with the `region:define` tag's `id` and `scope` attributes, respectively. The `region:define` tag also has a `template` attribute that specifies the template used by a region.

Like the `region:render` tag, `region:define` can contain `region:put` tags, which store section names and content in the region created by the `region:define` start tag.

Why would you want to define regions somewhere other than where they are rendered? Because that separation allows you to group region definitions in a single file, thereby giving you access to all of the regions defined by an application. That makes maintaining those regions significantly easier. Also, because regions can be nested—see "Nesting Regions" below—and can inherit from one another—see "Extending Regions" on page 112—it's easier to maintain multiple regions if they are all defined in one file.

Nesting Regions

Because sections and regions are implemented with the Composite design pattern, you can specify a region for a section's content; for example, the JSP page shown in Figure 4-5 nests one region inside another.

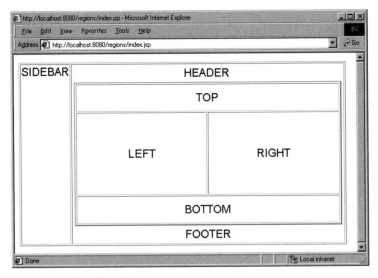

Figure 4-5 Nesting Regions

The JSP page shown in Figure 4-5 is identical to the JSP page listed in Example 4-5.a on page 109. That JSP page renders the preexisting SIDEBAR_REGION, which is defined in Example 4-5.c.

Example 4-5.c /regionDefinitions.jsp

```
<%@ taglib uri='regions' prefix='region' %>

<region:define id='SIDEBAR_REGION' scope='application'
        template='hscf.jsp'>
   <region:put section='header'  content='/header.jsp'/>
   <region:put section='sidebar' content='/sidebar.jsp'/>
   <region:put section='content' content='BORDER_REGION'/>
   <region:put section='footer'  content='/footer.jsp'/>
</region:define>

<region:define id='BORDER_REGION' scope='application'
        template='tlbr.jsp'>
   <region:put section='top'    content='/top.jsp'/>
   <region:put section='left'   content='/left.jsp'/>
   <region:put section='right'  content='/right.jsp'/>
   <region:put section='bottom' content='/bottom.jsp'/>
</region:define>
```

The SIDEBAR_REGION specifies the BORDER_REGION as the content for its content section, which nests the BORDER_REGION inside the SIDEBAR_REGION.

Notice that the BORDER_REGION does not need to be defined before it is specified in the SIDEBAR_REGION. That's because the SIDEBAR_REGION does not look for the BORDER_REGION until the SIDEBAR_REGION is rendered.

For completeness, the template used by the BORDER_REGION is listed in Example 4-5.d.

Example 4-5.d The Template Used by the BORDER_REGION in Example 4-5.c

```
<html><head>
  <%@ taglib uri='regions' prefix='region' %>
</head>

<table border='2' width='500'>
    <tr> <%-- Top Row --%>
        <td colspan='2' align='center' height='50'>
           <region:render section='top'/>
        </td>
    </tr>
```

```
<tr> <%-- Left and Right Rows --%>
    <td align='center' width='50%' height='150'>
        <region:render section='left'/>
    </td>
    <td align='center' width='50%' height='150'>
        <region:render section='right'/>
    </td>
</tr>

<tr> <%-- Bottom Row --%>
    <td colspan='2' align='center' height='50'>
        <region:render section='bottom'/>
    </td>
</tr>
</table>

</body></html>
```

The template listed in Example 4-5.d renders the top, left, right, and bottom sections defined in the BORDER_REGION.[6]

Extending Regions

Perhaps the most exciting feature of regions is that one region can extend another; for example, the JSP page shown in Figure 4-6 renders a region that extends the SIDEBAR_REGION used throughout this chapter.

The JSP page shown in Figure 4-6 is listed in Example 4-6.a.

Like the JSP page listed in Example 4-5.a on page 109, the JSP page listed in Example 4-6.a includes a JSP file that contains region definitions. The JSP page listed in Example 4-6.a subsequently renders the EXTENDED_SIDEBAR_REGION.

---

6.   The name BORDER_REGION comes from the AWT BorderLayout, which lays out components in a similar fashion.

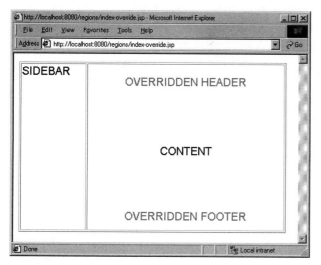

Figure 4-6 Overriding Sections

Example 4-6.a Extending an Existing Region

```
<%@ taglib uri='regions' prefix='region' %>
<%@ include file='/regionDefinitions-override.jsp' %>

<region:render region='EXTENDED_SIDEBAR_REGION'/>
```

The JSP page that defines the SIDEBAR_REGION and the
EXTENDED_SIDEBAR_REGION is listed in Example 4-6.b.

Example 4-6.b /regionDefinitions-override.jsp

```
<%@ taglib uri='regions' prefix='region' %>

<region:define id='SIDEBAR_REGION' scope='application'
        template='hscf.jsp'>
   <region:put section='header'  content='/header.jsp'/>
   <region:put section='sidebar' content='/sidebar.jsp'/>
   <region:put section='content' content='/content.jsp'/>
   <region:put section='footer'  content='/footer.jsp'/>
</region:define>

<region:define id='EXTENDED_SIDEBAR_REGION' scope='application'
           region='SIDEBAR_REGION'>
   <region:put section='header' content='/overridden-header.jsp'/>
   <region:put section='footer' content='/overridden-footer.jsp'/>
</region:define>
```

Usually, regions are defined with a template, as is the case for the
SIDEBAR_REGION defined in Example 4-6.b. But you can also define a region
with another region, as is the case for the EXTENDED_SIDEBAR_REGION, which
is defined with the SIDEBAR_REGION.

Defining one region in terms of another causes the newly defined region to
"inherit" from the specified region; for example, EXTENDED_SIDEBAR_REGION
is defined in terms of the SIDEBAR_REGION, so EXTENDED_SIDEBAR_REGION
inherits all of the SIDEBAR_REGION's content. Subsequently,
EXTENDED_SIDEBAR_REGION selectively overrides the content for the header
and footer sections defined in the SIDEBAR_REGION with region:put tags.

Combining Features

You may never need to create a web page with regions as complicated as those
shown in Figure 4-7, but the regions tag library discussed in this chapter lets you
combine nested and extended regions in all sorts of interesting ways.

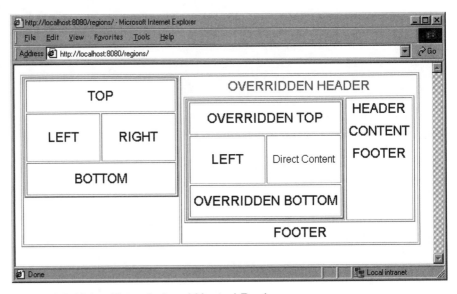

Figure 4-7 Using Extended and Nested Regions

The JSP page shown in Figure 4-7 is listed in Example 4-7.a.

Example 4-7.a /index.jsp

```
<%@ taglib uri='regions' prefix='regions' %>
<%@ include file='/regionDefinitions-override.jsp' %>

<region:render region='EXTENDED_SIDEBAR_REGION' />
```

The JSP file included above is listed in Example 4-7.b.

Example 4-7.b /regionDefinitions-override.jsp

```
<%@ taglib uri='regions' prefix='region' %>

<region:define id='SIDEBAR_REGION' scope='request'
         template='hscf.jsp'>
  <region:put section='header'  content='/header.jsp' />
  <region:put section='sidebar' content='EXTENDED_BORDER_REGION' />
  <region:put section='content' content='/content.jsp' />
  <region:put section='footer'  content='/footer.jsp' />
</region:define>

<region:define id='BORDER_REGION' scope='request'
         template='tlbr.jsp'>
  <region:put section='top'    content='/top.jsp' />
  <region:put section='bottom' content='/bottom.jsp' />
  <region:put section='left'   content='/left.jsp' />
  <region:put section='right'  content='/right.jsp' />
</region:define>

<region:define id='EXTENDED_SIDEBAR_REGION' scope='request'
           region='SIDEBAR_REGION'>
  <region:put section='header' content='/overridden-header.jsp' />
  <region:put section='sidebar' content='BORDER_REGION' />
  <region:put section='content' content='SIDEBAR_REGION' />
</region:define>

<region:define id='EXTENDED_BORDER_REGION' scope='request'
           region='BORDER_REGION'>
  <region:put section='top'    content='/overridden-top.jsp' />
  <region:put section='bottom' content='/overridden-bottom.jsp' />
  <region:put section='right'>
     <font size='4'>Direct Content</font>
  </region:put>
</region:define>
```

The regions defined in Example 4-7.b are so intertwined that they probably border on some kind of technology abuse; nonetheless, they demonstrate how powerful the regions custom tag library is.

The EXTENDED_SIDEBAR_REGION is the region that's rendered by the JSP page shown in Figure 4-7. That region extends SIDEBAR_REGION and overrides the header, sidebar, and content sections. The sidebar and content regions for the EXTENDED_SIDEBAR_REGION are the BORDER_REGION and SIDEBAR_REGION, respectively.

The SIDEBAR_REGION uses the EXTENDED_BORDER_REGION for its sidebar section. The EXTENDED_BORDER_REGION extends BORDER_REGION and overrides the top, bottom, and right sections. Notice that the right section for the EXTENDED_BORDER_REGION defines its content in the body of the region:put tag. That feature is discussed on page 130.

The regions defined above use the templates—hscf.jsp and tlbr.jsp—listed in Example 4-3.b on page 106 and Example 4-5.d on page 111, respectively, except that the table widths and heights for those templates were reduced to scale the JSP page shown in Figure 4-7 down to a reasonable size.

Region Tag Implementations

The regions custom tag library used in this chapter consists of four beans and three custom tags. The rest of this chapter explores the implementation of those beans and tags.

The Beans

The beans used by the regions custom tag library are listed in Table 4-1.

Table 4-1 Beans Used by the Regions Custom Tag Library[1]

Bean	Description
Content	Content that's rendered in a JSP PageContext
Section	Content that's part of a region
Region	A container that contains sections
RegionStack	A stack of regions maintained in application scope

1. All of the beans listed above are from the beans.regions package.

A class diagram for the beans listed in Table 4-1 is shown in Figure 4-8.

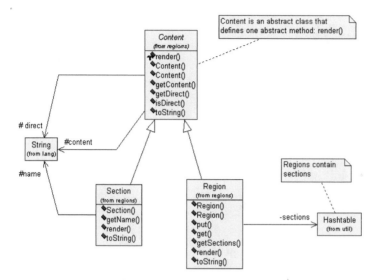

Figure 4-8 Region Beans

`Content` is an abstract class that's the superclass for `Section` and `Region`. Those three classes constitute an implementation of the Composite design pattern because the `Content` abstract class represents both primitives (sections) and their containers (regions).

The `Section` and `Region` classes both implement the `render` method, which is the only abstract method defined by the `Content` class. The `Region` class contains a hash table of its sections.

The `Content` class is listed in Example 4-8.a.

Example 4-8.a /WEB-INF/classes/beans/templates/Content.java

```
package beans.regions;

import javax.servlet.jsp.JspException;
import javax.servlet.jsp.PageContext;

public abstract class Content implements java.io.Serializable {
    protected final String content, direct;

    // Render this content in a JSP page
    abstract void render(PageContext pc) throws JspException;

    public Content(String content) {
        this(content, "false");
    }
```

```
public Content(String content, String direct) {
   this.content = content;
   this.direct  = direct;
}
public String getContent() {
   return content;
}
public String getDirect() {
   return direct;
}
public boolean isDirect() {
   return Boolean.valueOf(direct).booleanValue();
}
public String toString() {
   return "Content: " + content;
}
}
```

The Content class is a simple abstract class that defines a render abstract method. That class also maintains two properties: content and direct. The content property represents the content rendered by the render method, and the direct attribute specifies how that content is rendered. If the direct attribute is true, content is rendered directly by printing it. If the direct attribute is false, content is rendered by including it.

The Section class is listed in Example 4-8.b.

Example 4-8.b   /WEB-INF/classes/beans/templates/Section.java

```
package beans.regions;

import javax.servlet.jsp.JspException;
import javax.servlet.jsp.PageContext;

// A section is content with a name that implements
// Content.render. That method renders content either by including
// it or by printing it directly, depending upon the direct
// value passed to the Section constructor.
//
// Note that a section's content can also be a region;if so,
// Region.render is called from Section.Render().

public class Section extends Content {
   protected final String name;

   public Section(String name, String content, String direct) {
      super(content, direct);
```

```
      this.name = name;
   }
   public String getName() {
      return name;
   }
   public void render(PageContext pageContext)
                                    throws JspException {
      if(content != null) {
         // see if this section's content is a region
         Region region = (Region)pageContext.
                                    findAttribute(content);
         if(region != null) {
            // render the content as a region
            RegionStack.push(pageContext, region);
            region.render(pageContext);
            RegionStack.pop(pageContext);
         }
         else {
            if(isDirect()) {
               try {
                  pageContext.getOut().print(content.toString());
               }
               catch(java.io.IOException ex) {
                  throw new JspException(ex.getMessage());
               }
            }
            else {
               try {
                  pageContext.include(content.toString());
               }
               catch(Exception ex) {
                  throw new JspException(ex.getMessage());
               }
            }
         }
      }
   }
   public String toString() {
      return "Section: " + name + ", content= " +
                                    content.toString();
   }
}
```

The Section class extends Content and implements the render method. If a
section's direct attribute is true, that section prints its content to the implicit
out variable. If a section's direct attribute is false, that section uses the JSP
page context to include its content.

If a section's content is a region, the section pushes the region onto a stack—see Example 4-8.d for more information about the stack—and renders the region. After the region has been rendered, its section pops it off the stack.

The Region class is listed in Example 4-8.c.

Example 4-8.c /WEB-INF/classes/beans/templates/Region.java

```java
package beans.regions;

import java.util.Enumeration;
import java.util.Hashtable;
import javax.servlet.jsp.PageContext;
import javax.servlet.jsp.JspException;

// A region is content that contains a set of sections.

public class Region extends Content {
   private Hashtable sections = new Hashtable();

   public Region(String content) {
      this(content, null); // content is the name of a template
   }
   public Region(String content, Hashtable hashtable) {
      super(content);

      if(hashtable != null)
         sections = (Hashtable)hashtable.clone();
   }
   public void put(Section section) {
      sections.put(section.getName(), section);
   }
   public Section get(String name) {
      return (Section)sections.get(name);
   }
   public Hashtable getSections() {
      return sections;
   }
   public void render(PageContext pageContext)
                                 throws JspException {
      try {
         pageContext.include(content);
      }
      catch(Exception ex) { // IOException or ServletException
         throw new JspException(ex.getMessage());
      }
```

```
   }
   public String toString() {
      String s = "Region: " + content.toString() + "<br/>";
      int indent = 4;
      Enumeration e = sections.elements();

      while(e.hasMoreElements()) {
         Section section = (Section)e.nextElement();
         for(int i=0; i < indent; ++i) {
            s += " ";
         }
         s += section.toString() + "<br/>";
      }
      return s;
   }
}
```

Like the `Section` class, the `Region` class extends `Content` and implements the `render` method. Additionally, regions maintain a hash table of sections. A region's sections can be accessed with `Region.get` or with `Region.getSections`; the former returns a section given its name, and the latter returns the region's hash table of sections.

Regions are maintained on a stack in application scope. That stack is represented by the `RegionStack` class, which is listed in Example 4-8.d.

Example 4-8.d /WEB-INF/classes/beans/templates/RegionStack.java

```
package beans.regions;

import javax.servlet.jsp.PageContext;
import java.util.Stack;

public class RegionStack {
   private RegionStack() { } // no instantiations

   public static Stack getStack(PageContext pc) {
      Stack s = (Stack)pc.getAttribute("region-stack",
                              PageContext.APPLICATION_SCOPE);
      if(s == null) {
         s = new Stack();
         pc.setAttribute("region-stack", s,
                     PageContext.APPLICATION_SCOPE);
      }
      return s;
   }
}
```

```
public static Region peek(PageContext pc) {
    return (Region)getStack(pc).peek();
}
public static void push(PageContext pc, Region region){
    getStack(pc).push(region);
}
public static Region pop(PageContext pc) {
    return (Region)getStack(pc).pop();
}
}
```

Because nested templates could potentially overwrite their enclosing template's content, regions are stored on a stack. That stack is represented by the `RegionStack` class listed above, which provides `static` methods for pushing regions on the stack, popping them off, and peeking at the top region on the stack.

The Tag Handlers

The tag handlers from the regions custom tag library are listed in Table 4-2.

Table 4-2 Tags From the Regions Custom Tag Library[1]

Bean	Description
`RegionTag`	Is a base class for `RegionDefinitionTag` and `RenderTag`
`RegionDefinitionTag`	Creates a region and stores it in a specified scope
`RenderTag`	Renders a region or a section
`PutTag`	Creates a section and stores it in a region

    1. All of the tags listed above are from the `tags.regions` package.

A class diagram for the tags listed in Table 4-2 is shown in Figure 4-9.

Both the `region:render` and `region:define` tags, whose tag handlers are `RenderTag` and `RegionDefinitionTag`, respectively, create a region. That functionality is encapsulated in the `RegionTag` class, which is the base class for `RenderTag` and `RegionDefinitionTag`. All three of those classes ultimately extend `TagSupport`.

The `PutTag` class is the tag handler for the `region:put` tag. That tag handler extends `BodyTagSupport` so you can specify content in that tag's body.

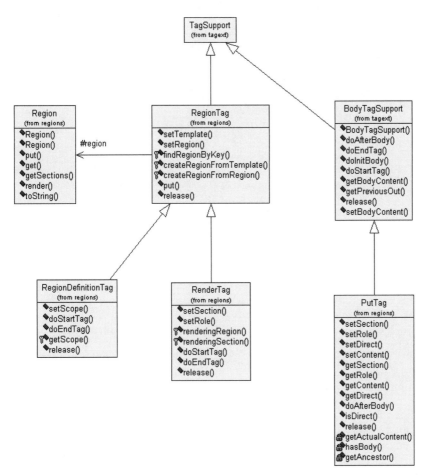

Figure 4-9 Region Tags

The RegionTag class is listed in Example 4-9.a.

Example 4-9.a   /WEB-INF/classes/tags/regions/RegionTag.java

```
package tags.regions;

import javax.servlet.jsp.JspException;
import javax.servlet.jsp.PageContext;
import javax.servlet.jsp.tagext.TagSupport;

import beans.regions.Section;
import beans.regions.Region;
```

```java
public class RegionTag extends TagSupport {
   protected Region region = null;
   protected String template = null;
     private String regionKey = null;

   public void setTemplate(String template) {
      this.template = template;
   }
   public void setRegion(String regionKey) {
      this.regionKey = regionKey;
   }
   protected boolean findRegionByKey() throws JspException {
      if(regionKey != null) {
         region = (Region)pageContext.findAttribute(regionKey);
         if(region == null) {
            throw new JspException("can't find page definition " +
                                   "attribute with this key: " +
                                   regionKey);
         }
      }
      return region != null;
   }
   protected void createRegionFromTemplate() throws JspException {
      if(template == null)
         throw new JspException("can't find template");

      region = new Region(template);
   }
   protected void createRegionFromRegion() throws JspException {
      findRegionByKey();

      if(region == null)
         return;

      region = new Region(region.getContent(),   // the template
                          region.getSections()); // sections
   }
   public void put(Section section) {
      region.put(section);
   }
   public void release() {
      super.release();
      region = null;
      regionKey = null;
      template = null;
   }
}
```

Regions can be created from a template or another region, both of which are specified with a `template` or `region` attribute. The `RegionTag` class provides setter methods for those attributes, implements methods for creating a region from a template or another region, and provides a method for locating an existing region given its name. All three of those methods are used by `RegionTag` subclasses.

The `RegionDefinitionTag` class is listed in Example 4-9.b.

Example 4-9.b /WEB-INF/classes/tags/regions/RegionDefinitionTag.java

```
package tags.regions;

import javax.servlet.jsp.JspException;
import javax.servlet.jsp.PageContext;
import javax.servlet.jsp.tagext.TagSupport;

import beans.regions.Content;
import beans.regions.Region;

public class RegionDefinitionTag extends RegionTag {
   private String scope = null;

   public void setScope(String scope) {
      this.scope = scope;
   }
   public int doStartTag() throws JspException {
      if(region != null && template != null)
         throw new JspException("regions can be created from " +
                                "a template or another region," +
                                "but not both");
      createRegionFromRegion();

      if(region == null)
         createRegionFromTemplate();

      return EVAL_BODY_INCLUDE;
   }
   public int doEndTag() throws JspException {
      pageContext.setAttribute(id, region, getScope());
      return EVAL_PAGE;
   }
   protected int getScope() {
      int constant = PageContext.PAGE_SCOPE;

      scope = (scope == null) ? "page" : scope;
```

```
        if("page".equalsIgnoreCase(scope))
           constant = PageContext.PAGE_SCOPE;
        else if("request".equalsIgnoreCase(scope))
           constant = PageContext.REQUEST_SCOPE;
        else if("session".equalsIgnoreCase(scope))
           constant = PageContext.SESSION_SCOPE;
        else if("application".equalsIgnoreCase(scope))
           constant = PageContext.APPLICATION_SCOPE;

        return constant;
     }
     public void release() {
        super.release();
        scope = "page";
     }
  }
```

The `RegionDefinitionTag` class extends `RegionTag` and creates a region, either from a template or another region. Notice that `RegionDefinitionTag.doStartTag` throws an exception if both `region` and `template` attributes are specified. That exception is thrown because a region can be created from a template or another region, but not both.

The `RenderTag` class is listed in Example 4-9.c.

Example 4-9.c /WEB-INF/classes/tags/regions/RenderTag.java

```
package tags.regions;

import javax.servlet.http.HttpServletRequest;
import javax.servlet.jsp.JspException;
import javax.servlet.jsp.PageContext;
import javax.servlet.jsp.tagext.TagSupport;

import beans.regions.Content;
import beans.regions.Section;
import beans.regions.Region;
import beans.regions.RegionStack;

public class RenderTag extends RegionTag {
   private String sectionName=null, role=null;

   public void setSection(String s)   { this.sectionName = s; }
   public void setRole(String s)       { this.role = s;        }

   protected boolean renderingRegion() {
      return sectionName == null;
   }
```

```
   protected boolean renderingSection() {
      return sectionName != null;
   }
   public int doStartTag() throws JspException {
      HttpServletRequest request = (HttpServletRequest)
                                   pageContext.getRequest();

      if(role != null && !request.isUserInRole(role))
         return SKIP_BODY;

      if(renderingRegion()) {
         if(!findRegionByKey()) {
            createRegionFromTemplate();
         }
         RegionStack.push(pageContext, region);
      }
      return EVAL_BODY_INCLUDE;
   }
   public int doEndTag() throws JspException {
      Region region = RegionStack.peek(pageContext);

      if(region == null)
         throw new JspException("Can't find region");

      if(renderingSection()) {
         Section section = region.get(sectionName);

         if(section == null)
            return EVAL_PAGE; // ignore missing sections

         section.render(pageContext);
      }
      else if(renderingRegion()) {
         try {
            region.render(pageContext);
            RegionStack.pop(pageContext);
         }
         catch(Exception ex) { // IOException or ServletException
            throw new JspException(ex.getMessage());
         }
      }
      return EVAL_PAGE;
   }
   public void release() {
      super.release();
      sectionName = role = null;
   }
}
```

The RenderTag class renders both sections and regions. If a section attribute is specified, that tag renders a section; otherwise, it renders a region. If a region is rendered, that region is pushed on the region stack in doStartTag and popped off the stack in doEndTag. See "The Beans" on page 116 for more information about that region stack.

The PutTag class is listed in Example 4-9.d.

Example 4-9.d   /WEB-INF/classes/tags/regions/PutTag.java

```java
package tags.regions;

import javax.servlet.http.HttpServletRequest;
import javax.servlet.jsp.JspException;
import javax.servlet.jsp.PageContext;
import javax.servlet.jsp.tagext.BodyTagSupport;
import javax.servlet.jsp.tagext.TagSupport;

import beans.regions.Content;
import beans.regions.Section;

public class PutTag extends BodyTagSupport {
   private String section, role, content, direct = null;

   public void setSection(String section){this.section = section;}
   public void setRole    (String role)   {this.role    = role;   }
   public void setDirect (String direct) {this.direct  = direct; }
   public void setContent(String cntnt)  {this.content = cntnt;  }

   public String getSection() { return section; }
   public String getRole()    { return role;    }
   public String getContent() { return content; }
   public String getDirect()  { return direct;  }

   public int doAfterBody() throws JspException {
      HttpServletRequest request =
                  (HttpServletRequest)pageContext.getRequest();

      if(role != null && !request.isUserInRole(role))
         return EVAL_PAGE;

      RegionTag regionTag = (RegionTag)getAncestor(
                                 "tags.regions.RegionTag");
      if(regionTag == null)
         throw new JspException("No RegionTag ancestor");

      regionTag.put(new Section(section, getActualContent(),
                                      isDirect()));
```

```
      return SKIP_BODY;
   }
   public String isDirect() {
      if(hasBody()) return "true";
      else          return direct == null ? "false" : "true";
   }
   public void release() {
      super.release();
      section = content = direct = role = null;
   }
   private String getActualContent() throws JspException {
      String bodyAndContentMismatchError =
         "Please specify template content in this tag's body " +
         "or with the content attribute, but not both.",
            bodyAndDirectMismatchError =
         "If content is specified in the tag body, the " +
         "direct attribute must be true.";

      boolean hasBody = hasBody();
      boolean contentSpecified = (content != null);

      if((hasBody && contentSpecified) ||
         (!hasBody && !contentSpecified))
         throw new JspException(bodyAndContentMismatchError);

      if(hasBody && direct != null &&
         direct.equalsIgnoreCase("false"))
         throw new JspException(bodyAndDirectMismatchError);

      return hasBody ? bodyContent.getString() : content;
   }
   private boolean hasBody() {
      if (bodyContent == null)
         return (false);

      return ! bodyContent.getString().equals("");
   }
   private TagSupport getAncestor(String className)
                              throws JspException {
      Class klass = null; // can't name variable "class"
      try {
         klass = Class.forName(className);
      }
      catch(ClassNotFoundException ex) {
         throw new JspException(ex.getMessage());
      }
      return (TagSupport)findAncestorWithClass(this, klass);
   }
}
```

The PutTag class creates a section and stores it in the region created by its enclosing region:define or region:render tag. The PutTag class extends BodyTagSupport because it allows content that's printed directly to be specified in the tag's body; for example, the region:put tag can be used like this:

```
<region:render template='/WEB-INF/jsp/templates/hscf.jsp'>
   <region:put section='title'>
     The Fruitstand
   </region:put>
   ...
</region:render>
```

If a region:put tag has a body, as is the case for the preceding code fragment, that body must be content that's printed directly. The PutTag class enforces that restraint by checking to make sure that the direct attribute is true if the tag has body content.

Conclusion

Components, containers, and layout managers are found in most window toolkits because they allow applications to be built from modular components. This chapter has demonstrated how to implement those types of objects for JSP-based web applications.

By using the sections, regions, and templates discussed in this chapter, you can implement web applications that are extensible, reusable, and maintainable. See "A Case Study" on page 390 for more information about using sections, regions, and templates in a nontrivial web application.

DESIGN

Topics in this Chapter

Chapter 5

Developing web pages in HTML is easy. Designing flexible and maintainable web applications that combine HTML, JSP, and Java and access databases or legacy systems is not. This chapter provides insights into the use of JSP, beans, and servlets by examining some common approaches to web application design.

The authors of the JSP specification designed JSP to be flexible. You can implement JSP-based web applications in many ways; for example, you can approach the project as follows:

- Freely mix HTML and JSP scriptlets
- Delegate functionality to beans
- Use servlets, JSP pages, and beans to implement a Model-View-Controller (MVC) architecture

The first approach—mixing copious amounts of Java code with HTML in JSP pages—leads to applications that are difficult to maintain and extend, and therefore is not recommended.

Delegating functionality to beans is a viable approach because it moves Java code from JSP pages to beans. This approach was first advocated in the 0.91 version of the JSP specification,[1] and is commonly known as the Model 1 architecture.

---

1. You can download the 0.91 and 0.92 JSP specifications from
   http://www.kirkdorffer.com/jspspecs.

The last approach—combining servlets, JSP pages, and beans in an MVC architecture—results in extensible and maintainable software because it encapsulates functionality and reduces the impact of change. This approach was also first advocated in the 0.91 JSP specification and is known as the Model 2 architecture.

This chapter begins with a brief discussion of the Model 1 architecture, followed by an in-depth examination of Model 2. In Chapter 6, we extend Model 2 with a framework that facilitates implementing Model 2 applications.

Model 1

The Model 1 architecture consists of JSP pages, beans, and business objects, as depicted in Figure 5-1.

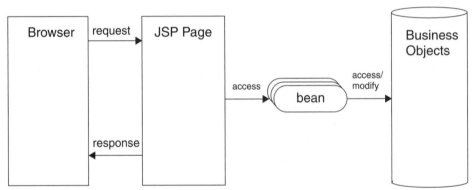

Figure 5-1 Model 1 Architecture: JSP Page, Beans, and Business Objects

The Model 1 architecture submits requests to JSP pages, which indirectly access business objects through beans. This indirect access insulates JSP pages from business object changes—which are typically frequent, especially for large projects—because those changes are dealt with by beans. As long as bean interfaces remain constant, JSP pages are independent of business object implementations.

Software developers implement the business objects and the beans. Ideally, web page authors would be responsible for JSP pages, resulting in a division of labor where business objects and web pages are developed in parallel by developers with different skill sets. That division of labor is difficult to achieve with the Model 1 architecture because JSP pages are responsible for content *generation*, which nearly always requires Java code, in addition to content *presentation*.

Because a division of labor between web page authors and software developers is difficult to achieve with the Model 1 architecture, that approach is only appropriate for small projects with a few developers, all of whom are fluent in Java, JSP, and HTML or XML.

For large projects, it's imperative to maintain a division of labor between web page authors and software developers. For those projects, a different approach must be taken. Most often, that approach is the Model 2 architecture.

JSP Tip

Model 1 Pros and Cons

The Model 1 architecture reduces dependencies between JSP pages and business objects, allowing web pages and business objects to be developed in parallel.

But with the Model 1 architecture, software developers are typically involved in the development of both web pages and business objects. That makes it difficult to achieve a division of labor where web page authors implement web pages and software developers provide underlying functionality. Such a division of labor is often crucial for large projects.

Model 2: An MVC Approach

The Model 2 architecture, like Model 1, separates business objects from JSP pages, as is essential for most web development projects where business objects are in a constant state of flux. Additionally, Model 2, illustrated in Figure 5-2, separates content generation from content presentation.

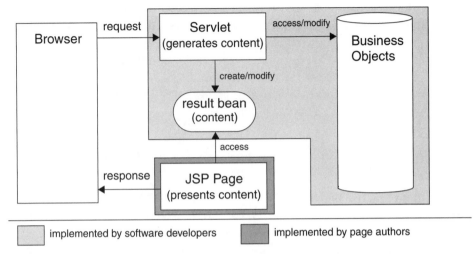

Figure 5-2 The Original Model 2 Architecture: An MVC Approach

The Model 2 architecture submits requests to a servlet, which accesses business objects to create content. That content is stored in a bean, which is accessed by a JSP page. That JSP page subsequently presents the content, typically in HTML.

Separating content generation from presentation is beneficial because Java code, for the most part, is restricted to content generation.[2] This encapsulation of Java code lets software developers concentrate on servlets and business objects and lets web page authors focus on corresponding JSP pages.

Model 2 is an MVC architecture, where business objects represent the model (data), servlets represent controllers (which handle requests), and JSP pages are views of the model. The MVC architecture, which originated in Smalltalk back in the stone age of computing, has stood the test of time because it separates business and presentation logic. That separation allows for pluggable components, resulting in flexible, reusable, and adaptable software.

Note: The Model 2 architecture is actually a modified MVC implementation because its model does not fire events to its views. That modification evolved because web applications typically do not display more than one view of their model at a time.

2. Java code in the presentation layer is easily replaced by custom tags; see "The Importance of Custom Tags" on page 175.

> ## JSP Tip
>
> The Benefits of MVC
>
> The MVC architecture has long been the foundation upon which Smalltalk applications are built, and for good reason.
>
> The most fundamental aspect of object-oriented development is identifying abstractions and encapsulating them in classes. For example, a payroll application would identify abstractions such as employees, salaries, etc. Encapsulating abstractions in classes allows for loose coupling between objects, thereby reducing dependencies and increasing flexibility and reuse.
>
> MVC encapsulates three general abstractions that are present in most graphical applications: models, views, and controllers. By encapsulating what other architectures intertwine, MVC applications are much more flexible and reusable than their traditional counterparts.

A Model 2 Example

This section discusses the implementation of a familiar web application: login and registration. The application is implemented with the Model 2 architecture and consists of two servlets—one for login and another for creating a new account—two beans, one custom tag, and six JSP pages, as shown in Figure 5-3. The application also includes a deployment descriptor (/WEB-INF/web.xml), which defines servlet mappings, and a tag library descriptor[3] (/WEB-INF/tlds/utilties.tld) that defines the application's lone custom tag.

---

3. See "Defining Custom Tags—The TLD" on page 6.

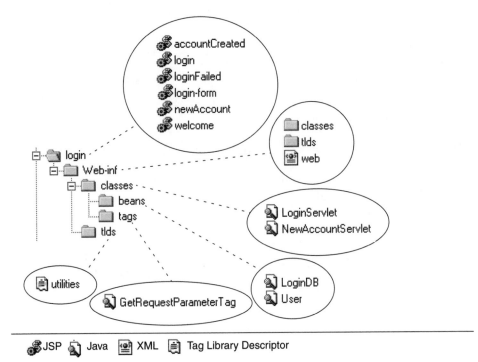

♨ JSP 🗋 Java 🗋 XML 📄 Tag Library Descriptor

Figure 5-3 Directory Structure and Files for the Model 2 Example

The Beans

The login and registration application contains two beans: one represents users, and the other represents a makeshift login database. The User class is listed in Example 5-1.a.

Example 5-1.a   /WEB-INF/classes/beans/User.java

```
package beans;

// Users are immutable

public class User implements java.io.Serializable {
   private final String userName, password, hint;

   public User(String userName, String password, String hint) {
      this.userName = userName;
      this.password = password;
      this.hint = hint;
```

```
    }
    public String getUserName() { return userName; }
    public String getPassword() { return password; }
    public String getHint()     { return hint; }

    public boolean equals(String uname, String pwd) {
        return getUserName().equals(uname) &&
               getPassword().equals(pwd);
    }
}
```

Users maintain three properties: a username, password, and a password hint, all of which are specified when a user is constructed. The User class provides accessors for those properties.

The User class also implements an equals method that returns true if the username and password passed to the method match.

Users are immutable because a user's properties can only be set by the User constructor. Immutability is one technique for guarding against multithreaded access; if an object cannot be changed after it is constructed, inconsistencies cannot arise from access by multiple threads.[4] The final keyword is used to emphasize that the properties cannot be changed after they are initialized.[5]

The login database is listed in Example 5-1.b.

Example 5-1.b /WEB-INF/classes/beans/LoginDB.java

```
package beans;

import java.util.Iterator;
import java.util.Vector;

public class LoginDB implements java.io.Serializable {
    private Vector users = new Vector();

    public void addUser(String uname, String pwd, String hint) {
        users.add(new User(uname, pwd, hint));
    }
    public User getUser(String uname, String pwd) {
        Iterator it = users.iterator();
        User bean;
```

4. See Lea, Doug. *Concurrent Programming in Java*, Addison-Wesley, 2000, page 71.
5. The User properties are known as blank finals; see Arnold and Gosling. *The Java Programming Language*, Addison-Wesley, 1998, page 111.

```
        synchronized(users) {
           while(it.hasNext()) {
              bean = (User)it.next();

              if(bean.equals(uname, pwd))
                 return bean;
           }
        }
        return null;
     }
     public String getHint(String uname) {
        Iterator it = users.iterator();
        User bean;

        synchronized(users) {
           while(it.hasNext()) {
              bean = (User)it.next();

              if(bean.getUserName().equals(uname))
                 return bean.getHint();
           }
        }
        return null;
     }
  }
```

The LoginDB class maintains a vector of users and provides methods for adding and retrieving users, in addition to a method that returns a password hint for a specified username.

The LoginDB class guards against multithreaded access by synchronizing critical code segments that iterate over its vector. The java.util.Vector class is synchronized, so, for example, LoginDB.addUser doesn't need to be. However, iterators are not synchronized and will throw an exception if a collection is modified while an iterator iterates over a collection.

The Deployment Descriptor

Web applications have a deployment descriptor that defines a web application's configuration and deployment information, such as:

- Servlet context initialization parameters
- Session configuration
- Servlet/JSP definitions
- Servlet/JSP mappings
- Mime type mappings

- Welcome file list
- Error pages
- Security

Deployment descriptors are defined in an application's /WEB-INF directory in a file named web.xml.[6] Example 5-1.c lists the deployment descriptor for the login and registration application.

Example 5-1.c /WEB-INF/web.xml

```xml
<?xml version="1.0" encoding="ISO-8859-1"?>

<!DOCTYPE web-app
    PUBLIC "-//Sun Microsystems, Inc.//DTD Web Application 2.2//EN"
    "http://java.sun.com/j2ee/dtds/web-app_2.2.dtd">

<web-app>
    <servlet>
        <servlet-name>login</servlet-name>
        <servlet-class>LoginServlet</servlet-class>
    </servlet>

    <servlet>
        <servlet-name>new-account</servlet-name>
        <servlet-class>NewAccountServlet</servlet-class>
    </servlet>

    <servlet-mapping>
        <servlet-name>new-account</servlet-name>
        <url-pattern>/new-account</url-pattern>
    </servlet-mapping>

    <servlet-mapping>
        <servlet-name>login</servlet-name>
        <url-pattern>/login</url-pattern>
    </servlet-mapping>

    <taglib>
     <taglib-uri>utilities</taglib-uri>
     <taglib-location>/WEB-INF/tlds/utilities.tld</taglib-location>
    </taglib>
 </web-app>
```

---

6. The Servlet Specification, which can be downloaded from
    http://java.sun.com/products/servlet, provides more information on
    deployment descriptors.

The deployment descriptor listed in Example 5-1.c defines servlet mappings and provides information about the application's tag library descriptor. The servlet mappings associate servlet names with URL patterns and servlet classes. For example, the login and new account servlets can be referenced with the servlet names—login and new-account, like this:

```
<form action='<%= response.encodeURL("login") %>'>
<form action='<%= response.encodeURL("new-account") %>'>
```

JSP pages can access the utilities tag library with the URI specified in the deployment descriptor as follows:

```
<%@ taglib uri='utilities' prefix='util' %>
```

The rest of this section discusses the two use cases implemented by the application: *successful login* and *opening a new account*.

JSP Tip

Use Cases

Use cases, first popularized by Ivar Jacobsen's book,[1] are essentially the formalization of written requirements. A use case is a collection of related scenarios that achieve a particular user goal, such as logging in to a web site.

Although use cases are widely used to describe system requirements, they are especially suited to web applications because of the way HTTP requests are handled: HTTP requests often correspond to a single use case or use case scenario.

---

1. Jacobsen, Ivar. *Object-Oriented Software Engineering*, Addison-Wesley, 1992.

Successful Login Use Case

The following sequence describes the *successful login* use case:

1. The user fills in the name and password fields in the login JSP page.

2. The login servlet determines whether the user is listed in the login database.

3. If the user is found in the login database, the request is forwarded to a welcome page.

Figure 5-4 illustrates a successful login.

Figure 5-4 Successful Login

Figure 5-5 further illustrates the sequence of events for a successful login.

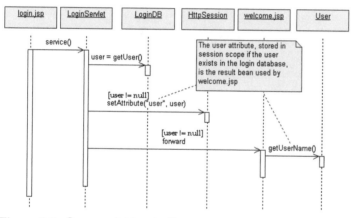

Figure 5-5   Successful Login Sequence

The login page shown in the left picture in Figure 5-4 invokes the login servlet when its form is submitted. That servlet determines whether the username and password correspond to a user listed in the database. If so, the servlet stores a User object in session scope and forwards to the welcome page, which subsequently accesses the username to create the welcome message.

Example 5-1.d lists the login JSP page.

Example 5-1.d /login.jsp

```
<html><head><title>Login Page</title></head>
<body>
    <%@ include file='login-form.jsp' %>
</body>
</html>
```

Because the login form is used by two other JSP pages in the application—see Example 5-1.h on page 150 and Example 5-1.k on page 152—it's encapsulated in a JSP page of its own and included by login.jsp.

The login form is listed in Example 5-1.e.

Example 5-1.e /login-form.jsp

```
<%@ taglib uri='utilities' prefix='util' %>

<font size='5' color='blue'>Please Login</font><hr>

<form action='<%= response.encodeURL("login") %>' method='post'>
    <table>
        <tr>
            <td>Name:</td>
            <td><input type='text' name='userName'
                value='<util:requestParameter property='userName' />'>
            </td>
        </tr><tr>
            <td>Password:</td>
            <td><input type='password' name='password' size='8'></td>
        </tr>
    </table>
    <br>
    <input type='submit' value='login'>
</form>
```

Because the login form is included by other JSP pages, it does not contain the usual preamble of HTML tags, such as <html>, <head>, and <body>—those tags are supplied by JSP pages that include the form.

The form's action is login—the name defined by the application's deployment descriptor for the login servlet. That name is encoded by HttpServletResponse.encodeURL in case cookies or session tracking are disabled.

The login form uses the application's only custom tag to retain the value in the Name field when the page is redisplayed. That tag's implementation is discussed in "Tags with Attributes" on page 14.

When the login form is submitted, the request is forwarded to the login servlet, which is listed in Example 5-1.f.

Example 5-1.f /WEB-INF/classes/LoginServlet.java

```java
import javax.servlet.ServletConfig;
import javax.servlet.ServletException;
import javax.servlet.http.HttpServlet;
import javax.servlet.http.HttpServletRequest;
import javax.servlet.http.HttpServletResponse;

import beans.LoginDB;
import beans.User;

public class LoginServlet extends HttpServlet {
    private LoginDB loginDB;

    public void init(ServletConfig config)
                              throws ServletException {
        super.init(config);
        config.getServletContext().setAttribute("loginDB",
                                    loginDB = new LoginDB());
    }
    public void service(HttpServletRequest req,
                    HttpServletResponse res)
                    throws java.io.IOException, ServletException {
        User user = loginDB.getUser(req.getParameter("userName"),
                                req.getParameter("password"));

        if(user != null) { // user is in the login database
            req.getSession().setAttribute("user", user);

            getServletContext().getRequestDispatcher(
                res.encodeURL("/welcome.jsp")).forward(req,res);
        }
        else { // user must open a new account or retry login
            getServletContext().getRequestDispatcher(
                res.encodeURL("/loginFailed.jsp")).forward(req,res);
        }
    }
}
```

The login servlet has two responsibilities: initializing the login database and handling requests. The former is handled by the `init` method, which creates the database and stores it in application scope.

The `service` method handles requests by accessing the login database to determine whether the username and password supplied to the login form correspond to a user in the database. If the user is listed in the database, the corresponding `User` instance is stored in session scope and control is forwarded to the welcome page. If the user is not listed in the database, control is forwarded to a login failed page, which is listed in Example 5-1.h on page 150.

Although a reference to the login database is maintained by the login servlet as a class member and is therefore susceptible to multithreaded access, the login servlet itself is not concerned with threading issues because the `LoginDB` class is thread safe. See "The Beans" on page 138 for a discussion of the `LoginDB` class and threading issues.

The welcome page is listed in Example 5-1.g.

Example 5-1.g /welcome.jsp

```
<html><head><title>Welcome</title></head>
<body>

<jsp:useBean id='user' scope='session' class='beans.User' />
Welcome <%= user.getUserName() %>

</body>
</html>
```

The welcome page uses the `User` bean in session scope to access the username. That bean is the result bean depicted in Figure 5-2 on page 136.

JSP Tip

Model 2 Encapsulates Java Code in Servlets

Notice how the Model 2 architecture encapsulates Java code in servlets. Nearly all of the Java code in this section is contained in the login servlet listed in Example 5-1.f on page 145; the corresponding JSP files, listed in Example 5-1.d on page 144 and Example 5-1.e on page 144, contain no Java code. This encapsulation of Java code allows software developers to concentrate on servlets and allows web page authors to implement JSP pages.

You may argue that the welcome page listed in Example 5-1.g on page 146 contains Java code to access the user's username, and you would be correct. If simple accessors like the one listed in Example 5-1.g are unacceptable for a project's web page authors, software developers can provide custom tags to replace them; see "The Importance of Custom Tags" on page 175.

Creating a New Account

If login fails, the user is given the opportunity to create a new account. The *new account* use case can be described as follows:

1. The user fills in the name and password fields in the login JSP page.

2. The login servlet determines whether the user is listed in the login database.

3. If the user is not in the login database, the request is forwarded to a login failed page, where the user can retry login or open a new account.

4. If the user chooses to open a new account, control is forwarded to a new account JSP page.

5. The user fills in the fields on the new account page and submits the form to a servlet. That servlet creates a new account in the login database and forwards the request to a new account JSP page, where the user can subsequently login.

Figure 5-6 illustrates the steps involved in creating a new account. That figure shows the JSP pages presented to the user for the *new account* use case, starting with the upper-left picture, and proceeding clockwise: the login page, the login failed page, the new account page, and the account created page.

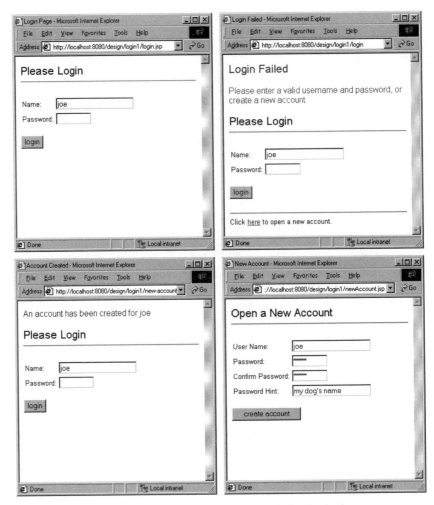

Figure 5-6 Creating a New Account, from top-left, clockwise

Figure 5-7 further illustrates the sequence of events for a failed login and the subsequent creation of a new account.

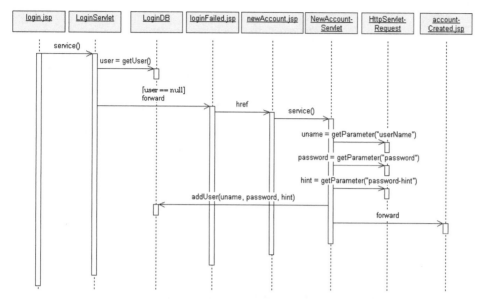

Figure 5-7 New Account Sequence Diagram

Like the *successful login* use case, the login form invokes the login servlet when the form is submitted; the servlet checks whether the user is listed in the login database.

If the user is not listed in the login database, the request is forwarded to the login failed page, which lets the user retry login or create a new account. The login failed page contains a link that points to a new account JSP page, which contains a form whose action is the new account servlet. The new account servlet retrieves information from the form, creates a new user, and adds it to the login database.

After creating a new user, the new account servlet forwards the request to the account created JSP page.

The login failed JSP page is listed in Example 5-1.h.

Example 5-1.h   /loginFailed.jsp

```
<html><head><title>Login Failed</title></head>
<body>

<font color='red' size='5'>Login Failed</font>
<font color='red' size='4'><p>
   Please enter a valid username and password, or create
   a new account
</font></p>

<%@ include file='/login-form.jsp' %>

<hr>Click <a href='<%= response.encodeURL("newAccount.jsp") %>' >
here</a> to open a new account.

</body>
</html>
```

The login failed page is unremarkable; it displays an error message, includes the login form, and provides a link to the new account page.

The new account page is listed in Example 5-1.i.

Example 5-1.i   /newAccount.jsp

```
<html><head><title>New Account</title></head>
<body>
<font size='5' color='blue'>Open a New Account</font>
<hr>
<form action='<%= response.encodeURL("new-account") %>'
      method='post'>
   <table><tr>
        <td> User Name: </td>
        <td><input type='text' name='userName'></td>
     </tr><tr>
        <td> Password: </td>
        <td><input type='password' name='password' size='8'></td>
     </tr><tr>
        <td> Confirm Password: </td>
        <td><input type='password' name='confirm-password'
                   size='8'></td>
     </tr><tr>
        <td> Password Hint: </td>
        <td><input type='text' name='password-hint'>
        </td>
     </tr>
   </table>
```

```
    <br>
    <input type='submit' value='create account'>
</form>
</body>
</html>
```

The new account page contains a form for entering a username, a password, and a password hint. That form's action is specified as `new-account`, which is the name for the new account servlet specified in the application's deployment descriptor. See "The Deployment Descriptor" on page 140 for more details.

The new account servlet is listed in Example 5-1.j.

Example 5-1.j /WEB-INF/classes/NewAccountServlet.java

```java
import javax.servlet.ServletException;
import javax.servlet.http.HttpServlet;
import javax.servlet.http.HttpServletRequest;
import javax.servlet.http.HttpServletResponse;

import beans.LoginDB;

public class NewAccountServlet extends HttpServlet {
    public void doPost(HttpServletRequest req,
                  HttpServletResponse res)
                     throws java.io.IOException, ServletException {
        LoginDB loginDB = (LoginDB)getServletContext().
                      getAttribute("loginDB");

        loginDB.addUser(req.getParameter("userName"),
                   req.getParameter("password"),
                   req.getParameter("password-hint"));

        getServletContext().getRequestDispatcher(
           res.encodeURL("/accountCreated.jsp")).forward(req, res);
    }
}
```

The new account servlet accesses the login database and the parameters from the new account form. That servlet subsequently adds a new user to the database with `LoginDB.addUser`, then forwards the request to the account-created page.

The new account servlet should check to make sure the password and password-confirmation parameters from the new account form are the same; however, in the interests of simplicity, it does not do so.

The account-created JSP page is listed in Example 5-1.k.

Example 5-1.k   /accountCreated.jsp

```
<html><head><title>Account Created</title></head>
<body>

<font size='4' color='blue'>
   An account has been created for
   <%= request.getParameter("userName") %>
</font>

<p><%@ include file='login-form.jsp' %></p>

</body>
</html>
```

The account-created page displays a message indicating that a new account has been created and includes the login form so the user can try out the new account.

Conclusion

There are many ways to implement JSP-based web applications. This chapter has illustrated two of them: Model 1 and Model 2. For extensibility, maintainability, and reusability, the latter is preferred over the former.

The next chapter demonstrates a simple Model 2 framework that simplifies web application development.

A MODEL 2
FRAMEWORK

Chapter 6

Because the Model 2 architecture is a Model-View-Controller implementation and because it allows for a division of labor between page authors and software developers, it's an excellent choice for developing web applications. But we can do better by encapsulating general code in a framework, thereby significantly reducing the amount of code required to implement applications.

This chapter discusses a simple Model 2 framework that simplifies web application development and lets software developers and page authors work independently. This framework is similar in concept to the Apache Struts framework; see http://www.apache.org for more information about Struts.

This chapter retrofits the Model 2 application discussed in "A Model 2 Example" on page 137 to the framework introduced in this chapter; therefore, that discussion is a prerequisite for this chapter.

A Model 2 Framework

The framework discussed in this chapter uses a single servlet that acts as a controller. That servlet is known as the action servlet. All HTTP requests ending in .do are handled by the action servlet, which dispatches requests to Java beans, known as actions, as shown in Figure 6-1.

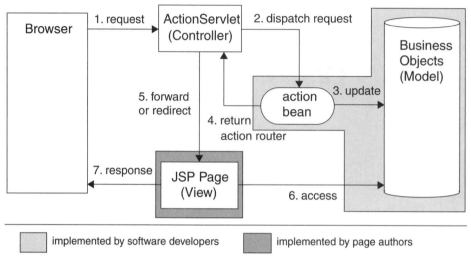

Figure 6-1 A Model 2 Framework

Action beans update business objects and return an action router to the action servlet. The action servlet uses that router to forward or redirect requests to a JSP page. That JSP page subsequently accesses business objects—often with custom tags—and sends a response back to the browser.

The framework shown in Figure 6-1 contains four types of objects, summarized in Table 6-1.

Table 6-1 Model 2 Framework Classes and Interfaces[1]

Name	Description
Action	Application-specific actions implement this interface
ActionFactory	Creates action instances
ActionServlet	Maps requests to actions
ActionRouter	Forwards or redirects requests to JSP pages

1. *italics* indicates an interface.

Figure 6-2 shows how the types of objects listed in Table 6-1 work together.

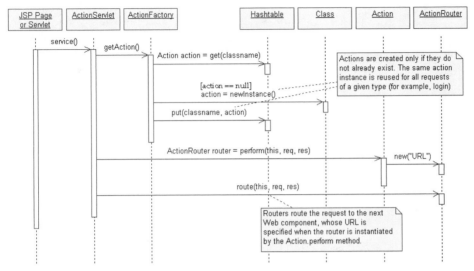

Figure 6-2 ActionServlet Sequence Diagram

The action servlet is typically invoked from a JSP page or another servlet, as the result of a form submission or link activation. That servlet retrieves the appropriate type of action, depending upon the request, from the action factory.

Because typical web applications handle numerous requests, the action factory maintains one action instance for each action type, and those actions are reused for a given type of request. Reusing a single action for multiple requests greatly reduces the number of actions that the framework must instantiate.

Keep in mind that multiple threads can issue identical requests concurrently, meaning that a single action instance can be accessed concurrently; therefore, actions must be thread safe. The easiest way to implement thread-safe actions is to avoid maintaining intrinsic state. That is accomplished by the use of local variables instead of class members, because local variables can only be accessed by one thread at a time.

After the action servlet obtains an action from the action factory, it invokes the action's `perform` method, which implements application-specific functionality, typically updating business objects. `Action.perform` returns an action router that maintains a URI and a `boolean` variable indicating whether the request should be forwarded or redirected to that URI.

With an action router in hand, the action servlet invokes the router's `route` method, which forwards or redirects the request to the appropriate web component. That web component is typically a JSP page, an HTML page, or another servlet, and that component usually contains a form or a link whose submission or activation, respectively, issues a request. Thus, the cycle begins anew.

The rest of this section begins with a discussion of the classes listed in Table 6-1 on page 156. Subsequently, we'll look at modifications to the Model 2 example discussed in "A Model 2 Example" on page 137 that are necessary to retrofit that example to our framework. Finally, we'll explore some refinements to our framework's design.

The Action Interface

The `Action` interface is listed in Example 6-1.a.

Example 6-1.a   /WEB-INF/classes/actions/Action.java

```
package actions;

import javax.servlet.http.HttpServlet;
import javax.servlet.http.HttpServletRequest;
import javax.servlet.http.HttpServletResponse;

// Application-specific actions implement this interface

public interface Action {
   public ActionRouter perform(HttpServlet servlet,
                               HttpServletRequest req,
                               HttpServletResponse res)
                       throws java.io.IOException,
                               javax.servlet.ServletException;
}
```

The `Action` interface defines a single method—`perform`—that's passed references to the action servlet and the HTTP request and response.

The Action Factory

The `ActionFactory` class is listed in Example 6-1.b.

Example 6-1.b   /WEB-INF/classes/actions/ActionFactory.java

```java
package actions;

import java.util.Hashtable;

public class ActionFactory {
   private Hashtable actions = new Hashtable();

   // This method is called by the action servlet

   public Action getAction(String classname,
                           ClassLoader loader)
                           throws ClassNotFoundException,
                                  IllegalAccessException,
                                  InstantiationException {
      Action action = (Action)actions.get(classname);

      if(action == null) {
         Class klass = loader.loadClass(classname);
         action = (Action)klass.newInstance();
         actions.put(classname, action);
      }
      return action;
   }
}
```

The action factory maintains a hash table of actions, and the factory's `getAction` method, invoked by the action servlet, returns an action corresponding to a specific class name. If that action is not stored in the factory's hash table, the factory creates it and stores it in its hash table. The factory handles subsequent requests for the same action by returning a reference from the hash table.

Action Routers

The `ActionRouter` class is listed in Example 6-1.c.

Example 6-1.c /WEB-INF/classes/actions/ActionRouter.java

```
package actions;

import javax.servlet.GenericServlet;
import javax.servlet.http.HttpServlet;
import javax.servlet.http.HttpServletRequest;
import javax.servlet.http.HttpServletResponse;

// Action routers are immutable

public class ActionRouter {
   private final String url;
   private final boolean isForward;

   public ActionRouter(String url) {
      this(url, true); // forward by default
   }
   public ActionRouter(String url, boolean isForward) {
      this.url = url;
      this.isForward = isForward;
   }

   // This method is called by the action servlet

   public void route(GenericServlet servlet,
                     HttpServletRequest req,
                     HttpServletResponse res)
                           throws javax.servlet.ServletException,
                                  java.io.IOException {
      if(isForward) {
         servlet.getServletContext().getRequestDispatcher(
         res.encodeURL(url)).forward(req, res);
      }
      else {
         res.sendRedirect(res.encodeRedirectURL(url));
      }
   }
}
```

Action routers forward or redirect requests; how those requests are handled can only be specified when a router is constructed.

The Action Servlet

A deployment descriptor maps URLs that end in .do to the action servlet, like
this:

```
// From /WEB-INF/web.xml
...
<web-app>
   <servlet>
      <servlet-name>action</servlet-name>
      <servlet-class>ActionServlet</servlet-class>
   </servlet>

   <servlet-mapping>
      <servlet-name>action</servlet-name>
      <url-pattern>*.do</url-pattern>
   </servlet-mapping>
...
</web-app>
```

The .do suffix is easy to remember because it indicates that the application is
about to *do* something. Immediately preceding the .do suffix is the name of an
action; for example, for a login action class named LoginAction from the
actions package, the URL for the login action would be specified as follows:

```
<form action='<%= response.encodeURL("actions.LoginAction.do") %>'
      method='post'>
```

Let's see how the action servlet, listed in Example 6-1.d, maps URLs into action
classes.

Example 6-1.d /WEB-INF/classes/ActionServlet.java

```
import javax.servlet.ServletException;
import javax.servlet.http.HttpServlet;
import javax.servlet.http.HttpServletRequest;
import javax.servlet.http.HttpServletResponse;

import actions.Action;
import actions.ActionFactory;
import actions.ActionRouter;

public class ActionServlet extends HttpServlet {
   private ActionFactory factory = new ActionFactory();
```

```
public void service(HttpServletRequest req,
                    HttpServletResponse res)
              throws java.io.IOException,
                       javax.servlet.ServletException {
   try {
      Action action = factory.getAction(getClassname(req),
                                   getClass().getClassLoader());
      ActionRouter router = action.perform(this,req,res);
      router.route(this, req, res);
   }
   catch(Exception e) {
      throw new ServletException(e);
   }
}
private String getClassname(HttpServletRequest req) {
   String path = req.getServletPath();
   int slash = path.lastIndexOf("/"),
       period = path.lastIndexOf(".");

   if(period > 0 && period > slash)
    path = path.substring(slash+1, period);

   return path;
}
}
```

The `ActionServlet.service` implementation is straightforward: An action is obtained from the action factory, and its `perform` method is invoked. The action's `perform` method returns an action router, which routes the request.

`ActionServlet.getClassname` is responsible for mapping URLs to action class names. That method obtains a reference to the servlet path and subsequently extracts the string between the forward slash and the period. For the login URL discussed in "The Action Servlet" on page 161, the servlet path is `/actions.LoginAction.do`, and the class name is `actions.LoginAction`.

Retrofitting the Original Model 2 Example

This section retrofits the login and registration example from the previous chapter: "A Model 2 Example" on page 137 to this chapter's Model 2 framework. Figure 6-3 shows the directory structure and files for the retrofitted application— Figure 5-3 on page 138 is a similar diagram for the original example.

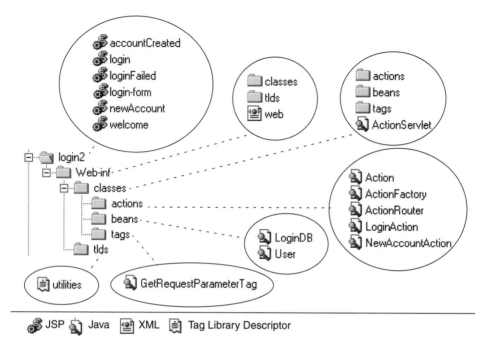

JSP 📇 Java 📄 XML 📄 Tag Library Descriptor

Figure 6-3 Directory Structure and Files for the ActionServlet Example

Once the framework is in place—meaning the action servlet is in /WEBINF/classes and the supporting action classes are in /WEBINF/classes/actions—only two changes need to be made to the original application. First, servlet URLs are replaced in login.jsp and newAccount.jsp; the URLs used in the original JSP files looked like this:

```
<%-- this is from the original login.jsp --%>
<form action='<%= response.encodeURL("login") %>' method='post'>

<%-- this is from the original newAccount.jsp --%>
<form action='<%= response.encodeURL("new-account") %>'
      method='post'>
```

The modified URLs look like this:

```
<%-- this is from the new login.jsp --%>
<form action='<%= response.encodeURL("actions.LoginAction.do") %>'
      method='post'>

<%-- this is from the new newAccount.jsp --%>
<form
action='<%= response.encodeURL("actions.NewAccountAction.do") %>'
method='post'>
```

Second, the original application's login and new account servlets are rewritten as actions. Those actions are listed in Example 6-2.a and Example 6-2.b, respectively.

Example 6-2.a   /WEB-INF/classes/actions/LoginAction.java

```
package actions;

import javax.servlet.*;
import javax.servlet.http.*;
import beans.LoginDB;
import beans.User;

public class LoginAction implements Action {
   public ActionRouter perform(HttpServlet servlet,
           HttpServletRequest req, HttpServletResponse res)
           throws java.io.IOException, ServletException {
      LoginDB loginDB = getLoginDB(servlet.getServletContext());
      User user = loginDB.getUser(req.getParameter("userName"),
                                  req.getParameter("password"));

      if(user != null) { // user is in the login database
         req.getSession().setAttribute("user", user);
         return new ActionRouter("/welcome.jsp");
      }
      else
         return new ActionRouter("/loginFailed.jsp");
   }
   private LoginDB getLoginDB(ServletContext context) {
      LoginDB loginDB = (LoginDB)context.getAttribute("loginDB");

      if(loginDB == null)
         context.setAttribute("loginDB", loginDB = new LoginDB());

      return loginDB;
   }
}
```

Example 6-2.b   /WEB-INF/classes/actions/NewAccountAction.java

```
package actions;

import javax.servlet.http.HttpServlet;
import javax.servlet.http.HttpServletRequest;
import javax.servlet.http.HttpServletResponse;

import beans.LoginDB;
import beans.User;
```

```
public class NewAccountAction implements Action {
    public ActionRouter perform(HttpServlet servlet,
                                HttpServletRequest req,
                                HttpServletResponse res)
                        throws java.io.IOException,
                                javax.servlet.ServletException{
        LoginDB loginDB = (LoginDB)servlet.getServletContext().
                        getAttribute("loginDB");
        String uname = req.getParameter("userName");

        loginDB.addUser(uname, req.getParameter("password"),
                        req.getParameter("password-hint"));
        req.setAttribute("userName", uname);

        return new ActionRouter("/accountCreated.jsp");
    }
}
```

Both actions are similar to their servlet counterparts, listed in Example 5-1.f on page 145 and Example 5-1.j on page 151, except the actions return action routers.

Refining the Design

Like any design, the Model 2 architecture discussed in "A Model 2 Framework" on page 155 has plenty of room for improvement; for example, JSP pages must explicitly refer to action classes, as illustrated by the form tag used by login-form.jsp:

```
<form action='<%= response.encodeURL("actions.LoginAction.do") %>'
      method='post'>
```

And actions must explicitly refer to JSP pages, as the following excerpt from LoginAction.java illustrates:

```
if(user != null) { // user is in the login database
    req.getSession().setAttribute("user", user);
    return new ActionRouter("/welcome.jsp");
}
else
    return new ActionRouter("/loginFailed.jsp");
```

This coupling between JSP pages and actions is undesirable, because changing the name of a JSP file results in a change to an action, and changing the name of an action—or even moving an action to a different package—results in a change to a JSP page.

Ideally, JSP pages and actions should be decoupled with logical names; for example, JSP pages could use logical names, like this:

```
<form action='<%= response.encodeURL("login-action") %>'
     method='post'>
```

Actions could also use logical names, like this:

```
if(user != null) { // user is in the login database
   req.getSession().setAttribute("user", user);
   return new ActionRouter("welcome-page");
}
else
   return new ActionRouter("login-failed-page");
```

We can easily use a resource bundle[1] to map logical names to action classes and JSP pages. First, we define a properties file, listed in Example 6-3.a, that resides in /WEB-INF/classes:

Example 6-3.a /WEB-INF/classes/actions.properties

```
# Action mappings used by ActionServlet

login-action=actions.LoginAction
new-account-action=actions.NewAccountAction

# JSP mappings used by Routers

login-failed-page=/loginFailed.jsp
welcome-page=/welcome.jsp
account-created-page=/accountCreated.jsp
```

We then add an `init` method to the action servlet, listed in Example 6-3.b, that creates a resource bundle from that properties file. That resource bundle is stored in application scope, for subsequent access by the action servlet and action routers.

Example 6-3.b /WEB-INF/classes/ActionServlet.java

```
import java.util.MissingResourceException;
import java.util.ResourceBundle;

import javax.servlet.ServletConfig;
import javax.servlet.ServletException;
import javax.servlet.http.HttpServlet;
import javax.servlet.http.HttpServletRequest;
```

1. See "Resource Bundles" on page 213 for more information on resource bundles.

```java
import javax.servlet.http.HttpServletResponse;

import actions.Action;
import actions.ActionFactory;
import actions.ActionRouter;

public class ActionServlet extends HttpServlet {
   private ActionFactory factory = new ActionFactory();

   public void init(ServletConfig config) throws ServletException{
      super.init(config);

      ResourceBundle bundle = null;

      try {
         bundle = ResourceBundle.getBundle("actions");
      }
      catch(MissingResourceException e) {
         throw new ServletException(e);
      }
      getServletContext().setAttribute("action-mappings", bundle);
   }
   public void service(HttpServletRequest req,
                       HttpServletResponse res)
                  throws java.io.IOException, ServletException {
      try {
         String actionClass = getActionClass(req);
         Action action = factory.getAction(actionClass,
                                getClass().getClassLoader());
         ActionRouter router = action.perform(this,req,res);
         router.route(this, req, res);
      }
      catch(Exception e) {
         throw new ServletException(e);
      }
   }
   private String getClassname(HttpServletRequest req) {
      String path = req.getServletPath();
      int slash = path.lastIndexOf("/"),
          period = path.lastIndexOf(".");

      if(period > 0 && period > slash)
       path = path.substring(slash+1, period);

      return path;
   }
   private String getActionClass(HttpServletRequest req) {
      ResourceBundle bundle = (ResourceBundle)getServletContext().
```

```
                                    getAttribute("action-mappings");
         return (String)bundle.getObject(getActionKey(req));
      }
      private String getActionKey(HttpServletRequest req) {
         String path = req.getServletPath();
         int slash = path.lastIndexOf("/"),
             period = path.lastIndexOf(".");

         if(period > 0 && period > slash)
            path = path.substring(slash+1, period);

         return path;
      }
   }
}
```

The action servlet's `service` method obtains the action class name through `getActionClass`, which uses the resource bundle to map logical names to action class names.

The `ActionRouter` class, listed in Example 6-3.c, is also modified to map logical names to JSP pages.

Example 6-3.c /WEB-INF/classes/actions/ActionRouter.java

```
package actions;

import java.util.ResourceBundle;
import javax.servlet.GenericServlet;
import javax.servlet.http.HttpServletRequest;
import javax.servlet.http.HttpServletResponse;

// Action routers are immutable

public class ActionRouter {
   private final String key;
   private final boolean isForward;

   public ActionRouter(String key) {
      this(key, true); // forward by default
   }
   public ActionRouter(String key, boolean isForward) {
      this.key = key;
      this.isForward = isForward;
   }
```

```
// This method is called by the action servlet

public synchronized void route(GenericServlet servlet,
                               HttpServletRequest req,
                               HttpServletResponse res)
                throws java.io.IOException,
                               javax.servlet.ServletException {
   ResourceBundle bundle = (ResourceBundle)servlet.
                               getServletContext().
                               getAttribute("action-mappings");
   String url = (String)bundle.getObject(key);

   if(isForward) {
      servlet.getServletContext().getRequestDispatcher(
      res.encodeURL(url)).forward(req, res);
   }
   else {
      res.sendRedirect(res.encodeRedirectURL(url));
   }
}
}
```

Now that the action servlet and action routers can map logical names, actions and JSP pages can use those names; for example, Example 6-3.d lists the NewAccountAction class and Example 6-3.e lists `login-form.jsp`.

Example 6-3.d   /WEB-INF/classes/actions/NewAccountAction.java

```
...
public class NewAccountAction implements Action {
   public ActionRouter perform(HttpServlet servlet,
            HttpServletRequest req, HttpServletResponse res)
            throws java.io.IOException, ServletException {
      LoginDB loginDB = (LoginDB)servlet.getServletContext().
                        getAttribute("loginDB");
      String uname = req.getParameter("userName");

      loginDB.addUser(uname, req.getParameter("password"),
                        req.getParameter("password-hint"));
      req.setAttribute("userName", uname);

      return new ActionRouter("account-created-page");
   }
}
```

Example 6-3.e /login-form.jsp

```
<%@ taglib uri='utilities' prefix='util' %>

<font size='5' color='blue'>Please Login</font><hr>

<form action='<%= response.encodeURL("login-action.do") %>'
        method='post'>
   ...
</form>
```

Many other improvements can be made to this framework; for example, the action servlet listed in Example 6-3.b on page 166 hardcodes the name of the properties file; if that name changes, the action servlet must be modified and recompiled. That dependency can be eliminated with a servlet initialization parameter.

The deployment descriptor specifies that initialization parameter:

```
<web-app>
   <servlet>
      <servlet-name>action</servlet-name>
      <servlet-class>ActionServlet</servlet-class>
         <init-param>
            <param-name>action-mappings</param-name>
            <param-value>actions</param-value>
         </init-param>
   </servlet>
 ...

</web-app>
```

The action servlet undergoes a simple modification, listed below, to use the initialization parameter.

```
public class ActionServlet extends HttpServlet {
   ...
   public void init(ServletConfig config) throws ServletException{
      super.init(config);

      ResourceBundle bundle = null;

      try {
         bundle = ResourceBundle.getBundle(
                  config.getInitParameter("action-mappings"));
      }
      catch(MissingResourceException e) {
         throw new ServletException(e);
      }
      ...
   }
}
```

Using an initialization parameter eliminates the dependency between the properties file and the action servlet but creates a dependency between the properties file and the deployment descriptor. Because changes to deployment descriptors do not involve code changes or recompilation, the latter dependency is preferred over the former.

Logical names can also be mapped with XML files. Because XML is widely used for configuration, in this case it's probably preferable to a properties file; however, we opted for a properties file because it's a simpler solution. See "XML" on page 330 for more information about XML and JSP.

Adding Use Cases

One measure of a framework's usefulness is the ease with which applications can be modified or extended. For the framework discussed in this chapter, adding use cases to an application involves the following steps:

1. **Implement an action** that manipulates business objects (the model) and perhaps stores beans in an appropriate scope for a JSP page (the view) to access. *(software developers)*

2. **Implement a JSP page** that accesses business objects (that may have been modified in step #1) and beans from a specific scope (that may have been created in step #1). *(web page authors)*

3. **Add mappings** to the application's properties file that equate the action and JSP page from steps #1 and #2 to logical names. *(web page authors or software developers)*

Notice the division of labor in the steps listed above: Software developers are responsible for actions, and web page authors are responsible for JSP pages.

Depending upon the use case, additional steps may be required, for example, modify existing actions *(software developers)* and JSP pages *(web page authors)*, or implement custom tags *(software developers)* and use custom tags *(web page authors)*. But for many use cases, the steps listed above will suffice.

This section extends the web application discussed in "A Model 2 Example" on page 137 and "Retrofitting the Original Model 2 Example" on page 162 with a *password hint* use case. That use case can be described as follows:

1. Login fails because of an incorrect password for an existing user.

2. The action servlet forwards to the login failed page, which provides a link to a password hint action.

3. The user activates the password hint link, which submits a request, through the action servlet, to the password hint action.

4. The password hint action retrieves the hint for the specified user from the login database, and stores the username and hint in request scope.

5. The action servlet forwards to a JSP page that displays the username and hint stored in request scope. That JSP page includes the login form so the user can retry login.

Figure 6-4 shows the login failed and password hint JSP pages.

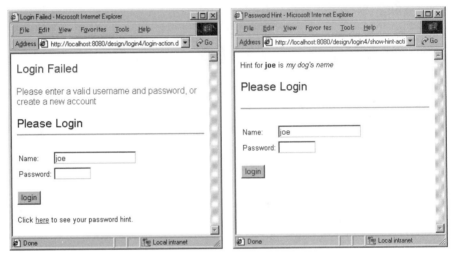

Figure 6-4 Showing a Password Hint

Let's look at the steps involved in adding this use case to our application.

Step #1: Implement a Password Hint Action

The password hint action—`ShowHintAction`—is listed in Example 6-4.a.

Example 6-4.a /WEB-INF/classes/actions/ShowHintAction.java

```
package actions;

import javax.servlet.ServletContext;
import javax.servlet.http.HttpServlet;
import javax.servlet.http.HttpServletRequest;
import javax.servlet.http.HttpServletResponse;

import beans.LoginDB;

public class ShowHintAction implements Action {
```

```
public ActionRouter perform(HttpServlet servlet,
        HttpServletRequest req, HttpServletResponse res)
        throws IOException, ServletException {
  LoginDB loginDB = getLoginDB(servlet.getServletContext());
  String  uname = (String)req.getSession().
                      getAttribute("userName");

  req.setAttribute("hint", loginDB.getHint(uname));
  req.setAttribute("userName", uname);

  return new ActionRouter("show-hint-page");
}
private LoginDB getLoginDB(ServletContext context) {
  LoginDB loginDB = (LoginDB)context.getAttribute("loginDB");

  if(loginDB == null)
      context.setAttribute("loginDB", loginDB = new LoginDB());

  return loginDB;
}
}
```

The action listed in Example 6-4.a implements use case step 4 listed above by storing the username and password hint in request scope. A logical name—show-hint-page—is specified for the router returned from the perform method. That logical name is mapped to the show hint JSP page in the application's properties file.

Step #2: Implement a Password Hint JSP Page

The password hint JSP page—showHintAction.jsp—is listed in Example 6-4.b.

Example 6-4.b   /showHintAction.jsp

```
<html><title>Password Hint</title>
<body>

Hint for <b><%= request.getAttribute("userName") %></b> is
<i><%= request.getAttribute("hint") %></i>

<p><font size='5' color='blue'>Please Login</font></p><hr>

<form action='<%= response.encodeURL("login-action.do") %>'
      method='post'>
  <table>
    <tr>
```

```
      <td>Name:</td>
      <td><input type='text' name='userName'
         value='<%= request.getAttribute("userName") %>'>
      </td>
   </tr><tr>
      <td>Password:</td>
      <td><input type='password' name='password' size='8'></td>
   </tr>
   </table>
   <br>
   <input type='submit' value='login'>
</form>

</body>
</html>
```

The JSP page listed in Example 6-4.a implements use case step 5 listed above by retrieving the username and hint from request scope and displaying them to the user.

The login form's action is specified as a logical name—login-action—which, like the logical name used by the show hint action, is defined in the application's properties file.

Step #3: Add Mappings to the Properties File

Example 6-4.c lists the application's properties file.

Example 6-4.c /WEB-INF/classes/actions.properties

```
# Action mappings used by ActionServlet

login-action=actions.LoginAction
new-account-action=actions.NewAccountAction
show-hint-action=actions.ShowHintAction

# JSP mappings used by Routers

login-failed-page=/loginFailed.jsp
welcome-page=/welcome.jsp
account-created-page=/accountCreated.jsp
show-hint-page=/showHint.jsp
```

Step #4: Modify the Login Failed JSP Page

The login failed page is modified, as listed in Example 6-4.d, to provide different links depending upon whether a password hint exists for the username specified in the login form.

Example 6-4.d /loginFailed.jsp

```
<html><head><title>Login Failed</title></head>
<body>

<font color='red' size='5'>Login Failed</font>
<font color='red' size='4'><p>
   Please enter a valid username and password, or create
   a new account
</font></p>

<%@ include file='/login-form.jsp' %>

<jsp:useBean id='loginDB' class='beans.LoginDB'
                scope='application'/>

<%if(loginDB.getHint(request.getParameter("userName")) != null){%>
   Click <a href='<%=response.encodeURL("show-hint-action.do")%>'>
   here</a> to see your password hint.
<% } else { %>
   Click <a href='<%=response.encodeURL("newAccount.jsp")%>'>
   here</a> to open a new account.
<% } %>

</body>
</html>
```

The JSP page listed above accesses the login database to determine whether a password hint exists for the specified user. If so, a link is provided to the show hint action; if not, a link to the new account JSP page is provided.

The Importance of Custom Tags

One of the main benefits of the Model 2 architecture is that Java code is encapsulated in servlets—see "Model 2 Encapsulates Java Code in Servlets" on page 147. This encapsulation of Java code is critical for large web development projects, where web page authors code HTML and JSP pages, and software developers provide underlying functionality. Keeping JSP pages free of Java code allows web page authors and software developers to work in parallel with few dependencies.

Even with a Model 2 framework, such as the one discussed in this chapter, it's not uncommon for some Java code to creep into JSP pages. For example, the login failed JSP page listed in Example 6-4.d contains a small amount of Java code, listed below.

```
<html><head><title>Login Failed</title></head>
...
<jsp:useBean id='loginDB' class='beans.LoginDB'
                scope='application'/>
...
<%if(loginDB.getHint(request.getParameter("userName")) != null){%>
    Click <a href='<%=response.encodeURL("show-hint-action.do")%>'>
    here</a> to see your password hint.
<% } else { %>
    Click <a href='<%=response.encodeURL("newAccount.jsp")%>'>
    here</a> to open a new account.
<% } %>
...
```

Application-specific custom tags can replace Java code in JSP pages; for example, the login failed page listed below uses two custom tags to replace Java code.

```
<html><head><title>Login Failed</title></head>
...
<%@ taglib uri='application-tags' prefix='app' %>
...
<app:hintAvailable>
    Click <a href='<%=response.encodeURL("show-hint-action.do")%>'>
    here</a> to see your password hint.
</app:hintAvailable>

<app:hintNotAvailable>
    Click <a href='<%=response.encodeURL("login.jsp")%>'>
    here</a> to retry login.
</app:hintNotAvailable>
...
```

If a hint is available, the body of the `hintAvailable` tag is included in the generated HTML; otherwise, the body of the `hintNotAvailable` tag is included.

Most custom tags, such as those used above, are easy to implement. For example, Example 6-5.a lists the hint available tag, and Example 6-5.b lists the hint not available tag.

Example 6-5.a /WEB-INF/classes/tags/HintAvailableTag.java

```
package tags;

import javax.servlet.ServletRequest;
import javax.servlet.jsp.JspException;
import javax.servlet.jsp.tagext.TagSupport;
import beans.LoginDB;

public class HintAvailableTag extends TagSupport {
    public int doStartTag() throws JspException {
        ServletRequest req = pageContext.getRequest();
        LoginDB loginDB = (LoginDB)pageContext.
                                findAttribute("loginDB");

        if(loginDB.getHint(req.getParameter("userName")) != null)
            return EVAL_BODY_INCLUDE;
        else
            return SKIP_BODY;
    }
}
```

Example 6-5.b /WEB-INF/classes/tags/HintNotAvailableTag.java

```
package tags;

import javax.servlet.jsp.JspException;

public class HintNotAvailableTag extends HintAvailableTag {
    public int doStartTag() throws JspException {
        int available = super.doStartTag();
        return available == EVAL_BODY_INCLUDE ?
                        SKIP_BODY : EVAL_BODY_INCLUDE;
    }
}
```

Both tags listed above access the login database to determine whether a hint is available for a specified username. Subsequently, those tags return either SKIP_BODY or EVAL_BODY_INCLUDE, which determines whether the body of the tag is included in the generated HTML. See "Custom Tag Fundamentals" on page 2 and "Custom Tag Advanced Concepts" on page 32 for more information on implementing custom tags.

JSP custom tags neatly encapsulate functionality for web page authors. One of the most important uses of custom tags is eliminating Java code from JSP pages. This use of custom tags is one reason why they are the single most important JSP feature.

JSP Scripts

Conventional wisdom advocates eliminating Java code from JSP pages. For the most part, that's excellent advice, especially when JSP pages are used as views in an MVC architecture. But there are times when JSP pages crammed with Java can be quite useful; those types of JSP pages are referred to in this book as JSP scripts. Fortunately, JSP is flexible enough to support many different design philosophies.

JSP scripts are JSP pages that contain mostly Java sprinkled with HTML. Like custom tags, JSP scripts encapsulate functionality useful to web page authors; for example, consider the script listed in Example 6-6.a that prints request parameters, something that's useful for debugging.

Example 6-6.a   /showRequestParameters.jsp: A JSP Script

```
<%
   java.util.Enumeration e = request.getParameterNames();
   boolean hasParams = false;

   while(e.hasMoreElements()) {
      String name = (String)e.nextElement();
      String[] values = request.getParameterValues(name);

      hasParams = true;

      for(int i=0; i < values.length; ++i) {
         String next = values[i];
         if(i == 0) { %>
            <b><%= name %>:</b> <%= next %>
<%       }
         else { %>
            , <%= next %>
<%       }
      } %>
<% }
   if(!hasParams) { %>
      <i>No parameters with this request</i>
<% } %>
```

Figure 6-5 shows a JSP page that uses the script listed in Example 6-6.a.

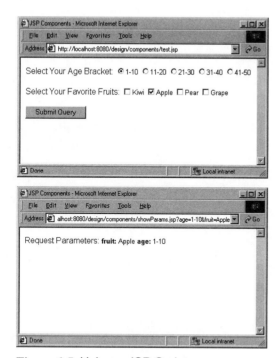

Figure 6-5 Using a JSP Script

The top picture shown in Example 6-6.a is an HTML page, listed in Example 6-6.b.

Example 6-6.b test.html

```html
<html><title>JSP Scripts</title>
<body>

<form action='showParams.jsp'>
    <font size='4' color='blue'>Select Your Age Bracket:</font>

    <input type='radio' name='age' value='1-10'>1-10</input>
    <input type='radio' name='age' value='11-20'>11-20</input>
    <input type='radio' name='age' value='21-30'>21-30</input>
    <input type='radio' name='age' value='31-40'>31-40</input>
    <input type='radio' name='age' value='41-50'>41-50</input>
    <p>
    <font size='4' color='blue'>Select Your Favorite Fruits:</font>

    <input type='checkbox' name='fruit' value='Kiwi'>Kiwi</input>
    <input type='checkbox' name='fruit' value='Apple'>Apple</input>
    <input type='checkbox' name='fruit' value='Pear'>Pear</input>
```

```
    <input type='checkbox' name='fruit' value='Grape'>Grape</input>
    </p>
    <p><input type='submit'/></p>
</form>

</body>
</html>
```

In Example 6-6.b, showParams.jsp is specified as the form's action; that file is listed in Example 6-6.c.

Example 6-6.c /showParams.jsp

```
<html><title>JSP Scripts</title>
<body>

<font size='4' color='blue'>Request Parameters:</font>
<%@ include file='showRequestParameters.jsp' %>

</body>
</html>
```

JSP scripts are included by another JSP page, as is the case for the JSP page listed in Example 6-6.c.

Both JSP scripts and custom tags encapsulate functionality useful to web page authors. Custom tags are more difficult to develop because they require coding and compilation, in addition to a tag library descriptor definition. In contrast, although JSP scripts are easier to develop, they're not as natural as custom tags for web page authors because they require the use of the JSP include directive. All other things being equal, custom tags are more reusable than JSP scripts, but the latter can be useful tools in the JSP developer's toolchest.

Conclusion

Some would have you believe that JSP is not viable for developing complex Web applications because it's too easy to mix Java code with HTML in JSP pages.[2] I disagree. Although I would not want to develop a large JSP-based web application without a Model 2 architecture, I would be more than comfortable using the techniques discussed in this chapter to implement any application.

---

2. See http://www.servlets.com/soapbox/problems-jsp.html.

This chapter provides insights into object-oriented design, the Model-View-Controller architecture and use cases, all of which are proven techniques for developing complex software systems. Books and articles on those topics abound; here is a short list of good references:

Object-Oriented Design:

Gamma, Helm, Johnson, Vlissides. *Design Patterns*, Addison-Wesley, 1992.

Wirfs-Brock, Wilkerson, Wiener. *Designing Object-oriented Software*, Prentice Hall, 1990.

Meyer, Bertand. *Object-Oriented Software Construction*, Prentice Hall, 1997.

Budd, Timothy. *An Introduction to Object-oriented Programming*, Addison-Wesley, 1991.

Model-View-Controller:

Alpert, Brown, Woolf. *The Design Patterns Smalltalk Companion*, Addison-Wesley, 1998.

Gamma, Helm, Johnson, Vlissides. *Design Patterns*, Addison-Wesley, 1992.

Use Cases:

Fowler, Scott. *UML Distilled Second Edition*, Addison-Wesley, 2000.

Schneider, Winters. *Applying Use Cases, a Practical Guide*, Addison-Wesley, 2000.

EVENT HANDLING AND SENSITIVE FORM RESUBMISSIONS

Topics in this Chapter

Chapter 7

Event handling is a mainstay of traditional graphical user interfaces; for example, Swing provides numerous event handlers for a wide variety of events, such as mouse, window, and focus events.

Prior to the Servlet 2.3 Specification, servlet containers only fired events when objects were placed in, or removed from, a session.[1] The Servlet 2.3 Specification adds support for application life cycle events, so developers can react to the creation and invalidation of servlet contexts and sessions. At the time this book was written, the Servlet 2.3 Specification had not been finalized, and the details of application life cycle events were still in flux. Please refer to an introductory servlets book that covers the Servlet 2.3 Specification for more information concerning application life cycle events.

Application life cycle events are fired by a *servlet container* and handled by *applications*. This chapter shows how Model 2 applications can fire, and handle, *their own events*. The event handling discussed in this chapter is an extension of the Model 2 framework discussed in "A Model 2 Framework" on page 154; therefore, an understanding of that chapter is a prerequisite for this discussion.

---

1. Events are fired if those objects implement `HttpSessionBindingListener`.

In this chapter, "Event Handling for a Model 2 Framework" demonstrates how event handling can be incorporated into a Model 2 framework. "Trapping Form Resubmissions with a Model 2 Framework" on page 191 illustrates how to use that event handling mechanism to trap sensitive form resubmissions, which can occur through misuse of bookmarks or the `Reload` button.

All web applications should trap sensitive form resubmissions regardless of whether those applications use a Model 2 framework with event handling. Because of this requirement, "Trapping Form Resubmissions Without a Framework" on page 201 shows how to trap sensitive form resubmissions without the benefit of a Model 2 framework or event handling.

Event Handling for a Model 2 Framework

Model 2 frameworks are well suited to web applications because, among other things, they separate business logic from presentation logic, which allows software developers and page authors to work in parallel.[2] But a Model 2 framework that fires events to applications is even better because applications can extend that framework's capabilities—without modifying that framework—by responding to events. For example, if a Model 2 framework fires events just before and immediately after every action is performed, applications can handle those events to perform a variety of tasks, such as authentication, internationalization, or trapping sensitive form resubmissions.

This section illustrates extending the Model 2 framework discussed in "A Model 2 Framework" on page 154 to fire events before and after an action's `perform` method is invoked. That event handling extension is implemented with Java's delegation event model. Under that model, *event sources* fire *events* to *event listeners*.

The event handling extension discussed in this section implements actions as event sources: Actions fire events to listeners that implement an `ActionListener` interface. Those events are instances of an `ActionEvent` class. Figure 7-1 shows the sequence of events that takes place every time an action is performed.

---

2. See "A Model 2 Framework" on page 154 for more information on the benefits of the Model 2 architecture.

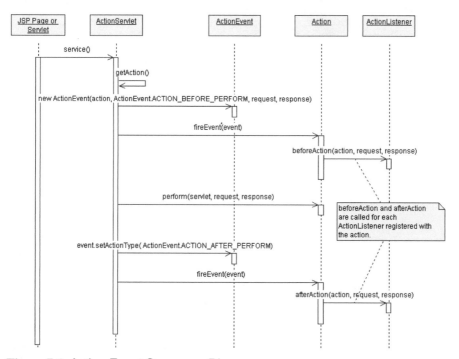

Figure 7-1 Action Event Sequence Diagram

Before performing an action, the action servlet creates an action event, specifying `ActionEvent.ACTION_BEFORE_PERFORM` as the type of the event. That event is passed to the action's `fireEvent` method, which invokes `beforeAction` for every action listener registered with the action.

After performing an action, the action servlet sets the action event's type to `ActionEvent.ACTION_AFTER_PERFORM`. That event is once again passed to the action's `fireEvent` method, and this time, that method calls `afterAction` for all registered listeners.

Example 7-1.a lists the `ActionListener` interface.[3]

---

3.   The `Action` class and `ActionListener` interface are unrelated to the AWT
    `Action` and `ActionListener`.

Example 7-1.a   /WEB-INF/classes/actions/events/ActionListener.java

```
package actions.events;

import javax.servlet.ServletException;

public interface ActionListener extends java.util.EventListener {
   public void beforeAction(ActionEvent event)
                            throws ServletException;
   public void afterAction(ActionEvent event)
                            throws ServletException;
}
```

The `ActionListener` interface extends `java.util.EventListener`, which is a tagging interface for all event listeners. By convention, all event listeners should implement the `EventListener` interface because some event sources will expect them to do so. In this case, it's not strictly necessary to extend that tagging interface.[4]

Two methods are defined by the `ActionListener` interface: `beforeAction` and `afterAction`. As illustrated in Figure 7-1, those methods are invoked before and after an action's `perform` method is called, respectively.

Both `ActionListener` methods may throw servlet exceptions, which lets those methods veto actions; for example, in "Sensitive Form Resubmissions" on page 190, an action listener throws a servlet exception when a sensitive form is resubmitted.

Both `ActionListener` methods are passed action events. Example 7-1.b lists the `ActionEvent` class.

Example 7-1.b /WEB-INF/classes/actions/events/ActionEvent.java

```
package actions.events;

import javax.servlet.http.HttpServletRequest;
import javax.servlet.http.HttpServletResponse;
import actions.Action;

public class ActionEvent extends java.util.EventObject {
   public static final int BEFORE_ACTION=0, AFTER_ACTION=1;

   private int eventType;
   private HttpServletRequest request;
   private HttpServletResponse response;
```

---

4.   Tagging interfaces do not define any methods.

```
   public ActionEvent(Action action, int eventType,
                      HttpServletRequest request,
                      HttpServletResponse response) {
      super(action);  // sets action as the source of the event
      this.eventType = eventType;
      this.request = request;
      this.response = response;
   }
   public int                 getEventType() { return eventType; }
   public HttpServletRequest  getRequest()   { return request;   }
   public HttpServletResponse getResponse()  { return response;  }

   public void setEventType(int eventType) {
      this.eventType = eventType;
   }
}
```

Action events are constructed with an action, event type, the request, and the response. That action is passed to the superclass—java.util.EventObject—constructor, thereby designating it as the event source. You can retrieve that action with the inherited getSource method.

The Action interface, originally discussed in "The Action Interface" on page 158, is listed again in Example 7-1.c, this time with support for firing action events. You can add action listeners to an action, and you can fire events to those listeners, in registration order, with Action.fireEvent.

Example 7-1.c /WEB-INF/classes/actions/Action.java

```
package actions;

import javax.servlet.http.HttpServlet;
import javax.servlet.http.HttpServletRequest;
import javax.servlet.http.HttpServletResponse;
import actions.events.ActionEvent;
import actions.events.ActionListener;

// Application-specific actions implement this interface

public interface Action {
   ActionRouter perform(HttpServlet servlet,
                        HttpServletRequest req,
                        HttpServletResponse res)
                        throws javax.servlet.ServletException;

   void addActionListener(ActionListener listener);
   void fireEvent(ActionEvent event)
                  throws javax.servlet.ServletException;
}
```

Default implementations of `Action.addActionListener` and
`Action.fireEvent` are provided by the `ActionBase` class, which is listed in
Example 7-1.d.

Example 7-1.d   /WEB-INF/classes/actions/ActionBase.java

```java
package actions;

import java.util.Enumeration;
import java.util.Vector;
import javax.servlet.ServletException;
import actions.events.ActionEvent;
import actions.events.ActionListener;

public abstract class ActionBase implements Action {
    protected boolean isSensitive = false,
                      hasSensitiveForms = false;
    private Vector listeners = new Vector();

    public ActionBase() {
        addActionListener(new SensitiveActionListener());
    }
    public void addActionListener(ActionListener listener) {
        listeners.addElement(listener);
    }
    public void removeActionListener(ActionListener listener) {
        listeners.remove(listener);
    }
    public void fireEvent(ActionEvent event)
                                        throws ServletException {
        Enumeration it = listeners.elements();

        while(it.hasMoreElements()) {
            ActionListener listener =
                        (ActionListener)it.nextElement();

            switch(event.getEventType()) {
                case ActionEvent.BEFORE_ACTION:
                        listener.beforeAction(event);
                        break;
                case ActionEvent.AFTER_ACTION:
                        listener.afterAction(event);
                        break;
            }
        }
    }
}
```

Finally, the action servlet, originally listed in Example 6-3.b on page 166, is modified in Example 7-1.e to fire action events.

Example 7-1.e /WEB-INF/classes/ActionServlet.java

```
// see Example 6-3.b on page 166 for the rest of this listing
...
import actions.events.ActionEvent;

public class ActionServlet extends HttpServlet {
    ...
    public void service(HttpServletRequest req,
                        HttpServletResponse res)
                          throws ServletException {
        Action action = getAction(req);
        ActionEvent event = new ActionEvent(action,
                    ActionEvent.BEFORE_ACTION,req, res);

        action.fireEvent(event);

        ActionRouter router = performAction(action, req, res);

        action.setEventType(ActionEvent.AFTER_ACTION);
        action.fireEvent(event);

        // routers could fire events in a manner similar to actions
        routeAction(router, req, res);
    }
    ...
}
```

Now that we've seen how to add event handling to a Model 2 framework, let's put that event handling to good use by trapping sensitive form resubmissions.

JSP Tip

Extend Your Framework Without Modifying It

If your framework fires events, you can extend that framework without modifying it by handling those events. The previous section—"Event Handling for a Model 2 Framework" on page 184—illustrated how to add event handling to a Model 2 framework. The next section—"Sensitive Form Resubmissions" on page 190—shows how to use that event handling mechanism to extend that framework.

Sensitive Form Resubmissions

It's easy to inadvertently resubmit forms with bookmarks or the `Reload` button. Because of this potential for mischief, web applications must guard against sensitive form resubmissions.

Figure 7-2 illustrates the potential for sensitive form resubmissions. Starting with the upper-left picture moving clockwise, Figure 7-2 shows the sequence of events as a hypothetical Timothy creates a new account.

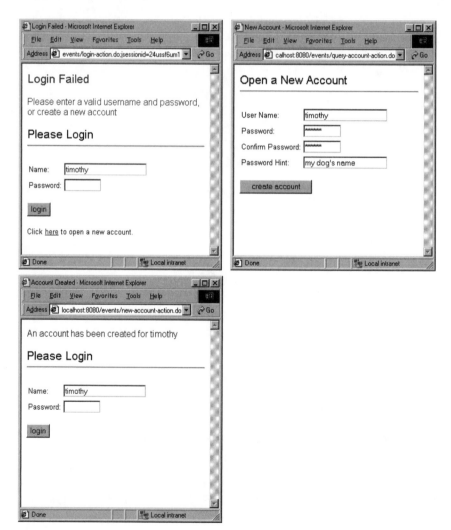

Figure 7-2 Sensitive Form Resubmissions: top left, clockwise

First, Timothy tries to log in, but since he doesn't have an account, he's forwarded to the Login Failed page.

Timothy clicks on the open new account link in the Login Failed page and is forwarded to the Open a New Account page, where he fills in the form and clicks the create account button.

At this point, Timothy's account has been created and he's forwarded to the Please Login page, but what if he reloads that page instead of logging in? Or what if he hits the Back button and clicks on the create account button without changing the form's data? In both cases, Timothy creates a duplicate request, and duplicate requests are hardly ever anticipated or welcome.

This section illustrates two ways that you can handle duplicate requests: with a Model 2 framework and event handling or with JSP custom tags. The former is discussed in "Trapping Form Resubmissions with a Model 2 Framework" on page 191, and the latter is discussed in "Trapping Form Resubmissions Without a Framework" on page 201. Both implementations trap sensitive form resubmissions by throwing a servlet exception, as shown in Figure 7-3.

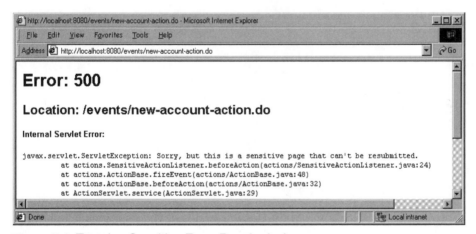

Figure 7-3 Trapping Sensitive Form Resubmissions

Trapping Form Resubmissions with a Model 2 Framework

From the discussion in "Sensitive Form Resubmissions" on page 190, it's apparent that some actions are sensitive to bookmarks or the Reload button. The bottom picture in Figure 7-2 on page 190 shows the result of the new-account-action (notice the Address bar). That action is sensitive because reloading that page will submit a duplicate new-account-action.

It's easy to identify sensitive actions because resubmitting a sensitive action results in an error or an undesired state; for example, if the `new-account-action`, listed in Example 7-2.a, is resubmitted, two identical accounts would be created.

Example 7-2.a /WEB-INF/classes/actions/NewAccountAction.java

```java
package actions;

import javax.servlet.ServletException;
import javax.servlet.http.HttpServlet;
import javax.servlet.http.HttpServletRequest;
import javax.servlet.http.HttpServletResponse;

import beans.LoginDB;
import beans.User;

public class NewAccountAction extends ActionBase {
   public NewAccountAction() {
      isSensitive = true; // this is a sensitive action
   }
   public ActionRouter perform(HttpServlet servlet,
                               HttpServletRequest req,
                               HttpServletResponse res)
                               throws ServletException {
      LoginDB loginDB = (LoginDB)servlet.getServletContext().
                        getAttribute("loginDB");
      String uname = req.getParameter("userName");

      loginDB.addUser(uname, req.getParameter("password"),
                             req.getParameter("password-hint"));
      req.setAttribute("userName", uname);

      return new ActionRouter("account-created-page");
   }
}
```

In addition to *sensitive actions*, we also speak of *sensitive forms*. A form is sensitive if it forwards to a sensitive action; for example, the form for opening a new account shown Figure 7-2 on page 190 is sensitive because it forwards to a sensitive action: `new-account-action`.

Some actions forward to JSP pages with sensitive forms; for example, the query-account-action listed in Example 7-2.b forwards to the JSP page shown in Figure 7-2 on page 190. That page has a sensitive form, so query-account-action forwards to a JSP page with a sensitive form. We refer to those types of actions as *actions that have sensitive forms*.

Example 7-2.b /WEB-INF/classes/actions/QueryAccountAction.java

```
package actions;

import javax.servlet.ServletException;
import javax.servlet.http.*;

// this action forwards to a JSP page with sensitive forms

public class QueryAccountAction extends ActionBase {
   public ActionRouter perform(HttpServlet servlet,
                               HttpServletRequest req,
                               HttpServletResponse res)
                               throws ServletException {
      // query-account-page is a logical name for the
      // upper-right JSP page shown in Figure 7-2 on page 190

      return new ActionRouter("query-account-page");
   }
}
```

Trapping sensitive form resubmissions requires us to keep track of sensitive actions and actions that have sensitive forms. That requires changes to the Action interface and the ActionBase class, which are partially listed in Example 7-2.a and Example 7-3.b, respectively.

Example 7-3.a Action.java with Support for Sensitive Forms

```
// see Example 7-1.c on page 187 for the rest of this listing

package actions;
...

public interface Action extends ActionListener {
   ...
   public boolean hasSensitiveForms();
   public boolean isSensitive();
}
```

Example 7-3.b ActionBase.java with Support for Sensitive Forms

```
// see Example 7-1.d on page 188 for the rest of this listing

package actions;
...

public abstract class ActionBase implements Action {
   protected boolean isSensitive = false,
                     hasSensitiveForms = false;
   ...
   public ActionBase() {
      addActionListener(new SensitiveActionListener());
   }
   ...
   public boolean isSensitive() {
      return isSensitive;
   }
   public boolean hasSensitiveForms() {
      return hasSensitiveForms;
   }
   ...
}
```

Now that we can identify sensitive actions and actions that have sensitive forms, let's see how to put that functionality to use with tokens.

Tokens As Used by a Listener

We will trap sensitive form resubmissions with an action listener that gives special treatment to sensitive actions and actions with sensitive forms.[5] For every action that has a sensitive form, the listener creates a unique string, called a token. Then the listener places that token in both the request and the session.

When the sensitive form is submitted, a new request is generated and a sensitive action is performed. But before that sensitive action is performed, that action's listener checks to see if both tokens are present and identical. If so, the sensitive action is performed; otherwise, a servlet exception is thrown. After a sensitive action is performed, both tokens are removed from their respective scopes.

Using tokens in this manner ensures that sensitive actions can only be invoked by a sensitive form. If a user attempts to submit a sensitive action with the Reload button or a bookmark, a servlet exception will be thrown.

---

5. See "Event Handling for a Model 2 Framework" on page 184 for more information concerning action listeners.

Example 7-4.a lists the Token class.

Example 7-4.a /WEB-INF/classes/beans/Token.java

```
package beans;

import javax.servlet.ServletException;
import javax.servlet.http.HttpServletRequest;
import javax.servlet.http.HttpSession;
import java.security.MessageDigest;

public class Token {
    private String token;

    public Token(HttpServletRequest req) throws ServletException {
        HttpSession session = req.getSession(true);
        long systime = System.currentTimeMillis();
        byte[] time  = new Long(systime).toString().getBytes();
        byte[] id = session.getId().getBytes();
        try {
            MessageDigest md5 = MessageDigest.getInstance("MD5");
            md5.update(id);
            md5.update(time);
            token = toHex(md5.digest());
        }
        catch(Exception ex) {
            throw new ServletException(ex);
        }
    }
    public String toString() {
        return token;
    }
    private String toHex(byte[] digest) {
        StringBuffer buf = new StringBuffer();

        for(int i=0; i < digest.length; i++)
            buf.append(Integer.toHexString((int)digest[i] & 0x00ff));

        return buf.toString();
    }
}
```

The token class creates a unique, encrypted string based on the user's session and the current time. But as far as we're concerned, tokens are black boxes—you give them a request and they return a unique string.[6]

6. For more on tokens, see Fields and Kolb. *Web Development with JSP*, Manning 2000.

The action listener that traps sensitive form resubmissions as described above is an instance of `SensitiveActionListener`. Each action has a sensitive action listener added to its list of action listeners by the `ActionBase` constructor, like this:

```
// see Example 7-3.b on page 194 for the rest of this listing

public abstract class ActionBase implements Action {
   ...
   public ActionBase() {
      addActionListener(new SensitiveActionListener());
   }
   ...
}
```

Figure 7-4 shows the sequence of events that take place when a sensitive action listener's `beforeAction` method is called.

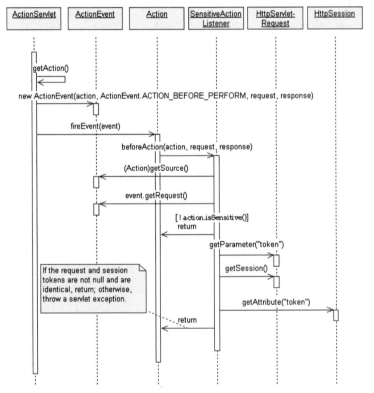

Figure 7-4 Filtering Actions Before They Are Performed

Sensitive action listeners act as a filter, filtering out sensitive actions before they are performed to make sure those actions were submitted by a sensitive form.

After an action is performed, sensitive action listeners check to see if that action has sensitive forms; if so, the listener creates a token and stores it in the request and the session, as illustrated in Figure 7-5.

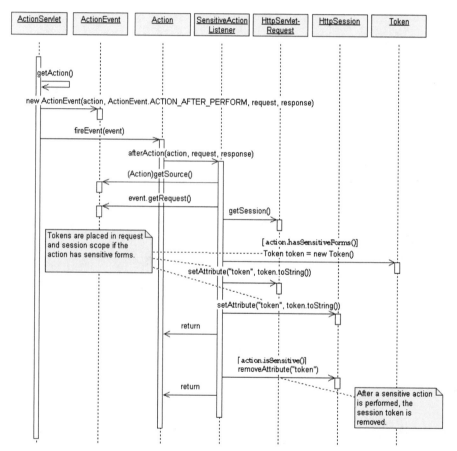

Figure 7-5 Filtering Actions After They Are Performed

The SensitiveActionListener class is listed in Example 7-4.b.

Example 7-4.b   /WEB-INF/classes/actions/SensitiveActionListener.java

```java
package actions;

import javax.servlet.ServletException;
import javax.servlet.http.HttpServletRequest;
import javax.servlet.http.HttpSession;
import actions.Action;
import actions.events.ActionEvent;
import actions.events.ActionListener;
import beans.Token;

public class SensitiveActionListener implements ActionListener {
   public void beforeAction(ActionEvent event)
                                        throws ServletException {
      Action action = (Action)event.getSource();

      if(action.isSensitive()) {
         HttpServletRequest req = event.getRequest();
         String requestToken = (String)req.getParameter("token"),
                sessionToken = (String)req.getSession().
                                        getAttribute("token");

         if(sessionToken == null || requestToken == null ||
                         !sessionToken.equals(requestToken)) {
            throw new ServletException(
                    "Sorry, but this is a sensitive page " +
                    "that can't be resubmitted.");
         }
      }
   }
   public void afterAction(ActionEvent event)
                                        throws ServletException {
      Action action = (Action)event.getSource();
      HttpServletRequest req = event.getRequest();
      HttpSession session = req.getSession();

      if(action.hasSensitiveForms()) {
         Token token = new Token(req);

         session.setAttribute("token", token.toString());
         req.setAttribute("token", token.toString());
      }
      if(action.isSensitive()) {
         session.removeAttribute("token");
      }
   }
}
```

Tokens As Used by a Programmer

Now that we've seen how tokens are used by sensitive action listeners, let's see how to put them to use. First, we identify sensitive actions, such as new-account-action discussed in "Trapping Form Resubmissions with a Model 2 Framework" on page 191, like this:

```
// see Example 7-2.a on page 192 for the rest of this listing

public class NewAccountAction extends ActionBase {
    public NewAccountAction() {
        isSensitive = true; // this is a sensitive action
    }
    ...
}
```

Likewise, the query-account-action is identified as an action that has sensitive forms:

```
// see Example 7-2.b on page 193 for the rest of this listing

public class QueryAccountAction extends ActionBase {
    public QueryAccountAction() {
        // this action forwards to a JSP page with sensitive forms
        hasSensitiveForms = true;
    }
    ...
}
```

newAccount.jsp, listed in Example 7-4.c, has a sensitive form that forwards to new-account-action. Before that JSP page is loaded, a sensitive action listener has stored tokens in the request and the session. Because submitting the sensitive form will result in a new request, the request token is stowed away, with the help of a custom tag, in the new request as a hidden field.

Example 7-4.c /newAccount.jsp

```
<html><head><title>New Account</title>
    <%@ taglib uri='/WEB-INF/tlds/utilities.tld' prefix='util' %>
</head>
<body>
<font size='5' color='blue'>Open a New Account</font>
<hr>
<form action=' <%=response.encodeURL("new-account-action.do")%> '
        method='post'>
```

```
<table><tr>
    <td> User Name: </td>
    <td><input type='text' name='userName'></td>
</tr><tr>
    <td> Password: </td>
    <td><input type='password' name='password' size='8'></td>
</tr><tr>
    <td> Confirm Password: </td>
    <td><input type='password' name='confirm-password'
                size='8'></td>
</tr><tr>
    <td> Password Hint: </td>
    <td><input type='text' name='password-hint'>
    </td>
</tr>
</table>
<br>
<input type='submit' value='create account'>
<util:token/>
</form>
</body>
</html>
```

When the form in Example 7-4.c is submitted and `new-account-action` is invoked, the sensitive action listener associated with that action will check request and session tokens. That means that `new-account-action` can only be invoked from a sensitive form, which renders it inaccessible with a bookmark or the `Reload` button.

The only thing left to discuss is the `util:token` custom tag used above. The tag handler for that tag is listed in Example 7-5.

Example 7-5 /WEB-INF/classes/tags/TokenTag.java

```
package tags;

import javax.servlet.ServletRequest;
import javax.servlet.jsp.JspException;
import javax.servlet.jsp.tagext.TagSupport;

public class TokenTag extends TagSupport {
    private String property;

    public int doStartTag() throws JspException {
        ServletRequest req = pageContext.getRequest();
        String value = (String)req.getAttribute("token");
```

```
      if(value == null)
         throw new JspException("No token in request scope");

      try {
         pageContext.getOut().print("<input type='hidden' " +
            "name='token' " + "value ='" + value + "'>");
      }
      catch(java.io.IOException ex) {
         throw new JspException(ex.getMessage());
      }
      return SKIP_BODY;
   }
}
```

The `token` tag handler generates HTML for a hidden field whose value is the token stored in the original request by a sensitive action handler.

JSP Tip

Be Diligent About Trapping Sensitive Form Resubmissions

Bookmarks and the Back button are the scourge of web developers because they allow random access to an application's views. Misuse of bookmarks and the Back button often results in sensitive form resubmissions, which should always be trapped.

The previous section—"Trapping Form Resubmissions with a Model 2 Framework" on page 191—illustrates how to trap sensitive form resubmissions with a Model 2 framework and event handling. The next section—"Trapping Form Resubmissions Without a Framework" on page 201—shows how to trap sensitive form resubmissions with custom tags alone.

Trapping Form Resubmissions Without a Framework

Not everyone will use a Model 2 framework with event handling as discussed in this book. But everyone should trap sensitive form resubmissions; therefore, we conclude this chapter by illustrating how to trap sensitive form resubmissions with custom tags alone. Those tags use the tokens discussed in "Tokens As Used by a Listener" on page 194.

Three custom tags, listed in Table 7-1 can be used to trap sensitive form resubmissions.

Table 7-1 Custom Tags for Trapping Sensitive Form Resubmissions

Tag	Description
create-tokens	Creates tokens and stores them in the request and the session
token	Places the request token in a form as a hidden field
check-tokens	Checks token validity

The tags listed in Table 7-1 are easy to use; for example, Example 7-6.a lists a JSP page that uses the first and second custom tags listed in Table 7-1.

Example 7-6.a Using the `create-tokens` and `token` Tags

```
<html><head><title>New Account</title>
   <%@ taglib uri='/WEB-INF/tlds/utilities.tld' prefix='util' %>
   <%@ taglib uri='/WEB-INF/tlds/tokens.tld' prefix='tokens' %>
   <tokens:create-tokens/>
</head>

<body>
<font size='5' color='blue'>Open a New Account</font>
<hr>
<form action='createAccount.jsp' method='post'>
   <table>
      <tr>
         <td>User Name:</td>
         <td><input type='text' name='userName'></td>
      </tr>
      <tr>
         <td>Password:</td>
         <td><input type='password' name='password' size='8'></td>
      </tr>
      <tr>
         <td>Confirm Password:</td>
         <td><input type='password' name='confirm-password'
                                    size='8'></td>
      </tr>
      <tr>
         <td>Password Hint:</td>
         <td><input type='text' name='password-hint'></td>
      </tr>
   </table>
   <br>
   <input type='submit' value='create account'>
   <tokens:token/>
</form>
</body>
</html>
```

In the JSP page listed above, the `create-tokens` tag creates session and request tokens, and the `token` tag passes that request token to the new account action as a hidden field.[7] That `token` tag is listed in Example 7-5 on page 200.

The `check-tokens` tag checks to make sure that there are identical tokens in the request and the session; if not, that tag throws an exception. The JSP page listed in Example 7-6.b uses that tag to make sure that duplicate accounts are not created.

Example 7-6.b Using the `check-tokens` and `remove-session-token` Tags

```
<%@ taglib uri='/WEB-INF/tlds/utilities.tld' prefix='util' %>
<%@ taglib uri='/WEB-INF/tlds/tokens.tld' prefix='tokens' %>

<tokens:check-tokens/>

<jsp:useBean id='bean' class='beans.CreateAccountBean'/>
<% bean.createAccount(request, application); %>

<font size='4' color='blue'>
   An account has been created for
   <%= request.getParameter("userName") %>
</font>

<p><%@ include file='login-form.jsp' %></p>
```

The tag handler for the `create-tokens` tag is listed in Example 7-6.c.

Example 7-6.c /WEB-INF/classes/tags/CreateTokensTag.java

```
package tags;

import javax.servlet.ServletRequest;
import javax.servlet.http.HttpServletRequest;
import javax.servlet.jsp.JspException;
import javax.servlet.jsp.PageContext;
import javax.servlet.jsp.tagext.TagSupport;
import beans.Token;

public class CreateTokensTag extends TagSupport {
   private String property;

   public int doEndTag() throws JspException {
      ServletRequest request = pageContext.getRequest();

      try {
         Token token = new Token((HttpServletRequest)request);
```

---

7.   The form submission creates a new request, which necessitates the hidden field.

```
                pageContext.setAttribute("token", token.toString(),
                                     PageContext.SESSION_SCOPE);

                pageContext.setAttribute("token", token.toString(),
                                     PageContext.REQUEST_SCOPE);
         }
         catch(Exception ex) {
            throw new JspException(ex.getMessage());
         }
         return EVAL_PAGE;
      }
   }
```

The `create-tokens` tag handler creates a token and copies it into request and session scopes.

The tag handler for the `check-tokens` tag is listed in Example 7-6.d.

Example 7-6.d   /WEB-INF/classes/tags/CheckTokensTag.java

```
   package tags;

   import javax.servlet.ServletRequest;
   import javax.servlet.jsp.JspException;
   import javax.servlet.jsp.tagext.TagSupport;

   public class CheckTokensTag extends TagSupport {
      private String property;

      public int doEndTag() throws JspException {
         ServletRequest  req = pageContext.getRequest();
         String sessionToken = (String)req.getParameter("token");
         String requestToken = (String)pageContext.getSession().
                            getAttribute("token");

         if(requestToken == null || requestToken == null ||
            !sessionToken.equals(requestToken))
            throw new JspException("Sorry, but this sensitive page" +
                               " can't be resubmitted.");

         return EVAL_PAGE;
      }
   }
```

The `check-tokens` tag handler retrieves the two tokens and compares them. If either of the tokens is not present or the two tokens are not equal, that tag handler throws an exception.

Conclusion

This chapter consists of three major themes:

- Adding event handling to a Model 2 framework
- Using that event handling to handle sensitive form resubmissions
- Handling sensitive form resubmissions without event handling or a Model 2 framework

The first theme listed above is really about using Java's delegation event model with some kind of framework that employs the Front Controller design pattern. That design pattern features centralized request handling, usually implemented with a servlet. This chapter uses the Model 2 framework discussed in "Design" on page 132, but you can easily adapt the event handling mechanism discussed in this chapter to other frameworks that use the Front Controller design pattern.

Adding event handling to a web application framework lets you extend that framework without modifying it. This chapter has illustrated extending the Model 2 framework discussed in "Design" on page 132 to handle sensitive form resubmissions, but you can use that event handling mechanism to extend your framework in many interesting ways, such as authenticating users or setting a locale for internationalization.

Whether you use a framework or event handling, you should be diligent about handling sensitive form resubmissions. This chapter has discussed two ways to do that: With a Model 2 framework and event handling and with custom tags alone.

I18N

Chapter 8

At the end of the 20th century, with the World Wide Web in its infancy, most web sites are in English, but that's starting to change as more web sites offer content in multiple languages. Web sites that adapt to a reader's native language and customs have an obvious competitive advantage over those that do not.

This chapter is concerned with *internationalization*—often abbreviated as i18n—and *localization*, which is sometimes referred to as l10n.[1] Internationalization is the process of implementing applications that accommodate multiple languages and customs, whereas localization involves adapting applications to support a specific region, known as a *locale*.

Starting with version 4.0, both Netscape Communicator and Internet Explorer allow users to select a prioritized list of preferred languages. The principal goal of this chapter is to illustrate internationalizing dynamic content based upon those preferred languages. This chapter shows how to find out what those languages are—see "Browser Language Preferences" on page 233—and how to provide appropriate content for them. In addition to discussing how to support multiple languages, we also explore how to format locale-sensitive objects,

---

1. Those abbreviations come from the first and last characters and the number of characters in between.

such as dates and numbers. The chapter concludes with two custom tags that can access localized text and format locale-sensitive objects. But before all that, we must discuss the underpinnings of internationalization: Unicode and charsets.

Unicode

Internally, the Java programming language uses Unicode to store characters. Unicode is a character coding system that assigns unique numbers for every character for every major language of the world. [2]

Java's use of Unicode means that JSP pages can store strings containing all characters found in commonly used written languages. It also means that you can use Unicode escape sequences to represent characters that you may not find on your keyboard. For example, Figure 8-1 shows a JSP page that displays "Are your applications internationalized?" in Spanish.[3]

Figure 8-1 Using Unicode Escape Sequences

The JSP page shown in Figure 8-1 is listed in Example 8-1.

Example 8-1 Using Unicode Escape Sequences

```
<html><head><title>Unicode Escape Sequences</title>
   <%@ page contentType='text/html; charset=ISO-8859-1' %>
   <% response.setHeader("Content-Language", "es"); %>
</head>
<body>

<font size='4'>
   <%= "\u00BFSus usos son internacionalizados?" %>
```

2. See http://www.unicode.org/ for more information about Unicode.
3. Most translations in this chapter are from online translation services.

```
</font>

</body>
</html>
```

The JSP page listed in Example 8-1 uses the Unicode escape sequence `\u00BF` for the inverted question mark. All Unicode escape sequences are of the form `\uXXXX`; see `http://www.unicode.org/charts/PDF/U0000.pdf` for a list of escape sequences for printable Latin-1 characters.

As an alternative to Unicode escape sequences, you can use HTML character entities; for example, the HTML character entity for the inverted question mark is `&iquest`.[4] Because HTML character entities are only valid for HTML, Unicode escape sequences are preferable to HTML character entities for servlets and JSP pages, which often produce output in other formats, such as plain text.

The JSP page listed in Example 8-1 sets the `Content-Language` response header to `es`, meaning that the response is in Spanish. Strictly speaking, that header should always be set, even though it is widely ignored; for example, both Netscape and Internet Explorer will produce the same result if that header is not set in Example 8-1.

Charsets

Browsers map bytes to characters or glyphs; for example, in Example 8-1, `\u00BF` is mapped to an inverted question mark. Those mappings are facilitated by a *charset*, which is defined as *a method of converting a sequence of octets into a sequence of characters*.[5] The charset used in Example 8-1 is `ISO-8859-1`, which maps bytes to characters for Latin-based languages. That charset is the default, and therefore the directive in Example 8-1 specifying `ISO-8859-1` is not strictly necessary.

Non-Latin-based JSP Pages

If your content is displayed in a Latin-based language, such as English, Spanish, or French, there's no need to specify a charset; however, if you need to display content in a language that's not Latin based, such as Japanese, you must specify the appropriate charset or the output will be unreadable. Figure 8-2 shows a JSP page that displays Good Morning in Korean by using the Korean charset.

---

4. See `http://www.utoronto.ca/webdocs/HTMLdocs/NewHTML/iso_table.html` for a list of HTML character entities.
5. The definition comes from RFC 2278—see `http://www.cis.ohiostate.edu/htbin/rfc/rfc2278.html`.

Advanced JavaServer Pages

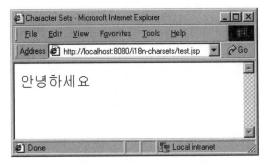

Figure 8-2 Using the Korean Charset

The JSP page shown in Figure 8-2 is listed in Example 8-2.

Example 8-2 Specifying a Charset

```
<html><head><title>Character Sets</title>
   <%@ page contentType='text/html; charset=EUC-KR' %>
   <% response.setHeader("Content-Language", "ko"); %>
</head>
<body>

<%= "\uc548\ub155\ud558\uc138\uc694" %>

</body>
</html>
```

The JSP page shown in Figure 8-2 uses the charset EUC-KR, which maps a sequence of bytes—in this case, "\uc548\ub155\ud558\uc138\uc694"—to Korean glyphs. For the JSP page shown in Figure 8-2 to display correctly, your browser must support the EUC-KR charset and have access to Korean fonts. Because of this requirement, you may need to install additional software for your browser; following are web sites with installation instructions:

- Netscape Communicator: http://home.netscape.com/eng/intl
- Internet Explorer: http://www.microsoft.com/ie/intlhome.htm

You can find a list of the most commonly used charsets here: http://www.w3.org/International/0-charset-lang.html.

As of the Servlet 2.2 specification, you can set charsets indirectly with ServletResponse.setLocale; see "Locales" on page 211 for more information.

Multilingual JSP Pages

If you need to display multiple languages, then you need the Universal Character Set (UCS), defined in 1993 by the ISO and IEC.[6]

The UCS can encode all of the characters and symbols for all of the written languages of the world, with room to spare. With 31 bits to represent each character or symbol, the UCS has room for a whopping 2 billion of them. That's the bad news, though, because most applications can only handle 16-bit encodings. The good news for the UCS is that it's Unicode compatible.

The majority of applications can't handle the UCS encoding, but because of its usefulness and compatibility with Unicode, a few transform encodings were developed, the most popular of which is UTF-8 (UCS Transformation Format 8). UTF-8 transforms UCS into one-, two-, or three-byte encodings, and because it preserves the US ASCII range, UTF-8 can transmit US ASCII as single bytes, which is much more efficient than the UCS. Those properties make UTF-8 the most widely used format for displaying multiple languages.

Four applications discussed in this chapter use UTF-8 to display more than one language; for example, see Figure 8-4 on page 226 and Figure 8-9 on page 239.

Locales

The most basic internationalization task is identifying geographical, political, or cultural regions, known as locales. In the Java programming language, locales are represented by the `java.util.Locale` class; instances of that class are used by locale-sensitive objects to format information. Java provides a number of locale-sensitive objects such as `java.util.DateFormat`—see "Dates and Times" on page 225—and Java's internationalization workhorse, `java.util.ResourceBundle`—see "Resource Bundles" on page 213.

The `Locale` class provides two constructors:

- `Locale(String language, String country)`
- `Locale(String language, String country, String variant)`

---

6.   ISO = International Standards Organization; IEC = International Electrotechnical Commission.

The first two arguments to both constructors are ISO codes, the first representing a language and the second representing a country. Those codes are listed at `http://www.ics.uci.edu/pub/ietf/http/related/iso639.txt` and `http://userpage.chemie.fuberlin.de/diverse/doc/ISO_3166.html` respectively.

The third argument for the second constructor listed above is a variant. Variants are vendor- and browser-specific; for example, WIN can be specified for Windows, and MAC for Macintosh. In practice, variants are seldom specified.

The Locale class provides static constants, listed in Table 8-1, for frequently used locales.

Table 8-1 Locale Constants for Frequently Used Locales

Country or Language	Country Code	Language Code
Locale.CANADA	CA	en
Locale.CHINA	CN	zh
Locale.CHINESE	zh	--
Locale.ENGLISH	--	en
Locale.FRANCE	FR	fr
Locale.GERMANY	DE	de
Locale.ITALY	IT	it
Locale.JAPAN	JP	ja
Locale.KOREA	KP	ko
Locale.SIMPLIFIED_CHINESE	--	--
Locale.TAIWAN	TW	--
Locale.TRADITIONAL_CHINESE	--	--
Locale.UK	UK	en
Locale.US	US	en

You can use the constants listed in Table 8-1 in lieu of constructing locales; for example, both of the following lines of code provide access to a locale representing United States English:

```
Locale locale_1 = new Locale("US", "en");
Locale locale_2 = Locale.US;
```

It's often the case that locales are accessed by country only, but the `Locale` class does not provide a constructor that takes a single argument representing a country. If you need to construct a locale associated with a country but not a specific language, you can specify an empty string for the language, like this:

```
// Construct a locale for Bulgaria:
Locale locale = new Locale("BG", "");
```

The Servlet 2.2 specification adds `setLocale` and `getLocale` methods to the `ServletResponse` class. The `setLocale` method sets the `Content-Language` header and an appropriate charset for the content type. Example 8-3 illustrates the use of that method by setting the response locale to Korean; that example is functionally identical to Example 8-2 on page 210, which explicitly sets the `Content-Language` header and charset.

Example 8-3   Setting the Response Locale

```
<html><head><title>Character Sets</title>
    <% response.setLocale(java.util.Locale.KOREAN); %>
</head>
<body>

<%= "\uc548\ub155\ud558\uc138\uc694" %>

</body>
</html>
```

The output of the JSP page listed in Example 8-3 is identical to what's shown in Figure 8-2 on page 210.

Resource Bundles

We've seen how to use Unicode escape sequences to display characters specific to one or more languages and how to specify charsets for displaying content in languages that are not Latin based. We've also seen how to specify geographical, political, or cultural regions as locales. But how do you actually provide localized content for your web applications?

Providing localized content can be accomplished in one of two ways. The most obvious solution is to provide separate JSP pages for different locales; however, that's a brute force method requiring high maintenance because those JSP pages must be kept in sync. That doesn't mean that it's not a viable solution, however. In cases where different locales require programmatic differences, such as different page layouts, it can be perfectly acceptable to implement a JSP page for each locale.

Most of the time, the best way to provide localized content is to separate locale-sensitive information from the JSP pages that use that information. In that case, a single JSP page can be used for many locales by retrieval of locale-sensitive information from a repository. That repository is a resource bundle.

Conceptually, resource bundles—represented by `java.util.ResourceBundle`—are hash tables that store key/value pairs for a specific locale. Resource bundles are located according to a base name, as outlined below.

Resource bundle keys are strings that uniquely identify a resource, whereas the values can be any Java object, although they too are typically strings (or string arrays) that have been translated for a particular locale. The most commonly used `ResourceBundle` methods are listed below.

- `static ResourceBundle getBundle(String base)`
- `static ResourceBundle getBundle(String base, Locale)`
- `Object getObject(String key)`
- `String getString(String key)`
- `String[] getStringArray(String key)`

The first two methods listed above are `static` methods that try to locate a resource bundle based on a locale. The first method starts the search with the default locale, and the second method uses the specified locale, followed by the default locale if a bundle associated with the specified locale cannot be found.

Both `static` methods listed above search for resource bundles named *package.Bundle_la_CO_va*, where *package.Bundle* is the **base name** specified with the `base` argument, *la* is a two-letter language code, *CO* is a two-letter country code, and *va* is a list of variants separated by underscores. If that search is not successful, the last component is dropped and the search is repeated. For example, consider the following statement:

```
ResourceBundle bundle = ResourceBundle.getBundle("Resources",
                                    new Locale("fr","CH"));
```

The code fragment listed above begins its search by looking for a resource bundle for Swiss French. If the default locale is Australian English, the longest possible search for the code fragment listed above would be:

```
Resources_fr_CH
Resources_fr
Resources_en_AU
Resources_en
Resources
```

The first resource bundle that is found is considered the best match and returned. If no match is found, a `MissingResourceException` is thrown.

Once you have a resource bundle, you can use the last three `ResourceBundle` methods listed above to extract locale-sensitive information from that bundle. For example, the following statements extract an object, string, and string array, respectively, from a resource bundle:

```
Object object = bundle.getObject("key_1");
String string = bundle.getString("key_2");
String[] array = bundle.getStringArray("key_3");
```

All three methods are passed a key, and all three methods return the key's associated value or throw a `MissingResourceException` if the key is not present in the bundle.

The resource bundles located by `ResourceBundle.getBundle` are either list resource bundles or property resource bundles. The next two sections illustrate how you create and use those types of resource bundles.

List Resource Bundles

List resource bundles are instances of `java.util.ListResourceBundle`, an abstract extension of `ResourceBundle`; for example, Example 8-4.a and Example 8-4.b list two list resource bundles.

Example 8-4.a /WEB-INF/classes/Resources.java

```java
import java.util.ListResourceBundle;

// This is the fallback resource bundle because it's not
// associated with a particular locale.

public class Resources extends ListResourceBundle {
    static final Object[][] contents = {
        { "message.welcome", "Welcome" },
        { "picture.flag", "graphics/usa_flag.gif" },
    };
    public Object[][] getContents() {
        return contents;
    }
}
```

Example 8-4.b   /WEB-INF/classes/Resources_fr.java

```java
import java.util.ListResourceBundle;

// This is a resource bundle for the French locale

public class Resources_fr extends ListResourceBundle {
   static final Object[][] contents = {
       { "message.welcome", "Bienvenue" },
       { "picture.flag", "graphics/french_flag.gif" }
   };
   public Object[][] getContents() {
      return contents;
   }
}
```

The resource bundle listed in Example 8-4.a is the bundle that will be found if no locale-specific bundles are located, because the resource bundle's class name corresponds to the resource bundle's base name. That type of bundle is sometimes referred to as a *fallback* bundle because it's the last resort. The bundle listed in Example 8-4.b is for a French locale, signified by the class name, which ends in _fr.

Both resource bundles listed above specify a welcome message and a GIF image. And both resource bundles implement getContents(), the lone abstract method defined by ListResourceBundle, which returns an array of key/value pairs.

Figure 8-3 shows a JSP page that uses the bundles listed above.

The application shown in Figure 8-3 consists of two JSP pages, one for selecting a language and one that displays a flag and welcome message based upon that selection. The latter page uses the resource bundles listed in Example 8-4.a and Example 8-4.b to access the images and welcome messages.

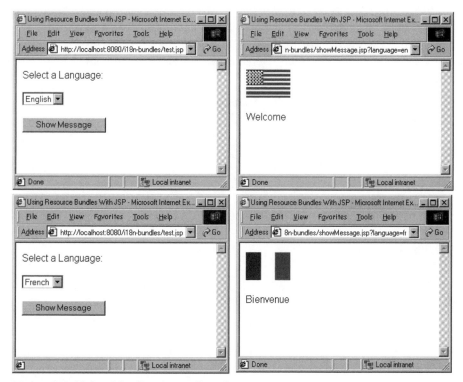

Figure 8-3 Using List Resource Bundles

The JSP page shown on the left in Figure 8-3 is listed in Example 8-4.c.

Example 8-4.c /test.jsp

```
<html><title>Using Resource Bundles With JSP</title>
<head><%@ page import='java.util.Locale' %></head>
<body>

<font size='4'>Select a Language:</font>
<p>
<form action='showMessage.jsp'>
   <select name='language'>
      <option value='en'><%= Locale.ENGLISH.getDisplayName() %>
      <option value='fr'><%= Locale.FRENCH.getDisplayName() %>
   </select>
   <p><input type='submit' value='Show Message'/></p>
</form>
</p>
</body>
</html>
```

The JSP page listed in Example 8-4.c uses `Locale.getDisplayName` to populate the drop-down list with names for English and French locales. That method returns a string appropriate for the default locale; for example, if the default locale is en_US, `getDisplayName` will return *English*, but if the default locale is `fr`, it will return *anglais*.

The action for the form listed in Example 8-4.c is `showMessage.jsp`, which is listed in Example 8-4.d.

Example 8-4.d   /showMessage.jsp

```
<html><title>Using Resource Bundles With JSP</title>
<head>
   <%@ page import='java.util.Locale' %>
   <%@ page import='java.util.ResourceBundle' %>
</head>
<body>

<% String language = request.getParameter("language");
   Locale locale = new java.util.Locale(language, "");
   ResourceBundle bundle =
                 ResourceBundle.getBundle("Resources", locale);%>

<img src='<%= bundle.getString("picture.flag") %>'>

<p>
<font size='4'>
  <%= bundle.getString("message.welcome") %>
</font>
</p>

</body>
</html>
```

The JSP page listed in Example 8-4.d retrieves the selected language from a request parameter and uses that language to construct a locale. That locale is subsequently used to locate a resource bundle, which in turn is used to access the URL for the flag and the welcome message.

Because the resource bundle listed in Example 8-4.a is the fallback bundle, it will be used for any locale other than French. If the JSP page listed in Example 8-4.c specified Spanish and French locales, the American flag and English welcome message would be shown if Spanish were selected because there is no Spanish resource bundle. An alternative would be to name the `Resources` bundle `Resources_en`. That bundle would then only be used for the English locale;

however, that approach would leave us without a fallback bundle, and so a
MissingResourceException would be thrown if Spanish were selected. In
general, it's advisable to implement a fallback bundle to avoid exceptions.

Using Constants for Resource Keys

The resource bundles listed in Example 8-4.a on page 215 and Example 8-4.b use
string literals to represent keys, and the JSP page listed in Example 8-4.d uses
those strings to access the key's associated values. That use of string literals
means that misspelled keys will not be caught until runtime, when a
MissingResourceException will be thrown. A better approach is to use
constants for resource keys because misspellings will be caught by the compiler.[7]

The JSP page listed in Example 8-5.a is a new version of the JSP page listed in
Example 8-4.d on page 218, revised to use string constants.

Example 8-5.a /showMessage.jsp

```
<html><title>Using Resource Bundles With JSP</title>
<head>
   <%@ page import='java.util.Locale' %>
   <%@ page import='java.util.ResourceBundle' %>
</head>
<body>

<% String language = request.getParameter("language");
   Locale locale = new java.util.Locale(language, "");
   ResourceBundle bundle =
                  ResourceBundle.getBundle("Resources", locale);%>

<img src='<%= bundle.getString(Resources.FLAG_PICTURE) %>'>

<p>
<font size='4'>
  <%= bundle.getString(Resources.WELCOME) %>
</font>
</p>

</body>
</html>
```

---

7. Resource key constants are best suited to precompiled JSP pages so that those
    errors are handled by the developer.

In Example 8-5.a, `ResourceBundle.getString` is passed a string constant instead of a string literal. Those constants are defined in the fallback bundle class, which is listed in Example 8-5.b.

Example 8-5.b   /WEB-INF/classes/Resources.java

```
import java.util.ListResourceBundle;

// This is the fallback resource bundle because it's not
// associated with a particular locale.

public class Resources extends ListResourceBundle {
   public static final String WELCOME = "message.welcome";
   public static final String FLAG_PICTURE = "picture.flag";

   static final Object[][] contents = {
      { WELCOME, "Welcome" },
      { FLAG_PICTURE, "graphics/usa_flag.gif" },
   };
   public Object[][] getContents() {
      return contents;
   }
}
```

A new version of the resource bundle listed in Example 8-4.b on page 216 is listed in Example 8-5.c, revised to use the string constants defined in Example 8-5.b.

Example 8-5.c   /WEB-INF/classes/Resources_fr.java with Constant Keys

```
import java.util.ListResourceBundle;

// This is a resource bundle for the French locale

public class Resources_fr extends ListResourceBundle {
   static final Object[][] contents = {
      { Resources.WELCOME, "Bienvenue" },
      { Resources.FLAG_PICTURE, "graphics/french_flag.gif" }
   };
   public Object[][] getContents() {
      return contents;
   }
}
```

Property Resource Bundles

Instead of implementing resource bundles as Java classes, you can specify key/value pairs in a properties file; for example, Example 8-6.a and Example 8-6.b list properties files that serve as replacements for the list resource bundles listed in Example 8-4.a on page 215 and Example 8-4.b, respectively.

Example 8-6.a /WEB-INF/classes/Resources.properties

```
message.welcome=Welcome
picture.flag=usa_flag.gif
```

Example 8-6.b /WEB-INF/classes/Resources_fr.properties

```
message.welcome=Bienvenue
picture.flag=french_flag.gif
```

Besides searching for resource bundle *classes* as described in "Resource Bundles" on page 213, the ResourceBundle.getBundle methods also search for *properties files* containing key/value pairs in the form of *key=value*.[8] If a properties file is found, a PropertyResourceBundle is instantiated and the values in the properties file are copied to the bundle, which is subsequently returned.

Using properties files is easier than implementing resource bundles as Java classes, but there is a price to be paid for this ease of use. First, properties files can only contain strings, whereas resource bundle classes can contain any type of object. Second, class constants cannot be referred to in a properties file, so string literals must be used for keys; see "Using Constants for Resource Keys" on page 219 for a description of the advantages of string constants vs. string literals. Even with these drawbacks, properties files are a popular choice for specifying resource bundle key/value pairs.

Multiple Resource Bundles

Internationalized applications often use multiple resource bundles; for example, one bundle could be used for localized text, and another for error messages. If you use multiple resource bundles, you can more easily maintain a large number of locale-sensitive objects by encapsulating different types of objects in different bundles.

---

8.   Resource bundle classes have precedence over properties files.

Example 8-7.a lists a JSP page that's functionally identical to the JSP page listed in Example 8-4.d on page 218, but Example 8-7.a uses multiple resource bundles: one for messages and another for image URLs.

Example 8-7.a   Using Multiple Resource Bundles

```
<html><title>Using Resource Bundles With JSP</title>
<head>
   <%@ page import='java.util.Locale' %>
   <%@ page import='java.util.ResourceBundle' %>
</head>
<body>

<% String language = request.getParameter("language");
   Locale locale = new java.util.Locale(language, "");
   ResourceBundle messages_bundle =
                 ResourceBundle.getBundle("messages",locale);
   ResourceBundle pictures_bundle =
                 ResourceBundle.getBundle("pictures",locale);%>

<img src='<%= pictures_bundle.getString("pictures.flag") %>'>

<p>
<font size='4'>
  <%= messages_bundle.getString("message.welcome") %>
</font>
</p>

</body>
</html>
```

As Example 8-7.a illustrates, using multiple resource bundles is straightforward, but it can be difficult for complex applications to keep track of a large number of resource bundles, especially among multiple JSP pages. Instead of maintaining references to multiple resource bundles, a better approach is to implement a Java class—a bundle cache—that maintains those references for you.

A Bundle Cache

The JSP page listed in Example 8-7.b, which is functionally identical to Example 8-7.a, uses multiple resource bundles with the help of a bundle cache.

Example 8-7.b   Using a Bundle Cache

```
<html><title>Using Resource Bundles With JSP</title>
<head><%@ page import='java.util.Locale' %></head>
<body>

<jsp:useBean id='bundleCache' scope='request'
                            class='beans.i18n.BundleCache'/>

<% String language = request.getParameter("language");
   Locale locale = new java.util.Locale(language, ""); %>

<img src='<%= bundleCache.getString("pictures", locale,
                                "pictures.flag") %>'>
<p>
<font size='4'>
  <%= bundleCache.getString("messages", locale,
                            "message.welcome") %>
</font>
</p>

</body>
</html>
```

The bundle cache used in Example 8-7.b provides access to multiple resource bundles without referencing those bundles directly.

Example 8-7.c lists the bundle cache used in Example 8-7.b.

Example 8-7.c   /WEB-INF/classes/beans/i18n/BundleCache.java

```
package beans.i18n;

import java.util.Hashtable;
import java.util.Locale;
import java.util.MissingResourceException;
import java.util.ResourceBundle;

public class BundleCache {
   private Hashtable bundles = new Hashtable();

   public Object getObject(String base, Locale locale, String key)
                                throws MissingResourceException {
      return getBundle(base, locale).getObject(key);
   }
```

```
public String getString(String base, Locale locale, String key)
                         throws MissingResourceException {
   return getBundle(base, locale).getString(key);
}
public String[] getStringArray(String base, Locale locale,
               String key) throws MissingResourceException {
   return getBundle(base, locale).getStringArray(key);
}
public ResourceBundle getBundle(String base, Locale locale)
                         throws MissingResourceException {
   String key = base + "_" + locale.toString();
   ResourceBundle bundle = (ResourceBundle)bundles.get(key);

   if(bundle == null) {
      bundle = ResourceBundle.getBundle(base, locale);
      bundles.put(bundle, key);
   }
   return bundle;
}
public void addBundle(ResourceBundle bundle, String base) {
   Locale locale = bundle.getLocale();
   bundles.put(bundle, base + "_" + locale.toString());
}
}
```

The bundle cache listed in Example 8-7.c maintains a hash table of resource bundles and provides methods to extract objects, strings, and string arrays from those bundles without referencing those bundles directly.

The bundle cache offers two advantages over directly accessing multiple resource bundles. First, accessing multiple bundles is simplified because applications do not have to maintain references to them. Second, accessing bundles is more efficient because they are cached in a hash table.

Formatting Locale-Sensitive Information

Besides localizing text, it's important for internationalized applications to format locale-sensitive objects, such as dates and numbers, according to a user's local customs.

The `java.text` package provides a set of classes and interfaces for iterating over text, searching and sorting strings, and formatting locale-sensitive objects. The full capabilities of the `java.text` package are beyond the scope of this book, but this section introduces date, number, and message formatting.

Dates and Times

Locales format dates and times according to local customs; for example, in the United States, dates are represented by *mm/dd/yy*, with *mm* representing the month, *dd* representing the day, and *yy* the year. On the other hand, in England, dates are formatted as *dd/mm/yy*.

The java.text.DateFormat class provides numerous methods for formatting and parsing dates as expressed in a particular locale. That class also provides the static methods listed below, which return an instance of DateFormat suitable for dates, times, or both.

- static DateFormat getInstance()
- static DateFormat getDateInstance()
- static DateFormat getDateTimeInstance()
- static DateFormat getTimeInstance()

Dates and times can be formatted according to one of four styles: short, medium, long, or full. The first method listed above returns a date/time format for the default locale that uses the short format for both date and time. The other three methods listed above return a format with a default style for the default locale. The DateFormat class also provides two other variations of the last three methods listed above that allow a locale or a style to be specified.

Table 8-2 lists the DateFormat style constants.

Table 8-2 DateFormat Constants

Constant	Description	Example Date and Time for US Locale
SHORT	Numeric	10/19/00 6:07 PM
MEDIUM	Longer than SHORT	Oct 19, 2000 6:05:55 PM
LONG	Longer than MEDIUM	October 19, 2000 6:07:01 PM MDT
FULL	Completely specified	Thursday, October 19, 2000 6:04:33 PM MDT

Figure 8-4 shows a JSP page that formats dates and times for United States English, French, and Japanese.

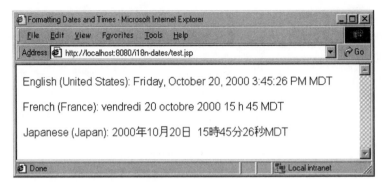

Figure 8-4 Formatting Dates and Times

The JSP page shown in Figure 8-4 is listed in Example 8-8.

Example 8-8 Formatting Dates and Times

```
<html><head><title>Formatting Dates and Times</title>
<%@ page contentType='text/html; charset=UTF-8'%>
<%@ page import='java.text.DateFormat' %>
<%@ page import='java.util.*' %>
</head>
<body>

<% DateFormat frenchFormat = DateFormat.getDateTimeInstance(
                                    DateFormat.FULL,
                                    DateFormat.FULL,
                                    Locale.FRANCE);

   DateFormat englishFormat = DateFormat.getDateTimeInstance(
                                    DateFormat.FULL,
                                    DateFormat.FULL,
                                    Locale.US);

   DateFormat japaneseFormat = DateFormat.getDateTimeInstance(
                                    DateFormat.FULL,
                                    DateFormat.FULL,
                                    Locale.JAPAN); %>

<font size='4'>
   <%= Locale.US.getDisplayName() %>:
   <%= englishFormat.format(new Date()) %><p>
```

```
   <%= Locale.FRANCE.getDisplayName() %>:
   <%= frenchFormat.format(new Date()) %></p><p>

   <%= Locale.JAPAN.getDisplayName() %>:
   <%= japaneseFormat.format(new Date()) %></p>
</font>

</body>
</html>
```

The JSP page listed in Example 8-8 obtains references to date and time formats, specifying the FULL style for both date and time. The format method is invoked for those formats and passed a date. The format method returns a formatted string representing that date and time.

The JSP page shown in Figure 8-4 also illustrates how to display output in multiple languages with the UTF-8 charset. See "Charsets" on page 209 for more information concerning charsets.

Numbers, Currency, and Percents

Like dates and times, numbers, currency, and percents are also formatted according to their locales. The java.text package contains a NumberFormat class, analogous to DateFormat, that provides methods for formatting and parsing numbers. Like the DateFormat class, NumberFormat provides static methods, listed below, that return number formats.

- static NumberFormat getInstance()
- static NumberFormat getCurrencyInstance()
- static NumberFormat getNumberInstance()
- static NumberFormat getPercentInstance()

The getNumberInstance method returns a general-purpose number format for the default locale. Like DateFormat, NumberFormat overloads the last three methods listed above with methods that are passed a specific locale; for example, you would use getNumberInstance() for the default locale, and getNumberInstance(Locale) for a specific locale. Unlike date and time formats, number formats don't have styles.

Example 8-9 shows a JSP page that formats numbers for English and German, currency for English and Japanese, and percents for English and Korean.

Advanced JavaServer Pages

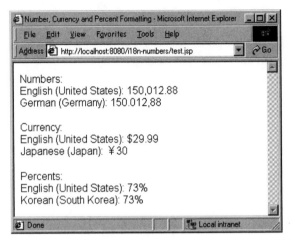

Figure 8-5 Formatting Numbers, Currency, and Percents

The JSP page shown in Figure 8-5 is listed in Example 8-9.

Example 8-9 Formatting Numbers and Currency

```
<html><head><title>Number, Currency and Percent Formatting</title>
<%@ page contentType='text/html; charset=UTF-8' %>
<%@ page import='java.text.*' %>
<%@ page import='java.util.Locale' %>
</head>
<body>
<%
   NumberFormat en_number_fmt =
               NumberFormat.getNumberInstance(Locale.US);
   NumberFormat fr_number_fmt =
               NumberFormat.getNumberInstance(Locale.GERMANY);

   NumberFormat en_currency_fmt =
               NumberFormat.getCurrencyInstance(Locale.US);
   NumberFormat fr_currency_fmt =
               NumberFormat.getCurrencyInstance(Locale.JAPAN);

   NumberFormat en_percent_fmt =
               NumberFormat.getPercentInstance(Locale.US);
   NumberFormat fr_percent_fmt =
               NumberFormat.getPercentInstance(Locale.KOREA);
%>
```

```
<font size='4'>
   Numbers:<br>
   <%= Locale.US.getDisplayName() %>:
   <%= en_number_fmt.format(150012.88) %><br>
   <%= Locale.GERMANY.getDisplayName() %>:
   <%= fr_number_fmt.format(150012.88) %>

   <p>Currency:<br>
   <%= Locale.US.getDisplayName() %>:
   <%= en_currency_fmt.format(29.99) %><br>
   <%= Locale.JAPAN.getDisplayName() %>:
   <%= fr_currency_fmt.format(29.99) %></p>

   <p>Percents:<br>
   <%= Locale.US.getDisplayName() %>:
   <%= en_percent_fmt.format(.73) %><br>
   <%= Locale.KOREA.getDisplayName() %>:
   <%= fr_percent_fmt.format(.73) %></p>
</font>

</body>
</html>
```

The JSP page listed in Example 8-9 obtains references to number formats that format numbers, currency, or percents. The `NumberFormat.format` method formats numbers as numbers, currency, or percents, according to the specified locale.

Messages

When you go to the store, you might say "I'm going to {0}", where {0} represents the store; after all, there are only so many ways to say that you're going to the store. Sometimes you might say "I'm going to {0} to get {1}".

This phenomenon, known as *parameterized text,* is commonplace; in fact, you can find many occurrences of "The JSP page shown in {0} is listed in {1}." scattered throughout this book.

The `java.text.MessageFormat` class lets you parameterize text. You supply a *pattern*—a string that contains {0},{1},...{n}—representing arguments in an array, and an array of argument values, like this:

```
MessageFormat fmt = new MessageFormat("I'm going to {0} for {1}");
Object[] parameters = {"the drugstore", "razors"}; %>
...
```

`MessageFormat` instances are constructed with a pattern. That pattern is formatted with `MessageFormat.format`, which substitutes parameters for occurrences of {n}; for example, for the preceding code fragment, the `formattedString` below is "I'm going to the drugstore for razors".

```
String formattedString = fmt.format(parameters);
```

Parameters are not restricted to strings, either. You can use dates, numbers, and choices for parameters, and you can specify styles for them all; for example, here's a format that uses a date:[9]

```
MessageFormat fmt = new MessageFormat("I went to {0} on {1,date}");
Object[] parameters = {"the drugstore", new java.util.Date()}; %>
String formattedString = fmt.format(parameters);
```

The code fragment above uses a *style* to format the date. You can specify styles analogous to constants defined by `DateFormat` and `NumberFormat`; for example, you could use {n, time} for a date or {n, percent} for a number. See "Formatting Locale-Sensitive Information" on page 224 for more information on `DateFormat` and `NumberFormat`.

Message formats use other formats, such as date and number formats, to format styled parameters; for example, if you specify {n, time}, a message format uses a date format to format that parameter. These helper formats are based on the locale of their message format, which you can set with `MessageFormat.setLocale`. If you set a message format's locale, you must subsequently call `MessageFormat.applyPattern`, which updates formats according to the newly set locale.

Figure 8-6 shows a JSP page that displays a localized message parameterized with a disk number and a date.

---

9.   Choices format ranges of numbers.

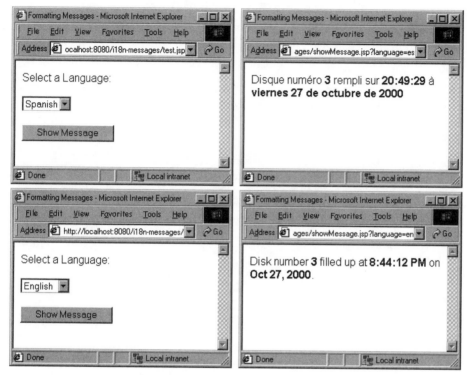

Figure 8-6 Formatting Messages

The application shown in Figure 8-6 consists of two JSP pages, one that selects a language (locale), and another that displays a parameterized message. The JSP page shown on the left is listed in Example 8-10.a.

Example 8-10.a /test.jsp

```
<html><title>Formatting Messages</title>
<head><%@ page import='java.util.Locale' %></head>

<body>

<font size='4' color='blue'>Select a Language:</font>
<p>
<form action='showMessage.jsp'>
   <select name='language'>
      <option value='en'>
         <%= (new Locale("en","")).getDisplayName() %>
      <option value='es'>
         <%= (new Locale("es","")).getDisplayName() %>
   </select>
```

```
   <p><input type='submit' value='Show Message'/></p>
</form>
</p>
</body>
</html>
```

The form for the JSP page listed in Example 8-10.a specifies showMessage.jsp as the form's action. That JSP page is listed in Example 8-10.b.

Example 8-10.b /showMessage.jsp

```
<html><head><title>Formatting Messages</title>
   <%@ page import='java.text.MessageFormat' %>
   <%@ page import='java.util.Locale' %>
   <%@ page import='java.util.ResourceBundle' %>
</head>
<body>

<% // get references to language, locale, and bundle
   String language = request.getParameter("language");
   Locale locale = new java.util.Locale(language, "");
   ResourceBundle bundle = ResourceBundle.getBundle(
                                "message_formats", locale);

   // get message pattern from resource bundle and ...
   String pattern = bundle.getString("message.diskFull");

   // ... create a message format using that string
   MessageFormat fmt = new MessageFormat(pattern);

   // when the pattern is applied, these parameters are inserted
   // into the pattern, replacing {0} {1} ... {n}
   // with parameters[0] parameters[1] ... parameters[n]
   Object[] parameters = {new Long(3), new java.util.Date()}; %>

<font size='4'>
   <% // the date parameter (parameters[1] -- see above) will
      // be formatted according to this locale
      fmt.setLocale(locale);

      // inserts parameters and formats them as necessary
      // with the locale set above
      fmt.applyPattern(pattern); %>

   <%= fmt.format(parameters) %></p>
</font>

</body>
</html>
```

The JSP page listed in Example 8-10.b obtains a format from a resource bundle associated with an English or Spanish locale, and that format is passed to the MessageFormat constructor. The format method subsequently formats parameters and inserts them into the pattern. Those parameters are substituted for occurrences of {0} and {1} that are found in the pattern.

Example 8-10.c and Example 8-10.d list the English and Spanish properties files, respectively.

Example 8-10.c /WEB-INF/classes/app_en.properties

```
message.formatString=Disk number <b>{0}</b> on computer <b>{1}</b>
is full
```

Example 8-10.d /WEB-INF/classes/app_es.properties

```
message.formatString=El número <b>{0}</b> de disco sobre la com-
putadora el <b>{1}</b> es lleno
```

Browser Language Preferences

Starting with version 4.0, both Netscape and Internet Explorer allow users to specify a prioritized list of preferred languages. The next section discusses how to detect those languages, and "Locating Resource Bundles" on page 235 illustrates how to obtain associated resource bundles. Once you have those resource bundles, you can apply the techniques discussed in "Resource Bundles" on page 213 to provide localized content for a user's preferred locale.

Detecting Locales

If users go to the trouble of configuring a browser for their preferred locales, you should respect their wishes as best you can. You can determine those locales with ServletRequest.getLocales and ServletRequest.getLocale. The former returns an enumeration of the user's preferred locales, and the latter returns the most preferred.

Figure 8-7 shows the Language Preference dialog box for Internet Explorer and a JSP page that detects those languages.

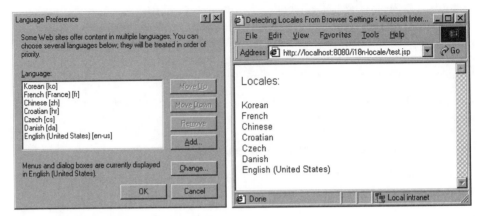

Figure 8-7 Browser Locale Detection

The JSP page shown in Figure 8-7 is listed in Example 8-11.

Example 8-11 Detecting Locales

```
<html><title>Detecting Locales From Browser Settings</title>
<head>
     <%@ page import='java.util.Enumeration' %>
     <%@ page import='java.util.Locale' %>
     <%@ page import='java.util.Vector' %>
</head>
<body>

<font size='4'>Locales:</font>
<p>
<% Enumeration en = request.getLocales();

   while(en.hasMoreElements()) {
      Locale locale = (Locale)en.nextElement(); %>
      <%= locale.getDisplayName() %><br>
<%   } %>
</p>

</body>
</html>
```

The JSP page listed above obtains an enumeration of locales from
`request.getLocales`, and prints each locale's display name.

Locating Resource Bundles

Now that we can discover a user's preferred locales—see "Detecting Locales" on page 233—we can put them to good use by searching for corresponding resource bundles. The search starts with the most preferred locale and ends with the least preferred; the first resource bundle that's found is considered the best match.

Figure 8-8 shows a JSP page that, like Figure 8-7 on page 234, prints the user's preferred locales. In addition, the JSP page shown in Figure 8-8 searches for the best-match resource bundle. Figure 8-8 shows two independent uses of that JSP page. For the left picture, the application had a single resource bundle in English; in the right picture, it was a Czech bundle.

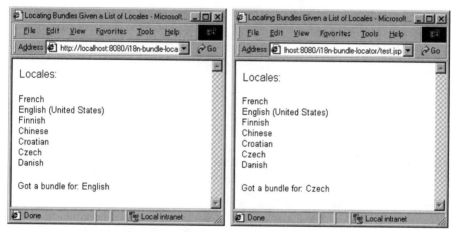

Figure 8-8 Locating Resource Bundles from Browser Locales

The JSP page shown in Figure 8-8 is listed in Example 8-12.a.

Example 8-12.a /test.jsp

```
<html><title>Locating Bundles Given a List of Locales</title>
<head>
<%@ taglib uri='/WEB-INF/tlds/i18n.tld' prefix='i18n' %>
<%@ page import='java.util.*' %>
</head>

<body>

<font size='4'>Locales:</font>
```

```
<p>
<% Enumeration en = request.getLocales();

   while(en.hasMoreElements()) {
       Locale locale = (Locale)en.nextElement(); %>
       <%= locale.getDisplayName() %><br>
<%   } %>
</p>

<jsp:useBean id='locator' scope='request'
         class='beans.i18n.BundleLocator' />

<% ResourceBundle bundle = locator.locateBundle(request, "app");

    if(bundle == null) { %>
    No bundle found
<% } else { %>
    Got a bundle for: <%= bundle.getLocale().getDisplayName() %>
<% } %>

</body>
</html>
```

The JSP page listed in Example 8-12.a gets the user's preferred locales with `HttpServletRequest.getLocales`, which is discussed in "Detecting Locales" on page 233. Those locales are passed to the `BundleLocator` constructor and subsequently used to search for a research bundle.

Example 8-12.b lists the bundle locator.

Example 8-12.b   /WEB-INF/classes/beans/i18n/BundleLocator.java

```
package beans.i18n;

import java.util.Enumeration;
import java.util.Locale;
import java.util.MissingResourceException;
import java.util.ResourceBundle;

import javax.servlet.ServletRequest;
import javax.servlet.jsp.JspException;

public class BundleLocator {
    public ResourceBundle locateBundle(ServletRequest request,
                                       String base)
                                  throws JspException {

        Enumeration en = request.getLocales();
        Locale defaultLocale = Locale.getDefault();
```

```
ResourceBundle fallbackBundle = null;

try {
    fallbackBundle = ResourceBundle.getBundle(base,
                                        defaultLocale);
}
catch(MissingResourceException ex) {
    throw new JspException(ex.getMessage());
}

while(en.hasMoreElements()) {
    Locale locale = (Locale)en.nextElement();
    ResourceBundle bundle = null;

    try {
        bundle = ResourceBundle.getBundle(base, locale);
    }
    catch(MissingResourceException ex2) {
        // ignore missing bundles ...
        continue;
    }
    if(bundle != fallbackBundle)
        return bundle;

    if(fallbackBundle != null && bundle == fallbackBundle) {
        String lang = locale.getLanguage();
        String defaultLanguage = defaultLocale.getLanguage();

        if(lang.equals(defaultLanguage))
            return bundle;
    }
}
return null;
    }
}
```

The bundle locator cycles through locales, looking for a match. If no bundle is found for a particular locale, the search continues with the next locale. If a bundle is found and it's not the fallback bundle, it's a match. If a bundle is the fallback bundle and the corresponding locale is the default locale, then it's also a match. If no bundle matches, BundleLocator.locateBundle returns null.

Custom Tags

The JSP pages throughout this chapter have used a great deal of unsightly Java code to illustrate internationalization. Two custom tags sweep JSP pages clean of internationalization code: a message tag and a format tag.

A Message Tag

This tag retrieves a string from a resource bundle; it's used like this:

```
<%@ taglib uri='/WEB-INF/tlds/i18n.tld prefix='i18n' %>
...
<i18n:message base='Resources' key='messages.welcome'/>
...
<i18n:message base='Resources' key='messages.welcome'
            locale='<%= Locale.UK %>'/>
...
```

The `base` attribute represents the base for a resource bundle; for example, if you have two resource bundles: `Resources_es.properties` and `Resources_fr.properties`, the base would be `Resources`. The `message` tag uses the `key` attribute to look up a message from a resource bundle.

The most interesting aspect of the `message` tag is how it locates resource bundles. If you specify a locale, as in the second tag listed above, the `message` tag tries to find a resource bundle for that locale only. If no locale is specified, as in the first tag listed above, the `message` tag tries to find a resource bundle that's a best match based on the user's preferred languages.

The `message` tag also does message formatting. To use it, specify a `params` attribute that's an array of objects; the string from the resource bundle then becomes a pattern, which is formatted with those objects.

See "Messages" on page 229 for more on message formatting, including an explanation of the best-match algorithm for locating resource bundles.

Figure 8-9 shows a JSP page that exercises all of the `message` tag's features. That JSP page displays multiple languages courtesy of UTF-8[10] and produces different results depending upon browser language preferences. Those preferences are shown on the left, and the corresponding output from the JSP page is shown on the right.

---

10. See "Multilingual JSP Pages" on page 211 for more information on UTF-8.

Figure 8-9 Using the message Tag

The JSP page shown in Figure 8-9 generates its strings like this:

```
...
<%@ taglib uri='/WEB-INF/tlds/i18n.tld' prefix='i18n' %>
<%@ page contentType="text/html; charset=UTF-8" %>
...
<i18n:message base='app' key='messages.welcome'/>
...
<i18n:message base='app' key='messages.introduction'
                  locale='<%= java.util.Locale.KOREAN %>'/>
...
<hr>
<i18n:message base='app' key='messages.today'
        locale='<%= java.util.Locale.ENGLISH %>'
        params='<%= new Object[] { new java.util.Date() } %>'/>
...
<i18n:message key='errors.test' base='errors'/>
```

The two middle tags listed above specify locales, so their language is always fixed: Korean for the second tag and English for the third. The first and last tags don't specify a locale, so their resource bundles are based on browser language preferences.

The third tag performs message formatting, which is evident from the `params` attribute, as discussed above. Instead of displaying a string from a resource bundle, like the `message` tag usually does, this tag formats the string before displaying it.

The last tag listed above uses a different base—`errors`—and therefore a different resource bundle than the other tags.

Here are the resource bundles associated with the JSP page shown in Figure 8-9:

```
WEB-INF/classes/app_en.properties
WEB-INF/classes/app_fr.properties
WEB-INF/classes/app_ko.properties

WEB-INF/classes/errors_fr.properties
WEB-INF/classes/errors_en.properties
```

The best-match resource bundle for the first tag in the top picture in Figure 8-9 is Korean, because it's the first language from the top in the language preferences that has a resource bundle properties file.

The best match for the last tag in the top picture is English, because the `errors` bundle only has French and English properties files, and English is higher on the preferred locale list than French.

In the bottom picture in Figure 8-9, the best match for the both the first and last tags is French.

Example 8-12.c through Example 8-12.g list the resource bundle properties files associated with the JSP page shown in Figure 8-9.

Example 8-12.c /WEB-INF/classes/app_en.properties

```
messages.welcome=Good Morning
messages.introduction=Welcome to the meeting
```

Example 8-12.d /WEB-INF/classes/app_fr.properties

```
messages.welcome=Bonjour
messages.introduction=Bienvenue a meeting
```

Example 8-12.e /WEB-INF/classes/app_ko.properties

```
messages.welcome=\uc548\ub155\ud558\uc138\uc694
messages.introduction=\ud68c\uc758 \ucc38\uc11d \uc744
\ud658\uc601\ud569\ub2c8\ub2e4
```

Example 8-12.f /WEB-INF/classes/errors_en.properties

```
errors.test=A test error message
```

Example 8-12.g /WEB-INF/classes/errors_fr.properties

```
errors.test=Un message d'erreur d'essai
```

The message tag handler is listed in Example 8-12.h.

Example 8-12.h /WEB-INF/classes/tags/i18n/MessageTag.java

```java
package tags.i18n;

import java.text.MessageFormat;

import java.util.Locale;
import java.util.ResourceBundle;

import javax.servlet.jsp.JspException;

import javax.servlet.http.HttpServletRequest;
import javax.servlet.jsp.tagext.TagSupport;

import beans.i18n.BundleLocator;
import beans.i18n.BundleCache;

public class MessageTag extends TagSupport {
   private static BundleCache bundles = new BundleCache();

   private String base, key;
   private Locale locale;
   private Object[] params;

   public void setBase(String base)      { this.base = base; }
   public void setLocale(Locale locale) { this.locale = locale; }
   public void setKey(String key)        { this.key = key; }
   public void setParams(Object[] params) { this.params = params;}

   public int doEndTag() throws JspException {
      MessageFormat fmt = null;
```

```java
        String message = null;

        if(locale != null)
           message = bundles.getString(base, locale, key);

        if(message == null)
           message = getMessageUsingBrowserLocales();

        if(params != null) {
           fmt = new MessageFormat(message);

           if(locale != null) {
              fmt.setLocale(locale);
              fmt.applyPattern(message);
           }
           message = fmt.format(params);
        }
        try {
           pageContext.getOut().write(message);
        }
        catch(Exception ex) { // IO or MissingResource
           throw new JspException(ex.getMessage());
        }
        return EVAL_PAGE;
     }
     private String getMessageUsingBrowserLocales()
                                         throws JspException {
        String message = null;
        BundleLocator locator = new BundleLocator();
        ResourceBundle bundle = locator.locateBundle(
                           pageContext.getRequest(), base);
        if(bundle != null) {
           bundles.addBundle(bundle, base);
           message = bundle.getString(key);
        }
        return message;
     }

     // prepare this tag handler for reuse

     public void release() {
        base = key = null;
        locale = null;
        params = null;
     }
  }
```

The message tag has four attributes: base, key, locale, and params. The first two parameters are required, and the last two are optional. The message tag does three things:

1. Locates a resource bundle and a string inside that bundle

2. Optionally formats the string from step #1

3. Prints the string to the out implicit variable

If the locale attribute is specified, a bundle cache tries to locate a bundle associated with the specified locale; if the bundle is found, the string associated with the key is returned. If the bundle is not found or it doesn't contain the key, the cache returns null. See "A Bundle Cache" on page 222 for more information about bundle caches.

If the bundle cache can't find the string, getMessageUsingBrowserLocales is called. That method uses a bundle locator to search for a resource bundle according to browser language preferences. See "Browser Language Preferences" on page 233 for more information about that utility bean.

If the params attribute has been specified, the message tag creates a message format, which formats the string obtained from the resource bundle.

Finally, the tag prints the string to the implicit out variable, which points to the tag's body content.[11]

A Format Tag

The format tag discussed in this section can format numbers, currencies, percents, dates, and times. This tag nicely complements the message tag discussed in "A Message Tag" on page 238. Together, those two tags provide basic functionality for internationalizing dynamic content.

Figure 8-10 shows two JSP pages that use the format tag.

---

11. See "Body Content" on page 46 for more information about tags and body content.

Figure 8-10 Formatting Tags for Dates and Numbers

The JSP page shown on the left in Figure 8-10 uses the `format` tag like this:

```
<i18n:format currency='134588.99'/>
...
<i18n:format currency='134588.99' locale='<%= Locale.UK %>'/>
...
<i18n:format number='134588.99'/>
...
<i18n:format number='134588.99' locale='<%= Locale.UK %>'/>
...
<i18n:format percent='.99'/>
...
<i18n:format percent='.88' locale='<%= Locale.KOREAN %>'/>
```

The JSP page shown on the right in Figure 8-10 uses the `format` tag like this:

```
<i18n:format time='<%= new java.util.Date() %>'/>
...
<i18n:format time='<%= new java.util.Date() %>'
         locale='<%= java.util.Locale.FRENCH %>'/>
...
<i18n:format time='<%= new java.util.Date() %>'
         locale='<%= java.util.Locale.CHINESE %>'
       dateStyle='<%= java.text.DateFormat.FULL %>'/>
```

```
<i18n:format date='<%= new java.util.Date() %>'/>
...
<i18n:format date='<%= new java.util.Date() %/>
        dateStyle='<%= java.text.DateFormat.SHORT %>'/>
...
<i18n:format date='<%= new java.util.Date() %>'
          locale='<%= java.util.Locale.CHINESE %>'
        dateStyle='<%= java.text.DateFormat.FULL %>'/>


...
<i18n:format dateTime='<%= new java.util.Date() %>'/>
...
<i18n:format dateTime='<%= new java.util.Date() %>'
              locale='<%= java.util.Locale.JAPANESE %>'/>
...
<i18n:format dateTime='<%= new java.util.Date() %>'
              locale='<%= java.util.Locale.JAPANESE %>'
           timeStyle='<%= java.text.DateFormat.FULL %>'
           dateStyle='<%= java.text.DateFormat.FULL %>'/>
```

The format tag is quite handy. The tag handler for the format tag is listed in
Example 8-13. That tag handler is rather lengthy, mainly because the format tag
has nine attributes, but it's a simple class.

Example 8-13 /WEB-INF/classes/tags/i18n/FormatTag

```
package tags.i18n;

import java.text.*;
import java.util.Date;
import java.util.Locale;
import javax.servlet.jsp.JspException;
import javax.servlet.jsp.tagext.*;

public class FormatTag extends TagSupport {
   private static DateFormat dateFormat;
   private static NumberFormat numberFormat;
   private static final int UNASSIGNED=-1,
                            TIME=0, DATE=1, DATE_TIME=2,
                            NUMBER=3, CURRENCY=4, PERCENT=5;
   private Date date;
   private double number = (double)UNASSIGNED;

   private Locale locale = null;
```

```java
private int dateStyle = UNASSIGNED,
            timeStyle = UNASSIGNED,
          formatStyle = UNASSIGNED,
          numberStyle = UNASSIGNED;

// doEndTag()

public int doEndTag() throws JspException {
   if(date != null) { // date attribute was set
      if(formatStyle == TIME)           processTime();
      else if(formatStyle == DATE)      processDate();
      else if(formatStyle == DATE_TIME) processDateTime();

      showFormatted(dateFormat.format(date));
   }
   if(number != UNASSIGNED) { // number attribute was set
      if(numberStyle == NUMBER)         processNumber();
      else if(numberStyle == CURRENCY)  processCurrency();
      else if(numberStyle == PERCENT)   processPercent();

      showFormatted(numberFormat.format(number));
   }
   return EVAL_PAGE;
}
private void showFormatted(String string) throws JspException {
   try {
      pageContext.getOut().write(string);
   }
   catch(Exception ex) {
      throw new JspException(ex.getMessage());
   }
}

// Attribute Setter Methods:

public void setLocale(Locale locale){ this.locale = locale; }
public void setDateStyle(int style) { this.dateStyle = style; }
public void setTimeStyle(int style) { this.timeStyle = style; }

public void setNumber(Double number){
   this.number = number.doubleValue(); numberStyle = NUMBER;
}
public void setCurrency(Double number) {
   setNumber(number); numberStyle = CURRENCY;
}
public void setPercent(Double number) {
   setNumber(number); numberStyle = PERCENT;
}
```

```java
public void setDate(Date date) {
   this.date = date; formatStyle = DATE;
}
public void setDateTime(Date date) {
   this.date = date; formatStyle = DATE_TIME;
}
public void setTime(Date date) {
   this.date = date; formatStyle = TIME;
}

// Processing Methods

private void processNumber() {
   numberFormat = (locale == null) ?
               NumberFormat.getNumberInstance() :
               NumberFormat.getNumberInstance(locale);
}
private void processCurrency() {
   numberFormat = (locale == null) ?
               NumberFormat.getCurrencyInstance() :
               NumberFormat.getCurrencyInstance(locale);
}
private void processPercent() {
   numberFormat = (locale == null) ?
               NumberFormat.getPercentInstance() :
               NumberFormat.getPercentInstance(locale);
}
private void processTime() {
   if(timeStyle == UNASSIGNED) {
      dateFormat = DateFormat.getTimeInstance();
   }
   else {
      dateFormat = (locale == null) ?
               DateFormat.getTimeInstance(timeStyle) :
               DateFormat.getTimeInstance(timeStyle,locale);
   }
}
private void processDate() {
   if(dateStyle == UNASSIGNED) {
      dateFormat = DateFormat.getDateInstance();
   }
   else {
      dateFormat = (locale == null) ?
               DateFormat.getDateInstance(dateStyle) :
               DateFormat.getDateInstance(dateStyle,locale);
   }
}
private void processDateTime() throws JspException {
```

```
      if(timeStyle == UNASSIGNED && dateStyle == UNASSIGNED) {
         dateFormat = DateFormat.getDateTimeInstance();
      }
      else {
         if(timeStyle == UNASSIGNED || dateStyle == UNASSIGNED) {
            throw new JspException("You must assign both" +
                                   "timeStyle and dateStyle, or" +
                                   "neither");
         }
         dateFormat = (locale == null) ?
                      DateFormat.getDateTimeInstance(
                                     timeStyle, dateStyle) :
                      DateFormat.getDateTimeInstance(
                                     timeStyle, dateStyle, locale);
      }
   }

   // Prepare this tag handler for reuse

   public void release() {
      numberFormat = null;
      dateFormat = null;

      date = null;
      number = (double)UNASSIGNED;
      locale = null;

      dateStyle = timeStyle =
      formatStyle = numberStyle = UNASSIGNED;
   }
}
```

`FormTag.doEndTag` is where the action begins. That method, depending upon the `date` and `number` attributes, calls an appropriate method that creates either a date or number format. Those formats are subsequently used to format a date or number, respectively.

Conclusion

As you can tell from the length of this chapter, the Java programming language strongly supports internationalization. That support, coupled with JSP's capacity for defining custom tags, allows web page authors to easily create internationalized web sites.

The advent of the World Wide Web has drawn increased attention to internationalization, as it has for security. Many companies that are moving legacy systems to the Web find that retrofitting internationalization to web applications is a tedious task. It's much easier to design for internationalization from the outset. This chapter illustrates that process.

SECURITY

Topics in this Chapter

- Servlet Authentication
  - Principals and Roles
  - Declarative Authentication
  - Portability
  - Types of Authentication
- Basic Authentication
- Digest Authentication
- Form-Based Authentication
- SSL and Client Certificate Authentication
- Web Application Security Elements
- Customizing Authentication
  - Resin
  - Tomcat 4.0
- Programmatic Authentication

Chapter

Computer security used to be the domain of hackers and their antagonists, but with the advent of the World Wide Web, it's become an issue for the rank and file setting up shop on the net. Because of this growing awareness, software developers today are far more likely to deal with security than were their counterparts of the late 20th century.

Many books have been written about the wide ranging topic of computer security, including Java security, and this chapter is a substitute for none of them. This discussion is restricted to protecting web application resources with the authentication mechanisms described in the servlet specification.[1]

Servlet Authentication

Servlet authentication looks simple:

1. A user tries to access a protected resource, such as a JSP page.

2. If the user has been authenticated, the servlet container makes the resource available; otherwise, the user is asked for a username and password.

3. If the name and password cannot be authenticated, an error is displayed and the user is given the opportunity to enter a new username and password.

---

1. This chapter is based upon the 2.2 Servlet specification; for specification links, see http://java.sun.com/products/servlet/download.html.

The steps outlined above are simple, but vague. It's not apparent who asks for a username and password, who does the authentication, how it's performed, or even how the user is asked for a username and password. Those steps are unspecified because the servlet specification leaves them up to applications and servlet containers. This vagueness in the servlet specification has an effect on portability; see "Portability" on page 254 for more information.

Principals and Roles

In security-speak, the user in the steps listed on page 251 is a *principal*. Principals are named entities that can represent anything; most often, they represent individuals or corporations.

Principals can fill one or more roles; for example, a customer could also be an employee. Security constraints in `WEB-INF/web.xml` associate *roles* with protected *resources*, like this:

```
<web-app>
...
  <security-constraint>
     <!-- web resources that are protected -->
     <web-resource-collection>
        <web-resource-name>Protected Resource</web-resource-name>
        <url-pattern>/page_1.jsp</url-pattern>
     </web-resource-collection>

     <auth-constraint>
        <!-- role-name indicates roles that are allowed
             to access the web resources specified above -->
        <role-name>customer</role-name>
     </auth-constraint>
  </security-constraint>
...
  <security-constraint>
     <!-- web resources that are protected -->
     <web-resource-collection>
        <web-resource-name>Protected Resource2</web-resource-name>
        <url-pattern>/page_2.jsp</url-pattern>
     </web-resource-collection>

     <auth-constraint>
        <!-- role-name indicates roles that are allowed
             to access the web resources specified above -->
        <role-name>employee</role-name>
     </auth-constraint>
  </security-constraint>
<web-app>
```

Two security constraints are specified above that restrict access to `/page_1.jsp` and `/page_2.jsp` to principals that are in roles `customer` or `employee`, respectively.

Security constraints, like those listed above, associate resources with roles. It's up to servlet containers or applications to associate roles with principals; for example, with Tomcat, you edit a `tomcat-users.xml` file that has entries like this:

```
<tomcat-users>
   ...
   <user name="rwhite" password="tomcat" roles="customer", "other"/>
   ...
</tomcat-users>
```

Here, `rwhite` has a password of `tomcat` and can fill roles `customer` or `other`; thus, `rwhite` can access `/page_1.jsp`, but not `/page_2.jsp` according to the security constraints listed above.

Other servlet containers provide different mechanisms for associating principals with roles; for example, "Resin" on page 264 illustrates how it's done with Resin for basic authentication.

Table 9-1 lists `HttpServletRequest` methods that allow you to retrieve information about principals and roles.

Table 9-1 `HttpServletRequest` Methods for Principals and Roles

Method	Description
`Principal getUserPrincipal()`	Returns a reference to a `java.security.Principal`
`boolean isUserInRole(String)`	Determines whether a user is in a role, specified by the string argument
`String getRemoteUser()`	Returns the username that was used for login

The servlet API does not provide corresponding setter methods for the getter methods listed in Table 9-1; therefore, principals and roles can only be set by servlet containers, meaning that applications cannot set them. This can be a consideration if you implement programmatic authentication—see "Programmatic Authentication" on page 271 for more information.

Table 9-2 lists other `ServletRequest` methods that provide security information.

Table 9-2   Other `ServletRequest` Security Methods[1]

Method	Description
`String getAuthType()`	Returns the authentication type: `BASIC`, `SSL`, or `null`
`boolean isSecure()`	Returns `true` if the connection is `HTTPS`
`String getScheme()`	Scheme represents transport mechanism: `http`, `https`...

1. `getAuthType()` is from `HttpServletRequest`.

Like the methods listed in Table 9-1 on page 253, the servlet API does not provide corresponding setter methods for those methods listed in Table 9-2. This means that the authentication type and transport scheme can only be set by servlet containers.

Declarative Authentication

Declarative authentication requires no programming because authentication is *declared* with XML tags in a deployment descriptor and implemented by the servlet container. Declarative authentication is attractive because it's easy, but it's not as flexible as other approaches that require you to write code.

At one end of the spectrum is declarative authentication, with 100% servlet container implemented and 0% application code; at the other end is programmatic authentication, with 0% servlet container and 100% application code.

Most servlet containers provide access to the middle of that spectrum by providing hooks so that you can replace their default authentication mechanism.

"Basic Authentication" on page 256 provides an example of declarative authentication, "Customizing Authentication" on page 263 illustrates customizing authentication, and programmatic authentication is discussed in "Programmatic Authentication" on page 271.

Portability

The servlet specification leaves enough security details unspecified that servlet containers must fill in the gaps with nonportable functionality. For example, the servlet specification does not specify a default authentication mechanism, so servlet containers implement their own; for example, Tomcat uses an XML file to specify usernames and passwords, whereas Resin requires you to implement an authenticator.

Because of nonportable security aspects of servlet containers and depending upon your choice for authentication, you may need to write some nonportable code, such as a Resin authenticator or a Tomcat realm, both of which are discussed in "Customizing Authentication" on page 263.

On the other hand, you can use declarative authentication to minimize any code you have to write.

Types of Authentication

A servlet-based web application can choose from the following types of authentication, from least secure to most:

- Basic authentication
- Form-based authentication
- Digest authentication
- SSL and client certificate authentication

All of the authentication mechanisms listed above are discussed in this chapter. Basic and digest authentication are discussed in much detail in RFC2617, which can be found at `ftp://ftp.isi.edu/in-notes/rfc2617.txt`.

You select one of the authentication mechanisms listed above in `/WEBINF/web.xml`, like this:

```
<web-app>
...
   <login-config>
      <auth-method>BASIC</auth-method>
      <realm-name>Basic Authentication Example</realm-name>
   </login-config>
...
</web-app>
```

Although basic and form-based authentication are not secure, you can use them in combination with SSL for secure transport.

You can find out the authentication method for a request with `HttpServletRequest.getAuthType`—see Table 9-2 on page 254.

Basic Authentication

Basic authentication is defined by the HTTP/1.1 specification. When a client attempts to access a protected resource, the server prompts for a username and password. If the server can authenticate that username and password, access is granted to the resource; otherwise, the process repeats. The server retries a server-specific number of times, three being typical.

The most notable aspect of basic authentication is its total lack of security. Passwords are transmitted with base64 encoding, which provides no encryption, thus making the passwords vulnerable.

Figure 9-1 illustrates basic authentication with Tomcat 4.0.

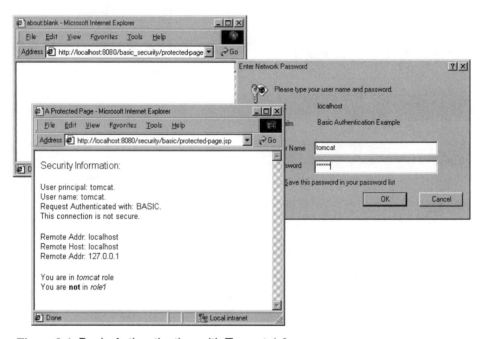

Figure 9-1 Basic Authentication with Tomcat 4.0

From top to bottom in Figure 9-1: An attempt is made to access a protected JSP page—/`protected-page.jsp`—and the user is presented with a dialog. After the dialog is filled out and the username and password are authenticated, the JSP page is displayed. That JSP page is listed in Example 9-1.a.

Example 9-1.a /protected-page.jsp

```
<html><head><title>A Protected Page</title></head>
<body>

<%@ include file='show-security.jsp' %></p>
<p>
<% if(request.isUserInRole("tomcat")) { %>
    You are in <i>tomcat</i> role<br/>
<% } else {%>
    You are <b>not</b> in <i>tomcat</i><br/>
<% } %>

<% if(request.isUserInRole("role1")) { %>
    You are in <i>role1</i><br/>
<% } else {%>
    You are <b>not</b> in <i>role1</i><br/>
<% } %>
</p>

</body>
</html>
```

The JSP page listed in Example 9-1.a prints security information and the principal's role—tomcat or role1. Security information is printed by a JSP page that's listed in Example 9-1.b.

Example 9-1.b /show-security.jsp

```
<font size='4' color='blue'>
    Security Information:
</font><br>
<p>
User principal: <%= request.getUserPrincipal().getName() %>.<br/>
User name: <%= request.getRemoteUser() %>.<br/>
Request Authenticated with: <%= request.getAuthType() %>.<br/>

<% if(request.isSecure()) { %>
    This connection is secure.<br/>
<% } else { %>
    This connection is not secure.<br/>
<% } %>
</p>
Remote Addr: <%= request.getServerName() %><br/>
Remote Host: <%= request.getRemoteHost() %><br/>
Remote Addr: <%= request.getRemoteAddr() %>
```

The JSP page listed in Example 9-1.b can be handy for debugging authentication.

The protected JSP page listed in Example 9-1.b is specified as a protected resource in the application's deployment descriptor, which is listed in Example 9-1.c.

Example 9-1.c   /WEB-INF/web.xml

```
<?xml version="1.0" encoding="ISO-8859-1"?>

<!DOCTYPE web-app
   PUBLIC "-//Sun Microsystems, Inc.//DTD Web Application 2.2//EN"
   "http://java.sun.com/j2ee/dtds/web-app_2.2.dtd">

<web-app>
   <security-constraint>
      <!-- web resources that are protected -->
      <web-resource-collection>
         <web-resource-name>A Protected Page</web-resource-name>
         <url-pattern>/protected-page.jsp</url-pattern>
      </web-resource-collection>

      <auth-constraint>
         <!-- role-name indicates roles that are allowed
              to access the web resource specified above -->
         <role-name>tomcat</role-name>
         <role-name>role1</role-name>
      </auth-constraint>
   </security-constraint>

   <login-config>
      <auth-method>BASIC</auth-method>
      <realm-name>Basic Authentication Example</realm-name>
   </login-config>
</web-app>
```

The deployment descriptor listed above restricts access to /protectedpage.jsp to principals in either tomcat or role1 roles, and BASIC is specified as the authentication method.

With Tomcat, usernames and passwords are associated with roles in $TOMCAT_HOME/conf/tomcat-users.xml, which is listed in Example 9-1.d.

Example 9-1.d $TOMCAT_HOME/conf/tomcat-users.xml

```
<tomcat-users>
   <user name="tomcat" password="tomcat" roles="tomcat" />
   <user name="role1"  password="tomcat" roles="role1"  />
   <user name="both"   password="tomcat" roles="tomcat,role1" />
</tomcat-users>
```

The configuration file listed in Example 9-1.d binds the username `tomcat` and password `tomcat`, which were used in the application shown in Figure 9-1 on page 256, to the `tomcat` role. That's why the application shows that the principal is in `tomcat` role, but not in `role1`.

The entry for username `both` in Example 9-1.d illustrates how you can associate a single principal with multiple roles using Tomcat. In Figure 9-1 on page 256, if we had logged in as `both`, we would be in both `tomcat` and `role1` roles.

Digest Authentication

Digest authentication is just like basic authentication, except digest authentication uses encryption to protect passwords. In fact, digest authentication transmits a password's hash value, not the password itself.[2]

Figure 9-2 illustrates digest authentication with Tomcat. Notice the differences between the dialog in Figure 9-2, which declares this web site to be secure, and the dialog in Figure 9-1 on page 256, which does not.

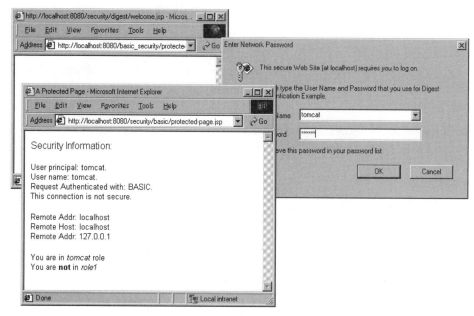

Figure 9-2 Digest Authentication with Tomcat

---

2. Digest authentication is also specified by the HTTP/1.1 specification; see
`ftp://ftp.isi.edu/in-notes/rfc2617.txt`.

Digest authentication is specified in an application's deployment descriptor, like this:

```
<login-config>
      <auth-method>DIGEST</auth-method>
      <realm-name>Digest Authentication Example</realm-name>
   </login-config>
</web-app>
```

The only difference between basic and digest authentication is the specification of the authentication method, as listed above.

Note: The digest authentication example discussed in this section works with Tomcat 4.0, but not with Tomcat 3.2.1.

Form-Based Authentication

Form-based authentication allows you to control the look and feel of the login page. Form-based authentication works like basic authentication, except that you specify a login page that is displayed instead of a dialog and an error page that's displayed if login fails.

Like basic authentication, form-based authentication is not secure because passwords are transmitted as clear text. Unlike basic and digest authentication, form-based authentication is defined in the servlet specification, not the HTTP specification.

Form-based login allows customization of the login page, but not the authentication process itself. If you're interested in customizing the authentication of usernames and passwords, see "Customizing Authentication" on page 263.

Form-based authentication requires the following steps:

1.   Implement a login page.

2.   Implement an error page that will be displayed if login fails.

3.   In the deployment descriptor, specify form-based authentication and the login and error pages from step #2.

Figure 9-3 shows an application that illustrates form-based authentication.

The top pictures in Figure 9-3 show a failed login, and the bottom pictures show subsequent success. Notice that the login form is displayed in the browser, not in a dialog, as is the case for basic and digest authentication.

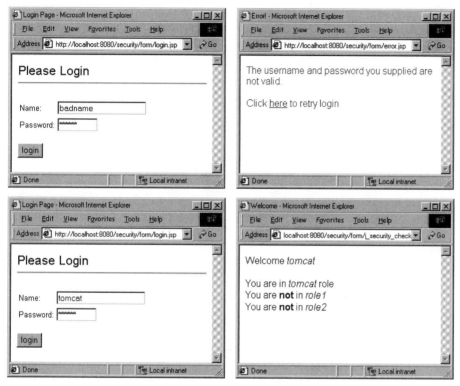

Figure 9-3 Form-Based Authentication with Tomcat

The login form used in Figure 9-3 is listed in Example 9-2.a.

Example 9-2.a /login.jsp

```
<html><head><title>Login Page</title></head>
<body>
<font size='5' color='blue'>Please Login</font><hr>

<form action='j_security_check' method='post'>
<table>
  <tr><td>Name:</td>
      <td><input type='text' name='j_username'></td></tr>
  <tr><td>Password:</td>
      <td><input type='password' name='j_password' size='8'></td>
  </tr>
</table>
<br>
    <input type='submit' value='login'>
</form></body>
</html>
```

The login page listed in Example 9-2.a is unremarkable except for the names of the name and password fields and the form's action. Those names, j_username, j_password, and j_security_check, respectively—which are defined in the Servlet Specification—must be used for form-based login. Table 9-3 summarizes those names.

Table 9-3 Login Form Attributes for Form-Based Login

Attribute	Description
j_username	The name of the username field
j_password	The name of the password field
j_security_check	The login form's action

The error page for the application shown in Figure 9-3 is listed in Example 9-2.b.

Example 9-2.b /error.jsp

```
<html> <head> <title>Error!</title></head>
<body>

<font size='4' color='red'>
   The username and password you supplied are not valid.
</p>
Click <a href='<%= response.encodeURL("login.jsp") %>'>here</a>
to retry login

</body>
</form>
</html>
```

The error page displays an error message and provides a link back to the login page. The deployment descriptor for the application shown in Figure 9-3 is listed in Example 9-2.c.

Example 9-2.c /WEB-INF/web.xml

```
<?xml version="1.0" encoding="ISO-8859-1"?>

<!DOCTYPE web-app
   PUBLIC "-//Sun Microsystems, Inc.//DTD Web Application 2.2//EN"
   "http://java.sun.com/j2ee/dtds/web-app_2.2.dtd">

<web-app>
   <security-constraint>
      <web-resource-collection>
```

```
            <web-resource-name>A Protected Page</web-resource-name>
            <url-pattern>/protected-page.jsp</url-pattern>
        </web-resource-collection>

        <auth-constraint>
            <role-name>tomcat</role-name>
        </auth-constraint>
    </security-constraint>

    <login-config>
        <auth-method>FORM</auth-method>
        <form-login-config>
            <form-login-page>/login.jsp</form-login-page>
            <form-error-page>/error.jsp</form-error-page>
        </form-login-config>
    </login-config>
</web-app>
```

The deployment descriptor listed in Example 9-2.c specifies a security constraint that restricts access to /protected-page.jsp to principals in the role of tomcat. The authentication method is specified as FORM, and the login and error pages are identified.

SSL and Client Certificate Authentication

Secure sockets layer (SSL) is a secure transport mechanism that ensures privacy and data integrity through encryption. Additionally, SSL allows verification of client and server identity. For more information on SSL, see http://home.netscape.com/eng/ssl3/3-SPEC.HTM.

SSL is designed so that it can be layered on top of existing servers. The details of adding SSL to a web server are server dependent; see your server documentation for details. Resin's technical FAQ provides detailed instructions for layering SSL on stand-alone Resin; it can be found at http://www.caucho.com/products/resin/ref/faq.xtp.

Client certificate authentication is implemented with SSL and requires the client to possess a public key certificate. Although Tomcat 4.0 plans to support client certificate authentication, at the time of this writing it did not.

Customizing Authentication

There are two aspects to authentication: *challenging* principals for usernames and passwords and *authenticating* usernames and passwords. The servlet specification requires servlet containers to allow customization of the former with form-based authentication, as discussed in "Form-Based Authentication" on page 260. The servlet specification does not require servlet containers to allow customization of the latter, but most servlet containers let you do so.

Because the servlet specification does not provide a standard mechanism for customizing authentication of usernames and passwords, that kind of customization is inherently nonportable. This section describes how to customize authentication with Resin and Tomcat and should give you a good idea of what to look for if you are using a different servlet container.

Resin

Resin authenticates usernames and passwords with authenticators, which are classes that implement the Resin `Authenticator` interface.

The default Resin authenticator will authenticate any combination of username and password—a useful feature if you are using Resin in combination with Apache or IIS, because you can rely on the web server's authentication. If you are using Resin in stand-alone mode, then you need to implement an authenticator for basic authentication.

Figure 9-4 shows a basic authentication example with Resin.

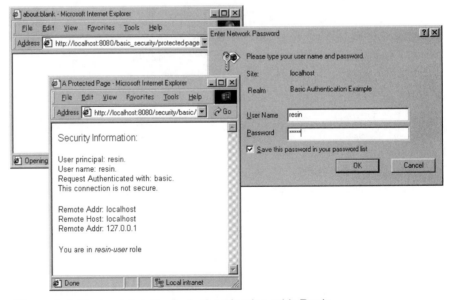

Figure 9-4 Customizing Basic Authentication with Resin

The protected page shown in Figure 9-4 is listed in Example 9-3.a.

Example 9-3.a /protected-page.jsp

```
<html><head><title>A Protected Page</title></head>
<body>

<%@ include file='show-security.jsp' %></p>
<p>
<% if(request.isUserInRole("resin-user")) { %>
   You are in <i>resin-user</i> role<br/>
<% } else {%>
   You are <b>not</b> in <i>resin-user</i> role<br/>
<% } %>
</p>
</body>
</html>
```

The JSP page listed in Example 9-3.a relies on the `show-security` JSP page to print security information; see "Basic Authentication" on page 256 for more information about that page. The JSP page listed in Example 9-3.a also verifies the user's role.

Example 9-3.b lists the deployment descriptor for the application shown in Figure 9-4.

Example 9-3.b /WEB-INF/web.xml

```
<?xml version="1.0" encoding="ISO-8859-1"?>

<!DOCTYPE web-app
   PUBLIC "-//Sun Microsystems, Inc.//DTD Web Application 2.2//EN"
   "http://java.sun.com/j2ee/dtds/web-app_2.2.dtd">

<web-app>
   <security-constraint>
      <!-- web resources that are protected -->
      <web-resource-collection>
         <web-resource-name>A Protected Page</web-resource-name>
         <url-pattern>/protected-page.jsp</url-pattern>
      </web-resource-collection>

      <auth-constraint>
         <role-name>resin-user</role-name>
      </auth-constraint>
   </security-constraint>
```

```
<login-config>
    <auth-method>BASIC</auth-method>
    <realm-name>Basic Authentication Example</realm-name>
        <!-- The authenticator tag is Resin-specific -->
        <authenticator id='beans.SimpleAuthenticator' />
</login-config>
</web-app>
```

The deployment descriptor listed in Example 9-3.b restricts access to
/protected-page.jsp to principals in the role of resin-user and specifies
BASIC as the authentication method. That deployment descriptor also contains a
Resin-specific authenticator tag that specifies the authenticator to use for this
authentication. That authenticator is listed in Example 9-3.c.

Example 9-3.c   /WEB-INF/classes/beans/SimpleAuthenticator.java

```
package beans;

import com.caucho.server.http.AbstractAuthenticator;
import com.caucho.server.http.BasicPrincipal;
import java.security.Principal;

public class SimpleAuthenticator extends AbstractAuthenticator {
    public Principal authenticate(String user, String password) {
        boolean valid = password != null &&
                        password.equals("resin") &&
                        user != null && user.equals("resin");

        if(valid) return new BasicPrincipal(user);
        else        return null;
    }
    public boolean isUserInRole(Principal user, String role) {
        return user.getName().equals("resin") &&
                role.equals("resin-user");
    }
}
```

The authenticator listed in Example 9-3.c extends the Resin
AbstractAuthenticator class and overrides the authenticate and
isUserInRole methods, both of which are defined in the Authenticator
interface and given default implementations in AbstractAuthenticator.

The authenticate method returns an instance of BasicPrincipal, which is a
Resin-specific class from com.caucho.server.http, if the username and
password are authentic; otherwise, the method returns null.

Tomcat 4.0

Tomcat 4.0 uses realms, which are similar in principle to Resin's authenticators, to authenticate usernames and passwords. Unlike Resin, Tomcat does not require special tags in /WEB-INF/web.xml; instead, Tomcat specifies a realm in $TOMCAT_HOME/conf/server.xml, like this:

```
...
<!-- From $TOMCAT_HOME/conf/server.xml -->
<!-- Example Server Configuration File -->
<!-- Note that component elements are nested corresponding to their
     parent-child relationships with each other -->

<Server port="8005" shutdown="SHUTDOWN" debug="0">
...
    <!-- Because this Realm is here, an instance will be
         shared globally
    <Realm className="org.apache.catalina.realm.MemoryRealm" />
      -->
    <Realm className="CustomRealm"/>
...
</Server>
```

Just inside the Server start tag, Tomcat specifies a default realm—org.apache.catalina.realm.MemoryRealm—which is shared by all contexts.[3] To replace the default realm, comment out the default and insert your own, as listed above.

Tomcat custom realms typically extend the Tomcat RealmBase abstract class, which implements the Realm interface. RealmBase defines three abstract methods that extensions must implement. Those methods are listed in Table 9-4.

Table 9-4 Tomcat 4.0 RealmBase **Abstract Methods**

Method	Intent
boolean hasRole(Principal principal, String role)	Returns true if a role is suitable for a principal
String getPassword(String user)	Returns a password associated with a user
Principal getPrincipal(String user)	Returns a principal associated with a user

---

3.   Tomcat realms can also be specified for individual web applications.

The CustomRealm class referred to in the server.xml file listed above is listed in Example 9-4.

Example 9-4 A Tomcat Custom Realm

```java
import java.security.Principal;
import org.apache.catalina.realm.RealmBase;

public class CustomRealm extends RealmBase {
   public boolean hasRole(Principal principal, String role) {
      String name = principal.getName();

      if(name.equals("tomcat"))
         return role.equals("tomcat");

      if(name.equals("role1"))
         return role.equals("role1");

      if(name.equals("both"))
         return role.equals("tomcat") || role.equals("role1");

      return false;
   }
   protected String getPassword(String username) {
      return "tomcat";
   }
   protected Principal getPrincipal(String username) {
      return new CustomPrincipal(username);
   }
   class CustomPrincipal implements Principal {
      private final String name;

      public CustomPrincipal(String name) {
         this.name = name;
      }
      public String getName() {
         return name;
      }
      public String toString() {
         return getName();
      }
   }
}
```

The custom realm listed in Example 9-4 is designed to work with the default entries from $TOMCAT_HOME/conf/tomcat-users.xml, which is listed in Example 9-1.d on page 258. For example, hasRole returns true if the principal and role correspond to those specified in `tomcat-users.xml`. The `getPassword` method returns `tomcat`, which is the password used for all of the users defined in `tomcat-users.xml`. The `getPrincipal` method returns a custom principal, which is a simple implementation of the `java.security.Principal` interface.

Custom realms must be made available to Tomcat at startup, which requires that custom realm classes reside in a JAR file in `$TOMCAT_HOME/server`. So, for the example listed above to work, `CustomRealm.java` is compiled, yielding two class files. Those class files are placed in a JAR file and copied to `$TOMCAT_HOME/server`.

Note: The code in this section is based on a beta version of Tomcat 4.0, so that code may need to be modified by the time you read this.

Web Application Security Elements

This section provides a reference to security elements from the Servlet 2.2 specification. A number of the examples in this chapter have illustrated the use of most of these elements; for example, see Example 9-1.c on page 258.

Table 9-5 lists the elements contained within a `security-constraint` element, which is the outermost security element in a deployment descriptor.

Table 9-5 `<security-constraint>` Elements

Element	Type[1]	Description
web-resource-collection	+	A subset of a web application's resources to which security constraints apply
auth-constraint	?	Authorization constraints placed on one or more web resource collections
user-data-constraint	?	A specification of how data sent between a client and a container should be protected

1. + = one or more? = one, optional

Web resource collections identify one or more protected resources, and authorization constraints specify one or more roles that can access those resources. User data constraints specify how data should be protected while in transit.

Table 9-6 lists web resource collection elements.

Table 9-6 `<web-resource-collection>` Elements

Element	Type[1]	Description
web-resource-name	1	The name of a web resource
description	?	A description of a web resource
url-pattern	*	A url pattern associated with a web resource
http-method	?	An HTTP method associated with a web resource

1. 1 = one, required? = zero or more* = one or more

Each web resource collection is associated with the name of a resource and an optional description of that resource. One or more URL patterns are associated with a resource name.

HTTP methods may also be associated with a web resource collection; for example, if GET is specified as the HTTP method, the security constraint is only enforced for GET requests. If no HTTP methods are specified, the corresponding security constraint applies to all HTTP requests for the specified resources.

Table 9-7 lists authorization constraint elements.

Table 9-7 `<auth-constraint>` Elements

Element	Type[1]	Description
description	?	A description of an authorization constraint
role-name	*	The role(s) to which a constraint applies

1. ? = zero or more* = one or more

Authorization constraints specify one or more roles that are allowed access to protected resources. Optionally, those roles can be accompanied by a description.

Table 9-8 lists user data constraint elements.

Table 9-8 `<user-data-constraint>` Elements

Element	Type[1]	Description
description	?	A description of a user data constraint
transport-guarantee	1	NONE, INTEGRAL, or CONFIDENTIAL

1. ? = zero or more 1 = one, required

User data constraints consist of a `transport-guarantee` and an optional description. That guarantee can be either NONE, INTEGRAL, or CONFIDENTIAL. A guarantee of NONE means there are no restrictions on the transport of data, and INTEGRAL means the servlet container must ensure that data cannot be changed in transit. A value of CONFIDENTIAL means that the data cannot be read while in transit.

The servlet specification does not specify how servlet containers should implement transport guarantees; however, a value of INTEGRAL or CONFIDENTIAL typically indicates a secure transport layer, such as SSL. Resin, for example, will only provide access to confidential data if ServletRequest.isSecure returns true.[4]

Programmatic Authentication

The word programmatic here means implemented from scratch, which is a good choice for authentication if you must have portability or if you want total control. Because it's more work than relying on your servlet container, programmatic authentication can be a bad choice if you are not interested in those benefits.

Another drawback to programmatic authentication is that HttpServletRequest.getUserPrincipal, HttpServletRequest.getRemoteUser, and HttpServletRequest.isUserInRole are rendered useless for applications with programmatic authentication. Programmatic authentication requires you to implement, and use, your own API because setting principals and roles is strictly for servlet containers. See "Principals and Roles" on page 252 for more information about setting principals and roles.

The rest of this section discusses an authentication mechanism implemented from scratch; if you're interested in something similar, you can use it for ideas or perhaps as a starting point.

The authentication mechanism discussed in this section entails protecting JSP pages with a custom tag, like this:

```
<!--A protected JSP page-->
...
<%@ taglib='/WEB-INF/tlds/security' prefix='security' %>
...
<!-- errorPage is optional; if unspecified, control goes back to
     loginPage if login fails -->

<security:enforceLogin loginPage='/login.jsp'
                        errorPage='/error.jsp' />

<!--The rest of the file is accessed only if a user has logged
     into this session -->
...
```

---

4. See page 465 for more information on the CONFIDENTIAL transport guarantee and SSL.

The enforceLogin tag looks for a user in session scope. If the user is in the session, the tag does nothing; if not, the tag forwards to the login page. The login page is specified with the loginPage attribute.

If login fails, control is forwarded to the error page. The errorPage attribute is optional; without it, the login page is redisplayed if login fails.

When login succeeds, a user is created and placed in session scope, and the rest of the page after the enforceLogin tag is evaluated.

Figure 9-5 provides a more visual representation of the sequence of events initiated by the enforceLogin tag.

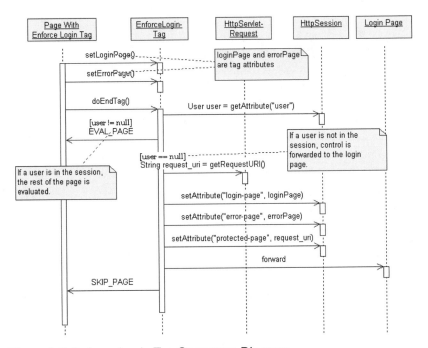

Figure 9-5 Enforce Login Tag Sequence Diagram

If no user is in session scope, three session attributes, listed in Table 9-9, are set by the enforceLogin tag.

The attributes listed in Table 9-9 determine how the request is subsequently handled; the first two correspond to the loginPage and errorPage attributes of the enforceLogin tag, respectively. The protected-page attribute represents the URI of the protected page.

Table 9-9 Session Attributes Set by the `enforceLogin` Tag

Attribute Name	Description
`login-page`	The `enforceLogin` tag forwards to this page if there's no user in the session. If login subsequently fails and no error page is specified, control is returned to this page.
`error-page`	An optional error page that's displayed when login fails
`protected-page`	The page with the `enforceLogin` tag; when login succeeds, the rest of the page after that tag is evaluated.

The login page submits the login form to a servlet. If that servlet authenticates the username and password, it redirects the request to the protected page; otherwise, it forwards to the error page, if specified, or back to the login page, if not.

Figure 9-6 shows an example that uses the programmatic authentication discussed in this section.

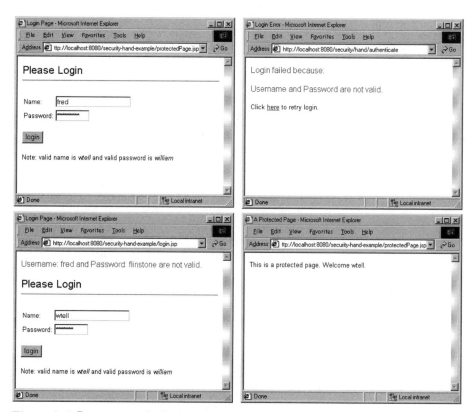

Figure 9-6 Programmatic Authentication

The top two pictures in Figure 9-6 show a failed login, and the bottom two show subsequent success. Figure 9-7 shows the files involved in the application shown in Figure 9-6.

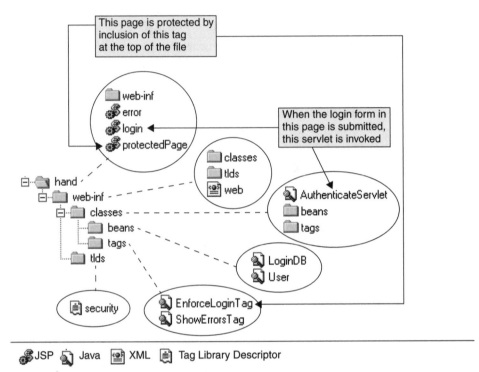

JSP   Java   XML   Tag Library Descriptor

Figure 9-7 Files for the Programmatic Authentication Example

The application maintains a makeshift database of users. That database is an instance of LoginDB and users are User instances; those classes are listed in Example 5-1.b on page 139 and Example 5-1.a on page 138, respectively. This implementation of LoginDB adds a default user, as listed in Example 9-5.a.

Example 9-5.a /WEB-INF/classes/beans/LoginDB.java

```
// The User class is listed in Example 5-1.a on page 138.
...
public class LoginDB implements java.io.Serializable {

   private Vector users = new Vector();
   private User[] defaultUsers = {
      new User("wtell", "william", "my first name"),
   };
```

```
   public LoginDB() {
      for(int i=0; i < defaultUsers.length; ++i)
         users.add(defaultUsers[i]);
   }
   public void addUser(String uname, String pwd, String hint) {
      users.add(new User(uname, pwd, hint));
   }
   // The rest of this class is identical to LoginDB listed in
   // Example 5-1.b on page 139.
   ...
}
```

The application shown in Figure 9-6 has one protected page, listed in Example 9-5.b.

Example 9-5.b /protectedPage.jsp

```
<html><head><title>A Protected Page</title></head>
<%@ taglib uri='security' prefix='security' %>
</body>

<!-- Without the errorPage attribute, control is forwarded back
     to the login page if login fails.  -->

<security:enforceLogin loginPage='/login.jsp'
                       errorPage='/error.jsp'/>

<jsp:useBean id='user' type='beans.User' scope='session'/>

This is a protected page. Welcome <%= user.getUserName() %>.

</body>
</html>
```

The protected page accesses the user in the session to display a welcome message. The enforceLogin tag handler is listed in Example 9-5.c.

Example 9-5.c /WEB-INF/classes/tags/EnforceLoginTag.java

```
package tags;

import javax.servlet.http.HttpServletRequest;
import javax.servlet.http.HttpSession;
import javax.servlet.jsp.JspException;
import javax.servlet.jsp.PageContext;
import javax.servlet.jsp.tagext.TagSupport;

public class EnforceLoginTag extends TagSupport {
   private String loginPage, errorPage;
```

```
public void setLoginPage(String loginPage) {
    this.loginPage = loginPage;
}
public void setErrorPage(String errorPage) {
    this.errorPage = errorPage;
}
public int doEndTag() throws JspException {
    HttpSession session = pageContext.getSession();
    HttpServletRequest req = (HttpServletRequest)pageContext.
                                          getRequest();
    String protectedPage = req.getRequestURI();

    if(session.getAttribute("user") == null) {
        session.setAttribute("login-page",      loginPage);
        session.setAttribute("error-page",      errorPage);
        session.setAttribute("protected-page", protectedPage);

        try {
            pageContext.forward(loginPage);
            return SKIP_PAGE;
        }
        catch(Exception ex) {
            throw new JspException(ex.getMessage());
        }
    }
    return EVAL_PAGE;
}
public void release() {
    loginPage = errorPage = null;
}
}
```

If there's a user in the session, the tag handler listed in Example 9-5.c returns EVAL_PAGE and the rest of the page after the tag is evaluated. If the user is not in the session, the attributes listed in Table 9-9 on page 273 are set and control is forwarded to the login page.

The login page is listed in Example 9-5.d.

Example 9-5.d   /login.jsp

```
<html><head><title>Login Page</title></head>
<%@ taglib uri='/WEB-INF/tlds/security.tld' prefix='security' %>
<body>

<font size='4' color='red'><security:showErrors/></font>

<p><font size='5' color='blue'>Please Login</font><hr>
<form action='<%= response.encodeURL("authenticate") %>'
```

```
    method='post'>
  <table>
    <tr>
       <td>Name:</td>
       <td><input type='text' name='userName'/>
       </td>
    </tr><tr>
       <td>Password:</td>
       <td><input type='password' name='password' size='8'></td>
    </tr>
  </table>
  <br>
  <input type='submit' value='login'>
</form></p>

Note: valid name is <i>wtell</i> and valid
password is <i>william</i>

</body>
</html>
```

The login form is submitted to the `authenticate` servlet, which generates error messages in session scope if authentication fails. Those messages are displayed by the `security:showErrors` tag at the top of the login page. The mappings between the name `authenticate` and the authenticate servlet are specified in `web.xml`, which is listed in Example 9-5.e.

Example 9-5.e /WEB-INF/web.xml

```
<?xml version="1.0" encoding="ISO-8859-1"?>

<!DOCTYPE web-app
   PUBLIC "-//Sun Microsystems, Inc.//DTD Web Application 2.2//EN"
   "http://java.sun.com/j2ee/dtds/web-app_2.2.dtd">

<web-app>
   <servlet>
      <servlet-name>authenticate</servlet-name>
      <servlet-class>AuthenticateServlet</servlet-class>
   </servlet>

   <servlet-mapping>
      <servlet-name>authenticate</servlet-name>
      <url-pattern>/authenticate</url-pattern>
   </servlet-mapping>

   <taglib>
    <taglib-uri>/WEB-INF/tlds/security.tld</taglib-uri>
```

```
        <taglib-location>/WEB-INF/tlds/security.tld</taglib-location>
    </taglib>
</web-app>
```

Example 9-5.f lists the authenticate servlet.

Example 9-5.f /WEB-INF/classes/AuthenticateServlet.java

```java
import javax.servlet.ServletConfig;
import javax.servlet.ServletException;
import javax.servlet.http.HttpServlet;
import javax.servlet.http.HttpServletRequest;
import javax.servlet.http.HttpServletResponse;
import javax.servlet.http.HttpSession;
import java.io.IOException;
import beans.LoginDB;
import beans.User;

public class AuthenticateServlet extends HttpServlet {
    private LoginDB loginDB;

    public void init(ServletConfig config) throws ServletException{
        super.init(config);
        loginDB = new LoginDB();
    }
    public void service(HttpServletRequest req,
                        HttpServletResponse res)
                            throws IOException, ServletException {
        HttpSession session = req.getSession();
        String      uname   = req.getParameter("userName");
        String      pwd     = req.getParameter("password");
        User        user    = loginDB.getUser(uname, pwd);

        if(user != null) { // authorized
            String protectedPage = (String)session.
                                    getAttribute("protected-page");
            session.removeAttribute("login-page");
            session.removeAttribute("error-page");
            session.removeAttribute("protected-page");
            session.removeAttribute("login-error");

            session.setAttribute("user", user);
            res.sendRedirect(res.encodeURL(protectedPage));
        }
        else { // not authorized
            String loginPage = (String)session.
                                getAttribute("login-page");
            String errorPage = (String)session.
                                getAttribute("error-page");
```

```
String forwardTo = errorPage != null ? errorPage :
                                        loginPage;
session.setAttribute("login-error",
        "Username and Password are not valid.");

getServletContext().getRequestDispatcher(
    res.encodeURL(forwardTo)).forward(req,res);
    }
  }
}
```

The authenticate servlet obtains the username and password from the request and attempts to obtain a reference to a corresponding user in the login database. If the user exists in the database, session attributes generated by the servlet and the enforceLogin tag are removed from the session and the request is redirected to the protected page. Figure 9-8 shows the sequence of events for a successful login.

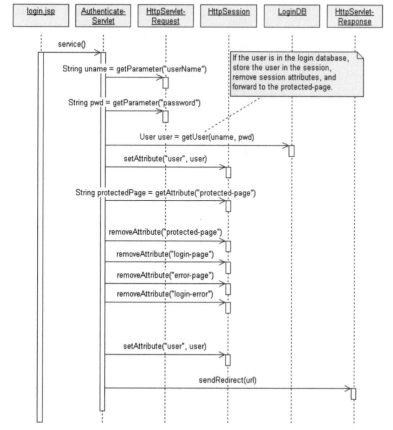

Figure 9-8 Login Succeeds Sequence Diagram

If the user is not in the login database, a `login-error` session attribute is set and the request is forwarded to the error page, if specified, or back to the login page, if not. Figure 9-9 shows the sequence of events for a failed login.

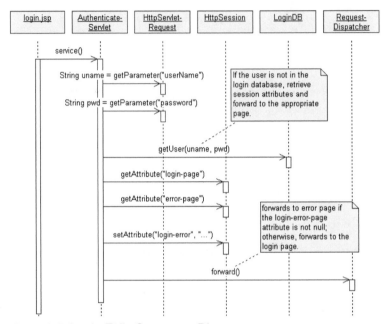

Figure 9-9 Login Fails Sequence Diagram

The error page for the application in Figure 9-6 on page 273 is listed in Example 9-5.g.

Example 9-5.g /error.jsp

```
<html><head><title>Login Error</title></head>
<%@ taglib uri='/WEB-INF/tlds/security.tld' prefix='security' %>
<body>

<font size='4' color='red'>
Login failed because:<p>
<security:showErrors/></font></p>

Click <a href='login.jsp'>here</a> to retry login.

</body>
</html>
```

Like the login page, the error page uses the `security:showErrors` tag, whose handler is listed in Example 9-5.h.

Example 9-5.h /WEB-INF/classes/tags/ShowErrorsTag.java

```java
package tags;

import javax.servlet.jsp.JspException;
import javax.servlet.jsp.PageContext;
import javax.servlet.jsp.tagext.TagSupport;

public class ShowErrorsTag extends TagSupport {
    public int doStartTag() throws JspException {
        String error = (String)pageContext.getSession().
                                getAttribute("login-error");
        if(error != null) {
            try {
                pageContext.getOut().print(error);
            }
            catch(java.io.IOException ex) {
                throw new JspException(ex.getMessage());
            }
        }
        return SKIP_BODY;
    }
}
```

The `showErrors` tag handler prints the value of the `login-error` session attribute that was set by the authenticate servlet.

Conclusion

Security is an important aspect of applications that transport sensitive data over the Internet. Because of this requirement, the servlet specification requires servlet containers to provide implementations of basic and digest authentication, as defined in the HTTP/1.1 specification. Additionally, servlet containers must provide form-based security that allows developers to control the look and feel of login screens. Finally, servlet containers may provide SSL and client certificate authentication, although containers that are not J2EE compliant are not required to do so.

Unlike other aspects of web applications implemented with JSP and the Java programming language, security typically requires some nonportable code. If portability is a high priority, you can implement security from scratch by using JSP and servlets, as illustrated in "Programmatic Authentication" on page 271.

DATABASES

Topics in this Chapter

- Database Creation
- Database Custom Tags
  - The Query Tag
  - The ColumnNames Tag
  - The Rows Tag
  - The Release Tag
  - The Release Tag
- Connection Pooling
  - Using a Connection Pool
  - Implementing a Simple Connection Pool
- Prepared Statements
- Transactions
- Scrolling Through Result Sets

Chapter 10

The vast majority of commercial web sites are driven by relational databases. Servlets and JSP pages are excellent choices for database access because they can use JDBC (Java Database Connectivity), which provides a simple and portable way to access databases. Additionally, the servlet life cycle allows servlets and JSP pages to maintain database connections that span multiple requests. Because of the overhead involved in creating a database connection, the ability to maintain open connections can result in substantial performance benefits.

This chapter assumes that readers are familiar with relational databases and the basics of SQL and JDBC. Those topics are adequately covered in most introductory JSP books; if you need more in-depth coverage of JDBC, see the *JDBC API Tutorial and Reference* from Addison-Wesley.

JSP custom tags for database access are the major theme of this chapter. In all, eight custom tags, summarized in Table 10-1, are discussed, ranging from a `Query` tag that executes a database query, to tags that execute prepared statements and transactions. Those tags illustrate the use of JDBC for most common database tasks, and they can also be used as a starting point for your own database tags.

Table 10-1 Custom Tags Discussed in This Chapter

Tag Name	Description	See Page(s)
query	Obtains a database connection and executes a query. Tag body is interpreted as SQL.	289, 302
rows	Iterates over a result set's rows	299, 327
columns	Iterates over a result set's columns	301
columnNames	Iterates over a result set's column names	293
release	Recycles the connection obtained by query	301, 302
prepareStatement	Creates a prepared statement and stores it in a specified scope	317
executePreparedStatement	Executes a prepared statement created by prepareStatement	319
transaction	Executes a transaction. The body of the tag is interpreted as SQL statements that constitute the transaction.	319

Additionally, "Connection Pooling" on page 302 discusses an implementation of a connection pool, which allows database connections to be reused. "Scrolling Through Result Sets" on page 324 shows how to scroll through result sets, which can be crucial for queries that return result sets with a large number of rows.

Database Creation

This section discusses a stand-alone Java application, listed in Example 10-1, that creates a database. That database is used throughout this chapter.

Example 10-1 Creating a Database

```java
import java.sql.Connection;
import java.sql.DriverManager;
import java.sql.Statement;
import java.sql.SQLException;

public class CreateDB {
   private Connection conn;
   private Statement stmt;

   public static void main(String args[]) {
      new CreateDB();
   }
```

```
public CreateDB() {
    try {
        loadJDBCDriver();
        conn = getConnection("F:/databases/sunpress");
        stmt = conn.createStatement();

        createTables(stmt);
        populateTables(stmt);

        stmt.close();
        conn.close();
        DriverManager.getConnection(
                        "jdbc:cloudscape:;shutdown=true");
    }
    catch(SQLException ex) {
        ex.printStackTrace();
    }
}
private void createTables(Statement stmt) {
    try {
        stmt.execute("CREATE TABLE Customers (" +
                        "Customer_ID  INTEGER, " +
                        "Name         VARCHAR(25), " +
                        "Phone_Number VARCHAR(30))");

        stmt.execute("CREATE TABLE Orders (" +
                        "Customer_ID  INTEGER, " +
                        "Order_ID     INTEGER, " +
                        "Amount       FLOAT)");
    }
    catch(SQLException ex) {
        ex.printStackTrace();
    }
}
private void populateTables(Statement stmt) {
    try {
        stmt.execute("INSERT INTO Customers VALUES " +
            "(1, 'William Dupont',     '(652)482-0931')," +
            "(2, 'Kris Cromwell',      '(652)482-0932')," +
            "(3, 'Susan Randor',       '(652)482-0933')," +
            "(4, 'Jim Wilson',         '(652)482-0934')," +
            "(5, 'Lynn Seckinger',     '(652)482-0935')," +
            "(6, 'Richard Tatersall',  '(652)482-0936')," +
            "(7, 'Gabriella Sarintia', '(652)482-0937')," +
            "(8, 'Lisa Hartwig',       '(652)482-0938')");

        stmt.execute("INSERT INTO Orders VALUES " +
            "(1, 1, 29.99)," + "(2, 2, 49.86)," +
```

```
                         "(1,  3,  39.99)," + "(3,  4,  99.13)," +
                         "(1,  5,  24.87)," + "(3,  6,  112.22)," +
                         "(8,  7,  29.99)," + "(2,  8,  49.86)," +
                         "(1,  9,  39.99)," + "(3,  10, 99.13)," +
                         "(1,  11, 24.87)," + "(3,  12, 112.22)," +
                         "(7,  13, 21.12)," + "(1,  14, 27.49)");
        }
        catch(SQLException ex) {
            ex.printStackTrace();
        }
    }
    private void loadJDBCDriver() {
        try {
            Class.forName("COM.cloudscape.core.JDBCDriver");
        }
        catch(ClassNotFoundException e) {
            e.printStackTrace();
        }
    }
    private Connection getConnection(String dbName) {
        Connection con = null;
        try {
            con = DriverManager.getConnection(
                "jdbc:cloudscape:" + dbName + ";create=true");
        }
        catch(SQLException sqe) {
            System.err.println("Couldn't access " + dbName);
        }
        return con;
    }
}
```

The application listed in Example 10-1 is lengthy but straightforward. The
`CreateDB` constructor loads a JDBC driver and obtains a database connection.
Subsequently, that constructor obtains a statement from the connection with
`Connection.createStatement`. The constructor uses that statement to create
and populate database tables, after which the statement and its associated
connection are closed. Finally, the constructor shuts down the database.

The last two methods listed in Example 10-1 load a JDBC driver and obtain a
database connection. Those methods specify a driver class and a database URL,
both of which will vary from one database vendor to another. The database that's
created in Example 10-1 is a Cloudscape database; to customize the application
for a different vendor, simply specify an appropriate driver and database URL for
that vendor.

Data Sources

Obtaining a database connection with a JDBC driver manager requires you to know three details about your database: the database name, the JDBC driver name, and the JDBC URL. If you use JDBC's `DataSource` interface and a naming and directory service, such as the Java Naming and Directory Interface (JNDI), you can access databases with their names alone. For example, the code fragment listed below shows how you would use a data source to obtain a database connection by using JNDI.

```
Context context = new InitialContext();
DataSource dataSource = (DataSource)context.lookup("sunpress_db");
Connection connection = dataSource.getConnection("uname", "pwd");
```

Using data sources shields your code from database details, so that changes to your database won't affect your code. On the other hand, you must provide access to that database through JNDI, which is often something that your system administrator must setup for you. Because of that requirement, this chapter obtains database connections with a JDBC driver manager instead of with data sources.

Database Custom Tags

Figure 10-1 shows two JSP pages, one that performs a database query (shown on the left), and another that displays the results of that query.

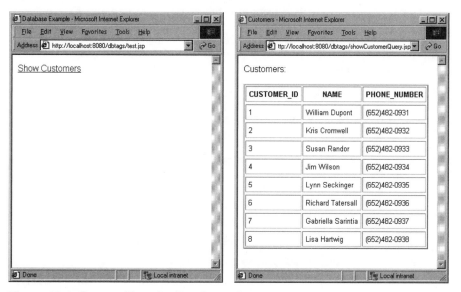

Figure 10-1 Custom Tags for Database Access

The JSP page shown on the left in Figure 10-1 is listed in Example 10-2.a.

Example 10-2.a /test.jsp

```
<html><head><title>Database Example</title>
   <%@ taglib uri='/WEB-INF/tlds/database.tld' prefix='database'%>
</head>
<body>

<database:query id='customers' scope='session'>
   SELECT * FROM Customers
</database:query>

<font size='4'>
   <a href='showCustomerQuery.jsp'>Show Customers</a><p>
</font>

</body>
</html>
```

The JSP page listed in Example 10-2.a uses a `query` custom tag to obtain a database connection and perform a query that selects all rows from the `Customers` table. The result of that query is given an identifier—`customers`—and is stored in session scope. That identifier is subsequently used by other custom tags to retrieve the result set associated with the query.

The `query` tag's `id` and `scope` attributes are similar to attributes of the same name associated with `jsp:useBean` and therefore should be intuitive to JSP developers.

The JSP page listed in Example 10-2.a provides a link to the JSP page—`showCustomerQuery.jsp`—shown on the right in Figure 10-1. `showCustomerQuery.jsp` is listed in Example 10-2.b.

Example 10-2.b /showCustomerQuery.jsp

```
<html><head><title>Customers</title>
   <%@ taglib uri='/WEB-INF/tlds/database.tld' prefix='database'%>
</head>
<body>

<p><font size='4'>Customers:</font></p>

<table border='2' cellpadding='5'>
   <database:columnNames query='customers' id='name'>
      <th><%= name %></th>
   </database:columnNames>
```

```
    <database:rows query='customers'><tr>
      <tr>
         <database:columns query='customers' id='value'>
            <td><%= value %></td>
         </database:columns>
      </tr>
    </database:rows>
  </table>
  </p>

  <database:release query='customers'/>

  </body>
  </html>
```

The JSP page listed in Example 10-2.b uses three custom tags to access the query: columnNames, rows, and columns. All three tags have a mandatory query attribute that identifies a query, and all three tags iterate over either the query's result set (rows) or the result set's metadata (columnNames and columns).

The columns and columnNames tags create scripting variables for the current column and column name, respectively. Those scripting variables are named by the developer with an id attribute and in Example 10-2.b are used to create the table shown in Figure 10-1 on page 287. See "Using Custom Tag IDs" on page 44 for more information about naming scripting variables with the id attribute.

The JSP page listed in Example 10-2.b uses a release tag, which closes the connection created by the query tag. Creating a connection for each query and closing that connection when the query has been processed are far from ideal from a performance standpoint. Instead of opening a new connection for every query, it's much more efficient for the query tag to obtain an open connection from a connection pool. That connection would subsequently be returned to the pool by the release tag. That scenario is discussed in "Connection Pooling" on page 302.

The Query Tag

The query tag used in Example 10-2.a interprets its body content as SQL and therefore specifies bodycontent as tagdependent in the tag library descriptor, like this:

```
<tag>
    <name>query</name>
    <tagclass>tags.jdbc.QueryTag</tagclass>
    <bodycontent>**tagdependent**</bodycontent>
    ...
</tag>
```

JSP containers do not evaluate body content for tagdependent tags. Such tags, like the query tag, typically have specialized content such as SQL that is interpreted only by the tag. See "Body Content" on page 46 for more information about tagdependent tags.

The tag handler for the query tag is listed in Example 10-3.a.

Example 10-3.a   /WEB-INF/classes/tags/jdbc/QueryTag.java

```java
package tags.jdbc;

import java.sql.Connection;
import java.sql.DriverManager;
import java.sql.Statement;
import java.sql.SQLException;
import java.sql.ResultSet;

import javax.servlet.jsp.JspException;
import javax.servlet.jsp.tagext.BodyTagSupport;

import beans.jdbc.Query;

public class QueryTag extends BodyTagSupport {
   private String scope = "page";
   private boolean update = false, driverLoaded = false;

   public void setScope(String scope) {
      this.scope = scope;
   }
   public void setUpdate(boolean update) {
      this.update = update;
   }
   public int doAfterBody() throws JspException {
      Connection conn = getConnection("f:/databases/sunpress");

      try {
         String query = bodyContent.getString();
         Statement statement = conn.createStatement(
                           ResultSet.TYPE_SCROLL_INSENSITIVE,
                           ResultSet.CONCUR_READ_ONLY);
         ResultSet rs = null;
         int rows = 0;

         if(update) {
            rows = statement.executeUpdate(query);
            Query.save(new Query(statement, rows),
                              pageContext, id, scope);
```

```
        }
        else {
           rs = statement.executeQuery(query);
           Query.save(new Query(statement, rs),
                                 pageContext, id, scope);
        }
     }
     catch(SQLException ex) {
        throw new JspException(ex.getMessage());
     }
     return SKIP_BODY;
  }
  private Connection getConnection(String dbName)
                                           throws JspException {
     Connection con = null;

     try {
        if(!driverLoaded) {
           Class.forName("COM.cloudscape.core.JDBCDriver");
           driverLoaded = true;
        }
        con = DriverManager.getConnection(
             "jdbc:cloudscape:" + dbName + ";create=false");
     }
     catch(Exception ex) {
        throw new JspException(ex.getMessage());
     }
     return con;
  }
}
```

Like the application listed in Example 10-1 on page 284, the query tag opens a database connection by loading a JDBC driver and subsequently invokes DriverManager.getConnection to obtain a connection. The query tag uses that connection to create a statement whose corresponding result set is scrollable and cannot be updated. That type of result set is only available for drivers that implement JDBC 2.0; therefore, the tags discussed in this chapter will only work with JDBC 2.0 drivers. That limitation is acceptable because nearly all database vendors provide JDBC 2.0-compliant drivers.

In addition to the id and scope attributes, the query tag defines an update attribute, which determines the type of query that's performed. If update is false (the default), Statement.executeQuery, which is used for queries that return a single result set, such as SELECT, is invoked. If update is true, Statement.executeUpdate, which is used for statements that affect one or more table rows, such as INSERT or UPDATE, is used.

After the query has been executed, a `Query` bean is stored in the specified scope using the specified identifier. The `Query` class is listed in Example 10-3.b.

Example 10-3.b   /WEB-INF/classes/beans/jdbc/Query.java

```java
package tags.jdbc.beans;

import java.sql.ResultSet;
import java.sql.Statement;

import javax.servlet.jsp.PageContext;
import javax.servlet.jsp.JspException;

public class Query {
   public static final String QUERY_PREFIX = "query-";
   private static final int UNASSIGNED = -1;

   private final Statement statement;
   private final ResultSet result;
   private final int updateCount;

   public Query(Statement statement, ResultSet result) {
      this.statement = statement;
      this.result = result;
      this.updateCount = UNASSIGNED;
   }
   public Query(Statement statement, int updateCount) {
      this.statement = statement;
      this.updateCount = updateCount;
      this.result = null;
   }
   public Statement getStatement() { return statement; }
   public ResultSet getResult()    { return result; }
   public int getUpdateCount()     { return updateCount; }

   public static void save(Query query, PageContext pageContext,
                        String name, String scope) {
      pageContext.setAttribute(QUERY_PREFIX + name, query,
                                    getConstantForScope(scope));
   }
   public static ResultSet getResult(PageContext pageContext,
                        String name) throws JspException {
      Query query = findQuery(pageContext, name);
      return query.getResult();
   }
   public static int getUpdateCount(PageContext pageContext,
                           String name) throws JspException {
```

```
      Query query = findQuery(pageContext, name);
      return query.getUpdateCount();
   }
   public static Query findQuery(PageContext pageContext,
                          String name) throws JspException {
      Query query = (Query)pageContext.findAttribute(
                               QUERY_PREFIX + name);

      if(query == null) { // session invalidated?
         throw new JspException("Query " + name + " not found." +
                          " Please retry the query");
      }
      return query;
   }
   private static int getConstantForScope(String scope) {
      int constant = PageContext.PAGE_SCOPE;

      if(scope.equalsIgnoreCase("page"))
         constant = PageContext.PAGE_SCOPE;
      else if(scope.equalsIgnoreCase("request"))
         constant = PageContext.REQUEST_SCOPE;
      else if(scope.equalsIgnoreCase("session"))
         constant = PageContext.SESSION_SCOPE;
      else if(scope.equalsIgnoreCase("application"))
         constant = PageContext.APPLICATION_SCOPE;

      return constant;
   }
 }
```

The Query class stores a statement and either a result set or an update count, depending upon the type of query that was performed.

The Query class also provides four public static methods, one that saves a Query instance in a specified scope, one that retrieves a stored query, and two others that return either a result set or update count associated with a stored query. The save method is used by QueryTag.doEndTag—see Example 10-3.a on page 290—and Query.getResult is used by the columns, columnNames, and rows tags, which access the result set associated with a query.

The ColumnNames Tag

The query tag, discussed in "The Query Tag" on page 289, obtains a database connection, executes a query and stores information about that query in a specified scope. That information is accessed by other database tags, including the columnNames tag, which iterates over column names.

The `columnNames` tag is used like this:

```
<database:columnNames query='customers' id='name'>
   <%= name %>
</database:columnNames>
```

The `columnNames` tag accesses the query identified by the `query` attribute and creates a scripting variable representing the name of the current column. That scripting variable is named with the tag's `id` attribute. The preceding code fragment uses that scripting variable to print the name of each column in the `customers` query.

Two of the database tags discussed in this chapter—`columnNames` and `columns`—iterate over a result set's columns. That behavior is encapsulated in an abstract base class—`ColumnIteratorTag`, listed in Example 10-4.a—that iterates over the columns in a result set and writes out its body content when that iteration is finished. The abstract designation for the `ColumnIteratorTag` class means `ColumnIteratorTag` is meant to be extended. `ColumnIteratorTag` does not define any abstract methods.

Example 10-4.a /WEB-INF/classes/tags/jdbc/ColumnIteratorTag.java

```
package tags.jdbc;

import java.sql.ResultSet;
import java.sql.ResultSetMetaData;
import java.sql.SQLException;

import javax.servlet.jsp.JspException;
import javax.servlet.jsp.tagext.BodyTagSupport;

import beans.jdbc.Query;

public abstract class ColumnIteratorTag extends BodyTagSupport {
   protected int columnCount, currentColumn;
   protected ResultSet rs;
   protected ResultSetMetaData rsmd;
   protected String query;

   public void setQuery(String query) {
      this.query = query;
   }
   public int doStartTag() throws JspException {
      rs = Query.getResult(pageContext, query);
```

```
   try {
      rsmd = rs.getMetaData();
      columnCount = rsmd.getColumnCount();
      currentColumn = 1;
   }
   catch(Exception ex) {
      throw new JspException(ex.getMessage());
   }
   if(columnCount > 0) return EVAL_BODY_TAG;
   else                return SKIP_BODY;
}
public int doAfterBody() throws JspException {
   if(++currentColumn <= columnCount) {
      return EVAL_BODY_TAG;
   }
   else {
      try {
         bodyContent.writeOut(getPreviousOut());
      }
      catch(java.io.IOException e) {
         throw new JspException(e.getMessage());
      }
   }
   return SKIP_BODY;
}
}
```

The column iterator start tag obtains a reference to the result set associated with the specified query, using the `static Query.getResult` method. See "The Query Tag" on page 289 for more information concerning that method.

With a result set in hand, `ColumnIteratorTag.doStartTag` obtains a reference to that result set's metadata to ascertain the number of columns in that result set. If that number is greater than zero, the body of the tag is evaluated.

`ColumnIteratorTag.doAfterBody` is called repeatedly until it runs out of columns from its result set. After the last column has been accessed, `doAfterBody` prints its body content to the previous out and returns `SKIP_BODY`, ending the iteration. See "Understanding How Body Content Works" on page 48 for more information about writing to the previous out in `doAfterBody`.

You can extend `ColumnIteratorTag` and override `BodyTag` methods. In those methods, you can access `ColumnIteratorTag` protected member variables. That's what the tag handler for the `columnNames` tag does. That tag handler is listed in Example 10-4.b.

Example 10-4.b   /WEB-INF/classes/tags/jdbc/ColumnNamesTag.java

```java
package tags.jdbc;

import java.sql.ResultSetMetaData;
import java.sql.SQLException;

import javax.servlet.jsp.JspException;

public class ColumnNamesTag extends ColumnIteratorTag {
   public void doInitBody() throws JspException {
      setAttribute();
   }
   public int doAfterBody() throws JspException {
      int whatNext = super.doAfterBody();

      if(whatNext == EVAL_BODY_TAG)
         setAttribute();

      return whatNext;
   }
   private void setAttribute() throws JspException {
      try {
         pageContext.setAttribute(getId(), rsmd.getColumnName(
                                      currentColumn));
      }
      catch(SQLException ex) {
         throw new JspException(ex.getMessage());
      }
   }
}
```

The ColumnNamesTag class, listed above, extends the ColumnIteratorTag class listed in Example 10-4.a and overrides doInitBody and doAfterBody. Those two methods store the current column name—identified by the tag's required id attribute—in page scope. The result set metadata used by the ColumnNamesTag class (rsmd in setAttribute) is a protected member of ColumnIteratorTag.

The columnNames tag creates a scripting variable, which requires an implementation of the TagExtraInfo class. Example 10-4.c lists the tag extra info for the columnNames tag. See "Scripting Variables" on page 41 for more information about creating scripting variables.

Example 10-4.c /WEB-INF/classes/tags/jdbc/ColumnNamesTagInfo.java

```java
package tags.jdbc;

import javax.servlet.jsp.tagext.TagData;
import javax.servlet.jsp.tagext.TagExtraInfo;
import javax.servlet.jsp.tagext.VariableInfo;

public class ColumnNamesTagInfo extends TagExtraInfo {
    public VariableInfo[] getVariableInfo(TagData data) {
        return new VariableInfo[] {
            new VariableInfo(data.getId(),
                             "java.lang.String",
                             true,
                             VariableInfo.NESTED)
        };
    }
}
```

The tag info class listed in Example 10-4.c specifies the name of the scripting variable, which corresponds to the tag's id attribute. The type of that scripting variable is specified as java.lang.String, and the true argument passed to the VariableInfo constructor indicates that the variable needs to be created. Finally, the VariableInfo.NESTED argument restricts the scope of the scripting variable to the body of the tag.

The Columns Tag

The columns tag is nearly identical to the columnNames tag—both tags iterate over a result set's columns, and both tags create scripting variables. The difference is that the columns tag makes the current column's *value* available as a scripting variable, whereas the columnNames tag makes the current column's *name* available as a scripting variable.

Like the tag handler for the columnNames tag, the tag handler for the columns tag extends ColumnIteratorTag and creates a scripting variable. The tag handler for the columns tag is listed in Example 10-5.a.

Example 10-5.a /WEB-INF/classes/tags/jdbc/ColumnsTag.java

```java
package tags.jdbc;

import java.sql.ResultSetMetaData;
import java.sql.SQLException;
```

```
import javax.servlet.jsp.JspException;

public class ColumnsTag extends ColumnIteratorTag {
   public void doInitBody() throws JspException {
      setAttribute();
   }
   public int doAfterBody() throws JspException {
      int whatNext = super.doAfterBody();

      if(whatNext == EVAL_BODY_TAG)
         setAttribute();

      return whatNext;
   }
   private void setAttribute() throws JspException {
      try {
         pageContext.setAttribute(getId(), rs.getString(
                                       currentColumn));
      }
      catch(SQLException ex) {
         throw new JspException(ex.getMessage());
      }
   }
}
```

The ColumnsTag class listed above uses the result set from its superclass to obtain column values. Also, like the columnNames tag, the columns tag has an associated tag info class that specifies the tag's scripting variable. That tag info class is listed in Example 10-5.b.

Example 10-5.b ColumnIteratorTagInfo.java

```
package tags.jdbc;

import javax.servlet.jsp.tagext.TagData;
import javax.servlet.jsp.tagext.TagExtraInfo;
import javax.servlet.jsp.tagext.VariableInfo;

public class ColumnsTagInfo extends TagExtraInfo {
   public VariableInfo[] getVariableInfo(TagData data) {
      return new VariableInfo[] {
         new VariableInfo(data.getId(),
                          "java.lang.String",
                          true,
                          VariableInfo.NESTED)
      };
   }
}
```

As was the case for the `columnNames` tag, the name of the scripting variable for the `columns` tag is set to the tag's `id` attribute, it's type is `java.lang.String`, the scripting variable needs to be created, and that variable is available only within the tag's body.

The Rows Tag

The `rows` tag iterates over each row of a result set associated with a specified query. The code fragment listed below shows how the `rows` tag is used.

```
<database:rows query='customers'>
   <database:columns query='customers' id='value'>
      <%= value %>
   </database:columns>
</database:rows>
```

In the preceding code fragment, the `rows` tag iterates over each row of the result set associated with the `customers` query. In that code fragment, the body of the `rows` tag contains a `columns` tag, which iterates over each column in the current row.

The tag handler for the `rows` tag is listed in Example 10-6.

Example 10-6 /WEB-INF/classes/tags/jdbc/RowsTag.java

```
package tags.jdbc;

import java.sql.ResultSet;
import java.sql.Statement;
import java.sql.SQLException;
import javax.servlet.jsp.JspException;
import javax.servlet.jsp.tagext.BodyTagSupport;

import beans.jdbc.Query;

public class RowsTag extends BodyTagSupport {
   private ResultSet rs;
   private boolean keepGoing;
   private String query;

   public void setQuery(String query) {
      this.query = query;
   }
   public int doStartTag() throws JspException {
      rs = Query.getResult(pageContext, query);

      try {
```

```
            keepGoing = rs.next(); // point to first row initially
        }
        catch(Exception ex) {
            throw new JspException(ex.getMessage());
        }
        if(keepGoing)  return EVAL_BODY_TAG;
        else           return SKIP_BODY;
    }
    public int doAfterBody() throws JspException {
        try {
            if(rs.isLast()) {
                rs.beforeFirst();

                try {
                    bodyContent.writeOut(getPreviousOut());
                }
                catch(Exception e) {
                    throw new JspException(e.getMessage());
                }
                return SKIP_BODY;
            }
            rs.next();
        }
        catch(java.sql.SQLException ex) {
            throw new JspException(ex.getMessage());
        }
        return EVAL_BODY_TAG;
    }
}
```

Like the `columnNames` tag listed in Example 10-4.a, the `rows` tag obtains a reference to the query's result set in `doStartTag`. That method subsequently invokes the result set's `next` method to point the result set's cursor to the first row.[1] `ResultSet.next` returns a `boolean` variable that indicates whether the result set's cursor points to a valid row. If that method returns `false` in `RowsTag.doStartTag`, the result set has no rows and `doStartTag` returns `SKIP_BODY`; otherwise, the body of the tag is evaluated.

`RowsTag.doAfterBody` checks to see if the cursor points to the last row; if so, the cursor is set to the first row and the iteration is terminated. If the cursor does not point to the last row, `doAfterBody` advances the cursor with `ResultSet.next`, and the iteration continues.

---

1.   A result set's cursor is initially positioned *before* the first row.

RowsTag.doAfterBody, like ColumnNames.doAfterBody, writes the tag's body content to the previous out.

The Release Tag

The release tag, whose tag handler is listed in Example 10-7, closes the connection opened by the query tag.

Example 10-7   /WEB-INF/classes/tags/jdbc/ReleaseTag.java

```
package tags.jdbc;

import java.sql.Connection;
import java.sql.Statement;
import javax.servlet.jsp.JspException;
import javax.servlet.jsp.tagext.TagSupport;

import beans.jdbc.Query;

public class ReleaseTag extends TagSupport {
   private String query = "null";

   public void setQuery(String query) {
      this.query = query;
   }
   public int doEndTag() throws JspException {
      Query q = Query.findQuery(pageContext, query);

      try {
         Connection con = q.getStatement().getConnection();

         if(con != null && !con.isClosed()) {
            con.close();
         }
      }
      catch(java.sql.SQLException sqlex) {
         throw new JspException(sqlex.getMessage());
      }
      pageContext.removeAttribute(query);

      return EVAL_PAGE;
   }
}
```

After the connection is closed, ReleaseTag.doEndTag removes the Query attribute from the scope it was stored in.

Connection Pooling

It can take upwards of a full second to open a database connection—that ranks database connections near the top of resources that are expensive to initialize. You can reduce that performance penalty by loaning out connections from a pool of open connections instead of repeatedly opening and closing them.

There are a number of ways you can add a connection pool to your web applications. First, there are numerous freely available connection pool implementations; a popular choice is PoolMan, which you can download from `http://poolman.sourceforge.net/PoolMan/index.shtml`.

Second, the JDBC 2.0 Optional Package API provides connection pooling, but it requires you to use a data source that's bound to a JNDI tree. See "Data Sources" on page 287 for more information about using data sources to obtain database connections.

The third option is implementing your own connection pool. This is a popular choice because implementing connection pools is fairly straightforward, and implementing your own connection pool gives you complete control over how it works. This section discusses a connection pool implementation that you may find useful as a starting point for your own.

Using a Connection Pool

The database tags discussed so far in this chapter are convenient, but the `query` and `release` tags, as listed in Example 10-3.a on page 290 and Example 10-7 on page 301, respectively, are inefficient because the former opens a database connection that's closed by the latter. Fortunately, it's easy to retrofit those tags with a connection pool.

The code fragment listed below shows how the `query` tag handler is modified to use a connection pool.

```
...
import beans.jdbc.DbConnectionPool;
import beans.util.ConnectionException;

public class QueryTag extends BodyTagSupport {
   ...
   public int doEndTag() throws JspException {
      DbConnectionPool pool = (DbConnectionPool)
                             pageContext.getServletContext().
                             getAttribute("db-connection-pool");
```

```
Connection conn;

try {
    conn = (Connection)pool.getResource();
}
catch(ConnectionException cex) {
    throw new JspException(cex.getMessage());
}
...

    }
}
```

`QueryTag.doEndTag` obtains a reference to the pool from application scope and invokes the pool's `getResource` method, which returns an available connection.

The `release` tag returns a connection to the pool with the pool's `recycleResource` method. A truncated listing of the updated `ReleaseTag` class is listed below.

```
...
import beans.jdbc.DbConnectionPool;

public class ReleaseTag extends TagSupport {
    ...
    public int doEndTag() throws JspException {
        Query q = (Query)pageContext.findAttribute(query);
        ServletContext app  = pageContext.getServletContext();
        DbConnectionPool pool = (DbConnectionPool)
                        pageContext.getServletContext().
                        getAttribute("db-connection-pool");
        try {
            pool.recycleResource(q.getStatement().getConnection());
        }
        catch(java.sql.SQLException ex) {
            throw new JspException(ex.getMessage());
        }
        ...
    }
}
```

Creating a Connection Pool

The connection pool accessed by the query and `release` tags is created by a servlet, which creates a connection pool and places it in application scope. That servlet is listed in Example 10-8.a.

Example 10-8.a   /WEB-INF/classes/SetupServlet.java

```java
import javax.servlet.ServletConfig;
import javax.servlet.ServletContext;
import javax.servlet.ServletException;
import javax.servlet.http.HttpServlet;
import beans.jdbc.DbConnectionPool;

public class SetupServlet extends HttpServlet {
   private DbConnectionPool pool;

   public void init(ServletConfig config) throws ServletException{
      super.init(config);

      ServletContext app = config.getServletContext();
      pool = new DbConnectionPool(
               config.getInitParameter("jdbcDriver"),
               config.getInitParameter("jdbcURL"),
               config.getInitParameter("jdbcUser"),
               config.getInitParameter("jdbcPwd"));

      app.setAttribute("db-connection-pool", pool);
   }
   public void destroy() {
      pool.shutdown();
      pool = null;
      super.destroy();
   }
}
```

The servlet listed in Example 10-8.a creates an instance of `DbConnectionPool` with four servlet initialization parameters: the JDBC driver name, the JDBC URL, and a name and a password. After the connection pool is created, it's stored in application scope under the name `db-connection-pool`.

The servlet's `destroy` method, which is invoked when the servlet is taken out of service, shuts down the pool, thereby closing all of the pool's open connections.

To ensure that the pool is stored in application scope before it's accessed, the servlet is loaded when the web application is started. That servlet loading is accomplished with a `load-on-startup` tag in the application's deployment descriptor. The pertinent sections of that descriptor are listed below.

```xml
   ...
   <web-app>
      <servlet>
         <servlet-name>setup</servlet-name>
         <servlet-class>SetupServlet</servlet-class>
```

```
    <init-param>
        <param-name>jdbcDriver</param-name>
        <param-value>COM.cloudscape.core.JDBCDriver</param-value>
    </init-param>

    <init-param>
        <param-name>jdbcURL</param-name>
        <param-value>
            jdbc:cloudscape:f:/databases/sunpress;create=false
        </param-value>
    </init-param>

    <init-param>
        <param-name>jdbcUser</param-name>
        <param-value>roymartin</param-value>
    </init-param>

    <init-param>
        <param-name>jdbcPassword</param-name>
        <param-value>royboy</param-value>
    </init-param>

    <load-on-startup/>
  </servlet>
  ...
</web-app>
```

The deployment descriptor listed above specifies the initialization parameters for the JDBC driver and URL, in addition to the `load-on-startup` directive.

Now that we've seen how the connection pool is used, let's see how it's implemented.

JSP Tip

Store Resource Pools in Application Scope

Resource pools, like the database connection pooled discussed in "Connection Pooling" on page 302, make recycled resources available to servlets, JSP pages, and custom tags. The best way to make those resources available is to store resource pools in application scope.

Implementing a Simple Connection Pool

Database connections are not the only resources appropriate for pooling. Substantial performance benefits can be obtained by pooling any resource that is expensive to initialize; for example, sockets or threads.

Because you may find it beneficial to pool resources other than database connections, the connection pool discussed here is implemented with a base class that can pool any type of object and an extension of that class specific to database connections. That base class is listed in Example 10-8.b.

Example 10-8.b   A Simple Resource Pool Base Class

```
package beans.util;

import java.util.Iterator;
import java.util.Vector;

public abstract class ResourcePool {
   protected final Vector availableResources = new Vector();
   protected final Vector inUseResources = new Vector();

   // Extensions must implement these three methods:
   public abstract Object  createResource()
                             throws ResourceException;
   public abstract boolean isResourceValid(Object resource);
   public abstract void    closeResource(Object resource);

   public Object getResource() throws ResourceException {
      Object resource = getFirstAvailableResource();

      if(resource == null) // no available resource
         resource = createResource();

      inUseResources.addElement(resource);
      return resource;
   }
   public void recycleResource(Object resource) {
      inUseResources.removeElement(resource);
      availableResources.addElement(resource);
   }
   public void shutdown() {
      closeResources(availableResources);
      closeResources(inUseResources);

      availableResources.clear();
      inUseResources.clear();
   }
   private Object getFirstAvailableResource() {
      Object resource = null;
```

```
   if(availableResources.size() > 0) {
      resource = availableResources.firstElement();
      availableResources.removeElementAt(0);
   }
   if(resource != null && !isResourceValid(resource))
      return getFirstAvailableResource(); // try again

   return resource;
   }
   private void closeResources(Vector resources) {
      Iterator it = resources.iterator();
      while(it.hasNext())
         closeResource(it.next());
   }
 }
```

The ResourcePool class is an abstract class that defines three abstract methods for subclasses to implement: createResource, isResourceValid, and closeResource. Those methods will vary depending upon the type of resource, so they are deferred to subclasses.

ResourcePool maintains two vectors, one for available resources and another for in-use resources. The latter is used to disconnect in-use resources when the pool is manually shut down with the shutdown method. The servlet listed in Example 10-8.a on page 304 calls that shutdown method.

The getResource and recycleResource methods retrieve an available resource from the pool and return a resource to the pool, respectively.

getResource tries to obtain a resource from the list of available resources by calling getFirstAvailableResource. If a resource is available, getFirstAvailableResource checks that resource's validity with the abstract isResourceValid method. Whether a resource is valid depends upon the type of resource; for example, database connections can time out if they're not used in a certain time period. If a resource is not valid, it's removed from the list of available resources, and getFirstAvailableResource calls itself recursively in search of a valid resource.

If there are no available resources, getResource creates one, adds it to the list of in-use resources, and returns it.

recycleResource makes a resource available by removing it from the list of in-use resources and adding it to the list of available resources.

That's how the ResourcePool class works; following are a few observations about that class. First, ResourcePool is thread safe because all of its class members are final, java.util.Vector is synchronized, and iterators are fail safe; the last means that an exception will be thrown if a vector is modified while an iterator iterates over it.

Second, the available resources and in-use resources are made available to ResourcePool subclasses. Among other things, this allows ResourcePool subclasses to allocate an initial cache of resources.

Third, createResource and getResource can throw a ResourceException if something goes wrong while a resource is being created. That exception is a simple extension of Exception, which is listed below.

```
package beans.util;

public class ResourceException extends Exception {
   public ResourceException(String s) {
      super(s);
   }
}
```

A More Capable Resource Pool

For the sake of illustration, the ResourcePool discussed in "Implementing a Simple Connection Pool" on page 305 is a very simple class that you can extend in many interesting ways, such as:

1. *Limiting the number of resources*, because a large number of open resources can degrade performance.

2. *Limiting the time spent waiting* for a recycled resource when the maximum resource limit has been reached—without that limit, a thread can wait indefinitely for a recycled resource.

3. *Creating resources in another thread* and waiting for either the new resource or a recycled one. Time is saved if a recycled resource becomes available before a new one is created.

A revised version of the ResourcePool class that implements the features listed above is listed in Example 10-8.c.

Example 10-8.c An Industrial-Strength Resource Pool Base Class

```
package beans.util;

import java.util.Iterator;
import java.util.Vector;

public abstract class ResourcePool implements Runnable {
   protected final Vector availableResources = new Vector(),
                              inUseResources = new Vector();
   private final int maxResources;
   private final boolean waitIfMaxedOut;
   private ResourceException error = null; // set by run()

   // Extensions must implement these three methods:
   public abstract Object  createResource ()
                        throws ResourceException;
   public abstract boolean isResourceValid(Object resource);
   public abstract void    closeResource  (Object resource);

   public ResourcePool() {
      this(10,     // by default, a max of 10 resources in pool
           false); // don't wait for resource if maxed out
   }
   public ResourcePool(int max, boolean waitIfMaxedOut) {
      this.maxResources = max;
      this.waitIfMaxedOut = waitIfMaxedOut;
   }
   public Object getResource() throws ResourceException {
      return getResource(0);
   }
   public synchronized Object getResource(long timeout)
                                    throws ResourceException {
      Object resource = getFirstAvailableResource();

      if(resource == null) { // no available resources
         if(countResources() < maxResources) {
            waitForAvailableResource();
            return getResource();
         }
         else { // maximum resource limit reached
            if(waitIfMaxedOut) {
               try {
                  wait(timeout);
```

```
                }
                catch(InterruptedException ex) {}
                return getResource();
            }
            throw new ResourceException("Maximum number " +
                "of resources reached. Try again later.");
        }
    }
    inUseResources.addElement(resource);
    return resource;
}
public synchronized void recycleResource(Object resource) {
    inUseResources.removeElement(resource);
    availableResources.addElement(resource);
    notifyAll(); // notify waiting threads of available con
}
public void shutdown() {
    closeResources(availableResources);
    closeResources(inUseResources);

    availableResources.clear();
    inUseResources.clear();
}
public synchronized void run() { // can't throw an exception!
    Object resource;
    error = null;
    try {
        resource = createResource(); // subclasses create
    }
    catch(ResourceException ex) {
        error = ex;   // store the exception
        notifyAll(); // waiting thread will throw an exception
        return;
    }
    availableResources.addElement(resource);
    notifyAll(); // notify waiting threads
}
private Object getFirstAvailableResource() {
    Object resource = null;

    if(availableResources.size() > 0) {
        resource = availableResources.firstElement();
        availableResources.removeElementAt(0);
    }
    if(resource != null && !isResourceValid(resource))
        resource = getFirstAvailableResource(); // try again
```

```
        return resource;
    }
    private void waitForAvailableResource()
                                    throws ResourceException {
        Thread thread = new Thread(this);
        thread.start(); // thread creates a resource: see run()

        try {
            wait(); // wait for new resource to be created
        }           // or for a resource to be recycled
        catch(InterruptedException ex) { }

        if(error != null) // exception caught in run()
            throw error;  // rethrow exception caught in run()
    }
    private void closeResources(Vector resources) {
        Iterator it = resources.iterator();
        while(it.hasNext())
            closeResource(it.next());
    }
    private int countResources() {
        return availableResources.size()+inUseResources.size();
    }
}
```

The differences between the ResourcePool class listed above and the one listed in Example 10-8.b on page 306 are mostly encapsulated in the getResource, waitForAvailableResource, and run methods.

If there are no available resources and the maximum resource limit has not been reached, getResource waits for an available resource; when one becomes available, getResource tries to get it by calling itself.

If the maximum resource limit has been reached and there are no available resources, getResource either waits for a resource to be recycled or throws an exception. The ResourcePool class provides a second getResource method that takes a timeout that represents the maximum time the resource pool will wait for a new resource when the pool is full. That timeout argument is an integer representing milliseconds.

The waitForResource method starts a thread that creates a new resource. That thread is constructed with a runnable, which happens to be the ResourcePool instance itself; so, when thread.start is invoked, the pool's run method is called.

The run method calls createResource, which is implemented by subclasses. That method may throw a ResourceException, but that exception can't be rethrown by run, because run is defined by the Runnable interface without a throws clause. Because run can't rethrow the exception, it stores it in a class member, notifies waiting threads that something has happened, and returns. One of the waiting threads will subsequently throw the exception from waitForAvailableResource.

Now that we have a resource pool base class, we can implement a database connection pool by extending it. Example 10-8.d lists that database connection pool class.

Example 10-8.d   /WEB-INF/classes/beans/jdbc/DbConnectionPool.java

```java
package beans.jdbc;

import java.sql.Connection;
import java.sql.DriverManager;
import java.sql.SQLException;

import beans.util.ResourcePool;
import beans.util.ResourceException;

public class DbConnectionPool extends ResourcePool {
   private final String driver, url, user, pwd;
   private final int initialConnections = 5;
   private boolean driverLoaded = false;

   public DbConnectionPool(String driver, String url) {
      this(driver, url, null, null);
   }
   public DbConnectionPool(String driver, String url,
                           String user, String pwd) {
      this.driver = driver;
      this.url    = url;
      this.user   = user;
      this.pwd    = pwd;

      try {
         for(int i=0; i < initialConnections; ++i)
            availableResources.addElement(createResource());
      }
      catch(Exception ex) {}
   }
   public Object createResource() throws ResourceException {
      Connection connection = null;
```

```
      try {
         if(!driverLoaded) {
            Class.forName(driver);
            driverLoaded = true;
         }
         if(user == null || pwd == null)
            connection = DriverManager.getConnection(url);
         else
            connection = DriverManager.getConnection(url, user,
                                                          pwd);
      }
      catch(Exception ex) {
         // ex is ClassNotFoundException or SQLException
         throw new ResourceException(ex.getMessage());
      }
      return connection;
   }
   public void closeResource(Object connection) {
      try {
         ((Connection)connection).close();
      }
      catch(SQLException ex) {
         // ignore exception
      }
   }
   public boolean isResourceValid(Object object) {
      Connection connection = (Connection)object;
      boolean valid = false;

      try {
         valid = ! connection.isClosed();
      }
      catch(SQLException ex) {
         valid = false;
      }
      return valid;
   }
}
```

DbConnectionPool instances are constructed with the name of a JDBC driver, a
JDBC URL, and an optional username and password. The DbConnectionPool
constructor preallocates five database connections.

DbConnectionPool implements the three abstract methods defined by its
superclass: createResource, isResourceValid, and closeResource.

createResource loads the JDBC driver if it hasn't been loaded previously and
creates a connection with one of two DriverManager.getConnection
methods, depending upon whether a username and password were supplied.

`DbConnectionPool.closeResource` closes a connection, and `isResourceValid` checks to see whether a connection is closed; if the connection is open and the call to `Connection.isClosed` does not throw an exception, the connection is valid.

Prepared Statements

Every time you execute a database query, that query's SQL statement is compiled and subsequently executed. For frequently used statements, it can be more efficient to precompile those statements. Precompiled statements, known as prepared statements, are compiled once and can be executed repeatedly without recompilation.

JDBC provides a `PreparedStatement` class that's an extension of `Statement`. You create instances of `PreparedStatement` with `Connection.prepareStatement`, like this:

```
String query = "SELECT * FROM Orders WHERE Amount > ?";
PreparedStatement pstate;

try {
   pstate = connection.prepareStatement(query);
}
catch(SQLException sqlEx) {
   // handle SQL exception
}
...
```

In a prepared statement, variables are specified with question marks; for example, in the preceding code fragment, *order amount* is a variable. Prepared statements can contain an unlimited[2] number of variables.

Once a prepared statement has been created, it can be executed just like a regular statement; for example, the prepared statement in the code fragment listed above can be executed like this:

```
...
pstate.setDouble(1, 100.00);

try {
   ResultSet result = pstate.executeQuery();
}
catch(SQLException sqlEx) {
   // handle SQL exception
}
```

2.   For all intents and purposes.

The PreparedStatement class has numerous setXXX methods for specifying variable values, where XXX specifies a type. Those methods have two arguments, one that specifies the position of the variable (starting with 1 for the first variable), and another that specifies the variable's value. For example, in the preceding code fragment, PreparedStatement.setDouble is used to set the first (and only) variable in the prepared statement to 100.00.

This section discusses two custom tags, one that creates a prepared statement and another that executes a prepared statement. Figure 10-2 shows two JSP pages that use those tags; the JSP page on the left creates a prepared statement that is executed by the JSP page on the right.

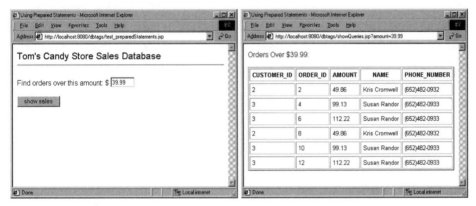

Figure 10-2 Using Prepared Statement Custom Tags

The JSP page shown on the left in Figure 10-2 is listed in Example 10-9.a.

Example 10-9.a /test_preparedStatements.jsp

```
<html><head><title>Using Prepared Statements</title>
   <%@ taglib uri='/WEB-INF/tlds/database.tld' prefix='database'%>
</head>
<font size='5'>Tom's Candy Store Sales Database
</font><hr>

<database:prepareStatement id='candyQuery' scope='application'>
   SELECT * FROM Orders JOIN Customers USING (Customer_ID)
   WHERE Amount > ?
</database:prepareStatement>

<font size='4'>

<form action='showPreparedStatementQuery.jsp'>
   Find orders over this amount: $
   <input type='text' name='amount' size='6'><p>
```

```
      <input type='submit' value='show sales'></p>
   </form>

   </font>
```

The JSP page listed in Example 10-9.a uses a `prepareStatement` tag to create a prepared statement. That tag has two attributes:

1. An identifier for the prepared statement.

2. The scope in which the prepared statement is stored.

The body of the `prepareStatement` tag is the prepared statement's SQL.

When the submit button is activated in the JSP page listed in Example 10-9.a, control is forwarded to `showPreparedStatementQuery.jsp`, which is listed in Example 10-9.b.

Example 10-9.b /showPreparedStatementQuery.jsp

```
<html><head><title>Using Prepared Statements</title>
   <%@ taglib uri='/WEB-INF/tlds/database.tld' prefix='database'%>
</head>
<body>

<% Double amount = new Double(request.getParameter("amount")); %>

<database:executePreparedStatement id='candyQuery' scope='session'
                  variables='<%= new Object[] {amount} %>'/>

<p><font size='4'>Orders Over $<%= amount %>:</font></p>

<table border='2' cellpadding='5'>
   <database:columnNames query='candyQuery' id='name'>
      <th><%= name %></th>
   </database:columnNames>

   <database:rows query='candyQuery'><tr>
      <tr>
         <database:columns query='candyQuery' id='value'>
         <td><%= value %></td>
         </database:columns>
      </tr>
   </database:rows>
</table>
</p>

<database:release query='candyQuery'/>
```

```
</body>
</html>
```

The JSP page listed in Example 10-9.b uses an `executeStatement` tag to execute the prepared statement created by the JSP page listed in Example 10-9.a. That tag has three attributes:

1. An identifier for the prepared statement.

2. The scope in which the *result of the query* is stored.

3. An array of objects, each of which is substituted for a question mark in the prepared statement.

After the prepared statement has been executed, the JSP page listed in Example 10-9.b uses the `columnNames`, `columns`, and `rows` tags to display the results of the query. See "Database Custom Tags" on page 287 for a discussion of those tags.

The tag handler for the `prepareStatement` tag is listed in Example 10-9.c.

Example 10-9.c /WEB-INF/classes/tags/jdbc/PrepareStatementTag.java

```
package tags.jdbc;

import java.sql.Connection;
import java.sql.PreparedStatement;
import java.sql.ResultSet;
import java.sql.SQLException;

import javax.servlet.jsp.JspException;
import javax.servlet.jsp.PageContext;
import javax.servlet.jsp.tagext.BodyTagSupport;

import beans.jdbc.DbConnectionPool;
import beans.util.ResourceException;

public class PrepareStatementTag extends BodyTagSupport {
   private String scope = "page";

   public void setScope(String scope) {
      this.scope = scope;
   }
   public int doAfterBody() throws JspException {
      DbConnectionPool pool = (DbConnectionPool)
                        pageContext.getServletContext().
                        getAttribute("db-connection-pool");
```

```
      Connection con;
      try {
         con = (Connection)pool.getResource();
      }
      catch(ResourceException ex) {
         throw new JspException(ex.getMessage());
      }
      PreparedStatement ps = prepareStatement(con);
      pageContext.setAttribute(id,ps,getConstantForScope(scope));

      return SKIP_BODY;
   }
   private PreparedStatement prepareStatement(Connection con)
                                         throws JspException {
      PreparedStatement pstate = null;
      try {
         pstate = con.prepareStatement(bodyContent.getString(),
                        ResultSet.TYPE_SCROLL_INSENSITIVE,
                        ResultSet.CONCUR_READ_ONLY);
      }
      catch(SQLException ex) {
         throw new JspException(ex.getMessage());
      }
      return pstate;
   }
   private int getConstantForScope(String scope) {
      int constant = PageContext.PAGE_SCOPE;

      if(scope.equalsIgnoreCase("page"))
         constant = PageContext.PAGE_SCOPE;
      else if(scope.equalsIgnoreCase("request"))
         constant = PageContext.REQUEST_SCOPE;
      else if(scope.equalsIgnoreCase("session"))
         constant = PageContext.SESSION_SCOPE;
      else if(scope.equalsIgnoreCase("application"))
         constant = PageContext.APPLICATION_SCOPE;

      return constant;
   }
}
```

The `prepareStatement.doAfterBody` method obtains a database connection from a connection pool; see "Connection Pooling" on page 302 for a discussion of that connection pool. That connection is used to create a prepared statement whose result sets are scrollable and cannot be updated.

After the prepared statement is created, it's stored in the scope specified by the tag's scope attribute under that tag's id. That prepared statement is subsequently accessed by the executePreparedStatement tag, whose tag handler is listed in Example 10-9.d.

Example 10-9.d /WEB-INF/classes/tags/jdbc/ExecutePreparedStatementTag.java

```
package tags.jdbc;

import java.sql.SQLException;
import java.sql.PreparedStatement;
import java.sql.ResultSet;

import javax.servlet.jsp.JspException;
import javax.servlet.jsp.tagext.TagSupport;

import beans.jdbc.Query;

public class ExecutePreparedStatementTag extends TagSupport {
   private Object[] variables = null;
   private String scope = "page";

   public void setScope(String scope) {
      this.scope = scope;
   }
   public void setVariables(Object[] variables) {
      this.variables = variables;
   }
   public int doEndTag() throws JspException {
      PreparedStatement ps = (PreparedStatement)
                              pageContext.findAttribute(id);
      if(ps == null) {
         throw new JspException("No prepared statement " + id);
      }
      try {
         setVariables(ps, variables);
         ResultSet rs = ps.executeQuery();

         Query query = new Query(ps, rs);
         Query.save(query, pageContext, id, scope);
      }
      catch(SQLException sqlex) {
         throw new JspException(sqlex.getMessage());
      }
      return EVAL_PAGE;
   }
   private void setVariables(PreparedStatement ps,
```

```
                              Object[] variables)
                              throws SQLException, JspException {
   for(int i=0; i < variables.length; ++i) {
      Object object = variables[i];

      if(object instanceof String) {
         ps.setString(i+1, (String)object);
      }
      if(object instanceof Integer) {
         int value = ((Integer)object).intValue();
         ps.setInt(i+1, value);
      }
      if(object instanceof Double) {
         double value = ((Double)object).doubleValue();
         ps.setDouble(i+1, value);
      }
      // Add more code here for other types of variables,
      // such as shorts, times, timestamps, etc. See
      // java.sql.PreparedStatement for valid types.
      else {
         throw new JspException("ExecuteStatementTag:" +
            "setVariables(): unkown parameter type");
      }
   }
  }
 }
```

The executePreparedStatement end tag obtains a reference to a prepared
statement with PageContext.findAttribute, using the tag's id. The
prepared statement's variables are specified with the values stored in the Object
array specified with the objects attribute. Subsequently, the prepared statement
is executed, and like the query tag discussed in "The Query Tag" on page 289, a
Query instance is stored in the scope specified by the tag's scope attribute. That
query can subsequently be accessed by the columnNames, columns, and rows
tags, as discussed in "Database Custom Tags" on page 287.

Transactions

A transaction is a group of SQL statements that must be executed atomically. If
one of the statements in a transaction fails, that transaction should be rolled back;
if all of the statements succeed, that transaction should be committed.

This section discusses a transaction tag that executes a group of SQL
statements as a transaction. Those statements can be specified in the body of the
tag, with statements separated by semicolons, like this:

```
<database:transaction>
     INSERT INTO Customers VALUES (100, 'Bill', '(882)863-4971');
     INSERT INTO Customers VALUES (101, 'Roy', '(882)863-4972');
     INSERT INTO Customers VALUES (102, 'Ron', '(882)863-4973')
</database:transaction>
```

Alternately, the `transaction` tag allows transactions to be specified in a file. In that case, the tag is used like this:

```
<database:transaction file='addCustomers.tx'/>
```

Example 10-10.a lists a JSP page that uses the `transaction` tag.

Example 10-10.a /test_transaction.jsp

```
<html><title>Database Example</title>
<head>
   <%@ taglib uri='/WEB-INF/tlds/database.tld' prefix='database'%>
</head>
<body>

<database:transaction file='addCustomers.tx'/>

<database:query id='addCustomers'>
   SELECT * FROM Customers
</database:query>

<table border='2' cellpadding='5'>
   <database:columnNames query='addCustomers' id='column_name'>
      <th><%= column_name %></th>
   </database:columnNames>

   <database:rows query='addCustomers'><tr>
   <tr><database:columns query='addCustomers' id='column_value'>
      <td><%= column_value %></td>
   </database:columns></tr>
   </database:rows>
</table>

</body>
</html>
```

The JSP page listed in Example 10-10.a uses the `transaction` tag to execute SQL statements stored in the file `addCustomers.tx`. Subsequently, the JSP page listed in Example 10-10.a displays the data contained in the `Customers` table with the `query`, `columnNames`, `columns`, and `rows` tags. See "Database Custom Tags" on page 287 for a discussion of those tags.

The tag handler for the `transaction` tag is listed in Example 10-10.b.

Example 10-10.b   /WEB-INF/classes/tags/jdbc/TransactionTag.java

```java
package tags.jdbc;

import java.sql.Connection;
import java.sql.Statement;
import java.sql.SQLException;

import java.io.BufferedReader;
import java.io.InputStreamReader;

import java.util.StringTokenizer;
import javax.servlet.jsp.JspException;
import javax.servlet.jsp.tagext.BodyTagSupport;

import beans.util.ResourceException;
import beans.jdbc.DbConnectionPool;

public class TransactionTag extends BodyTagSupport {
   private String file;

   public void setFile(String file) {
      this.file = file;
   }
   public int doAfterBody() throws JspException {
      Connection con = getConnection();
      String stmts = null;

      if(file != null) stmts = getStatementsFromFile();
      else             stmts = bodyContent.getString();

      try {
         executeTransaction(con, stmts);
      }
      catch(SQLException ex) {
         throw new JspException(ex.getMessage());
      }
      return SKIP_BODY;
   }
   private Connection getConnection() throws JspException {
      DbConnectionPool pool = (DbConnectionPool)
                         pageContext.getServletContext().
                         getAttribute("db-connection-pool");
      Connection con;
      try {
         con = (Connection)pool.getResource();
      }
      catch(ResourceException ex) {
```

```
          throw new JspException(ex.getMessage());
      }
      return con;
  }
  private String getStatementsFromFile() throws JspException {
      BufferedReader reader = new BufferedReader(
                             new InputStreamReader(
                                pageContext.getServletContext().
                                getResourceAsStream(file)));
      String stmts = "", line = null;

      try {
          while((line = reader.readLine()) != null) {
              stmts += line;
          }
      }
      catch(java.io.IOException ex) {
          throw new JspException(ex.getMessage());
      }
      return stmts;
  }
  private void executeTransaction(Connection con, String stmts)
                                         throws SQLException {
      boolean wasAutoCommit = con.getAutoCommit();

      try {
          StringTokenizer tok = new StringTokenizer(stmts, ";");

          con.setAutoCommit(false);

          while(tok.hasMoreElements()) {
              Statement stmt = con.createStatement();
              String query =(String)tok.nextElement();
              stmt.execute(query);
              stmt.close();
          }
      }
      catch(Exception ex) {
          con.rollback();
      }
      finally {
          con.commit();
      }
      con.setAutoCommit(wasAutoCommit);
  }
}
```

`TransactionTag.doAfterBody` gets a database connection from the connection pool discussed in "Connection Pooling" on page 302. If the `file` attribute was specified, the transaction's statements are read from that file; otherwise, those statements are read from the tag's body.

The `executeTransaction` method performs the following steps:

1. Store the connection's `autocommit` property.

2. Set the connection's `autocommit` property to `false`.

3. Execute each statement.

4. Roll back changes if an exception is thrown.

5. Commit changes if no exception is thrown.

6. Restore the connection's `autocommit` property.

Scrolling Through Result Sets

Sometimes it's desirable, usually for performance reasons, to let users scroll through the rows of a result set, instead of displaying them all at once.

This section illustrates scrolling through result sets by modifying the `Rows` tag listed in "The Rows Tag" on page 299, which iterates over the rows of a result set. That modification entails adding tag attributes for the start and end rows, which limits the tag's iteration. That modified tag is used in conjunction with a simple bean to scroll through a result set. Figure 10-3 shows an application that uses that tag.

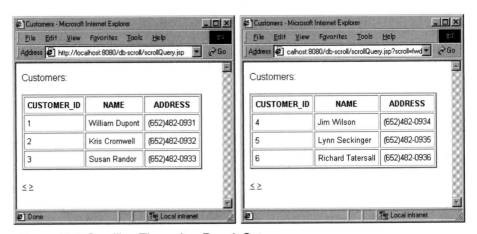

Figure 10-3 Scrolling Through a Result Set

The application shown in Figure 10-3 shows three rows of a result set at a time and provides links to the next and previous pages.

The query accessed by the JSP page shown in Figure 10-3 is created by the JSP page listed in Example 10-11.a.

Example 10-11.a /test_scroll.jsp

```
<html><title>Database Example</title>
<head>
   <%@ taglib uri='/WEB-INF/tlds/database.tld' prefix='database'%>
</head>
<body>

<database:query id='customers' scope='session'>
   SELECT * FROM Customers
</database:query>

<font size='4'>
   <a href='scrollQuery.jsp'>Show Customers</a><p>
</font>

</body>
</html>
```

The JSP page listed in Example 10-11.a uses the query tag discussed in "The Query Tag" on page 289 to execute a query and store the result of the query in session scope. That JSP page also provides a link to scrollQuery.jsp, which is listed in Example 10-11.b.

Example 10-11.b /scrollQuery.jsp

```
<html><title>Customers</title>
<head>
   <%@ taglib uri='/WEB-INF/tlds/database.tld' prefix='database'%>
</head>
<body>

<jsp:useBean id='scroller' class='beans.ScrollBean'
                         scope='session'>
  <jsp:setProperty name='scroller' property='position' value='1'/>
  <jsp:setProperty name='scroller' property='pageSize' value='3'/>
</jsp:useBean>

<% scroller.scroll(request.getParameter("scroll")); %>

<p><font size='4'>Customers:</font></p>
```

```
<table border='2' cellpadding='5'>
   <database:columnNames query='customers' id='name'>
      <th><%= name %></th>
   </database:columnNames>

   <database:rows query='customers'
              startRow='<%= scroller.getPosition() %>'
               endRow='<%= scroller.getEndPosition() %>'>
      <tr>
         <database:columns query='customers' id='value'>
            <td><%= value %></td>
         </database:columns>
      </tr>
   </database:rows>
</table>
</p>

<database:release query='customers'/>

<a href='scrollQuery.jsp?scroll=back'>&lt;</a>
<a href='scrollQuery.jsp?scroll=fwd'>&gt;</a>

</body>
</html>
```

The JSP page listed in Example 10-11.b uses the modified `rows` tag, specifying the start and end rows that the tag should display.

To track the start and end rows, the JSP page listed in Example 10-11.b uses an instance of `ScrollBean`, which keeps track of scroll position and page size. That bean has a `scroll` method that takes a string, which must be either "`fwd`" or "`back`". That `scroll` method adjusts the position, depending upon the page size and the direction in which we are scrolling—forward or back. The `ScrollBean` class is listed in Example 10-11.c.

Example 10-11.c /WEB-INF/classes/beans/util/ScrollBean.java

```
package beans.util;

public class ScrollBean {
   private int position, pageSize;

   public ScrollBean() {
      this(1, 4);
   }
   public ScrollBean(int start, int pageSize) {
      this.position = start;
```

```
         this.pageSize = pageSize;
      }
      public synchronized int scroll(String direction) {
         if("fwd".equalsIgnoreCase(direction)) {
            position += pageSize + 1;
         }
         else if("back".equalsIgnoreCase(direction)) {
            position -= pageSize;
            position = (position < 1) ? 1 : position;
         }
         else
            position = 1;

         return position;
      }
      public synchronized void setPosition(int position) {
         this.position = position;
      }
      public synchronized void setPageSize(int pageSize) {
         this.pageSize = pageSize;
      }
      public synchronized int getPosition() {
         return position;
      }
      public synchronized int getEndPosition() {
         return position + pageSize;
      }
   }
}
```

The rows tag handler is listed in Example 10-11.d.

Example 10-11.d   /WEB-INF/classes/tags/jdbc/RowsTag.java

```
package tags.jdbc;

import java.sql.ResultSet;
import java.sql.Statement;
import java.sql.SQLException;
import javax.servlet.jsp.JspException;
import javax.servlet.jsp.tagext.BodyTagSupport;
import tags.jdbc.beans.Query;

public class RowsTag extends BodyTagSupport {
   private static int UNASSIGNED=-1;

   private ResultSet rs;
   private boolean keepGoing;
   private String query;
```

```
   private int startRow = UNASSIGNED, endRow = UNASSIGNED;

   public void setQuery(String query) {
      this.query = query;
   }
   public void setStartRow(int startRow) {
      this.startRow = startRow;
   }
   public void setEndRow(int endRow) {
      this.endRow = endRow;
   }
   public int doStartTag() throws JspException {
      rs = Query.getResult(pageContext, query);

      try {
         if(startRow == UNASSIGNED) {
            keepGoing = rs.next(); // point to first row initially
         }
         else {
            if(startRow < 1)
               startRow = 1;

            keepGoing = rs.absolute(startRow);
         }
      }
      catch(Exception ex) {
         throw new JspException(ex.getMessage());
      }
      if(keepGoing) return EVAL_BODY_TAG;
      else          return SKIP_BODY;
   }
   public int doAfterBody() throws JspException {
      try {
         if(endRow == UNASSIGNED) {
            if(rs.isLast()) {
               rs.beforeFirst();
               writeBodyContent();
               return SKIP_BODY;
            }
         }
         else {
            if(rs.getRow() == endRow || rs.isLast()) {
               rs.beforeFirst();
               writeBodyContent();
               return SKIP_BODY;
            }
         }
         rs.next();
```

```
      }
      catch(java.sql.SQLException ex) {
         throw new JspException(ex.getMessage());
      }
      return EVAL_BODY_TAG;
   }
   public void writeBodyContent() throws JspException {
      try {
         bodyContent.writeOut(pageContext.getOut());
      }
      catch(Exception e) {
         throw new JspException(e.getMessage());
      }
   }
}
```

The tag handler for the rows tag listed above iterates over a specified subset of a result set's rows. That rows tag can specify a start and end row to delimit that subset.

Conclusion

This chapter has three themes:

- Basic database tags
- Resource and database connection pooling
- Specialized database tags

Although you may not use the database tags discussed in this chapter, the implementation of those tags illustrates how to use JDBC and how to implement JSP custom tags.

Sizable performance increases can be realized by pooling resources. This chapter has discussed ways to pool not only database connections, but resources in general. If you don't use the database connection pool discussed in this chapter, you may still find its implementation helpful for developing other types of resource pools.

XML

Topics in this Chapter

Chapter 11

Java and XML are the top contenders to power e-commerce in the early 21st century. Portable code and portable data, respectively, Java and XML are complemented by two synergistic technologies: JSP and XSLT. This chapter demonstrates all four technologies and shows how to use them together.

There are three fundamental ways to manipulate XML:

- Generate it from one or more data sources
- Parse it and create server-side objects or another XML document
- Transform it into other metalanguages, such as HTML or WML

Generating XML with JSP is easy because JSP template text[1] can be anything, including XML. This chapter begins by illustrating how to use JSP and beans to generate XML in "Generating XML" on page 333.

There are many ways to use JSP and XML together; for example, Figure 11-1 shows a Model 2 architecture that generates XML from information stored in a database. XSLT transforms that XML into a final document. That document could be HTML, JSP or another XML dialect such as WML (Wireless Meta-Language).

---

1. Template text is text in a JSP file that's not a JSP action, directive, expression or scriptlet. The term template is unrelated to JSP Templates, which are discussed in "Templates" on page 96.

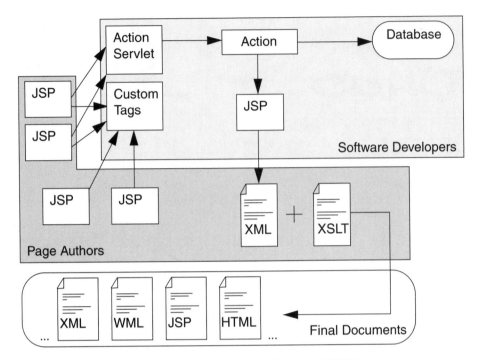

Figure 11-1 A JSP Model 2 Framework with XML and XSLT

Parsing XML to create server-side objects is typically done with an XML parser that uses the SAX (Simple API for XML) and DOM (Document Object Model) APIs. See "Parsing XML" on page 341 for more information about those APIs.

In addition to generating and parsing XML, it's common to transform XML into something else, perhaps a different XML dialect such as WML or another metalanguage such as HTML. The overwhelming choice for transforming XML is XSLT, which is a language specifically designed for XML transformations. In "Transforming XML" on page 374, we explore applying XSLT transformations at both compile time and runtime.

The code in this chapter was developed using the software listed below:

- Java Development Kit (JDK) 1.3
- Tomcat 3.2.1 Final
- Apache Xerces-Java version 1.2.2
- Apache Xalan-Java version 1.2.2

You'll find the JDK at `http://www.java.sun.com` and Tomcat from `http://jakarta.apache.org/tomcat/index.html`.

Xerces and Xalan are Apache's XML parser and XSLT processor, respectively; see `http://xml.apache.org/xalan/index.html` for more information about them.

Generating XML

Example 11-1 lists the simplest of JSP pages that produces XML, with a bare minimum of dynamic content.

Example 11-1 /date.jsp

```
<%@ page contentType='text/xml' %>

<?xml version="1.0" encoding="ISO-8859-1"?>
<document>
    <date>
        <%= new java.util.Date() %>
    </date>
</document>
```

The JSP page listed in Example 11-1 specifies `text/xml` as its content type, which you should always do for JSP pages that generate XML directly. Although JSP template text is usually HTML, it can be anything, including XML, as is the case for the JSP page listed in Example 11-1.

Figure 11-2 shows the XML generated by the JSP page listed in Example 11-1.

The date is the only dynamic content displayed by the JSP page listed in Example 11-1. As you can see from Figure 11-2, that date expression is evaluated and the resulting output is placed in the generated XML.

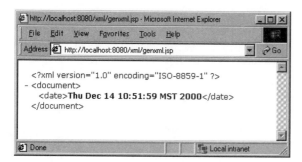

Figure 11-2 Generating XML with JSP

Generating XML with Beans

You can implement JSP pages that are mostly XML sprinkled with JSP scriptlets or custom tags that generate dynamic content, as illustrated in "Generating XML" on page 333. This section expands on that approach with a JSP page that generates dynamic content with beans. That JSP page is shown in Figure 11-3.

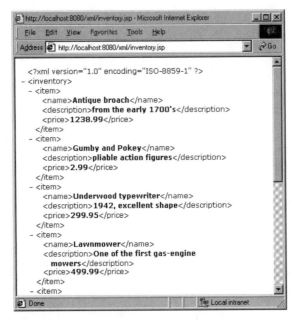

Figure 11-3 Generating XML using JSP and Java Beans

The JSP page shown in Figure 11-3 is listed in Example 11-2.a.

Example 11-2.a /inventory.jsp

```
<%@ page contentType='text/xml' %>
<%@ page import='beans.Inventory' %>
<%@ page import='beans.Item' %>

<jsp:useBean id='inventory' class='beans.Inventory' scope='page'/>

<% java.util.Iterator it = inventory.getItems();
   Item item = null;
%>
```

```
<?xml version="1.0" encoding="ISO-8859-1"?>
<inventory>
    <% while(it.hasNext()) { %>
        <% item = (Item)it.next(); %>
        <item>
            <name><%= item.getName() %></name>
            <description><%= item.getDescription() %></description>
            <price><%= item.getPrice() %></price>
        </item>
    <% } %>
</inventory>
```

The JSP page listed in Example 11-2.a iterates over items obtained from an inventory bean and generates XML as it sees fit for each item in the inventory. You should note that the JSP page listed in Example 11-2.a is responsible for the XML representation of an item. See "Beans That Generate Their Own XML" on page 337 to see how objects can generate their own XML.

The Inventory and Item classes referred to in Example 11-2.a are unremarkable. They are listed in Example 11-2.b and Example 11-2.c for completeness.

Example 11-2.b   /WEB-INF/classes/beans/Inventory.java

```java
package beans;

import java.util.Iterator;
import java.util.Vector;

public class Inventory implements java.io.Serializable {
    private Vector items = new Vector();

    public Inventory() {
        items.addElement(new Item("Antique broach",
                    "from the early 1700's",
                    (float)1238.99));

        // more items omitted for brevity

    }
    public Iterator getItems() {
        return items.iterator();
    }
}
```

Example 11-2.c /WEB-INF/classes/beans/Item.java

```
package beans;

public class Item implements java.io.Serializable {
   private String description, name;
   private float price;

   public Item(String name, String description, float price) {
       this.description = description;
       this.name = name;
       this.price = price;
   }
   public String getName()        { return name; }
   public float  getPrice()       { return price; }
   public String getDescription() { return description; }
}
```

As the examples in this section illustrate, it's easy to generate XML with JSP. But that's only half the battle because most of the time, you must postprocess XML generated by JSP files, instead of merely displaying that XML in a browser.

JSP Tip

Specify a Content Type of text/xml When Generating XML

JSP pages that generate XML should specify text/xml for their content type, even though it's not always necessary; for example, the JSP page listed in Example 11-1 on page 333 will display the same output—shown in Figure 11-2 on page 333—whether the content type is specified or not.

JSP pages that generate XML that is subsequently transformed into something other than XML should *not* specify text/xml for their content type; for example, consider the following code fragment:

```
<xslt:apply xsl='date.xsl'>
   <%@ include file='genXML.jsp' %>
</xslt:apply>
```

In the code fragment listed above, xslt:apply is a custom tag that applies an XSLT stylesheet to XML. That XML is generated by genXML.jsp, but genXML.jsp must not specify a content type of text/xml, because the stylesheet produces HTML.

Beans That Generate Their Own XML

Generating XML from a JSP page is straightforward, as illustrated in "Generating XML" on page 333. But as you can see from Example 11-2.a on page 334, JSP pages that generate XML tend to make liberal use of JSP expressions and scriptlets, which may violate your design sensibilities.[2]

As an alternative to directly generating XML in a JSP page, you can equip beans to generate their own XML representation. One pleasant feature of this simple design is that beans are responsible for their XML representation, not some unrelated JSP page; for example, consider the Inventory and Item beans listed below in Example 11-3.a and Example 11-3.b, respectively. Instead of a JSP page dictating an item's XML representation, as was the case in Example 11-2.a on page 334, the Inventory and Item classes listed below are responsible for their own XML representation.

Example 11-3.a /WEB-INF/classes/beans/Inventory.java

```
// The rest of this class is listed in Example 11-2.b on page 334
...
public class Inventory implements java.io.Serializable {
   ...
   public void printXml(PrintStream s) {
      s.println("<inventory>");

      Iterator it = getItems();
      while(it.hasNext()) {
         Item item = (Item)it.next();
         item.printXml(s, 1);
      }
      s.println("</inventory>");
   }
}
```

Example 11-3.b /WEB-INF/classes/beans/Item.java

```
// The rest of this class is listed in Example 11-2.c on page 334
...
public class Item implements java.io.Serializable {
   ...
   public void printXml(PrintStream s) {
      printXml(s, 2);
```

2. Custom tags can eliminate the need for scriptlets; see "The Importance of Custom Tags" on page 175.

```
  }
  public void printXml(PrintStream s, int indent) {
     doIndent(s,indent);      s.println("<item>");

     doIndent(s,indent, 2);      s.println("<name>");
     doIndent(s,indent, 3);      s.println(getName());
     doIndent(s,indent, 2);      s.println("</name>");

     doIndent(s,indent, 2);      s.println("<description>");
     doIndent(s,indent, 3);      s.println(getDescription());
     doIndent(s,indent, 2);      s.println("</description>");

     doIndent(s,indent, 2);      s.println("<price>");
     doIndent(s,indent, 3);      s.println(getPrice());
     doIndent(s,indent, 2);      s.println("</price>");

     doIndent(s,indent);      s.println("</item>");
  }
  private void doIndent(PrintStream s, int indent, int cnt) {
     for(int i=0; i < cnt; ++i) {
        doIndent(s,indent);
     }
  }
  private void doIndent(PrintStream s, int indent) {
     for(int i=0; i < indent; ++i) {
        s.print("   ");
     }
  }
}
```

Generating Beans from XML

There's a great deal of synergy between Java and XML that continually makes it easier to map XML to beans, and vice versa. At the time this book was written, Sun's project Adelard, which generates beans from XML, was on the verge of being released. Adelard was inspired by projects such as IBM's XML Productivity Kit for Java, which also generates beans from XML. You can read about Adelard and the XML Productivity Kit, respectively, at the following URLs:

- http://java.sun.com/xml/
- http://ww.alphaworks.ibm.com/tech/xmlproductivity

There are many ways to generate XML by using JSP. How you choose to generate XML will depend on many variables such as how your data is stored. If your data is stored in beans, you might want to implement JSP pages that generate XML from those beans. You might also want to consider modifying those beans to generate their own XML, which is a more reusable approach.

If your data is stored in XML to begin with, you might want to consider using software such as Adelard to generate beans from that XML. Those beans can subsequently be used by JSP pages to provide a view of that XML.

Postprocessing XML

You can process the output of a JSP page—whether that output is XML or not— in only one of two ways:[3]

- Use a custom tag to capture and process the desired output.
- Use a servlet filter to process the output (Servlet 2.3).

When this book was written, the Servlet 2.3 specification had not been finalized, so here we will stick to the custom tag solution. Example 11-4.a lists a JSP page that uses a custom tag to store the XML generated in Example 11-2.a on page 334 in a file.

Example 11-4.a /test.jsp

```
<%@ taglib uri='/WEB-INF/tlds/util.tld' prefix='util' %>

<jsp:useBean id='inventory' class='beans.Inventory' scope='page'/>

<% java.util.Iterator it = inventory.getItems();
   beans.Item item = null;
%>

<util:streamToFile file='f:/books/jsp/src/xml/inventory.xml'>
<?xml version="1.0" encoding="ISO-8859-1"?>
   <inventory>
      <% while(it.hasNext()) { %>
         <% item = (beans.Item)it.next(); %>
         <item>
            <name><%= item.getName() %></name>
            <description>
               <%= item.getDescription() %>
            </description>
```

---

3.   As of servlets 2.3 and JSP 1.2.

```
                <price><%= item.getPrice() %></price>
           </item>
        <% } %>
    </inventory>
</util:streamToFile>
```

The tag handler for `<util:streamToFile>` is listed in Example 11-4.b.

Example 11-4.b WEB-INF/classes/tags/util/StreamToFileTag.java

```java
package tags.util;

import java.io.File;
import java.io.FileWriter;
import javax.servlet.jsp.JspException;
import javax.servlet.jsp.tagext.BodyTagSupport;

public class StreamToFileTag extends BodyTagSupport {
   private String filename;

   public void setFile(String filename) {
      this.filename  = filename;
   }
   public int doAfterBody() throws JspException {
      try {
         FileWriter writer = new FileWriter(new File(filename));
         writer.write(bodyContent.getString().trim());
         writer.close();
      }
      catch(java.io.IOException e) {
         throw new JspException(e.getMessage());
      }
      return SKIP_BODY;
   }
}
```

Often, it's not apparent to JSP newcomers that JSP custom tags have a unique ability to capture the *evaluated* output of their body content.[4] That feature is evident in the tag handler listed in Example 11-4.b, which writes the tag's body content—*after that content has been evaluated*—to a file.

---

4. See "Body Content" on page 46 for more information about this feature.

The tag handler listed in Example 11-4.b writes its body content to a file to illustrate how to postprocess evaluated JSP. But there are other ways to postprocess JSP, such as applying XSLT transformations to XML generated by a JSP page. That topic is discussed in "Using XSLT in a Custom Tag to Produce HTML" on page 377.

Parsing XML

Now that we've seen how to produce XML, let's discuss how to consume it. Everything starts with parsing XML, and the parsing landscape is dominated by two APIs—SAX and DOM—that we will discuss in turn.

"Simple API for XML (SAX)" (see below) and "Document Object Model (DOM)" on page 354, respectively, discuss using SAX and DOM to parse XML.

Simple API for XML (SAX)

SAX is a de facto standard for parsing XML. SAX was developed by members of the XML-DEV mailing list, and the first version of SAX, known as SAX1, was released in May 1998.

SAX1 has subsequently been superseded by SAX2, which was released in May 2000. SAX2 is substantially different from SAX1, making the two incompatible. The SAX examples in this chapter conform to SAX2. See `http://www.megginson.com/SAX` for more information about SAX.

SAX is fast and cheap, because unlike the Document Object Model (DOM), SAX does not build an in-memory representation of an XML document. SAX is faster than DOM, because SAX does not incur the overhead of maintaining that in-memory representation.

SAX uses callbacks—methods that a SAX parser invokes on objects known as handlers—to notify handlers of things of interest, such as elements, attributes, or text. The SAX approach is similar to the delegation event model discussed in "Event Handling and Sensitive Form Resubmissions" on page 182.

SAX2 defines three types of handlers, represented by the following interfaces:[5]

- `org.xml.sax.ContentHandler`
- `org.xml.sax.DTDHandler`
- `org.xml.sax.ErrorHandler`

---

5. SAX2 also defines an `EntityReference` interface that is used like a handler for resolving external entities. That interface is beyond the scope of this book.

Using SAX is a five-step process:

1. Implement one or more handlers.

2. Create an XML reader (org.xml.sax.XMLReader).

3. Set handlers—created in step #1—for the reader created in step #2.

4. Create an input source (org.xml.sax.InputSource).

5. Call XMLReader.parse for the reader created in step #2, passing the input source created in step #4.

While parsing, the XML reader invokes methods on its handlers; for example, the ErrorHandler interface defines a warning method that's invoked by the reader when a SAX warning is generated.

Robust SAX applications often implement all handler interfaces, which would mean implementing 19 methods if it were not for the DefaultHandler class from org.xml.sax.helpers, which implements all three interfaces listed above with do-nothing methods that you can selectively override. Example 11-5.a lists a bean that encapsulates SAX parsing with Apache's Xerces SAX parser.

Example 11-5.a /WEB-INF/classes/beans/xml/sax/SAXParserBean.java

```java
package beans.xml.sax;

import java.io.FileReader;
import org.xml.sax.Attributes;
import java.io.IOException;
import java.util.Vector;
import org.xml.sax.Attributes;
import org.xml.sax.InputSource;
import org.xml.sax.SAXException;
import org.xml.sax.XMLReader;
import org.xml.sax.helpers.DefaultHandler;
import org.apache.xerces.parsers.SAXParser;

public class SAXParserBean extends DefaultHandler {
   private Vector vector = new Vector();
   private SAXElement currentElement = null;
   private String elementText;

   public Vector parse(String filename) throws SAXException,
                                                IOException {
      XMLReader xmlReader = new SAXParser();
      FileReader fileReader = new FileReader(filename);

      xmlReader.setContentHandler(this);
      xmlReader.parse(new InputSource(fileReader));
      return vector;
```

```
    }
    public void startElement(String uri, String localName,
                             String qName, Attributes attrs) {
       currentElement = new SAXElement(uri,localName,qName,attrs);
       vector.addElement(currentElement);
       elementText = new String();
    }
    public void characters(char[] chars, int start, int length) {
       if(currentElement != null && elementText != null) {
          String value = new String(chars, start, length);
          elementText += value;
       }
    }
    public void endElement(String uri, String localName,
                           String qName) {
       if(currentElement != null && elementText != null)
          currentElement.setValue(elementText.trim());

       currentElement = null;
    }
  }
```

Because SAXParserBean extends DefaultHandler, it implements all three SAX handler interfaces listed above. That takes care of step #1 listed above: Implement one or more handlers.

Like all SAX parsers, the Xerces parser used by SAXParserBean implements the XMLReader interface, so step #2 listed above—create an XML reader—is fulfilled by instantiation of a parser.

Steps #3, #4, and #5 listed above are implemented in Example 11-5.a by setting the parser's content handler and parsing the XML with an input source created from a file reader.

SAXParserBean overrides startElement, endElement, and characters, all of which are defined by the ContentHandler interface. In Example 11-5.a those three methods, which are called by Xerces for each element in the XML file, create a vector of beans that represent elements. Those beans are instances of SAXElement, which is listed in Example 11-5.b.

Example 11-5.b /WEB-INF/classes/beans/xml/sax/SAXElement.java

```
package beans.xml.sax;

import org.xml.sax.Attributes;

public class SAXElement {
   String namespace, localName, qualifiedName, value=null;
```

```
   Attributes attributes;

   public SAXElement(String namespace, String localName,
                     String qualifiedName, Attributes attributes){
      this.namespace     = namespace;
      this.localName     = localName;
      this.qualifiedName = qualifiedName;
      this.attributes    = attributes;
   }
   public void setValue(String value) {
      this.value = value;
   }
   public String getNamespace()     { return namespace; }
   public String getLocalName()     { return localName; }
   public String getQualifiedName() { return qualifiedName; }
   public String getValue()         { return value; }
   public Attributes getAttributes() { return attributes; }
}
```

Instances of the SAXElement class listed in Example 11-5.b are read-only objects that contain information about XML elements. That information comes from the ContentHandler.startElement method—see Example 11-5.a.

Figure 11-4 shows a JSP page that uses the bean listed in Example 11-5.a to parse an XML file representing a book inventory.

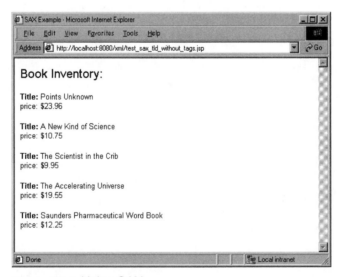

Figure 11-4 Using SAX

The XML file parsed by the application shown in Figure 11-4 is listed in Example 11-5.c.

Example 11-5.c   /bookInventory.xml

```xml
<?xml version="1.0" encoding="ISO-8859-1"?>

<inventory>
    <book>
        <ISBN>0393040009</ISBN>
        <title>Points Unknown</title>
        <price>$23.96</price>
    </book>
    <book>
        <ISBN>1579550088</ISBN>
        <title>A New Kind of Science</title>
        <price>$10.75</price>
    </book>
    <book>
        <ISBN>0416399760</ISBN>
        <title>The Accelerating Universe</title>
        <price>$19.55</price>
    </book>
</inventory>
```

The JSP page shown in Figure 11-4 is listed in Example 11-5.d.

Example 11-5.d   /test_sax.jsp

```jsp
<html><head><title>SAX Example</title>
    <%@ page import='java.util.Collection' %>
    <%@ page import='java.util.Iterator' %>
    <%@ page import='beans.xml.sax.SAXParserBean' %>
    <%@ page import='beans.xml.sax.SAXElement' %>
</head>
<body>

<jsp:useBean id='parser' class='beans.xml.sax.SAXParserBean'
                         scope='page' />

<% Collection elements = parser.parse(
                        "f:/books/jsp/src/xml/bookInventory.xml");
    Iterator it = elements.iterator();
%>
    <font size='5'>Book Inventory:</font><p>

<%  while(it.hasNext()) {
```

```
        SAXElement element = (SAXElement)it.next();
        String tagName = element.getLocalName();
        String showThis = null;

        if(tagName.equals("title")) {
            showThis = "<b>Title:</b> " +
                        element.getValue() + "<br/>";
        }
        else if(tagName.equals("price")) {
            showThis = "price: " + element.getValue() + "<p>";
        }
%>
        <%= showThis == null ? "" : showThis %>

<%  } %>
</p>
</body>
</html>
```

The JSP page listed in Example 11-5.d iterates over elements (`SAXElement`) that are created by the SAX parser bean (`SAXParserBean`). That page formats the data according to the XML tags it encounters. The local name represents the tag name, and tag values are obtained with `SAXElement.getValue`.

SAX Custom Tags

Three custom tags, used in Example 11-6, eradicate Java code from the JSP page listed in Example 11-5.d on page 345. The JSP page listed in Example 11-6 is functionally identical to the one listed in Example 11-5.d.

Example 11-6 /test_sax.jsp—Functionally Equivalent to Example 11-5.d

```
<html><head><title>SAX Example</title>
   <%@ taglib uri='/WEB-INF/tlds/sax.tld' prefix='sax' %>
   <%@ page import='beans.xml.sax.SAXElement' %>
</head>
<body>

<font size='5'>Book Inventory:</font><p>

<sax:iterateElements id='element'
              xmlFile='f:/books/jsp/src/xml/bookInventory.xml'>
   <sax:ifElementNameEquals element='<%= element %>'
                            names='title'>
     <b>Title:</b>  <%= element.getValue() %><br/>
   </sax:ifElementNameEquals>
```

```
      <sax:ifElementNameEquals element='<%= element %>'
                              names='price'>
         price: <%= element.getValue() %><p>
      </sax:ifElementNameEquals>
   </sax:iterateElements></p>
</body>
</html>
```

iterateElements uses the SAXParserBean listed in Example 11-5.a on page 342 to parse XML and iterate over elements, and ifElementNameEquals includes its body content depending upon the current element's name.

iterateElements creates a scripting variable for the current element. That variable's name is specified by the iterateElements tag's id attribute for the current element; so, in Example 11-7.b, each element from inventory.xml is available within the iterateElements tag as an element scripting variable.

The scripting variable generated by the iterateElements tag is passed to the ifElementNameEquals tag. That tag includes its body content if the name of an element matches one of the names specified with the names attribute.

Figure 11-5 shows a more complicated application that uses those tags to provide a view of a Tag Library Descriptor (TLD).

Figure 11-5 Using SAX with JSP Custom Tags

Example 11-7.a lists the TLD that is parsed by the JSP page shown in Figure 11-5.

Example 11-7.a   database.tld

```
<?xml version="1.0" encoding="ISO-8859-1" ?>
<!DOCTYPE taglib PUBLIC
   "-//Sun Microsystems, Inc.//DTD JSP Tag Library 1.1//EN"
   "http://java.sun.com/j2ee/dtds/web-jsptaglibrary_1_1.dtd">

<taglib>
   <tlibversion>1.0</tlibversion>
   <jspversion>1.1</jspversion>
   <shortname>
      Sun Microsystems Press Database Tag Library
   </shortname>
   <info>
      You can execute database queries and iterate over the
      results with the tags in this library. This library also
      includes tags for prepared statements and transactions.
   </info>
   <tag>
      <name>transaction</name>
      <tagclass>tags.jdbc.TransactionTag</tagclass>
      <bodycontent>tagdependent</bodycontent>
      <attribute>
         <name>file</name>
         <required>false</required>
         <rtexprvalue>true</rtexprvalue>
      </attribute>
   </tag>

   ... more tag definitions omitted for brevity ...

</taglib>
```

The JSP page shown in Figure 11-5 is listed in Example 11-7.b.

Example 11-7.b   /test_sax.jsp

```
<html><head><title>SAX Example</title>
   <%@ taglib uri='/WEB-INF/tlds/sax.tld' prefix='sax'%>
   <%@ page import='tags.util.IteratorTag' %>
   <% boolean inAttributes = false, bodyContentSpecified = false;
      String attributeData = null; %>
</head>
<body>

<%-- Display the tag lib's shortname and info --%>
```

```
<sax:iterateElements id='element'
              xmlFile='f:/books/jsp/src/xml/database.tld'>
   <sax:ifElementNameEquals element='<%=element%>'
                            names='shortname'>
      <font size='5'><%= element.getValue() %></font><p>
   </sax:ifElementNameEquals>

   <sax:ifElementNameEquals element='<%=element%>'
                            names='info'>
      <p><font size='4'><%= element.getValue() %></font></p>
   </sax:ifElementNameEquals>
</sax:iterateElements>


<%-- Display a table with the tag lib's name, tagclass,
     bodycontent, and attributes --%>
<table border='1' cellpadding='2'>
   <th>TagName</th>
   <th>Tag Class</th>
   <th>Body Content</th>
   <th>Attributes</th>

   <sax:iterateElements id='element'
              xmlFile='f:/books/jsp/src/xml/database.tld'>

      <% if( ! inAttributes) { %>
         <sax:ifElementNameEquals element='<%=element%>'
                                  names='name'>
         <tr><td><%= element.getValue() %></td>
         </sax:ifElementNameEquals>

         <sax:ifElementNameEquals element='<%=element%>'
                                  names='tagclass'>
         <td><%= element.getValue() %></td>
         </sax:ifElementNameEquals>

         <sax:ifElementNameEquals element='<%=element%>'
                                  names='bodycontent'>
         <td><%= element.getValue() %></td>
         <% bodyContentSpecified = true; %>
        </sax:ifElementNameEquals>

         <sax:ifElementNameEquals element='<%=element%>'
                                  names='attribute'>
         <% inAttributes = true;
            attributeData = new String();

            if( ! bodyContentSpecified) { %>
```

```
               <td>JSP</td>
           <% }
           bodyContentSpecified = false; %>
         </sax:ifElementNameEquals>
      <% }
      else {   // in attributes %>
         <sax:ifElementNameEquals element='<%=element%>'
                                  names='name'>
         <% attributeData += element.getValue() + " "; %>
         </sax:ifElementNameEquals>

         <sax:ifElementNameNotEquals element='<%=element%>'
                     names='attribute name required rtexprvalue'>
            <td><%= attributeData %></td>
            <% inAttributes = false; %>
         </sax:ifElementNameNotEquals>
   <%    } %>
   </sax:iterateElements>
   <td><%= attributeData %></td></tr>
</table></p>

</body>
</html>
```

The JSP page listed in Example 11-7.b iterates over the elements in
`database.tld` twice; once to process the `shortname` and `info` elements, and
again to build the HTML table. But that XML file (`database.tld`) is only parsed
once—see Example 11-7.c for details.

The body of the `iterateElements` tags in Example 11-7.b are essentially tag-
based switch statements that process the current element according to that
element's name; for example, a font size of 5 is used to display the value of the
`shortname` tag.

Example 11-7.c lists the tag handler for the `iterateElements` tag.

Example 11-7.c   /WEB-INF/classes/tags/xml/sax/SAXParserTag.java

```
package tags.xml.sax;

import java.util.Collection;
import java.util.Vector;
import javax.servlet.jsp.JspException;
import javax.servlet.jsp.PageContext;
import beans.xml.sax.SAXParserBean;
import tags.util.IteratorTag;
```

```
import org.xml.sax.SAXException;

public class SAXParserTag extends IteratorTag {
   private String xmlFile;

   public void setXmlFile(String xmlFile) {
      this.xmlFile = xmlFile;
   }
   public int doStartTag() throws JspException {
      setCollection(getCollection());
      return super.doStartTag();
   }
   public void release() {
      xmlFile = null;
   }
   private Collection getCollection() throws JspException {
      Collection collection = (Collection)
                              pageContext.getAttribute(
                                     xmlFile,
                                     PageContext.PAGE_SCOPE);
      if(collection == null) {
         try {
            SAXParserBean parserBean = new SAXParserBean();
            collection = parserBean.parse(xmlFile);
            setCollection(collection);
            pageContext.setAttribute(xmlFile,
                                 collection,
                                 PageContext.PAGE_SCOPE);
         }
         catch(java.io.IOException ex) {
               throw new JspException("IO Exception: " +
                                 ex.toString());
         }
         catch(SAXException ex) {
               throw new JspException("SAX Exception" +
                                 ex.toString());
         }
      }
      return collection;
   }
}
```

The tag handler—SAXParserTag—listed in Example 11-7.c extends
IteratorTag. That tag, which is discussed in "Iteration" on page 36, iterates
over a collection and creates two scripting variables: the current and next items in
the collection.

SAXParserTag uses the SAX parser bean discussed in "Simple API for XML (SAX)" on page 341 to parse the XML file. That bean's parse method returns a collection that contains all of the XML file's elements. That collection is subsequently set in SAXParserTag.doStartTag and iterated over by the IteratorTag superclass.

SAXParserTag only parses the specified XML file once per page. After that file is parsed, the resulting collection is stored in page scope. Subsequently, other iterateElements tags on the same page access that collection.

Scripting variables are defined by a tag info class, as discussed in "Scripting Variables" on page 41. The tag info class for the parse tag—SAXParserTagInfo—is listed in Example 11-7.d.

Example 11-7.d   /WEB-INF/classes/tags/xml/sax/SAXParserTagInfo.java

```
package tags.xml.sax;

import javax.servlet.jsp.tagext.TagData;
import javax.servlet.jsp.tagext.TagExtraInfo;
import javax.servlet.jsp.tagext.VariableInfo;
import beans.xml.sax.SAXElement;

public class SAXParserTagInfo extends TagExtraInfo {
   public VariableInfo[] getVariableInfo(TagData data) {
      return new VariableInfo[] {
         new VariableInfo(data.getId(),
                         "beans.xml.sax.SAXElement",
                         true, VariableInfo.NESTED),

         new VariableInfo("next", // scripting var's name
               "beans.xml.sax.SAXElement", // variable's type
               true, // whether variable is created
               VariableInfo.NESTED) // scope
      };
   }
}
```

SAXParserTagInfo defines the two scripting variables representing the current and next elements in a collection. The name of the scripting variable for the current element is specified with the iterateElements tag's mandatory id attribute.

The tag handler for `<sax:ifElementNameEquals>` is listed in Example 11-7.e.

Example 11-7.e   /WEB-INF/classes/tags/xml/sax/IfElementNameEqualsTag.java

```java
package tags.xml.sax;

import java.util.StringTokenizer;
import java.util.NoSuchElementException;
import javax.servlet.jsp.JspException;
import javax.servlet.jsp.tagext.TagSupport;
import beans.xml.sax.SAXElement;

public class IfElementNameEqualsTag extends TagSupport {
   private SAXElement element = null;
   private String names = null;

   public void setElement(SAXElement element) {
      this.element = element;
   }
   public void setNames(String names) {
      this.names = names;
   }
   public int doStartTag() throws JspException {
      StringTokenizer tok = new StringTokenizer(names);
      String nextName = null,
             elementName = element.getLocalName();
      boolean nameFound = false;

      try {
         while(!nameFound)
            nameFound = elementName.equals(tok.nextToken());
      }
      catch(NoSuchElementException ex) {
         // no more tokens
      }
      return nameFound ? EVAL_BODY_INCLUDE : SKIP_BODY;
   }
   public void release() {
      names = null;
      element = null;
   }
}
```

IfElementNameEqualsTag has two attributes: a SAX element—an instance of SAXElement—and a string representing one or more names separated by spaces. The tag includes its body only if one of those names matches the element's name.

The tag handler for <sax:ifElementNameNotEquals> is listed in Example 11-7.f.

Example 11-7.f /WEB-INF/classes/tags/.../IfElementNameNotEqualsTag.java

```
package tags.xml.sax;

import java.util.StringTokenizer;
import java.util.NoSuchElementException;
import javax.servlet.jsp.JspException;
import javax.servlet.jsp.tagext.TagSupport;
import beans.xml.sax.SAXElement;

public class IfElementNameNotEqualsTag extends
                                        IfElementNameEqualsTag {
   public int doStartTag() throws JspException {
      int rvalue = super.doStartTag();
      return rvalue == EVAL_BODY_INCLUDE ? SKIP_BODY :
                                        EVAL_BODY_INCLUDE;
   }
}
```

IfElementNameNotEquals extends IfElementNameEqualsTag and simply reverses its superclass's decision on what to return from doStartTag.

To recap, here's how all of the classes listed above work together: The iterateElements tag uses an instance of SAXParserBean to parse the elements in the specified XML file. That tag creates a scripting variable, which is an instance of SAXElement. That scripting variable is subsequently used by the ifElementNameEquals and ifElementNameNotEquals tags.

Document Object Model (DOM)

The Document Object Model is a language-neutral interface for accessing and updating documents. That interface represents a tree that you can access and modify. The Swing XML viewer shown in Figure 11-6 provides a visual representation of that tree.

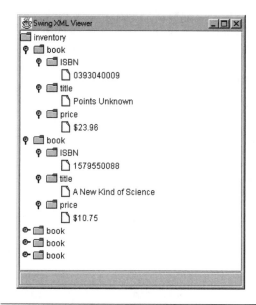

▭ element nodes ▯ text nodes

Figure 11-6 A DOM Tree

The DOM tree shown in Figure 11-6 corresponds to the following XML:

```
<?xml version="1.0" encoding="ISO-8859-1"?>
// See Example 11-5.c on page 345 for a complete listing
<inventory>
    <book>
        <ISBN>0393040009</ISBN>
        <title>Points Unknown</title>
        <price>$23.96</price>
    </book>
    <book>
        <ISBN>1579550088</ISBN>
        <title>A New Kind of Science</title>
        <price>$10.75</price>
    </book>
    ...

</inventory>
```

The Java application shown in Figure 11-6 uses a bean—DOMParserBean—to parse XML into a DOM tree. That bean, listed in Example 11-8.a, uses Apache's Xerces parser.[6]

Example 11-8.a   /WEB-INF/classes/beans/xml/dom/DOMParserBean.java

```java
package beans.xml.dom;

import java.io.IOException;
import java.io.FileInputStream;
import org.apache.xerces.parsers.DOMParser;
import org.xml.sax.InputSource;
import org.xml.sax.SAXException;
import org.w3c.dom.Document;

public class DOMParserBean {
    private DOMParserBean() {} // disallow instantiation

    public static Document getDocument(String file)
                                throws SAXException, IOException {
        DOMParser parser = new DOMParser();
        parser.parse(new InputSource(new FileInputStream(file)));
        return parser.getDocument();
    }
}
```

DOMParserBean.getDocument encapsulates parser-dependent code that takes a filename and produces a DOM document. That method is static because it's purely a utility method. The DOMParserBean class exists solely as a place to house the getDocument method, so DOMParserBean instances don't make sense;[7] that's why a private constructor disallows instantiation.

Once you have a document, such as the one returned from DOMParserBean.getDocument, you can access and modify any part of that document. After you're finished, you could walk that document and generate XML. The application shown in Figure 11-7 does just that with two JSP pages that allow you to change prices from the book inventory XML shown in Figure 11-6 on page 355.

---

6.   The Java application shown in Figure 11-6 is not discussed further in this book, but you can download it from this book's web site; see
     http://www.phptr.com/advjsp.
7.   Because you can't instantiate instances, DOMParserBean is not a true bean.

The application shown in Figure 11-7 illustrates three algorithms that most DOM applications implement:

- Parse XML into a (DOM) document
- Modify an existing document
- Generate XML from an existing document

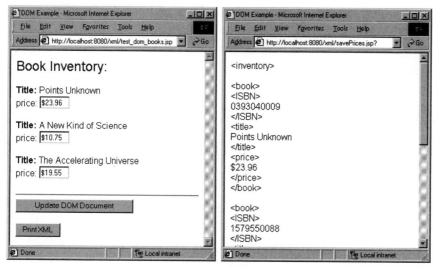

Figure 11-7 Accessing and Modifying XML Documents

The JSP page shown on the left in Figure 11-7 parses the book inventory XML and stores the resulting document in application scope. If a user activates the Update DOM Document button, the prices entered in the form are copied to the appropriate nodes in the document.

If a user activates the Print XML button, control is forwarded to the JSP page on the right. That page reads the book inventory from the document in application scope and displays it in XML. That JSP page could just as easily update the original book inventory XML file.

Example 11-8.b lists the JSP page shown on the left in Figure 11-7.

Example 11-8.b /test_dom_books.jsp

```
<html><head><title>DOM Example</title>
    <%@ taglib uri='/WEB-INF/tlds/dom.tld' prefix='dom'%>
    <%@ page import='org.w3c.dom.Document' %>
    <%@ page import='org.w3c.dom.Node' %>
    <%@ page import='org.w3c.dom.NodeList' %>
```

```jsp
   <%@ page import='beans.xml.dom.DOMParserBean' %>
   <%@ page import='javax.servlet.http.HttpServletRequest' %>
   <%@ page import='java.util.Enumeration' %>
</head>
<body>

<% Document document = (Document)application.getAttribute(
                                             "document");

   if(document == null) {
      document = DOMParserBean.getDocument(
                "f:/books/jsp/src/xml/bookInventory.xml");

      application.setAttribute("document", document);
   }
   updatePrices(document, request);
   showDocument(document, out);
   addButtons(out);
%>

<%! private void updatePrices(Node node,
                              HttpServletRequest request)
                              throws JspException {
      NodeList list = node.getChildNodes();
      int childCnt = list.getLength();

      if(childCnt > 0) {
         String lastTitle = null;

         for(int i=0; i < childCnt; ++i) {
            Node next = list.item(i);
            String value = next.getNodeValue();

            if(next.getNodeType() == Node.ELEMENT_NODE) {
               String nodeName = next.getNodeName();
               String text = getElementText(next);

               if(text != null) {
                  if(nodeName.equals("title")) {
                     lastTitle = text;
                   }
                   else if(nodeName.equals("price")) {
                      String pval = getParameterValue(request,
                                                   lastTitle);
                      if(pval != null && !pval.equals(text))
                         setElementText(next, pval);
                  }
               }
                 updatePrices(next, request);
```

```java
            }
        }
    }
}
private void showDocument(Node node, JspWriter out)
                                        throws JspException {
    NodeList list = node.getChildNodes();
    int childCnt = list.getLength();

    if(childCnt > 0) {
        String lastTitle = null;

        for(int i=0; i < childCnt; ++i) {
            Node next = list.item(i);
            try {
                String value = next.getNodeValue();

                if(next.getNodeType() == Node.ELEMENT_NODE) {
                    String nodeName = next.getNodeName();
                    String text = getElementText(next);

                    if(text != null) {
                        if(nodeName.equals("inventory")) {
                            out.print("<font size='5'>Book " +
                                    "Inventory:</font><form>");
                        }
                        else if(nodeName.equals("title")) {
                            lastTitle = text;
                            out.print("</p><b>Title: </b>" + text +
                                    "<br/>");
                        }
                        else if(nodeName.equals("price")) {
                            out.print("price: " +
                            "<input type='text' size='6' name='" +
                            lastTitle + "' value='" + text+ "'/><p>");
                        }
                    }
                }
            }
            catch(java.io.IOException ex) {
                throw new JspException(ex.getMessage());
            }
            showDocument(next, out);
        }
    }
}
private void addButtons(JspWriter out) throws JspException {
    try {
```

```
            out.print("<hr><input type='submit' " +
                        "value='Update DOM Document'/></form><p>");

            out.print("<form action='printXML.jsp'>");
            out.print("<input type='submit' value='Print XML'" +
                        "/></form></p>");
        }
        catch(java.io.IOException ex) {
            throw new JspException(ex.getMessage());
        }
    }
    private String getParameterValue(HttpServletRequest request,
                                            String param) {
        Enumeration parameterNames = request.getParameterNames();

        while(parameterNames.hasMoreElements()) {
            String next = (String)parameterNames.nextElement();

            if(next.equals(param))
                return request.getParameterValues(next)[0];
        }
        return null;
    }
    private String getElementText(Node element) {
        Node child = element.getFirstChild();
        String text = null;

        if(child != null)
            text = child.getNodeValue();

        return text;
    }
    private void setElementText(Node element, String text) {
        Node child = element.getFirstChild();

        if(child != null)
            child.setNodeValue(text);
    }
%>
</body>
</html>
```

The JSP page listed in Example 11-8.b contains a short scriptlet followed by a long declaration containing five methods. Three of those methods are called by that scriptlet. That scriptlet listing is repeated below for convenience.

```
<% Document document = (Document)application.getAttribute(
                                    "document");
    if(document == null) {
       document = DOMParserBean.getDocument(
                    "f:/books/jsp/src/xml/bookInventory.xml");

       application.setAttribute("document", document);
    }
    updatePrices(document, request);
    showDocument(document, out);
    addButtons(out);
%>
```

The preceding scriptlet checks to see whether a document exists in application scope; if not, the book inventory XML is parsed and the resulting document is stored in application scope. Then updatePrices, showDocument, and addButtons are invoked, in that order.

updatePrices and showDocument are recursive methods that walk the DOM tree. updatePrices copies requested parameters that represent book prices to appropriate nodes in the document, and showDocument prints XML to the browser. Both methods are passed a reference to a DOM node and are structured as listed in Example 11-8.c.

Example 11-8.c Walking the DOM Tree

```
// Both showDocument() and updatePrices() in Example 11-8.b use
// this algorithm to walk the nodes of a DOM tree.

NodeList list = node.getChildNodes();
int childCnt = list.getLength();

if(childCnt > 0) {
    ...
    for(int i=0; i < childCnt; ++i) {
       Node next = list.item(i);
       ...
       // do something with next
       ...
       // updatePrices(node) or showDocument(node, out)
       // is called here recursively
    }
    ...
}
```

Both `updatePrices` and `showDocument` obtain a list of child nodes from the node they are passed, and `updatePrices` or `showDocument` is called recursively for each child. In this manner, those methods walk the entire DOM tree.

`addButtons`, the last method called by the scriptlet, is a simple method that generates HTML for the two buttons shown in Figure 11-7 on page 357.

If a user activates the Print XML button in the application shown in Figure 11-7, control is forwarded to `printXML.jsp`, which is listed in Example 11-8.d.

Example 11-8.d /printXML.jsp

```
<html><head><title>DOM Example</title>
    <%@ taglib uri='/WEB-INF/tlds/dom.tld' prefix='dom'%>
    <%@ page import='org.w3c.dom.Document' %>
    <%@ page import='org.w3c.dom.Node' %>
    <%@ page import='org.w3c.dom.NodeList' %>
    <%@ page import='javax.servlet.jsp.JspWriter' %>
    <%@ page import='javax.servlet.http.HttpServletRequest' %>
    <%@ page import='java.util.Enumeration' %>
</head>
<body>

<% printXML((Document)application.getAttribute("document"),out);
%>

<%! private void printXML(Node node, JspWriter out)
                                        throws JspException {
        NodeList list = node.getChildNodes();
        int childCnt = list.getLength();

        for(int i=0; i < childCnt; ++i) {
          Node next = list.item(i);

          if(next.getNodeType() == Node.ELEMENT_NODE) {
             String name = next.getNodeName();
             try {
                out.print("&lt;" + name + "&gt;<br/>");
                if(name.equals("inventory"))
                   out.print("<br/>");
             }
             catch(Exception ex) {}
          }
        }
```

```
        String value = getElementText(next);

        if(value != null && value.charAt(0) != '\n') {
            try {
                out.print(value + "<br/>");
            }
            catch(Exception ex) {}
        }

        printXML(next, out);

        if(next.getNodeType() == Node.ELEMENT_NODE) {
            String name = next.getNodeName();
            try {
                out.print("&lt;" + "/" + name + "&gt;<br/>");

                if(name.equals("book"))
                    out.print("<br/>");
            }
            catch(Exception ex) {}
        }
    }
}
private String getElementText(Node element) {
    Node child = element.getFirstChild();
    String text = null;

    if(child != null)
        text = child.getNodeValue();

    return text;
}
%>
```

Like showDocument and updatePrices, printXML listed in Example 11-8.d is a recursive method that walks a document tree. That method prints start elements while recursing down the tree and prints end elements while recursing back up the call stack.

Most of the time, it's best to keep JSP pages free from scriptlets and declarations, as discussed in "Design" on page 132. The examples discussed in this section are the antithesis of that ideal to emphasize the basics of using DOM. "DOM Custom Tags" discusses a set of custom tags that encapsulates all of that code, allowing page authors easy access to DOM documents.

DOM Custom Tags

The svelte JSP page listed in Example 11-9.a is functionally identical to the monolith listed in Example 11-8.b on page 357. The output of both of those pages is identical to the left picture shown in Figure 11-7 on page 357.

Example 11-9.a   test_dom_books_with_tags.jsp

```
<html><head><title>DOM Custom Tags Example</title>
   <%@ taglib uri='/WEB-INF/tlds/dom.tld' prefix='dom'%>
   <%@ taglib uri='/WEB-INF/tlds/app.tld' prefix='app'%>
</head>
<body>

<dom:parse id='document'
      xmlFile='f:/books/jsp/src/xml/bookInventory.xml'/>

<app:updatePrices/>

<font size='5'>Book Inventory:</font>
<form>
  <dom:iterate node='<%= document %>' id='book'>
    <dom:ifNodeNameEquals node='<%= book %>' names='book'>
      <% String lastTitle = null; %>

      <dom:iterate node='<%= book %>' id='bookElement'>
        <dom:ifNodeIsElement node='<%= bookElement %>'>
          <dom:elementValue id='value'
                            element='<%= bookElement %>'/>

        <dom:ifNodeNameEquals node='<%= bookElement %>'
                              names='title'>
          <% lastTitle = value; %>
          </p><b>Title:</b> <%= value %><br/>
        </dom:ifNodeNameEquals>

        <dom:ifNodeNameEquals node='<%= bookElement %>'
                              names='price'>
          price: 
          <input type='text' size='5' value='<%= value %>'
          name='<%= lastTitle %>'/>
        </dom:ifNodeNameEquals>

      </dom:ifNodeIsElement>
    </dom:iterate>
  </dom:ifNodeNameEquals>
</dom:iterate>
```

```
    <p><hr><input type='submit' value='Update DOM Document'/></p>
</form>

<form action='printXML.jsp'>
   <input type='submit' value='Print XML'/>
</form>

</body>
</html>
```

The differences between the JSP page listed in Example 11-8.b on page 357 and the
page listed in Example 11-9.a are due solely to six custom tags. Those tags are
listed in Table 11-1.

Table 11-1 DOM Custom Tags used in Example 11-9.a on page 364

Tag Name	Description	Attributes
`<dom:parse>`	Parses an `xmlFile` and stores the resulting document in a scripting variable	`id xmlFile` `force`
`<dom:iterate>`	Iterates over the children of a `node` and makes children available in a scripting variable	`node id`
`<dom:ifNodeNameEquals>`	Includes body content if the `node`'s name equals one of the `names` specified	`node names`
`<dom:ifNodeIsElement>`	Includes body content if the `node` is an element	`node`
`<dom:elementValue>`	Stores an `element`'s value in a scripting variable	`id element`
`<app:updatePrices>`	Copies request parameters representing prices to the document created by `<dom:parse>`	

Each of the tag handlers for the custom tags listed in Table 11-1 is discussed in this
section. Example 11-9.b lists the tag handler for the `parse` tag.

Example 11-9.b /WEB-INF/classes/tags/xml/dom/DOMParserTag.java

```
package tags.xml.dom;

import javax.servlet.jsp.PageContext;
import javax.servlet.jsp.JspException;
import javax.servlet.jsp.tagext.TagSupport;
import org.w3c.dom.Document;
import beans.xml.dom.DOMParserBean;
```

```java
public class DOMParserTag extends TagSupport {
   private String xmlFile;
   private boolean force = false;

   public void setXmlFile(String xmlFile) {
      this.xmlFile = xmlFile;
   }
   public void setId(String id) {
      this.id = id;
   }
   public void setForce(boolean force) {
      this.force = force;
   }
   public int doStartTag() throws JspException {
      Document document = (Document)pageContext.
                          getServletContext().getAttribute(id);

      if(document == null || force)
         parse();

      return SKIP_BODY;
   }
   private void parse() throws JspException {
      try {
         pageContext.setAttribute(id,
                     DOMParserBean.getDocument(xmlFile),
                     PageContext.APPLICATION_SCOPE);
      }
      catch(Exception ex) {
         throw new JspException(ex.getMessage());
      }
   }
   public void release() {
      xmlFile = null;
      force = false;
   }
}
```

By default, the parse tag only parses the specified XML once. The resulting DOM document is placed in application scope and made available as a scripting variable for other tags to access. You can force the parse tag to parse the XML again by specifying true for the tag's force attribute, which is false by default.

The parse tag calls the static DOMParserBean.getDocument to do the actual parsing. That method, which encapsulates nonportable code, is discussed in "Document Object Model (DOM)" on page 354.

The tag info class for the parse tag defines the scripting variable for the DOM document. That class is listed in Example 11-9.c.

Example 11-9.c /WEB-INF/classes/tags/xml/dom/DOMParserTagInfo.java

```
package tags.xml.dom;

import javax.servlet.jsp.tagext.TagData;
import javax.servlet.jsp.tagext.TagExtraInfo;
import javax.servlet.jsp.tagext.VariableInfo;

public class DOMParserTagInfo extends TagExtraInfo {
    public VariableInfo[] getVariableInfo(TagData data) {
        return new VariableInfo[] {
            new VariableInfo(data.getId(),
                             "org.w3c.dom.Document",
                             true, VariableInfo.AT_END)
        };
    }
}
```

The document scripting variable is stored under the name assigned to the parse tag's id attribute.

The document created by the parse tag is modified by the updatePrices tag in Example 11-9.a on page 364. updatePrices is an application-specific tag that changes prices in the document to match request parameters that represent those prices. The tag handler for the updatePrices tag is listed in Example 11-9.d.

Example 11-9.d /WEB-INF/classes/tags/app/UpdatePricesTag.java

```
package tags.app;

import java.util.Enumeration;
import javax.servlet.ServletRequest;
import javax.servlet.jsp.JspException;
import javax.servlet.jsp.PageContext;
import javax.servlet.jsp.tagext.TagSupport;
import org.w3c.dom.Document;
import org.w3c.dom.Node;
import org.w3c.dom.NodeList;

public class UpdatePricesTag extends TagSupport {
```

```java
public int doEndTag() throws JspException {
    Document document = (Document)pageContext.getAttribute(
                            "document",
                            PageContext.APPLICATION_SCOPE);
    if(document != null)
        updatePrices(document);

    return EVAL_PAGE;
}
private void updatePrices(Node node) throws JspException {
    ServletRequest request = pageContext.getRequest();
    NodeList list = node.getChildNodes();
    int childCnt = list.getLength();

    if(childCnt > 0) {
        String lastTitle = null;

        for(int i=0; i < childCnt; ++i) {
            Node next = list.item(i);
            String value = next.getNodeValue();

            if(next.getNodeType() == Node.ELEMENT_NODE) {
                String nodeName = next.getNodeName();
                String text = getElementText(next);

                if(text != null) {
                    if(nodeName.equals("title")) {
                        lastTitle = text;
                    }
                    else if(nodeName.equals("price")) {
                        String pval = getParameterValue(request,
                                                        lastTitle);
                        if(pval != null && !pval.equals(text))
                            setElementText(next, pval);
                    }
                }
                updatePrices(next);
            }
        }
    }
}
private String getParameterValue(ServletRequest request,
                                 String param) {
    Enumeration parameterNames = request.getParameterNames();

    while(parameterNames.hasMoreElements()) {
        String next = (String)parameterNames.nextElement();
```

```
        if(next.equals(param))
            return request.getParameterValues(next)[0];
    }
    return null;
}
private String getElementText(Node element) {
    Node child = element.getFirstChild();
    String text = null;

    if(child != null)
        text = child.getNodeValue();

    return text;
}
private void setElementText(Node element, String text) {
    Node child = element.getFirstChild();

    if(child != null)
        child.setNodeValue(text);
}
}
```

In the preceding code, `updatePrices.doEndTag` looks for a document in application scope. If that document is found, it's passed to `updatePrices`, which recursively walks the document as listed in Example 11-8.c on page 361.

For every `price` element found in the document, `updatePrices` checks for a request parameter stored under the associated book's title. If that request parameter is found, the corresponding element in the document is updated with that parameter's value.

After parsing the XML file and updating prices, the JSP page listed in Example 11-8.c iterates over the child nodes of the document, using the `iterate` tag. The tag handler for that tag is listed in Example 11-9.e.

Example 11-9.e /WEB-INF/classes/tags/xml/dom/NodeIteratorTag.java

```
package tags.xml.dom;

import java.util.Collection;
import java.util.Vector;
import javax.servlet.jsp.JspException;
import org.w3c.dom.Document;
import org.w3c.dom.Node;
import org.w3c.dom.NodeList;

public class NodeIteratorTag extends tags.util.IteratorTag {
```

```
   private Node node;

   public void setNode(Node node) {
      this.node = node;
   }
   public int doStartTag() throws JspException {
      Node parent = node;

      if(node instanceof Document)
         parent = ((Document)node).getDocumentElement();

      setCollection(collection(parent.getChildNodes()));
      return super.doStartTag();
   }
   public void release() {
      node = null;
   }
   private Collection collection(NodeList list) {
      Vector vector = new Vector();
      int length = list.getLength();

      for(int i=0; i < length; ++i) {
         vector.addElement(list.item(i));
      }
      return vector;
   }
}
```

The tag handler listed in Example 11-9.e extends `tags.util.IteratorTag`, which is discussed in "Iteration" on page 36. That tag iterates over a collection and creates a scripting variable for the current item in the collection.

Other tag handlers that iterate over a collection, like `NodeIteratorTag` listed in Example 11-9.e, can extend `IteratorTag` by overriding `doStartTag` and calling `IteratorTag.setCollection` before returning `super.doStartTag`.

`NodeIteratorTag` iterates over DOM nodes. Those nodes are children of the node specified with the `node` attribute. If that parent node is a document, the parent is reset to the node returned from `Document.getDocumentElement`. That method returns the root element of the document.

The scripting variable created by `NodeIteratorTag` is defined by `NodeIteratorTagInfo`, which is listed in Example 11-9.f. The name of that scripting variable is defined by the `iterate` tag's mandatory `id` attribute.

Example 11-9.f /WEB-INF/classes/tags/xml/dom/NodeIteratorTagInfo.java

```
package tags.xml.dom;

import javax.servlet.jsp.tagext.TagData;
import javax.servlet.jsp.tagext.TagExtraInfo;
import javax.servlet.jsp.tagext.VariableInfo;

public class NodeIteratorTagInfo extends TagExtraInfo {
   public VariableInfo[] getVariableInfo(TagData data) {
      return new VariableInfo[] {
         new VariableInfo(data.getId(),
                          "org.w3c.dom.Node",
                          true, VariableInfo.NESTED)
      };
   }
}
```

The JSP page listed in Example 11-9.a on page 364 uses three utility tags:
ifNodeNameEquals, ifNodeIsElement, and elementValue. The first two
tags conditionally include their body content, depending upon a node's name or
whether that node is an element. The elementValue tag creates a scripting
variable with a specified element's value.

The tag handler for the ifNodeNameEquals tag is listed in Example 11-9.g.

Example 11-9.g /WEB-INF/classes/tags/xml/dom/IfNodeNameEqualsTag.java

```
package tags.xml.dom;

import java.util.StringTokenizer;
import java.util.NoSuchElementException;
import javax.servlet.jsp.JspException;
import javax.servlet.jsp.tagext.TagSupport;
import org.w3c.dom.Node;

public class IfNodeNameEqualsTag extends TagSupport {
   private Node node = null;
   private String names = null;

   public void setNode(Node node)      { this.node = node; }
   public void setNames(String names) { this.names = names; }

   public int doStartTag() throws JspException {
      StringTokenizer tok = new StringTokenizer(names);
      String nextName = null, nodeName = node.getNodeName();
      boolean nameFound = false;
```

```
        try {
           while(!nameFound)
              nameFound = nodeName.equals(tok.nextToken());
        }
        catch(NoSuchElementException ex) {
           // no more tokens
        }
        return nameFound ? EVAL_BODY_INCLUDE : SKIP_BODY;
     }
     public void release() {
        names = null;
        node = null;
     }
  }
```

The tag handler listed in Example 11-9.g compares a DOM node's name to a list of space-separated names. If the node's name matches one of the names in the list, that tag's body content is included; otherwise that body content is skipped.

The tag handler for the `ifNodeIsElement` tag includes its body content if a node is an element. That tag handler is listed in Example 11-9.h.

Example 11-9.h /WEB-INF/classes/tags/xml/dom/IfNodeIsElementTag.java

```
package tags.xml.dom;

import javax.servlet.jsp.JspException;
import javax.servlet.jsp.tagext.TagSupport;
import org.w3c.dom.Node;

public class IfNodeIsElementTag extends TagSupport {
   private Node node = null;

   public void setNode(Node node) {
      this.node = node;
   }
   public int doStartTag() throws JspException {
      return node.getNodeType() == Node.ELEMENT_NODE ?
            EVAL_BODY_INCLUDE : SKIP_BODY;
   }
   public void release() {
      node = null;
   }
}
```

Example 11-9.i lists the tag handler for the elementValue tag, which stores an element's value in a scripting variable.

Example 11-9.i /WEB-INF/classes/tags/xml/dom/GetElementValueTag.java

```java
package tags.xml.dom;

import javax.servlet.jsp.JspException;
import javax.servlet.jsp.tagext.TagSupport;
import org.w3c.dom.Element;
import org.w3c.dom.Node;

public class GetElementValueTag extends TagSupport {
   private Node element = null;

   public void setElement(Node element) {
      this.element = element;
   }
   public void setId(String id) {
      this.id = id;
   }
   public int doEndTag() throws JspException {
      if(element.getNodeType() == Node.ELEMENT_NODE) {
         String value = getElementText(element);
         pageContext.setAttribute(id, value);
      }
      else
         throw new JspException("Node must be an element");

      return EVAL_PAGE;
   }
   public void release() {
      element = null;
   }
   private String getElementText(Node element) {
      Node child = element.getFirstChild();
      String text = null;

      if(child != null)
         text = child.getNodeValue();

      return text;
   }
}
```

The tag info class for the `elementValue` tag—`GetElementValueTagInfo`— is listed in Example 11-9.j.

Example 11-9.j   /WEB-INF/classes/tags/xml/dom/GetElementValueTag.java

```
package tags.xml.dom;

import javax.servlet.jsp.tagext.TagData;
import javax.servlet.jsp.tagext.TagExtraInfo;
import javax.servlet.jsp.tagext.VariableInfo;

public class GetElementValueTagInfo extends TagExtraInfo {
   public VariableInfo[] getVariableInfo(TagData data) {
      return new VariableInfo[] {
         new VariableInfo(data.getId(),
                          "java.lang.String", true,
                          VariableInfo.AT_END)
      };
   }
}
```

The name of the scripting variable created by `GetElementValueTagInfo` is defined by the `elementValue` tag's mandatory `id` attribute.

As you can see by comparing Example 11-8.b on page 357 to Example 11-9.a on page 364, DOM custom tags can greatly simplify JSP pages and make them more accessible to page authors.

Transforming XML

As the Internet spreads to more devices, the capability for Web applications to transform their data into multiple formats, such as XML, HTML, or WML, will become increasingly important.

You can use XSLT to transform XML into any desired format. XSLT stands for Extensible Stylesheet Language: Transformations; as its name suggests, it's a language you use to create transformation stylesheets.

XSLT basics are easy to grasp, as evidenced by the following simple example that transforms the XML listed in Example 11-10.a.[8]

---

8.   That XML was generated by the JSP page listed in Example 11-2.a on page 334.

Example 11-10.a date.xml

```
<?xml version="1.0" encoding="ISO-8859-1"?>
<document>
   <date>
      Fri Dec 15 11:46:45 MST 2000
   </date>
</document>
```

In Example 11-10.b, the XSLT stylesheet listed below is applied to the XML listed in Example 11-10.a to produce the HTML shown in Figure 11-8.

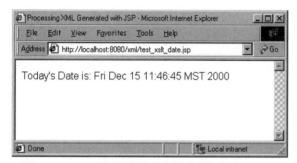

Figure 11-8 Using XSLT to Transform XML into HTML

Example 11-10.b /date.xsl

```
<xsl:stylesheet xmlns:xsl="http://www.w3.org/1999/XSL/Transform"
                version="1.0">

   <xsl:template match="/">
      <html><head>
         <title>Processing XML Generated with JSP</title>
      </head>
      <body><font size='4'>
         Today's Date is: <xsl:apply-templates/> </font>
      </body>
      </html>
   </xsl:template>

   <xsl:template match="date">
      <xsl:apply-templates/>
   </xsl:template>

</xsl:stylesheet>
```

XSLT is a declarative language based on template rules. Each template rule consists of a *pattern* and an *action* and is specified with `xsl:template`; for example, in the stylesheet listed in Example 11-10.a, there are two template rules:

```
<xsl:template match="/">...</xsl:template>
<xsl:template match="date">...</xsl:template>
```

The *patterns* for the two rules are "`/`", which matches the root element, and "`date`", which matches `date` elements. The *actions* for the two rules are specified by the body of each rule.

The action for the rule matching the root element—"`/`"—creates HTML that looks like this:

```
<html><head>
   <title>Processing XML Generated with JSP</title>
</head>
<body><font size='4'>
   Today's Date is: </font>
</body>
</html>
```

The date is not filled in by the rule that matches the root element; instead, that rule calls `xsl:apply-templates`, which recursively applies matching rules to the root element's children. In this case, the `date` element matches the "date" rule.

The "date" rule simply calls `xsl:apply-templates`. If an element has no children, as is the case for the `date` element, `xsl:apply-templates` inserts the body of that element into the output. In this case, that output is "Fri Dec 15 11:46:45 MST 2000".

The scope of this book includes this brief introduction to XSLT and how XSLT is used with JSP. Now that are done with the former, let's move on to the latter.

Using JSP and XSLT Together

There are many ways to use JSP and XSLT together. This discussion focuses on two of them, illustrated in Figure 11-9.

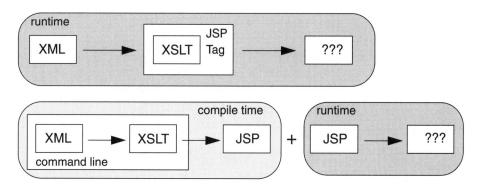

Figure 11-9 Two Ways to Transform XML with JSP and XSLT

As Figure 11-9 illustrates, you can use a JSP custom tag to apply XSLT to XML at runtime, or you can apply XSLT to XML at compile time to produce a JSP page. Let's take a look at each of those options.

Using XSLT in a Custom Tag to Produce HTML

One of the most flexible ways to use JSP and XSLT together is with a JSP custom tag that applies an XSLT stylesheet to its body, which is presumed to be XML. That tag could be used like this:

```
<xslt:apply xsl='inventory.xsl'>
   <%@ include file='inventory.xml' %>
</xslt:apply>
```

In the code fragment listed above, a stylesheet named `inventory.xsl` is applied to `inventory.xml`. Optionally, XML can be inserted directly into the tag's body, like this:

```
<xslt:apply xsl='inventory.xsl'>
   <?xml version='1.0' encoding='ISO-8859-1'?>
   ...
</xslt:apply>
```

Figure 11-10 shows a web application that uses `xslt:apply` to apply an XSLT stylesheet to an XML file. That XML file is listed in Example 11-11.a.

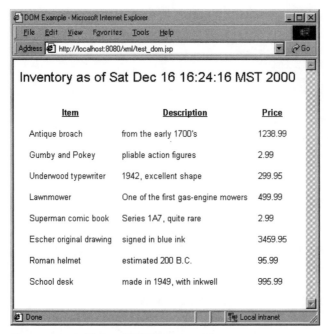

Figure 11-10 Using XSLT Custom Tags

Example 11-11.a /inventory.xml

```
<?xml version="1.0" encoding="ISO-8859-1"?>
   <inventory>
      <item>
         <name>Antique broach</name>
         <description>from the early 1700's</description>
         <price>1238.99</price>
      </item>
      <item>
         <name>Gumby and Pokey</name>
         <description>pliable action figures</description>
         <price>2.99</price>
      </item>

      ... other items omitted for brevity

   </inventory>
...
```

The JSP page shown in Figure 11-10 is listed in Example 11-11.b.

Example 11-11.b /test_xslt.jsp

```
<html><head><title>XSLT Example</title>
   <%@ taglib uri='/WEB-INF/tlds/xslt.tld' prefix='xslt' %>
</head>
<body>

<font size='5'>
   Inventory as of <%= new java.util.Date() %>
</font>
<p>

<xslt:apply xsl='inventory.xsl'>
   <%@ include file='inventory.xml' %>
</xslt:apply>

</p>
</body></html>
```

The JSP page listed in Example 11-11.b applies the inventory.xsl stylesheet to inventory.xml with the xslt:apply tag. That stylesheet is listed in Example 11-11.c.

Example 11-11.c /inventory.xsl

```
<xsl:stylesheet xmlns:xsl="http://www.w3.org/1999/XSL/Transform"
                version="1.0">

   <xsl:template match="/">
      <html>
         <head>
            <title>Inventory</title>
         </head>
         <body>
            <table cellspacing='15'>
               <th><u>Item</u></th>
               <th><u>Description</u></th>
               <th><u>Price</u></th>
               <xsl:apply-templates/>
            </table>
         </body>
      </html>
   </xsl:template>

   <xsl:template match="item">
      <tr><xsl:apply-templates/></tr>
   </xsl:template>
```

```
   <xsl:template match="item/*">
      <td><xsl:apply-templates/></td>
   </xsl:template>
</xsl:stylesheet>
```

The stylesheet listed in Example 11-11.c creates an HTML table. Most of the HTML is generated against the document's root element, including the table and table headers. The table rows are generated for each `item` element, and table data is generated for each `name`, `description`, and `price`.

The tag handler for `<xslt:apply>` is listed in Example 11-11.d.

Example 11-11.d   /WEB-INF/classes/tags/xml/xslt/XSLTApplyTag.java

```java
package tags.xml.xslt;

import java.io.StringReader;
import javax.servlet.ServletContext;
import javax.servlet.jsp.JspException;
import javax.servlet.http.HttpServletRequest;
import javax.servlet.http.HttpServletResponse;
import javax.servlet.jsp.tagext.BodyTagSupport;
import beans.xml.xslt.XSLTProcessorBean;

public class XSLTApplyTag extends BodyTagSupport {
   private String xsl;

   public void setXsl(String xsl) {
      this.xsl = xsl;
   }
   public int doAfterBody() throws JspException {
      XSLTProcessorBean xslBean = new XSLTProcessorBean();
      ServletContext context = pageContext.getServletContext();
      String body = bodyContent.getString().trim();

      try {
         if(body.equals("")) {
            throw new JspException("The body of this tag " +
                                   "must be XML.");
         }
         xslBean.process(new StringReader(body),
                         context.getResourceAsStream(xsl),
                         getPreviousOut());
      }
      catch(Exception ex) {
         throw new JspException(ex.getMessage());
      }
      return SKIP_BODY;
   }
}
```

The tag handler listed in Example 11-11.d uses a bean to perform the XSLT transformation. That tag handler throws an exception if the tag has no body; otherwise, it invokes the bean's `process` method to apply the transformation. That bean is listed in Example 11-11.e.

Example 11-11.e   /WEB-INF/classes/beans/xml/xslt/XsltProcessorBean.java

```
package beans.xml.xslt;

import java.io.InputStream;
import java.io.Reader;
import javax.servlet.ServletException;
import javax.servlet.http.HttpServletRequest;
import javax.servlet.http.HttpServletResponse;
import javax.servlet.jsp.JspWriter;

import org.apache.xalan.xslt.XSLTInputSource;
import org.apache.xalan.xslt.XSLTProcessor;
import org.apache.xalan.xslt.XSLTProcessorFactory;
import org.apache.xalan.xslt.XSLTResultTarget;

public class XSLTProcessorBean implements java.io.Serializable {
    public void process(Reader xmlrdr, InputStream xslstrm,
                            JspWriter writer)
                    throws java.io.IOException, ServletException {
        process(new XSLTInputSource(xmlrdr),
            new XSLTInputSource(xslstrm), writer);
    }
    public void process(XSLTInputSource xmlsrc,
                        XSLTInputSource xslsrc,
                            JspWriter writer)
                    throws java.io.IOException, ServletException {
        try {
            XSLTProcessorFactory.getProcessor().process(
                            xmlsrc, xslsrc,
                            new XSLTResultTarget(writer));
        }
        catch(Exception ex) {
            throw new ServletException(ex);
        }
    }
}
```

The bean listed in Example 11-11.e uses Apache's Xalan XSLT processor, so that bean encapsulates nonportable code. The bean's `process` method obtains an XSLT processor from the XSLT processor factory, and that processor applies the XSLT transformation and writes the result to a writer.

Using XSLT to Produce JSP at Compile Time

In "Using XSLT in a Custom Tag to Produce HTML" on page 377, a custom tag applies an XSLT transformation to an XML file at *runtime* with a JSP custom tag to produce the HTML shown in Figure 11-10 on page 378.

In this section, an XSLT transformation is applied to that same XML file at *compile* time to produce a JSP page. That JSP page produces the HTML shown in Figure 11-10 on page 378 at runtime.

Example 11-12.a lists the XSLT stylesheet that's applied to `inventory.xml` at compile time.

Example 11-12.a   An XSLT Stylesheet That Produces a JSP File

```
<xsl:stylesheet xmlns:xsl="http://www.w3.org/1999/XSL/Transform"
                version="1.0">

   <xsl:template match="/">
      <jsp:root xmlns:jsp="http://java.sun.com/jsp_1_2">
         <head>
            <title>Inventory</title>
         </head>
         <body>
            <font size='4'>
               Inventory as of <jsp:expression>
                                   new java.util.Date()
                               </jsp:expression>
            </font>
            <table cellspacing='15'>
               <th><u>Item</u></th>
               <th><u>Description</u></th>
               <th><u>Price</u></th>
               <xsl:apply-templates/>
            </table>
         </body>
      </jsp:root>
   </xsl:template>

   <xsl:template match="item">
      <tr><xsl:apply-templates/></tr>
   </xsl:template>

   <xsl:template match="item/*">
      <td><xsl:apply-templates/></td>
   </xsl:template>
</xsl:stylesheet>
```

The stylesheet listed in Example 11-12.a is applied on the command line, like this:

```
> java org.apache.xalan.xslt.Process -in inventory.xml -xsl
inventory.xsl -out inventory.jsp
```

inventory.xsl is listed in Example 11-12.a, and inventory.xml is listed in Figure 11-3 on page 334. The file produced by the transformation, inventory.jsp, is listed in Example 11-12.b.

Example 11-12.b A JSP Page Produced by an XSLT Stylesheet

```
<?xml version="1.0" encoding="UTF-8"?>
<jsp:root xmlns:jsp="http://java.sun.com/jsp_1_2"><head>
<title>Inventory</title></head><body><font size="4">
Inventory as of
    <jsp:expression>
        new java.util.Date()
    </jsp:expression>

</font><table cellspacing="15">
    <th><u>Item</u></th>
    <th><u>Description</u></th>
    <th><u>Price</u></th>

    <tr>
        <td>Antique broach</td>
        <td>from the early 1700's</td>
        <td>1238.99</td>
    </tr>
    <tr>
        <td>Gumby and Pokey</td>
        <td>pliable action figures</td>
        <td>2.99</td>
    </tr>

    ... more items omitted ...

</table></body>
</jsp:root>
```

The JSP page listed in Example 11-12.b produces the same HTML as the JSP page shown in Figure 11-10 on page 378, but the JSP page listed in Example 11-12.b is different because it uses the alternative JSP XML syntax. That alternative syntax must be used because XSLT can only process well-formed markup.[9]

---

9. The JSP 1.2 specification requires servlet containers to process that alternative JSP syntax.

> ## JSP Tip
>
> ### The Usefulness of JSP's XML Format
>
> Instead of using scriptlets and expressions, you can write JSP pages entirely in XML format. The JSP 1.1 specification provides XML tags for all of the JSP elements; for example, you would use a `jsp:scriptlet` tag instead of the usual scriptlet syntax.
>
> At first glance, it might not seem as though there is much reason to write JSP files in XML format. But that capability is essential if you are generating JSP pages from XML files using XSLT. That's because XSLT will only parse well-formed XML; if you try to process a normal JSP file with scriptlets and expressions, XSLT will produce an error.

Using XSLT at Compile Time Vs. Runtime

This section, which began at "Transforming XML" on page 374, has illustrated two ways to generate HTML from XML. The first uses a custom tag that performs an XSLT transformation at runtime for a specified XML file. That XSLT transformation generates HTML. The second performs an XSLT transformation on an XML file at compile time to produce a JSP file. That JSP page subsequently produces HTML at runtime.

Both of the methods discussed in "Transforming XML" on page 374 start with the same XML and end up with the same HTML. Applying transformations at runtime with custom tags is more flexible because it doesn't require an extra compilation step. But that flexibility comes at a rather steep price because XSLT transformations are very slow. Because of that performance penalty, it might make more sense to transform XML at compile time into a JSP page evaluated at runtime. That way, you avoid the performance penalty at runtime of transforming XML.

Using XPath

XPath is a language of its own that's used by XSLT stylesheets to match XML elements to a pattern. Recall that in "Transforming XML" on page 374, a template rule used the "/" pattern to match the XML root element, like this:

```
<xsl:template match="/">...</xsl:template>
```

That rule applies to elements that match the "/" XPath expression, meaning the root element. That rule uses the simplest XPath expression possible, but XPath expressions can be much more complicated.

Sometimes it's convenient to have the expressive power of XPath at your disposal to match elements in an XML document but inconvenient to incur the overhead of XSLT.

Because XPath is a stand-alone language, most XSLT processors allow you to use XPath without using XSLT. This section shows how to use XPath with Apache's Xalan XSLT processor.

The JSP page shown in Figure 11-11 uses a custom tag to select elements from an XML file. That tag uses a bean that uses XPath to locate elements in that XML file.

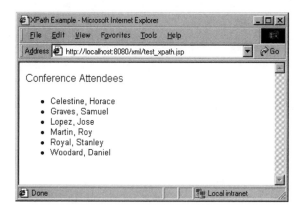

Figure 11-11 Using XPath Custom Tags

The JSP page shown in Figure 11-11 is listed in Example 11-13.a.

Example 11-13.a test_xpath.jsp

```
<html><head><title>XPath Example</title>
    <%@ taglib uri='xpath' prefix='xpath' %>
    <%@ page import='org.w3c.dom.Node' %>
</head>
<body>

<font size='4'>Conference Attendees</font><p>

<ul>
<xpath:selectNodes id='node'
            xmlFile='f:/books/jsp/src/xml/names.xml'
                expr='//name'>
```

```
<% Node first = node.getAttributes().getNamedItem("first");
   Node last  = node.getAttributes().getNamedItem("last"); %>

<li><%=last.getNodeValue()%>, <%=first.getNodeValue()%></li>
```

```
</xpath:selectNodes></p>
</ul>
```

```
</body></html>
```

The `selectNodes` custom tag used in Example 11-13.a iterates over a list of nodes from the specified XML file. Those nodes are selected according to the XPath expression. That tag makes a scripting variable available, representing the current node. That scripting variable is named `node` in Example 11-13.a.

The JSP page listed in Example 11-13.a iterates over a list of names from `names.xml`, which is listed in Example 11-13.b.

Example 11-13.b names.xml

```xml
<?xml version="1.0"?>
<doc>
  <name first="Horace" last="Celestine"/>
  <name first="Samuel" last="Graves"/>
  <name first="Jose" last="Lopez"/>
  <name first="Roy" last="Martin"/>
  <name first="Stanley" last="Royal"/>
  <name first="Daniel" last="Woodard"/>
</doc>
```

The tag handler for the `selectNodes` tag is listed in Example 11-13.c.

Example 11-13.c /WEB-INF/classes/tags/xml/xpath/XPathTag.java

```java
package tags.xml.xpath;

import java.util.Collection;
import java.util.Vector;
import javax.servlet.jsp.JspException;
import javax.servlet.jsp.PageContext;
import org.w3c.dom.Document;
import org.w3c.dom.Node;
import org.w3c.dom.NodeList;
import beans.xml.dom.DOMParserBean;
import beans.xml.xpath.XPathBean;
import tags.util.IteratorTag;
```

```java
public class XPathTag extends IteratorTag {
   private String file, expr;
   private boolean force = false;

   public void setXmlFile(String file) { this.file = file; }
   public void setExpr(String expr)    { this.expr = expr; }
   public void setForce(boolean force) { this.force = force; }

   public int doStartTag() throws JspException {
      Document document = (Document)pageContext.getAttribute(file,
                              PageContext.SESSION_SCOPE);
      NodeList list = null;

      if(force || document == null) {
         try {
            document = DOMParserBean.getDocument(file);
         }
         catch(Exception ex) {
            throw new JspException(ex.getMessage());
         }
         pageContext.setAttribute(file, document,
                              PageContext.SESSION_SCOPE);
      }
      try {
         setCollection(
               collection(XPathBean.process(document, expr)));
      }
      catch(Exception ex) {
         throw new JspException(ex.getMessage());
      }
      return super.doStartTag();
   }
   public void release() {
      file = expr = null;
      force = false;
   }
   private Collection collection(NodeList list) {
      Vector vector = new Vector();
      int length = list.getLength();

      for(int i=0; i < length; ++i) {
         vector.addElement(list.item(i));
      }
      return vector;
   }
}
```

Like the tag handler discussed in Example 11-9.e on page 369, the tag handler listed in Example 11-13.c extends `IteratorTag`, which is discussed in "Iteration" on page 36.

`XPathTag.doStartTag` creates an instance of `XPathBean`, which encapsulates XPath calls. That bean processes the XPath expression and returns a DOM `NodeList` containing a list of nodes that match the expression. `XPathTag.doStartTag` converts that list into a collection and passes it to `IteratorTag.setCollection`. Subsequently, `XPathTag.doStartTag` calls `super.doStartTag()`, and the `IteratorTag` superclass takes over from there, iterating over the collection set by the call to `setCollection`.

The `XPathBean` class is listed in Example 11-13.d.

Example 11-13.d   /WEB-INF/classes/beans/xml/xpath/XPathBean.java

```
package beans.xml.xpath;

import java.io.InputStream;
import java.io.FileInputStream;
import java.io.FileNotFoundException;
import javax.servlet.jsp.JspException;

import org.apache.xerces.parsers.DOMParser;
import org.w3c.dom.Node;
import org.w3c.dom.NodeList;
import org.xml.sax.InputSource;
import org.xml.sax.SAXException;

import org.apache.xalan.xpath.XPathSupport;
import org.apache.xalan.xpath.XPath;
import org.apache.xalan.xpath.XPathProcessorImpl;
import org.apache.xalan.xpath.xml.XMLParserLiaisonDefault;
import org.apache.xalan.xpath.xml.PrefixResolverDefault;
import org.apache.xalan.xpath.XObject;

public class XPathBean {
   private XPathBean() { } // defeat instantiation

   public static NodeList process(Node node, String expr)
                                          throws SAXException {
      XPathSupport s = new XMLParserLiaisonDefault();
      PrefixResolverDefault pr = new PrefixResolverDefault(node);
      XPathProcessorImpl processor = new XPathProcessorImpl(s);
      XPath xpath = new XPath();
```

```
        processor.initXPath(xpath, expr, pr);
        XObject xo = xpath.execute(s, node, pr);
        return xo.nodeset();
    }
}
```

Like the SAXParserBean, DOMParserBean, and XSLTProcessorBean classes discussed previously in this chapter, XPathBean encapsulates processor-specific code. That code—the static XPathBean.process—processes an XPath expression against a DOM node, which is presumed to be the root of a document or document fragment. That method returns a DOM NodeList containing all of the nodes that match the XPath expression.

Like the DOMParserBean discussed in "Document Object Model (DOM)" on page 354, XPathBean maintains no state and implements a single static method. Because of this implementation, XPathBean implements a private no-argument constructor to defeat instantiation.

Conclusion

This chapter has illustrated some of the ways to use JSP and XML together. As both of those technologies mature there will be even more ways for JSP-based applications to benefit from XML.

The authors of the JSP specification designed JSP with XML in mind. Because JSP template text can be anything, including XML, it's a simple matter for a JSP page to generate XML with dynamic content. JSP pages can also be specified as XML, which allows JSP pages to be generated from XSLT.

SAX and DOM, the two standard XML parsing APIs, are discussed at length in this chapter, including sets of custom tags for both. This chapter has also illustrated two ways to transform XML into HTML: by using XSLT to generate JSP at compile time that ultimately generates HTML at runtime, or by applying XSLT transformations to XML at runtime. The latter is usually chosen for performance reasons, whereas the former is more flexible.

A CASE STUDY

Topics in this Chapter

Chapter 12

This book has focused on singular techniques for implementing web applications, such as Model 2 frameworks, internationalization, and authentication. This chapter shows you how to use many of those techniques to implement a nontrivial Web application—an online fruitstand. That fruitstand:

- Is an e-commerce application with inventory, users, and shopping carts
- Is implemented with a Model 2 MVC architecture
- Is internationalized in three languages: English, German, and Chinese
- Implements custom authentication
- Uses JSP templates
- Accesses a database
- Uses XML and DOM
- Guards against sensitive form resubmissions

You can use this chapter in one of two ways:

- As a *guide to developing* nontrivial web applications using the concepts discussed in this book
- As an *introduction to the concepts* discussed in this book

Because of this chapter's dual role, you can read—or most likely skim—this chapter first, even though it's the last chapter in the book. If you do that, be aware that concepts are not explained in this chapter, so don't expect all of the code to make sense at first glance.

This chapter uses many of the 50 or so custom tags discussed throughout this book. Those tags are useful,[1] but the concepts behind those tags, and not the tags themselves, are the emphasis of this book.

The online fruitstand contains a significant amount of code, so we will cover it in three passes:

- **The main use case:** Homepage—>Storefront—>Checkout—>Purchase, starting at "The Homepage" on page 395
- **The MVC architecture:** The Model, Views, and Controllers, starting at "The Model 2 Framework" on page 416
- **Other features:** I18n, authentication, HTML forms, sensitive form resubmissions, SSL, and XML, starting at "Internationalization" on page 438

Because the topics listed above are discussed extensively elsewhere in this book, this chapter is purposely short on words and long on code and diagrams.

The Fruitstand

The online fruitstand provides one-stop shopping for 10 different fruits, as shown in Figure 12-1. The fruitstand's home page reveals its true intent by providing a summary of the JSP techniques used to develop the application. From the homepage, users can access the storefront, purchase fruit, and subsequently check out their purchase.

Figure 12-1 depicts a single use case for the fruitstand application; namely, a *logged-in user purchases fruit*. The fruitstand also implements a number of other use cases ranging from *user switches languages* to *user opens a new account*.

1.   You can use this book's custom tags for any purpose.

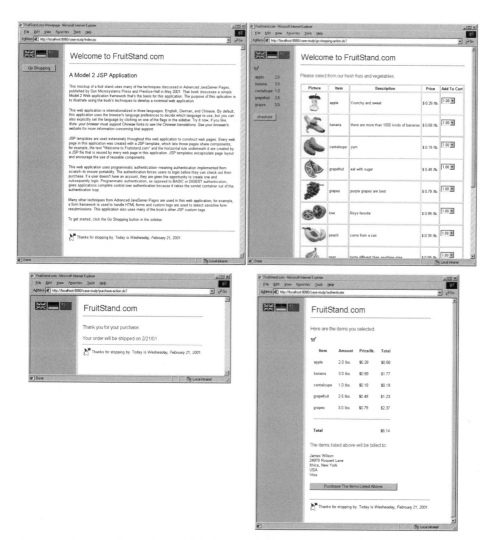

Figure 12-1 The Fruit Stand's Main Use Case: From top left, clockwise: The *homepage*, the *storefront*, the *checkout*, and the *purchase* JSP pages

The use case shown in Figure 12-1 can be described as follows:

1. A user accesses the homepage and activates the Go Shopping button.

2. The application forwards to the storefront page. That page accesses inventory from a database, lets the user select items, and displays those items in the sidebar's shopping cart.

3. The user activates the Checkout button in the storefront's sidebar.

4. The user has already logged in,[2] so the application forwards to the checkout page. That page displays an invoice of the items in the user's shopping cart.

5. The user activates the Purchase the Items Listed Above button in the checkout page.

6. The application forwards to a purchase page, which thanks the user for the purchase, and displays the expected ship date.

We will discuss the implementation of the use case listed above, starting with "The Homepage" on page 395. But first, take a look at Figure 12-2, which shows an overview of the fruitstand's directory structure.

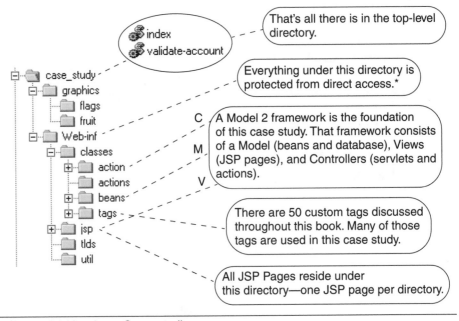

M = model, V = views, C = controllers
*Warning: Not all servlet containers enforce this rule.

Figure 12-2 Application Overview

Except for graphics and a couple of files in the top-level directory, the fruitstand's files all reside under /WEB-INF. According to the servlet specification, files under /WEB-INF must not be directly accessed, so nearly all of the fruitstand application is hidden from direct access by a browser.

2. See "Authentication" on page 443 for a discussion of the create account case.

The fruitstand application uses the Model 2 framework discussed in "A Model 2 Framework" on page 154. That framework is a Model-View-Controller (MVC) implementation that allows applications to be built from interchangeable parts. The fruitstand's model consists of a database and beans, the views are JSP pages, and the controllers—which orchestrate use cases—are servlets and actions.

The fruitstand's JSP files all reside under /WEB-INF/jsp, one JSP page per directory; for example, there's a /WEB-INF/jsp/homepage directory that contains the JSP files used by the home page.

The fruitstand application was developed and tested with both Resin 1.2.1 and Tomcat 3.2 final. You can run the application in one of two ways. The easiest way is to create a JAR file of the application and place that JAR file in $TOMCAT_HOME/webapps or $RESIN_HOME/webapps, for Tomcat and Resin, respectively, where $TOMCAT_HOME and $RESIN_HOME are the installation directories for those servlet containers. If you want to modify the application, it's best to specify that application in the Tomcat and Resin configuration files; for example, for Tomcat 3.2 final, you would add the following to $TOMCAT_HOME/conf/server.xml:

```
<Context path="/case-study"
    docBase="f:/books/jsp/src/case_study"/>
```

For Resin, you would add the following to $RESIN_HOME/conf/resin.conf:

```
<web-app id='case-study'
    app-dir='f:/books/jsp/src/case_study/final'/>
```

Now that we have a high-level view of how the fruitstand application is organized, let's explore the implementation of the *logged-in user purchases fruit* use case.

The Homepage

The fruitstand application defines a welcome file list containing one file: /index.jsp. That welcome file designation, from /WEB-INF/web.xml, is listed below:

```
<?xml version="1.0" encoding="ISO-8859-1"?>

<!DOCTYPE web-app
    PUBLIC "-//Sun Microsystems, Inc.//DTD Web Application 2.2//EN"
    "http://java.sun.com/j2ee/dtds/web-app_2.2.dtd">
    ...
```

```
<welcome-file-list>
   <welcome-file>index.jsp</welcome-file>
</welcome-file-list>
   ...
</web-app>
```

/index.jsp is invoked when the following URL is accessed with either Tomcat or Resin: http://localhost:8080/case-study.[3] Example 12-1.a lists /index.jsp.

Example 12-1.a   /index.jsp

```
<%@ page contentType='text/html; charset=UTF-8' %>
<%@ taglib uri='regions' prefix='region' %>
<%@ include file='/WEB-INF/jsp/regionDefinitions.jsp' %>

<region:render region='HOMEPAGE_REGION' />
```

Because the fruitstand supports Chinese, all of the application's JSP pages use the UTF-8 charset. See "Templates" on page 96 for more information concerning UTF-8 and support for non-Western languages.

/index.jsp uses the regions custom tag library discussed in "Templates" on page 96 and includes another JSP file—/WEBINF/jsp/regionDefinitions.jsp—that contains region definitions. Subsequently, /index.jsp renders the homepage region. The homepage is shown in Figure 12-3.

Like all the other JSP pages in the fruitstand application, the homepage comprises one region with four sections: header, sidebar, content, and footer. The homepage sidebar contains three flags—used to select a language—and the Go Shopping button. The header displays the Welcome to Fruitstand.com message and a horizontal rule. The homepage content is the main text, and the footer contains a horizontal rule and a greeting with the current date.

---

3.   The port number, in this case 8080, may change with other servlet containers.

Figure 12-3 The Fruit Stand Homepage

Each of the homepage sections is implemented with one or more JSP files, collectively known as a component. Every JSP page in this application is composed in this same way, with templates that insert interchangeable components. See "Templates" on page 96 for more information on templates and their benefits.

`regionDefinitions.jsp`, which defines all of the regions used in the fruitstand application, is partially listed in Example 12-1.b.[4]

---

4.   See Example 12-7.g on page 428 for a complete listing of `regionDefinitions.jsp`.

Example 12-1.b   /WEB-INF/jsp/regionDefinitions.jsp (partial listing)

```
<%@ taglib uri='regions' prefix='region' %>

<region:define id='STOREFRONT_REGION'
          template='/WEB-INF/jsp/templates/hscf.jsp'>
   <region:put section='title'
               content='FruitStand.com'
                direct='true'/>

   <region:put section='background'
               content='graphics/blueAndWhiteBackground.gif'
                direct='true'/>

   <region:put section='header'
               content='/WEB-INF/jsp/storefront/header.jsp'/>

   <region:put section='sidebar'
               content='/WEB-INF/jsp/storefront/sidebar.jsp'/>

   <region:put section='content'
               content='/WEB-INF/jsp/storefront/content.jsp'/>

   <region:put section='footer'
               content='/WEB-INF/jsp/storefront/footer.jsp'/>
</region:define>
...
<region:define id='HOMEPAGE_REGION' region='STOREFRONT_REGION'>
   <region:put section='sidebar'
               content='/WEB-INF/jsp/homepage/sidebar.jsp'/>

   <region:put section='content'
               content='/WEB-INF/jsp/homepage/content.jsp'/>
</region:define>
...
```

regionDefinitions.jsp defines a STOREFRONT_REGION for the application's storefront. That region is listed in Example 12-1.b because the HOMEPAGE_REGION extends it and overrides the sidebar and content sections. The homepage reuses the storefront's title, background, header, and footer sections.

Example 12-1.c and Example 12-1.d list the storefront header and footer JSP pages, respectively.

Example 12-1.c /WEB-INF/jsp/storefront/header.jsp

```
<%@ page contentType='text/html; charset=UTF-8' %>
<%@ taglib uri='i18n' prefix='i18n' %>

<font size='6' color='blue'>
   <i18n:message key="storefront.title"/>
</font>
<hr/>
<br/>
```

Example 12-1.d /WEB-INF/jsp/storefront/footer.jsp

```
<%@ page contentType='text/html; charset=UTF-8' %>
<%@ taglib uri='i18n' prefix='i18n' %>

<hr><p>
<table>
   <tr>
      <td><img src='graphics/duke.gif'/></td>
      <td>
         <i18n:message key='login.footer.message'/><i>
         <i18n:format date='<%=new java.util.Date()%>'
               dateStyle='<%=java.text.DateFormat.FULL%>'/></i>.
      </td>
   </tr>
</table>
</p>
```

All of the text displayed in the fruitstand application is rendered by the
i18n:message and i18n:format tags, which are used to internationalize text,
numbers, dates, and currency. Those tags are used by the storefront's header and
footer.

The i18n:message tag displays text defined in a properties file; for example, the
partial listing below is from /WEB-INF/classes/app_en.properties, which
is the English properties file for the fruitstand application.

```
...
storefront.title=Welcome to FruitStand.com
storefront.form.title=Please select from our fresh fruts.

storefront.table.header.picture=Picture
storefront.table.header.item=Item
storefront.table.header.description=Description
storefront.table.header.price=Price
storefront.table.header.addToCart=Add To Cart
...
```

The storefront application also has properties files for German and Chinese; see "Internationalization" on page 438 for more information about the storefront's internationalization capabilities.

The homepage content page is listed in Example 12-1.e.

Example 12-1.e /WEB-INF/jsp/homepage/content.jsp

```
<%@ page contentType='text/html; charset=UTF-8' %>
<%@ taglib uri='i18n' prefix='i18n'  %>

<font size='5' color='blue'>
   <i18n:message key='homepage.title'/>
</font>

<i18n:message key='homepage.text'/>
```

Although the text displayed in the homepage is rather lengthy, the JSP file that produces it is not. That's because the JSP file listed above also uses the i18n:message tag to retrieve the rather lengthy text associated with homepage.text.

Going Shopping

There are only two interesting things to do from the fruitstand's homepage: change languages by clicking on one of the flags, or go shopping by clicking on the Go Shopping button. Both the flags and the buttons are contained in the homepage's sidebar, which is listed in Example 12-2.a.

Example 12-2.a /WEB-INF/jsp/homepage/sidebar.jsp

```
<%@ page contentType='text/html; charset=UTF-8' %>
<jsp:include page='../shared/flags.jsp' flush='true'/>

<form action='go-shopping-action.do'>
   <input type='submit' value='Go Shopping'/>
</form>
```

The homepage sidebar includes another JSP file that displays the flags. That file—/WEB-INF/jsp/shared/flags.jsp—is used by all of the fruitstand's JSP pages so that users can change languages at any time. See "Internationalization" on page 438 for more information about flags.jsp.

The homepage sidebar also contains a simple form with a submit button. The action associated with that button is go-shopping-action.do. URIs that end in .do are handled by the fruitstand's action servlet. That servlet, which is part of a simple Model 2 framework discussed in "A Model 2 Framework" on page 154, forwards the `go-shopping-action.do` request to an action, which is listed in Example 12-2.b.

Example 12-2.b /WEB-INF/classes/actions/GoShoppingAction.java

```java
package actions;

import javax.servlet.ServletException;
import javax.servlet.http.HttpServlet;
import javax.servlet.http.HttpServletRequest;
import javax.servlet.http.HttpServletResponse;
import javax.servlet.http.HttpSession;

import beans.app.ShoppingCart;

import action.ActionBase;
import action.ActionRouter;

import beans.app.Item;

public class GoShoppingAction extends ActionBase
                       implements beans.app.Constants {
   public ActionRouter perform(HttpServlet servlet,
                               HttpServletRequest req,
                               HttpServletResponse res)
                               throws ServletException {
      HttpSession session = req.getSession();
      ShoppingCart   cart = (ShoppingCart)session.getAttribute(
                                        SHOPPING_CART_KEY);
      if(cart == null) {
         cart = new ShoppingCart();

         synchronized(this) {
            session.setAttribute(SHOPPING_CART_KEY, cart);
         }
      }
      return new ActionRouter("storefront-page");
   }
}
```

The `GoShoppingAction.perform` method, invoked by the action servlet, makes sure the user has a shopping cart in the session and returns an action router that the action servlet uses to forward the request to the storefront-page. That page is defined in the application's `actions.properties` file, which is listed in Example 12-2.c.

Example 12-2.c /WEB-INF/classes/actions.properties

```
# Action mappings used by the action servlet

go-shopping-action              =actions.GoShoppingAction
query-account-action            =actions.QueryAccountAction
new-account-action              =actions.NewAccountAction
show-hint-action                =actions.ShowHintAction
update-locale-action            =actions.UpdateLocaleAction
add-selection-to-cart-action=actions.AddToCartAction
checkout-action                 =actions.CheckoutAction
validate-account-action         =actions.ValidateAccountAction
purchase-action                 =actions.PurchaseAction

# JSP mappings used by Routers

storefront-page        =/WEB-INF/jsp/storefront/page.jsp
login-failed-page      =/WEB-INF/jsp/loginFailed/page.jsp
query-account-page     =/WEB-INF/jsp/createAccount/page.jsp
account-created-page=/WEB-INF/jsp/accountCreated/page.jsp
show-hint-page         =/WEB-INF/jsp/showHint/page.jsp
checkout-page          =/WEB-INF/jsp/checkout/page.jsp
purchase-page          =/WEB-INF/jsp/purchase/page.jsp
```

The `actions.properties` file defines two sets of logical names. The first set maps requests to actions; for example, the `go-shopping-action.do` request is mapped to the `actions.GoShoppingAction` class listed in Example 12-2.b. The `storefront-page` logical name used by that action is also defined in the `actions.properties` file.

The Storefront

Now we come to the fruitstand's storefront. Let's briefly review how we got here. First, the user accesses the fruitstand's homepage with the URL `http://localhost:8080/case_study`. That causes the welcome file— `/index.jsp`—to be displayed, which renders the homepage. The user clicks on the Go Shopping button, which submits a `go-shopping-action.do` request. That request is mapped to an action—`GoShoppingAction`—which creates a shopping cart and forwards the request to the storefront page. The storefront page is shown in Figure 12-4.

Figure 12-4 The Storefront

The storefront page is listed in Example 12-3.a.

Example 12-3.a /WEB-INF/jsp/storefront/page.jsp

```
<%@ taglib uri='regions' prefix='region' %>

<region:render region='STOREFRONT_REGION'/>
```

The storefront page renders the storefront region, which is defined in
/WEBINF/jsp/regionDefinitions.jsp. That JSP file is partially listed in
Example 12-1.b on page 398.

The storefront comprises four files: header.jsp, sidebar.jsp, content.jsp, and footer.jsp. Because the storefront header and footer are reused by the homepage, we've already seen their listings in Example 12-1.c and Example 12-1.d on page 399. The storefront sidebar is listed in Example 12-3.b.

Example 12-3.b /WEB-INF/jsp/storefront/sidebar.jsp

```
<%@ page contentType='text/html; charset=UTF-8' %>

<jsp:include page='../shared/flags.jsp' flush='true' /><p>
<jsp:include page='../shared/cart.jsp'  flush='true' /></p>
```

Like the homepage sidebar, the storefront sidebar includes flags.jsp, so the user can change languages. The storefront sidebar includes another shared component that displays the items in the user's shopping cart. That component—/WEB-INF/jsp/shared/cart.jsp—is listed in Example 12-4.b on page 408.

The main content displayed by the storefront is created by /WEBINF/jsp/storefront/content.jsp, which is listed in Example 12-3.c.

Example 12-3.c /WEB-INF/jsp/storefront/content.jsp

```
<%@ page contentType='text/html; charset=UTF-8' %>

<%@ taglib uri='database'   prefix='database' %>
<%@ taglib uri='html'       prefix='html'     %>
<%@ taglib uri='i18n'       prefix='i18n'     %>
<%@ taglib uri='logic'      prefix='logic'    %>

<font size='4' color='blue'>
   <i18n:message key='storefront.form.title' />
</font><p>

<database:query id='inventory' scope='session'>
   SELECT * FROM Inventory
</database:query>

<% String currentItem = null, currentSku = null; %>

<table border='1' cellpadding='5'>
   <tr><th><i18n:message key='storefront.table.header.picture' />
      </th>

      <database:columnNames query='inventory' id='name'>
         <logic:stringsNotEqual compare='SKU' to='<%= name %>'>
            <% String hdrKey = "storefront.table.header." +
                               name.toLowerCase(); %>
```

```
          <th><i18n:message key='<%= hdrKey %>'/></th>

          <logic:stringsEqual compare='NAME' to='<%= name %>'>
             <th><i18n:message
                      key='storefront.table.header.description'/>
             </th>
          </logic:stringsEqual>
       </logic:stringsNotEqual>
   </database:columnNames>

   <th><i18n:message key='storefront.table.header.addToCart'/>
   </th>
</tr>

<tr>
<database:rows query='inventory'>
   <database:columns query='inventory' columnName='name'
                                      columnValue='value'>
      <logic:stringsEqual compare='SKU' to='<%= name %>'>
         <% currentSku = value; %>
         <td><img src='<%= "graphics/fruit/" + currentSku +
                        ".jpg" %>'/></td>
      </logic:stringsEqual>

      <logic:stringsEqual compare='NAME' to='<%= name %>'>
         <% currentItem = value; %>
         <td><%= value %></td>
         <td><i18n:message key='<%=value + ".description"%>'/>
         </td>
      </logic:stringsEqual>

      <logic:stringsEqual compare='PRICE' to='<%= name %>'>
         <td><%= value %></td>
         <td>
            <form action='add-selection-to-cart-action.do'>
               <html:links name='<%= currentSku  + "-" +
                                     currentItem + "-" +
                                        value %>'>
                  <option value='0.00'>0.00</option>
                  <option value='1.00'>1.00</option>
                  <option value='1.50'>1.50</option>
                  <option value='2.00'>2.00</option>
                  <option value='2.50'>2.50</option>
                  <option value='3.00'>3.00</option>
                  <option value='3.50'>3.50</option>
                  <option value='4.00'>4.00</option>
                  <option value='4.50'>4.50</option>
                  <option value='5.00'>5.00</option>
                  <option value='5.50'>5.50</option>
```

```
              </html:links>
          </form>
        </td>
        </tr><tr>
      </logic:stringsEqual>

    </database:columns>
  </database:rows>
</table>
</p>

<database:release query='inventory'/>
```

The storefront content page listed in Example 12-3.c reads inventory from a database. Subsequently, the content page iterates over column names and the columns themselves to create a table, as shown in Figure 12-4 on page 403.

The storefront content page also uses the `html:links` custom tag discussed in "Custom Tag Advanced Concepts" on page 32 to create HTML options that generate a request when they are selected. That request is `add-selection-to-cart-action.do`, which is mapped to `actions.AddToCartAction` in the `actions.properties` file listed in Example 12-2.c on page 402. That action class is discussed next.

The Shopping Cart

When a selection is made from one of the options in the storefront page shown in Figure 12-4 on page 403, a request is generated that maps to the `actions.AddToCartAction` action class. That class is listed in Example 12-4.a

Example 12-4.a /WEB-INF/classes/AddToCartAction.java

```java
package actions;

import java.util.Enumeration;
import java.util.Iterator;
import java.util.StringTokenizer;

import javax.servlet.*;
import javax.servlet.http.*;

import beans.app.Item;
import beans.app.ShoppingCart;

import action.ActionBase;
import action.ActionRouter;
```

```
// sku stands for stock keeping unit, an accounting term for
// something that's in stock pending sale. This action's request
// has a parameter that looks like this: sku-fruit-price=amount;
// for example, 1002-banana-0.69=0.75.

public class AddToCartAction extends ActionBase
                            implements beans.app.Constants {
   public ActionRouter perform(HttpServlet servlet,
                               HttpServletRequest req,
                               HttpServletResponse res)
                               throws ServletException {
      Enumeration      e = req.getParameterNames();
      String skuAndFruit = (String)e.nextElement();
      String       amount = req.getParameterValues(skuAndFruit)[0];
      ShoppingCart  cart = (ShoppingCart)req.getSession().
                               getAttribute(SHOPPING_CART_KEY);

      if(cart == null) {
         throw new ServletException("No cart found");
      }

      StringTokenizer tok = new StringTokenizer(skuAndFruit, "-");
      String sku = (String)tok.nextElement(),
           fruit = (String)tok.nextElement(),
           price = (String)tok.nextElement();

      Iterator it = cart.getItems().iterator();
      boolean fruitWasInCart = false;

      while(it.hasNext()) {
         Item item = (Item)it.next();

         if(item.getName().equals(fruit)) {
            fruitWasInCart = true;
            item.setAmount(item.getAmount() +
                        Float.parseFloat(amount));
         }
      }
      if(!fruitWasInCart) {
         cart.addItem(new Item(Integer.parseInt(sku), fruit,
                            Float.parseFloat(price),
                            Float.parseFloat(amount)));
      }
      return new ActionRouter("storefront-page");
   }
}
```

The add-to-cart action listed in Example 12-4.a is invoked with a single request parameter of the form *sku-fruit-price=amount*; for example, if two pounds of grapefruit are selected at $0.49/lb, that request parameter will be 1004-grapefruit-0.49=2.0.[5] The add-to-cart action parses that parameter and uses the resulting information to update the user's shopping cart.

The action's `perform` method returns an action router that points back to the storefront page, which causes the storefront to be redisplayed and the contents of the cart in the sidebar to be updated. The JSP page for that cart is listed in Example 12-4.b.

Example 12-4.b   /WEB-INF/jsp/shared/cart.jsp

```
<%@ taglib uri='application' prefix='app' %>

<img src='graphics/cart.gif'/>

<table cellpadding='3'>
   <app:iterateCart id='cartItem'>
      <tr>
         <td><%= cartItem.getName()   %></td>
         <td><%= cartItem.getAmount() %></td>
      </tr>
   </app:iterateCart>
</table>

<form action='checkout-action.do'>
   <input type='submit' value='checkout'/>
</form>
```

The JSP page listed in Example 12-4.b uses an application-specific custom tag to iterate over the items in the user's cart. That custom tag is listed in Example 12-4.c.

---

5. Sku is an accounting term that stands for stock keeping unit, which simply means something in stock. Grapefruit was arbitrarily assigned an sku of 1004.

Example 12-4.c /WEB-INF/classes/tags/app/CartIteratorTag.java

```
package tags.app;

import javax.servlet.jsp.PageContext;
import javax.servlet.jsp.JspException;
import javax.servlet.jsp.tagext.TagSupport;

import beans.app.User;
import beans.app.Users;
import beans.app.ShoppingCart;

public class CartIteratorTag extends tags.util.IteratorTag
                             implements beans.app.Constants {
   public int doStartTag() throws JspException {
      ShoppingCart cart = (ShoppingCart)pageContext.getAttribute(
                           SHOPPING_CART_KEY,
                        PageContext.SESSION_SCOPE);
      if(cart == null) {
         throw new JspException("CartIteratorTag can't find " +
                              "cart");
      }
      setCollection(cart.getItems());
      return super.doStartTag();
   }
}
```

The custom tag listed in Example 12-4.c iterates over the items in the user's shopping cart and makes the current item available as a scripting variable named by the tag's id attribute. But none of that functionality is evident in Example 12-4.c because it's inherited from `IteratorTag`, which is discussed in "Iteration" on page 36. `CartIteratorTag.doStartTag` invokes the `setCollection` method defined in its superclass and calls `super.doStartTag` before returning. The `IteratorTag` superclass takes care of the rest.

The cart in the storefront's sidebar, which is listed in Example 12-4.b on page 408, contains a `Checkout` button that generates a `checkout-action.do` request. That request is mapped to the `actions.CheckoutAction` class in the `actions.properties` file; that properties file is listed in Example 12-2.c on page 402. The `CheckoutAction` class is listed in Example 12-5.a.

Example 12-5.a   /WEB-INF/classes/CheckoutAction.java

```java
package actions;

import javax.servlet.ServletException;
import javax.servlet.http.HttpServlet;
import javax.servlet.http.HttpServletRequest;
import javax.servlet.http.HttpServletResponse;
import javax.servlet.http.HttpSession;

import beans.app.ShoppingCart;

import action.ActionBase;
import action.ActionRouter;

public class CheckoutAction extends ActionBase
                      implements beans.app.Constants {
   public ActionRouter perform(HttpServlet servlet,
                               HttpServletRequest req,
                               HttpServletResponse res)
                               throws ServletException {
      HttpSession session = req.getSession();
      ShoppingCart  cart = (ShoppingCart)session.getAttribute(
                                        SHOPPING_CART_KEY);
      if(cart == null) {
         throw new ServletException("Cart not found");
      }
      return new ActionRouter("checkout-page");
   }
}
```

The checkout action checks to make sure the user has a shopping cart; if not, CheckoutAction.perform throws a servlet exception. After the shopping cart has been found, the checkout action returns an action router that forwards the request to the checkout page.

The Checkout

The checkout page, shown in Figure 12-5, displays an invoice of the items in the user's shopping cart and lists the billing address. To complete the transaction, the user must activate the Purchase The Items Listed Above button.

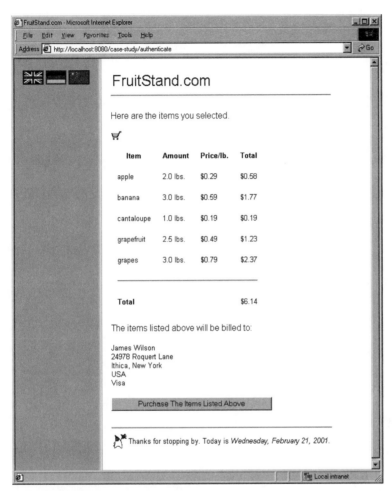

Figure 12-5 The Checkout Page

The checkout page shown in Figure 12-5 is listed in Example 12-5.b.

Example 12-5.b /WEB-INF/jsp/checkout/page.jsp

```
<%@ taglib uri='security' prefix='security'%>
<%@ taglib uri='regions' prefix='region' %>

<security:enforceLogin
   loginPage='/WEB-INF/jsp/login/page.jsp'
   errorPage='/WEB-INF/jsp/loginFailed/page.jsp'/>

<region:render region='CHECKOUT_REGION'/>
```

Like the storefront page listed in Example 12-3.a on page 403, the checkout page renders a region, in this case CHECKOUT_REGION, which is defined like this:

```
<region:define id='CHECKOUT_REGION' region='LOGIN_REGION'>
   <region:put section='content'
               content='/WEB-INF/jsp/checkout/content.jsp'/>
</region:define>
```

The CHECKOUT_REGION extends LOGIN_REGION and overrides only the content section. That means that the checkout region is identical to the login region, except for the main content of the page. The main content of the checkout region is supplied by /WEB-INF/jsp/checkout/content.jsp, which is listed in Example 12-5.c.

Example 12-5.c /WEB-INF/jsp/checkout/content.jsp

```
<%@ page contentType='text/html; charset=UTF-8' %>
<%@ page import='beans.app.User' %>

<%@ taglib uri='application' prefix='app'  %>
<%@ taglib uri='i18n'        prefix='i18n' %>

<font size='4' color='blue'>
   <i18n:message base='app' key='checkout.title'/>
</font><p>

<img src='graphics/cart.gif'/>

<table cellpadding='10'>
   <th><i18n:message base='app'
                   key='checkout.table.header.item'/></th>
   <th><i18n:message base='app'
                   key='checkout.table.header.amount'/></th>
   <th><i18n:message base='app'
                   key='checkout.table.header.pricePerLb'/></th>
   <th><i18n:message base='app'
                   key='checkout.table.header.price'/></th>

   <% double total = 0.0; %>

   <app:iterateCart id='item'>
      <% String  name = item.getName();
         float    amt = item.getAmount(),
               price = item.getPrice();
      %>
      <tr>
         <td><%= name %></td>
```

```
      <td><%= amt %> lbs.</td>
      <td><i18n:format currency='<%=new Double(price)%>'/></td>
      <td><i18n:format currency='<%=new Double(price*amt)%>'/>
      </td>
   </tr>
   <% total += price * amt; %>
</app:iterateCart>

<tr>
   <td colspan='4'><hr/></td>
</tr>
   <td><b><i18n:message base='app' key='checkout.table.total'/>
   </b></td>
   <td></td><td></td>
   <td><i18n:format currency='<%= new Double(total) %>'/></td>
</tr>
</table><p>

<% User user = (User)session.getAttribute(
               tags.security.Constants.USER_KEY); %>

<font size='4' color='blue'>
   <i18n:message base='app' key='checkout.billTo'/><p>
</font>
   <%= user.getFirstName() %> <%= user.getLastName() %><br/>
   <%= user.getAddress() %><br/>
   <%= user.getCity() %>, <%= user.getState() %><br/>
   <%= user.getCountry() %><br/>
   <%= user.getCreditCardType() %><br/>
</p>

<form action='purchase-action.do'>
   <input type='submit'
          value='<i18n:message key="checkout.purchase.button"/>'/>
</form>
```

Like the storefront sidebar listed in Example 12-4.b on page 408, the checkout content page uses the application-specific `CartIterator` custom tag to iterate over the items in the user's shopping cart. Those items are used to construct the invoice and display a total price.

To obtain billing and shipping information, the checkout content page accesses a `User` bean from the current session.[6] See "Authentication" on page 443 for more information about how that `User` bean is created and stored in session scope.

---

6. The fruitstand application assumes that billing and shipping information are the same.

The checkout content page also contains a form with a submit button that creates a `purchase-action.do` request, which maps to `actions.PurchaseAction`. That action class is listed in Example 12-5.d.

Example 12-5.d   /WEB-INF/classes/actions/PurchaseAction.java

```
package actions;

import javax.servlet.ServletException;
import javax.servlet.http.HttpServlet;
import javax.servlet.http.HttpServletRequest;
import javax.servlet.http.HttpServletResponse;
import javax.servlet.http.HttpSession;

import beans.app.ShoppingCart;
import beans.app.User;

import action.ActionBase;
import action.ActionRouter;

public class PurchaseAction extends ActionBase
                      implements beans.app.Constants,
                                 tags.security.Constants {
   public ActionRouter perform(HttpServlet servlet,
                               HttpServletRequest req,
                               HttpServletResponse res)
                               throws ServletException {
      HttpSession session = req.getSession();
      ShoppingCart   cart = (ShoppingCart)session.getAttribute(
                                          SHOPPING_CART_KEY);
      if(cart == null) {
         throw new ServletException("Cart not found");
      }
      return new ActionRouter("purchase-page");
   }
}
```

Like the checkout action listed in Example 12-5.a on page 410, the purchase action checks to make sure the user has a shopping cart in the session. If so, the purchase action forwards the request to the purchase page.

The Purchase

The purchase page is a simple JSP page that thanks the user for their purchase and displays an expected shipping date. That JSP page is shown in Figure 12-6.

Figure 12-6 The Purchase Page

The `purchase-page` referenced by the purchase action listed in Example 12-5.d maps to `/WEB-INF/jsp/purchase/content.jsp`, which is listed in Example 12-5.e.

Example 12-5.e /WEB-INF/jsp/purchase/page.jsp

```
<%@ taglib uri='regions' prefix='region' %>

<region:render region='PURCHASE_REGION'/>
```

The purchase page, like the homepage, storefront, and checkout pages, is defined by a region. That region is listed below:

```
<region:define id='PURCHASE_REGION' region='LOGIN_REGION'>
   <region:put section='content'
               content='/WEB-INF/jsp/purchase/content.jsp'/>
</region:define>
```

Like `CHECKOUT_REGION`, `PURCHASE_REGION` extends `LOGIN_REGION` and redefines only the content section. That section is generated by `/WEBINF/jsp/purchase/content.jsp`, which is listed in Example 12-5.f.

Example 12-5.f /WEB-INF/jsp/purchase/content.jsp

```
<%@ page contentType='text/html; charset=UTF-8' %>

<%@ taglib uri='i18n' prefix='i18n' %>

<font size='4' color='blue'>
   <i18n:message base='app' key='purchase.title'/><p>
```

```
<i18n:message base='app' key='purchase.willBeShippedOn'/>
<i18n:format date='<%= new java.util.Date() %>'
        dateStyle='<%= java.text.DateFormat.SHORT %>'/></p>
</font>
```

The purchase page uses the i18n:message tag to display its messages. That page also uses the i18n:format tag to predict an optimistic shipping date.

This concludes our walkthrough of the fruitstand's main use case. The rest of this chapter examines the fruitstand application from two other perspectives: the MVC framework upon which the application is built and an examination of some of the application's other features, such as internationalization and authentication.

The Model 2 Framework

From "The Fruitstand" on page 392, it's apparent that the fruitstand application is implemented with small chunks of functionality that are plugged into a framework. That framework is the Model 2 framework discussed in "A Model 2 Framework" on page 154 that allows web applications to be implemented in a Model-View-Controller (MVC) style. This section examines the fruitstand's use of that framework, starting with the model, followed by the views and controllers.

The Model

The fruitstand's model consists of a database and beans, as depicted in Figure 12-7. Those beans, which reside in WEB-INF/classes/beans/app, are listed below:

- User: A fruitstand customer
- Users: A collection of users initialized from a database
- Item: An item for sale
- Inventory: A collection of items
- Shopping Cart: An inventory of the items a user has selected

In addition to the beans listed above, the fruitstand application also defines a number of constants that are used throughout the application.

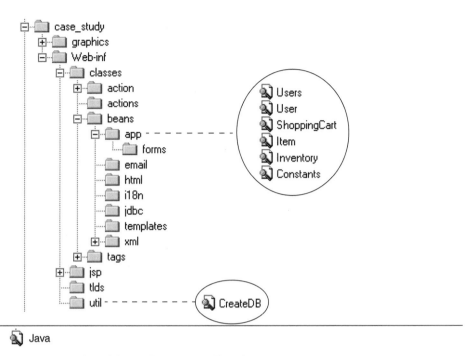

Figure 12-7 *The Model:* Beans and Database

The fruitstand application uses a database that maintains the fruitstand's inventory and list of users. That database is created by the CreateDB Java application that resides in the /WEB-INF/classes/util directory.

The Database

Figure 12-8 shows the inventory table from the fruitstand's database. That table maintains a stock keeping unit (sku), the name of the sku's corresponding fruit, and that fruit's price.

The fruitstand's database also maintains a table of users. That table has 14 columns, which is too wide to show effectively in Figure 12-8. The User table stores a user's first and last name, address, credit card information, username and password, and the user's role.

SKU	NAME	PRICE
1001	apple	0.29
1002	banana	0.69
1003	cantaloupe	0.19
1004	grapefruit	0.49
1005	grapes	0.79
1006	kiwi	0.99
1007	peach	0.39
1008	pear	0.69
1009	pineapple	0.29
1010	strawberry	0.89
1011	watermelon	0.29

Figure 12-8 The Inventory Table

The CreateDB application, which creates the fruitstand's database, is listed in Example 12-6.

Example 12-6 /WEB-INF/util/CreateDB.java

```java
import java.sql.Connection;
import java.sql.DriverManager;
import java.sql.SQLException;
import java.sql.Statement;

public class CreateDB {
   private Connection conn;
   private Statement stmt;

   public static void main(String args[]) {
      new CreateDB();
   }
   public CreateDB() {
      try {
         loadJDBCDriver();
         conn = getConnection("F:/databases/sunpress");
         stmt = conn.createStatement();

         createTables(stmt);
         populateTables(stmt);

         stmt.close();
         conn.close();
```

```
        DriverManager.getConnection(
                            "jdbc:cloudscape:;shutdown=true");
    }
    catch(SQLException ex) {
        ex.printStackTrace();
    }
}
private void createTables(Statement stmt) {
    try {
        stmt.execute("CREATE TABLE Users (" +
            "FIRST_NAME VARCHAR(15), " +
            "LAST_NAME VARCHAR(25), " +
            "ADDRESS VARCHAR(35), " +
            "CITY VARCHAR(15), " +
            "STATE VARCHAR(15), " +
            "COUNTRY VARCHAR(25), " +
            "CREDIT_CARD_TYPE VARCHAR(10), " +
            "CREDIT_CARD_NUMBER VARCHAR(20), " +
            "CREDIT_CARD_EXPIRATION VARCHAR(10), " +
            "USER_ID VARCHAR(15), " +
            "PASSWORD VARCHAR(15), " +
            "PASSWORD_HINT VARCHAR(15), " +
            "ROLES VARCHAR(99))");

        stmt.execute("CREATE TABLE Inventory (" +
            "SKU         INTEGER, " +
            "NAME        VARCHAR(30), " +
            "PRICE       FLOAT)");
    }
    catch(SQLException ex) {
        ex.printStackTrace();
    }
}
private void populateTables(Statement stmt) {
    try {
        stmt.execute("INSERT INTO Users VALUES " +
        "('James', 'Wilson', '24978 Roquert Lane', 'Ithica'," +
        " 'New York', 'USA', 'Visa', '124-3393-62975', '01/05',"+
        " 'jwilson', 's2pdpl8', 'license', 'customer')");

        stmt.execute("INSERT INTO Inventory VALUES " +
                        "('1001', 'apple', '0.29')," +
                        "('1002', 'banana', '0.69')," +
                        "('1003', 'cantaloupe', '0.19')," +
                        "('1004', 'grapefruit', '0.49')," +
                        "('1005', 'grapes', '0.79')," +
                        "('1006', 'kiwi', '0.99')," +
                        "('1007', 'peach', '0.39')," +
```

```
                                     "('1008', 'pear', '0.69')," +
                                     "('1009', 'pineapple', '0.29')," +
                                     "('1010', 'strawberry', '0.89')," +
                                     "('1011', 'watermelon', '0.29')");
            }
            catch(SQLException ex) {
                ex.printStackTrace();
            }
        }
        private void loadJDBCDriver() {
            try {
                Class.forName("COM.cloudscape.core.JDBCDriver");
            }
            catch(ClassNotFoundException e) {
                e.printStackTrace();
            }
        }
        private Connection getConnection(String dbName) {
            Connection con = null;
            try {
                con = DriverManager.getConnection(
                    "jdbc:cloudscape:" + dbName + ";create=true");
            }
            catch(SQLException sqe) {
                System.err.println("Couldn't access " + dbName);
            }
            return con;
        }
    }
}
```

The application listed in Example 12-6 connects to a Cloudscape database and creates a database in `f:/databases/sunpress`. The application subsequently populates the database with the fruitstand's two tables, shuts down the database, and exits.

It's easy to adapt the application listed in Example 12-6 for a different database vendor by changing the driver name used in the `loadJDBCDriver` method and the database URL used in `getConnection`.

The Beans

The beans used in the fruitstand application are simple versions of the canonical User, Users, Inventory, and Shopping Cart objects. The `User` class is listed in Example 12-7.a.

Example 12-7.a /WEB-INF/classes/beans/app/User.java

```java
package beans.app;

// Users are immutable to eliminate multithreading concerns.

public class User implements java.io.Serializable {
    private final String firstName, lastName, address, city, state;
    private final String country, creditCardType, creditCardNumber;
    private final String creditCardExpiration;
    private final String userName, password, pwdHint, roles;

    public User(String firstName, String lastName, String address,
                String city, String state, String country,
                String creditCardType, String creditCardNumber,
                String creditCardExpiration, String userName,
                String password, String pwdHint, String roles) {
        this.firstName          = firstName;
        this.lastName           = lastName;
        this.address            = address;
        this.city               = city;
        this.state              = state;
        this.country            = country;
        this.creditCardType     = creditCardType;
        this.creditCardNumber   = creditCardNumber;
        this.creditCardExpiration = creditCardExpiration;
        this.userName           = userName;
        this.password           = password;
        this.pwdHint            = pwdHint;
        this.roles              = roles;
    }
    public String getFirstName() { return firstName; }
    public String getLastName()  { return lastName;  }
    public String getAddress()   { return address;   }
    public String getCity()      { return city;      }
    public String getState()     { return state;     }
    public String getCountry()   { return country;   }

    public String getCreditCardType()   { return creditCardType; }
    public String getCreditCardNumber() { return creditCardNumber;}
    public String getCreditCardExpiration() {
        return creditCardExpiration;
    }

    public String getUserName() { return userName; }
    public String getPassword() { return password; }
    public String getPwdHint()  { return pwdHint;  }
    public String getRoles()    { return roles;    }
```

```
public boolean equals(String uname, String pwd) {
    return getUserName().equals(uname) &&
            getPassword().equals(pwd);
    }
}
```

The User class maintains read-only information about a single user. That class is immutable to eliminate multithreading concerns. If you want to change information about a user, the original User instance must be replaced. Because modifying user data is typically infrequent and multithreaded access to users can be common, an immutable User class makes sense in this case.

Users are maintained by a Users class, which is listed in Example 12-7.b.

Example 12-7.b   /WEB-INF/classes/beans/app/Users.java

```java
package beans.app;

import java.sql.ResultSet;
import java.sql.ResultSetMetaData;
import java.sql.SQLException;

import java.util.Enumeration;
import java.util.Hashtable;

public class Users {
    private final static int FIRST_NAME=1, LAST_NAME=2, ADDRESS=3,
                             CITY=4, STATE=5, COUNTRY=6,
                             CREDIT_TYPE=7, CREDIT_NUMBER=8,
                             CREDIT_EXPIRE=9, USER_NAME=10,
                             PASSWORD=11, PASSWORD_HINT=12,
                             ROLES=13;
    private final Hashtable users = new Hashtable();

    public Users(ResultSet rs) {
        try {
            ResultSetMetaData rsmd = rs.getMetaData();

            if(rsmd.getColumnCount() > 0) {
                boolean moreRows = rs.next(); // point to first
                                              // row initially
                while(moreRows) {
                    addUser(new User(
                        ((String)rs.getObject(FIRST_NAME)).trim(),
                        ((String)rs.getObject(LAST_NAME)).trim(),
                        ((String)rs.getObject(ADDRESS)).trim(),
                        ((String)rs.getObject(CITY)).trim(),
```

```
                    ((String)rs.getObject(STATE)).trim(),
                    ((String)rs.getObject(COUNTRY)).trim(),
                    ((String)rs.getObject(CREDIT_TYPE)).trim(),
                    ((String)rs.getObject(CREDIT_NUMBER)).trim(),
                    ((String)rs.getObject(CREDIT_EXPIRE)).trim(),
                    ((String)rs.getObject(USER_NAME)).trim(),
                    ((String)rs.getObject(PASSWORD)).trim(),
                    ((String)rs.getObject(PASSWORD_HINT)).trim(),
                    ((String)rs.getObject(ROLES)).trim()));

            moreRows = rs.next(); // move to next row
         }
      }
   }
   catch(SQLException ex) {
      // can't throw an exception from a constructor
   }
}
public int getNumberOfUsers() {
   return users.size();
}
public User addUser(User user) {
   users.put(user.getUserName(), user);
   return user;
}
public User getUser(String username, String password) {
   User user = getUser(username);
     boolean found = false;

   if(user != null) {
       found = user.equals(username, password);
   }
   return found ? user : null;
}
public User getUser(String username) {
   return (User)users.get(username);
}
public Hashtable getUsers() {
   return users;
}
public String getPasswordHint(String username) {
   User user = getUser(username);
   return user != null ? user.getPwdHint() : null;
}
}
```

Because users are stored in a database, the Users constructor is passed a ResultSet object, which is used to create users. Besides the constructor, the Users class provides a number of accessor methods for retrieving information associated with a user.

Like the User class, the Users class is thread safe because its members are immutable.

Example 12-7.c lists the Item class, which represents an item in an inventory.

Example 12-7.c /WEB-INF/classes/beans/app/Item.java

```java
package beans.app;

// This is an item in an inventory or shopping cart (same thing)
// with four properties: sku, (stock keeping unit) name, price,
// and amount. Items are nearly immutable to eliminate
// multithreading concerns.

public class Item implements java.io.Serializable {
    private final int sku; // stock keeping unit
    private final float price;
    private final String name;

    private float amount;

    public Item(int sku, String name, float price, float amount) {
        this.sku    = sku;
        this.name   = name;
        this.amount = amount;
        this.price  = price;
    }
    public int    getSku()   { return sku;   }
    public String getName()  { return name;  }
    public float  getPrice() { return price; }

    public synchronized float getAmount() {
        return amount;
    }
    public synchronized void setAmount(float amount) {
        this.amount = amount;
    }
}
```

The Item class maintains a stock keeping unit, name, price, and an amount for each item. All that information is read-only, except for the price, which is expected to change relatively frequently. The setter and getter methods for the amount are both synchronized, so the Item class is thread safe.

Items are maintained by an inventory; the Inventory class is listed in Example 12-7.d.

Example 12-7.d   /WEB-INF/classes/beans/app/Inventory.java

```
package beans.app;

import java.util.Iterator;
import java.util.Vector;

public class Inventory implements java.io.Serializable {
    final protected Vector items;

    public Inventory() {
        items = new Vector();
    }
    public void addItem(Item item) {
        items.add(item);
    }
    public void removeItem(Item item) {
        items.remove(item);
    }
    public Vector getItems() {
        return items;
    }
}
```

The Inventory class is a simple façade for a vector of items; it allows items to be added and removed from the inventory.[7] The Inventory class also provides a getItems method, for convenience, that returns the vector of items. The caller of that method should not modify that vector.

Example 12-7.e lists the ShoppingCart class.

Example 12-7.e   /WEB-INF/classes/beans/app/ShoppingCart.java

```
package beans.app;

public class ShoppingCart extends Inventory {
}
```

For the purposes of the fruitstand application, a shopping cart is the same thing as an inventory; however, the ShoppingCart class exists as a placeholder for functionality specific to shopping carts that may be added in the future.

---

7.   See "Façade Design Pattern for HTML Forms" on page 79 for more information about the Façade design pattern.

The fruitstand application uses a number of constants, which are defined in the Constants interface. That class is listed in Example 12-7.f.

Example 12-7.f /WEB-INF/classes/beans/app/Constants.java

```java
package beans.app;

// These constants are mostly used by this application's actions
// -- see /WEB-INF/classes/actions.

public interface Constants {
    // this prefix provides some degree of uniqueness for the
    // constants defined below.
    static final String prefix = "beans.app";

    static final String
        // Keys for attributes
        LOCALE_KEY            = prefix + ".locale",
        SHOPPING_CART_KEY     = prefix + ".cart",
        USERS_KEY             = prefix + ".users",
        USERNAME_KEY          = prefix + ".username",
        PASSWORD_KEY          = prefix + ".password",
        CONFIRM_PASSWORD_KEY  = prefix + ".cnfrmpwd",
        PASSWORD_HINT_KEY     = prefix + ".pwdhint",

        // Default values
        DEFAULT_I18N_BASE = "app";
}
```

The constants defined by the Constants interface are accessed by implementing that interface; for example, the PurchaseAction class listed in Example 12-5.d on page 414 implements the Constants interface and uses the SHOPPING_CART_KEY.

The Views—JSP Pages and Templates

The most dynamic and interesting aspect of the fruitstand application is its views, which are constructed with regions and templates. The goal of this section is to illustrate how the fruitstand application uses regions and templates. This section does not show how regions or templates work; for that discussion, see "Templates" on page 96.

Figure 12-9 shows the files used to create all nine of the fruitstand's JSP pages. Each directory under /WEB-INF/jsp, with the exception of the shared and templates directories, contains all of the JSP files specific to one JSP page; for example, /WEB-INF/jsp/accountCreated contains all of the JSP files— page.jsp and content.jsp—that are specific to the account-created JSP page.

The shared directory contains JSP files that are used by more than one JSP page, and the templates directory contains the fruitstand application's lone template.

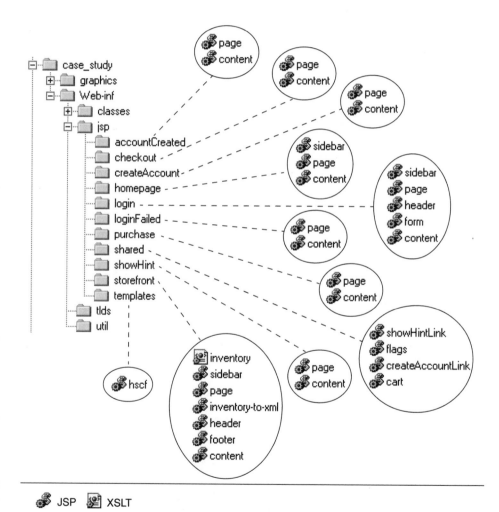

🐝 JSP   🖼 XSLT

Figure 12-9 *The Views:* JSP Pages

Each JSP page in the fruitstand application is defined by a region, which uses a template, and the content that's inserted into that template. All of the regions in the application use the same template: `/WEB-INF/jsp/templates/hscf.jsp`. That template displays four regions: header, sidebar, content, and footer; thus, the template is named `hscf.jsp`.

All of the fruitstand's regions are defined in one file, `/WEBINF/jsp/regionDefinitions.jsp`, which is listed in Example 12-7.g.

Example 12-7.g /WEB-INF/jsp/regionDefinitions.jsp

```
<%@ taglib uri='regions' prefix='region' %>

<region:define id='STOREFRONT_REGION'
          template='/WEB-INF/jsp/templates/hscf.jsp'>
   <region:put section='title'
               content='FruitStand.com'
                direct='true'/>

   <region:put section='background'
               content='graphics/blueAndWhiteBackground.gif'
                direct='true'/>

   <region:put section='header'
               content='/WEB-INF/jsp/storefront/header.jsp'/>

   <region:put section='sidebar'
               content='/WEB-INF/jsp/storefront/sidebar.jsp'/>

   <region:put section='content'
               content='/WEB-INF/jsp/storefront/content.jsp'/>

   <region:put section='footer'
               content='/WEB-INF/jsp/storefront/footer.jsp'/>
</region:define>

<region:define id='LOGIN_REGION' region='STOREFRONT_REGION'>
   <region:put section='header'
               content='/WEB-INF/jsp/login/header.jsp'/>

   <region:put section='sidebar'
               content='/WEB-INF/jsp/login/sidebar.jsp'/>

   <region:put section='content'
               content='/WEB-INF/jsp/login/content.jsp'/>
</region:define>
```

```
<region:define id='HOMEPAGE_REGION' region='STOREFRONT_REGION'>
    <region:put section='sidebar'
                content='/WEB-INF/jsp/homepage/sidebar.jsp'/>

    <region:put section='content'
                content='/WEB-INF/jsp/homepage/content.jsp'/>
</region:define>

<region:define id='CREATE_ACCOUNT_REGION' region='LOGIN_REGION'>
    <region:put section='content'
                content='/WEB-INF/jsp/createAccount/content.jsp'/>
</region:define>

<region:define id='LOGIN_FAILED_REGION' region='LOGIN_REGION'>
    <region:put section='content'
                content='/WEB-INF/jsp/loginFailed/content.jsp'/>
</region:define>

<region:define id='ACCOUNT_CREATED_REGION' region='LOGIN_REGION'>
    <region:put section='content'
                content='/WEB-INF/jsp/accountCreated/content.jsp'/>
</region:define>

<region:define id='CHECKOUT_REGION' region='LOGIN_REGION'>
    <region:put section='content'
                content='/WEB-INF/jsp/checkout/content.jsp'/>
</region:define>

<region:define id='PURCHASE_REGION' region='LOGIN_REGION'>
    <region:put section='content'
                content='/WEB-INF/jsp/purchase/content.jsp'/>
</region:define>

<region:define id='SHOW_HINT_REGION' region='LOGIN_REGION'>
    <region:put section='content'
                content='/WEB-INF/jsp/showHint/content.jsp'/>
</region:define>
```

Most of the regions defined in Example 12-7.g reuse content from another region; for example, the HOMEPAGE_REGION reuses the title, background, and footer from the STOREFRONT_REGION, as discussed in "The Homepage" on page 395. All the other regions reuse content from either LOGIN_REGION or STOREFRONT_REGION.

Defining all of an application's regions in one file eases maintenance of those regions; for example, it's easy to change the content displayed by any JSP page simply by modifying the file listed in Example 12-7.g. The ability for regions to extend each other enables regions to share content and facilitates a more readable definition of those regions.

The only template defined by the fruitstand application is listed in Example 12-7.h.

Example 12-7.h   /WEB-INF/jsp/templates/hscf.jsp

```
<html><head>
  <%@ taglib uri='regions' prefix='region' %>
  <title><region:render section='title' /></title>
</head>

<body background='<region:render section='background' />'>

<table>
   <tr valign='top'>
      <td><region:render section='sidebar' /></td>
      <td>
         <table>
            <tr><td><region:render section='header' /></td></tr>
            <tr><td><region:render section='content' /></td></tr>
            <tr><td><region:render section='footer' /></td></tr>
         </table>
      </td>
   </tr>
</table>

</body></html>
```

The template listed in Example 12-7.h uses an HTML table to display content. That content is supplied by JSP files that are referenced by a region. So, for example, when LOGIN_REGION is rendered, the template listed in Example 12-7.h uses the content defined in that region; namely, the storefront's title, background, and footer and the login page's content section.

Notice that each directory in the fruitstand application that corresponds to a JSP page contains a JSP file titled page.jsp. That page renders a corresponding region; for example, Example 12-7.i lists the page.jsp file for the login page. That JSP file renders the login region.

Example 12-7.i /WEB-INF/jsp/login/page.jsp

```
<%@ taglib uri='regions' prefix='region' %>

<region:render region='LOGIN_REGION'/>
```

The fruitstand's page.jsp files are responsible for features central to pages; for example, the page.jsp file listed in Example 12-7.j restricts access to the checkout page to users that have logged in.

Example 12-7.j /WEB-INF/jsp/checkout/page.jsp

```
<%@ taglib uri='security' prefix='security'%>
<%@ taglib uri='regions' prefix='region' %>

<security:enforceLogin
    loginPage='/WEB-INF/jsp/login/page.jsp'
    errorPage='/WEB-INF/jsp/loginFailed/page.jsp'/>

<region:render region='CHECKOUT_REGION'/>
```

The security:enforceLogin tag used in Example 12-7.j evaluates the rest of the JSP file only if the user has logged in; if not, the request is forwarded to the login page. You can read more about the security:enforceLogin tag in "Security" on page 250. Authentication for the fruitstand application is discussed in "Authentication" on page 443.

Templates are powerful because they separate page layout from page content, both of which can change frequently during development. Because of that separation, you can change the layout of multiple JSP pages by changing a single template. Conversely, you can make changes to content without affecting layout.

Regions specify content used by templates. The ability to specify regions somewhere other than where they are used, as is the case for the fruitstand application, lets you centralize an application's JSP page descriptions. That ability simplifies the implementation and maintenance of JSP pages.

Regions can also be defined in terms of another region. That allows one region to "inherit" sections from another region, thereby simplifying page construction and encouraging reuse.

Finally, both templates and regions encourage you to construct JSP pages out of small, reusable components, each of which represents a particular section of a region. Constructing JSP pages in that manner results in web applications that are flexible, malleable, and extensible.

Now that we've seen how the fruitstand's model and views are implemented, let's take a look at the application's controllers.

The Controllers—Servlets and Actions

In a Model-View-Controller (MVC) application, data is stored in a model and displayed by views. Controllers are the glue that connects models and views. Controllers react to events and may access the model before forwarding control to a view.

The fruitstand's controllers are servlets and actions, both of which are discussed in the following sections.

Servlets

The fruitstand uses four servlets that reside in /WEB-INF/classes, as shown by Figure 12-10.

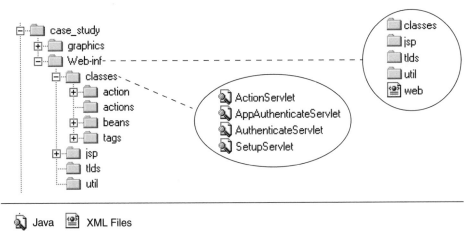

| <span></span> Java | <span></span> XML Files |

Figure 12-10 Servlets and web.xml

The `ActionServlet` is an integral part of the fruitstand's Model 2 framework and handles all HTTP requests that end in .do. Because that servlet is discussed extensively in "A Model 2 Framework" on page 154, it is not discussed here.

The `AuthenticateServlet` is an abstract base class that's extended by `AppAuthenticateServlet`. Those servlets are used to enforce authentication, as discussed in "Authentication" on page 443.

The `SetupServlet` loads at startup and initializes the database. That servlet is listed in Example 12-8.b on page 435.

All of the fruitstand's servlets are configured in the application's `web.xml` file, which is listed in Example 12-8.a.

Example 12-8.a /WEB-INF/web.xml

```xml
<?xml version="1.0" encoding="ISO-8859-1"?>

<!DOCTYPE web-app
  PUBLIC "-//Sun Microsystems, Inc.//DTD Web Application 2.2//EN"
  "http://java.sun.com/j2ee/dtds/web-app_2.2.dtd">

<web-app>
  <servlet>
     <servlet-name>authenticate</servlet-name>
     <servlet-class>AppAuthenticateServlet</servlet-class>
  </servlet>

  <servlet>
     <servlet-name>action</servlet-name>
     <servlet-class>ActionServlet</servlet-class>
     <init-param>
        <param-name>action-mappings</param-name>
        <param-value>actions</param-value>
     </init-param>
  </servlet>

  <servlet>
     <servlet-name>setup</servlet-name>
     <servlet-class>SetupServlet</servlet-class>
     <init-param>
        <param-name>jdbcDriver</param-name>
        <param-value>COM.cloudscape.core.JDBCDriver</param-value>
     </init-param>

     <init-param>
        <param-name>jdbcURL</param-name>
        <param-value>
           jdbc:cloudscape:f:/databases/sunpress;create=false
        </param-value>
     </init-param>

     <init-param>
        <param-name>jdbcUser</param-name>
        <param-value>roymartin</param-value>
```

```
        </init-param>

        <init-param>
            <param-name>jdbcPassword</param-name>
            <param-value>royboy</param-value>
        </init-param>

        <load-on-startup/>
    </servlet>

    <servlet-mapping>
        <servlet-name>action</servlet-name>
        <url-pattern>*.do</url-pattern>
    </servlet-mapping>

    <servlet-mapping>
        <servlet-name>authenticate</servlet-name>
        <url-pattern>/authenticate</url-pattern>
    </servlet-mapping>

    <welcome-file-list>
            <welcome-file>index.jsp</welcome-file>
    </welcome-file-list>

    <taglib>
      <taglib-uri>application</taglib-uri>
      <taglib-location>/WEB-INF/tlds/utilities.tld</taglib-location>
    </taglib>

    ... more taglib mappings that follow are omitted for brevity ...

  </web-app>
```

The `web.xml` file defines servlet names and classes and, where appropriate, servlet initialization parameters. The `SetupServlet` has initialization parameters for the JDBC URL and driver and a username and password for the application's database.

Additionally, `web.xml` specifies the custom tag libraries used by the fruitstand application. The listing in Example 12-8.a is truncated in the interests of brevity because the application uses a number of custom tag libraries. Besides the application custom tag library listed above, the fruitstand application uses the following tag libraries:

- database
- DOM

- html
- i18n
- template
- tokens

The custom tag libraries listed above are discussed throughout this book, and therefore are not covered here.

The SetupServlet, which initializes the database, is listed in Example 12-8.b.

Example 12-8.b   /WEB-INF/classes/SetupServlet.java

```java
import java.sql.Connection;
import java.sql.ResultSet;
import java.sql.ResultSetMetaData;
import java.sql.Statement;
import java.sql.SQLException;

import javax.servlet.ServletConfig;
import javax.servlet.ServletContext;
import javax.servlet.ServletException;
import javax.servlet.http.HttpServlet;

import beans.app.User;
import beans.app.Users;
import beans.jdbc.DbConnectionPool;

public class SetupServlet extends HttpServlet
                        implements beans.app.Constants,
                                   tags.jdbc.Constants {
    private DbConnectionPool pool;

    public void init(ServletConfig config) throws ServletException{
        super.init(config);

        ServletContext ctx = config.getServletContext();
        createDbConnectionPool(config, ctx);

        try {
            ctx.setAttribute(USERS_KEY, loadUsers(ctx));
        }
        catch(SQLException ex) {
            throw new ServletException(ex);
        }
    }
    public void destroy() {
```

```
        ServletContext ctx = getServletConfig().getServletContext();
        ctx.removeAttribute(DBPOOL_KEY);
        ctx.removeAttribute(USERS_KEY);

        pool.shutdown();
        pool = null;
        super.destroy();
    }
    private void createDbConnectionPool(ServletConfig config,
                                        ServletContext ctx) {
        pool = new DbConnectionPool(
                    config.getInitParameter("jdbcDriver"),
                    config.getInitParameter("jdbcURL"),
                    config.getInitParameter("jdbcUser"),
                    config.getInitParameter("jdbcPwd"));
        ctx.setAttribute(DBPOOL_KEY, pool);
    }
    private Users loadUsers(ServletContext ctx)
                                        throws SQLException {
        Connection conn = null;

        if(pool != null) {
            try {
                // wait for a maximum of 10 seconds for a connection
                // if pool is full
                conn = (Connection)pool.getConnection(10000);
            }
            catch(Exception ex) {
                throw new SQLException(ex.getMessage());
            }
            Statement stmt = conn.createStatement();
            ResultSet rs = stmt.executeQuery("SELECT * FROM USERS");
            Users users = new Users(rs);

            pool.recycleConnection(conn);
            return users;
        }
        return null;
    }
}
```

The servlet listed in Example 12-8.b creates a database connection pool with the initialization parameters specified in web.xml. The implementation and use of that database connection pool is discussed in "Connection Pooling" on page 302.

After creating the database connection pool, the SetupServlet performs a query on the database and constructs the application's users based on the results of that query.

The servlet container invokes `SetupServlet` when the application is first accessed, as specified by the `load-on-startup` tag in `web.xml`.

Servlets are only half of the fruitstand's controllers. Much of the responsibility for reacting to events and forwarding to views is shouldered by the fruitstand's actions.

Actions

When an HTTP request ending in .do is initiated in the fruitstand application, it is ultimately handled by an action. Exactly how that is implemented is discussed extensively in "A Model 2 Framework" on page 154 and therefore is not covered here. Nevertheless, actions are integral to a Model 2 web application, and the fruitstand uses them heavily, as you can see from Figure 12-11.

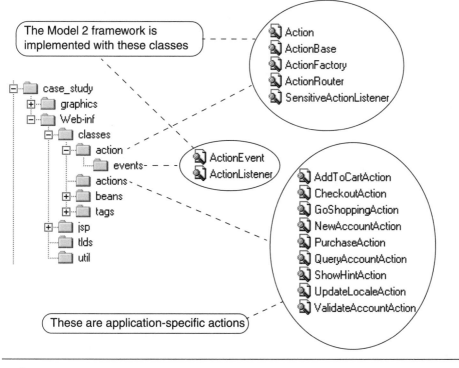

 Java

Figure 12-11 Model 2 Framework Action Classes

The `/WEB-INF/classes/action` and `/WEB-INF/classes/action/events` directories contain the classes that constitute the Model 2 framework. Those classes are discussed in "A Model 2 Framework" on page 154 and "Event Handling and Sensitive Form Resubmissions" on page 182.

The `/WEB-INF/classes/actions` directory houses the fruitstand's application-specific actions. Each of those nine actions represents a single use case, which is evident from their names. None of those actions are discussed further in this section, but you can find discussions of them throughout this chapter; for example, see "The Shopping Cart" on page 406 for a discussion of `AddToCartAction` and "The Checkout" on page 410 for a discussion of `CheckoutAction`.

Internationalization

We've already seen that the fruitstand application uses the custom tags discussed in "I18n" on page 206 to internationalize text, numbers, dates, and currency. This section explores how fruitstand users can change languages on the fly.

Figure 12-12 shows the fruitstand's login page in three different languages. To switch from one language to another, the user clicks on one of the flags in the sidebar; that action changes the application's locale and updates the current page.

The steps in the *user switches language* use case are listed below.

1. The user clicks on a flag in the fruitstand's sidebar.
2. The application updates its locale according to the selected flag.
3. The application redisplays the current page.

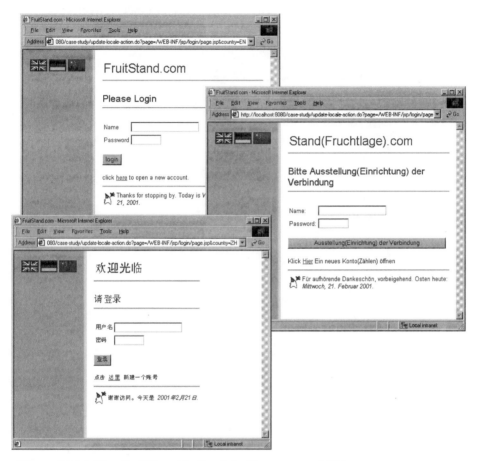

Figure 12-12 The FruitStand in English, German, and Chinese

Figure 12-13 shows the files involved in the use case outlined above.

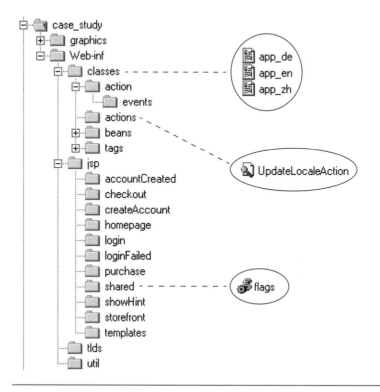

Figure 12-13 is preceded by the tree and legend.

Java   **JSP**   **Properties Files**

Figure 12-13 Files Involved in the User Changes Languages Case

The fruitstand application maintains three properties files that each define all of the text displayed by the application. Each of those files defines the same messages in a different language. The English properties file is partially listed in Example 12-9.a.

Example 12-9.a /WEB-INF/classes/app_en.properties

```
click=click
here=here

messages.login-header-title=FruitStand.com
messages.today=Today is {0, date}

homepage.title=A Model 2 JSP Application
```

```
homepage.text=<p>This mockup of a fruit stand uses many of the
techniques discussed in Advanced JavaServer Pages, published by Sun
Microsystems Press and Prentice-Hall in May 2001.

... the rest of homepage.title is omitted in the interests of
brevity ...

login.title=FruitStand.com

login.form.title=Please Login
login.button.submit=login
login.textfield.name=Name
login.textfield.pwd=Password
login.footer.message=Thanks for stopping by. Today is

login.failed.title=Login Failed
login.failed.message=Please enter a valid username and password, or
create a new account

... the rest of this file is omitted for brevity ...
```

In the interests of brevity, the properties files listed in this section are all truncated. The German properties file is listed in Example 12-9.b.

Example 12-9.b   /WEB-INF/classes/app_de.properties

```
click=Klick
here=Hier

messages.login-header-title=FruitStand.com
messages.today=Huite ist {0, date}

homepage.title=Eine Model 2 JSP Anwendung
...
```

Example 12-9.c lists the Chinese properties file, which unlike the English and German versions defines messages with Unicode escape sequences. See "Unicode" on page 208 for more information concerning Unicode.

Example 12-9.c /WEB-INF/classes/app_zh.properties

```
click=\u70b9\u51fb
here=\u8fd9\u91cc

messages.login-header-title=\u6b22\u8fce\u5149\u4e34
messages.today=\u4eca\u5929\u662f {0, date}

homepage.title=\u4e00\u4e2a\u6a21\u5f0f\u4e8cJSP\u8303\u4f8b
...
```

Example 12-9.d lists the `flags.jsp` file.

Example 12-9.d /WEB-INF/jsp/shared/flags.jsp

```
<% String thisPage = request.getServletPath();
   String updateLocaleAction = "update-locale-action.do?page=" +
                               thisPage + "&country="; %>
<table width='160'>
   <tr><td>
      <a href='<%= updateLocaleAction + "EN" %>'>
         <img src='graphics/flags/britain_flag.gif'/></a>

      <a href='<%= updateLocaleAction + "DE" %>'>
         <img src='graphics/flags/german_flag.gif'/></a>

      <a href='<%= updateLocaleAction + "ZH" %>'>
         <img src='graphics/flags/chinese_flag.gif'/></a></tr>
   </td><td height='25'></td>
</table>
```

The JSP file listed in Example 12-9.d constructs actions for each of the flags according to the current page and the country those flags represent; for example, the `flags.jsp` file is included by `/WEB-INF/jsp/storefront/sidebar`, so if a user clicks on the Chinese flag while viewing the storefront, the following action would be invoked:

```
http://localhost:8080/case-study/update-locale-
action.do?page=/WEB-INF/jsp/storefront/page.jsp&country=ZH
```

The actions associated with the flags from `flags.jsp` result in a call to the `UpdateLocaleAction`, which is listed in Example 12-9.e.

Example 12-9.e /WEB-INF/classes/actions/UpdateLocaleAction.java

```
package actions;

import java.util.Locale;

import javax.servlet.ServletException;
import javax.servlet.http.HttpServlet;
import javax.servlet.http.HttpServletRequest;
import javax.servlet.http.HttpServletResponse;

import action.ActionBase;
import action.ActionRouter;
```

```
public class UpdateLocaleAction extends ActionBase
                          implements beans.app.Constants {
   public ActionRouter perform(HttpServlet servlet,
                               HttpServletRequest req,
                               HttpServletResponse res)
                               throws ServletException {
      Locale locale = new Locale(req.getParameter("country"),"");
      String forwardTo = req.getParameter("page");

      req.getSession(true).setAttribute(LOCALE_KEY, locale);
      res.setLocale(locale);

      return new ActionRouter(forwardTo, true, false);
   }
}
```

The update locale action obtains the country associated with the desired language from a request parameter that is generated by the JSP file listed in Example 12-9.e on page 442. That action subsequently sets a session attribute that indicates the current locale, sets the response's locale, and then forwards the request to the original page.

When the original page is redisplayed, i18n custom tags render internationalized text. Those tags use the locale in the user's session.

Authentication

Anyone can shop at the fruitstand, but only logged-in users can check out their purchase. That security constraint is implemented with a use case called *authenticate user*. The steps involved in that use case are listed below.

1. When the user tries to check out, a custom tag checks to see that the user is logged in.
2. If the user is not logged in, the custom tag in step #1 forwards to the login page.
3. The user clicks on the create account link on the login page.
4. The application displays a form for creating a new account.
5. The user fills out the form and activates the create account button.
6. The application redisplays the login form and the user logs in.

The files that participate in the *authenticate user* use case are shown in Figure 12-14.

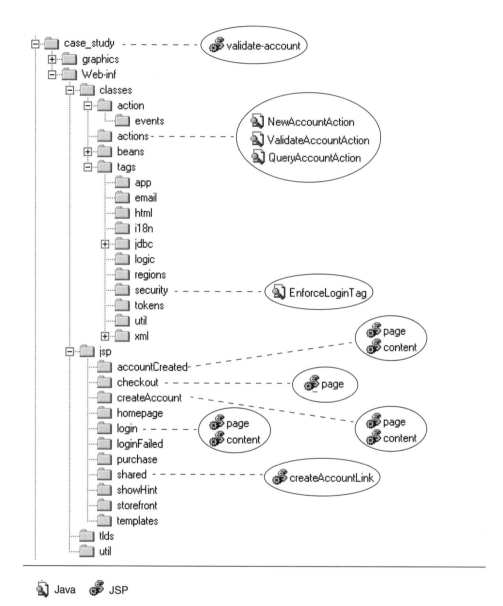

Java   JSP

Figure 12-14 Files Involved in the Authenticate User Use Case

Let's see how the files shown in Figure 12-14 are used to implement the *authenticate user* use case. First, users are directed to the checkout page when they activate the storefront's Checkout button, as discussed in "The Checkout" on page 410. That checkout page is listed in Example 12-10.a.

Example 12-10.a   /WEB-INF/jsp/checkout/page.jsp

```
<%@ taglib uri='security' prefix='security'%>
<%@ taglib uri='regions' prefix='region' %>

<security:enforceLogin
    loginPage='/WEB-INF/jsp/login/page.jsp'
    errorPage='/WEB-INF/jsp/loginFailed/page.jsp'/>

<region:render region='CHECKOUT_REGION'/>
```

The `security:enforceLogin` tag used in Example 12-10.a is listed in Example 12-10.b.

Example 12-10.b   /WEB-INF/jsp/classes/tags/security/EnforceLoginTag.java
                      (partial listing)

```
package tags.security;
...
public class EnforceLoginTag extends TagSupport
                             implements Constants {
    private String loginPage, errorPage;
    ...
    public int doEndTag() throws JspException {
        HttpSession session = pageContext.getSession();
        HttpServletRequest req = (HttpServletRequest)pageContext.
                                                  getRequest();
        String protectedPage = req.getServletPath();

        if(session.getAttribute(USER_KEY) == null) {
            session.setAttribute(LOGIN_PAGE_KEY,     loginPage);
            session.setAttribute(ERROR_PAGE_KEY,     errorPage);
            session.setAttribute(PROTECTED_PAGE_KEY, protectedPage);

            try {
               pageContext.forward(loginPage);
               return SKIP_PAGE;
            }
            catch(Exception ex) {
                throw new JspException(ex.getMessage());
            }
        }
        return EVAL_PAGE;
    }
    ...
}
```

The `security:enforceLogin` tag checks to see if there is a `User` object in session scope; if so, the rest of the checkout page is evaluated; otherwise, that tag forwards to the login page. The content for the login page is listed in Example 12-10.c.

Example 12-10.c /WEB-INF/jsp/login/content.jsp

```
<%@ page contentType='text/html; charset=UTF-8' %>

<%@ taglib uri='i18n' prefix='i18n' %>

<font size='5' color='blue'>
   <i18n:message key='login.form.title'/>
</font><hr>

<jsp:include page='form.jsp' flush='true'/>
<jsp:include page='../shared/createAccountLink.jsp' flush='true'/>
```

The JSP page listed in Example 12-10.c includes two other JSP files. The first file generates the login form and is a file of its own because it's used by another JSP page in the application. That form JSP page is listed in Example 12-10.k on page 453.

The second JSP page included by the login content page is `createAccountLink.jsp`, which is listed in Example 12-10.d.

Example 12-10.d /WEB-INF/jsp/shared/createAccountLink.jsp

```
<%@ taglib uri='i18n' prefix='i18n' %>
<%@ taglib uri='utilities' prefix='util' %>

<i18n:message base='app' key='click'/>
<a href='<util:encodeURL url="query-account-action.do"/>'>
<i18n:message base='app' key='here'/></a>
<i18n:message base='app' key='password.hint.toOpenAccount'/>
```

`createAccountLink.jsp` provides a link that forwards to the query account action. Figure 12-15 shows the login page.

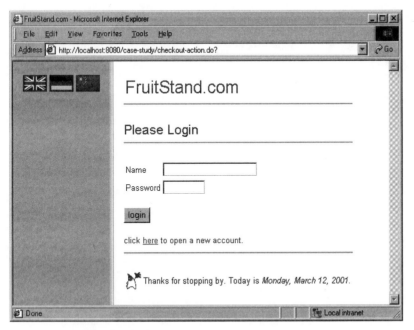

Figure 12-15 The Login Page

The link in `createAccountLink.jsp` listed in Example 12-10.d submits a `query-account-action.do` request that maps to `QueryAccountAction`. That action is listed in Example 12-10.e.

Example 12-10.e /WEB-INF/classes/QueryAccountAction.java

```
package actions;

import javax.servlet.ServletException;
import javax.servlet.http.HttpServlet;
import javax.servlet.http.HttpServletRequest;
import javax.servlet.http.HttpServletResponse;

import action.ActionBase;
import action.ActionRouter;
```

```
public class QueryAccountAction extends ActionBase {
   public QueryAccountAction() {
      // this action forwards to a JSP page with sensitive forms
      hasSensitiveForms = true;
   }
   public ActionRouter perform(HttpServlet servlet,
                               HttpServletRequest req,
                               HttpServletResponse res)
                               throws ServletException {
      return new ActionRouter("query-account-page");
   }
}
```

The QueryAccountAction.perform method does nothing other than forward to the query-account-page. That action class exists because it forwards to a JSP page that has sensitive forms, which is evident from the action's constructor, which sets hasSensitiveForms (an inherited member variable) to true. That designation is used to trap sensitive form resubmissions; see "Sensitive Form Resubmissions" on page 464 for more information about how that trapping is accomplished.

The query-account-page maps to /WEBINF/jsp/createAccount/page.jsp. The main content for that page is supplied by /WEB-INF/jsp/createAccount/content.jsp, which is listed in Example 12-10.f.

Example 12-10.f /WEB-INF/jsp/createAccount/content.jsp

```
<%@ page contentType='text/html; charset=UTF-8' %>
...

<form action='validate-account.jsp' method='post' >
   <table width='450'><tr>
      ...
      the rest of this table listing is omitted for brevity
      ...
   </table>
   <br>
   <input type='submit' value='create account'>
</form>
```

The JSP page listed in Example 12-10.f contains a rather lengthy table definition, which is truncated in the interests of brevity.[8] Figure 12-16 shows the JSP page listed in Example 12-10.f.

---

8.   That table is listed in its entirety in Example 12-11.a on page 455.

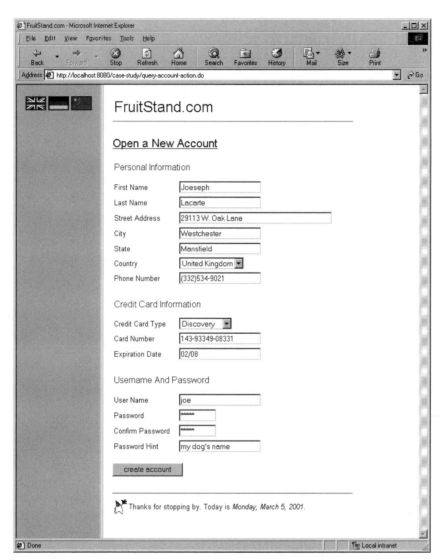

Figure 12-16 Opening a New Account

The table shown in Figure 12-16 resides in a form whose action is
validateaccount.jsp, so when the create account button is activated, the
browser forwards to that JSP page. That JSP page is listed in Example 12-10.g.

Example 12-10.g   /validate-account.jsp

```
<jsp:useBean id='form' scope='request'
                       class='beans.app.forms.CreateAccountForm'/>

<jsp:setProperty name='form' property='*'/>

<jsp:forward page='/validate-account-action.do'/>
```

The JSP page listed in Example 12-10.g creates a `CreateAccountForm` bean and
populates that bean with information from the form shown in Figure 12-16. That
bean is used to validate the form; see "HTML Forms" on page 455 for more
information on exactly how that validation is accomplished. Subsequently, the JSP
page listed in Example 12-10.g forwards to `validate-account-action.do`,
which maps to the action class listed in Example 12-10.h.

Example 12-10.h   /WEB-INF/classes/actions/ValidateAccountAction.java (partial
                      listing)

```
package actions;
...
public class ValidateAccountAction extends ActionBase
                        implements beans.app.Constants {
   public ActionRouter perform(HttpServlet servlet,
                               HttpServletRequest req,
                               HttpServletResponse res)
                               throws ServletException {
      CreateAccountForm form = (CreateAccountForm)
                               req.getAttribute("form");
      ...
      boolean errorDetected = false;
      ...
      return errorDetected ?
         new ActionRouter("query-account-page") :
         new ActionRouter("/new-account-action.do", true, false);
   }
}
```

`ValidateAccountAction` checks to see if the create account form was filled in
properly; if not, that action forwards to the `query-account-page`, which
redisplays the form shown in Figure 12-16 with appropriate error messages. If the
form was filled in properly, that action forwards to `new-account-action.do`,
which maps to the action class listed in Example 12-10.i.

Example 12-10.i   /WEB-INF/classes/actions/NewAccountAction.java

```java
package actions;

import javax.servlet.ServletException;
import javax.servlet.http.HttpServlet;
import javax.servlet.http.HttpSession;
import javax.servlet.http.HttpServletRequest;
import javax.servlet.http.HttpServletResponse;

import beans.app.User;
import beans.app.Users;

import action.ActionBase;
import action.ActionRouter;

public class NewAccountAction extends ActionBase
                           implements beans.app.Constants {
   public NewAccountAction() {
      isSensitive = true; // this is a sensitive action
   }
   public ActionRouter perform(HttpServlet servlet,
                             HttpServletRequest req,
                             HttpServletResponse res)
                             throws ServletException {
      Users users = (Users)servlet.getServletContext().
                  getAttribute(USERS_KEY);

      if(users == null) {
         throw new ServletException("Users not found " +
                                  "in application scope");
      }
      HttpSession session = req.getSession();

      String  firstName = req.getParameter("firstName");
      String  lastName  = req.getParameter("lastName");
      String  address   = req.getParameter("address");
      String  city      = req.getParameter("city");
      String  state     = req.getParameter("state");
      String  country   = req.getParameter("country");

      String  creditCardType = req.getParameter("creditCardType");
      String  creditCardNumber =
            req.getParameter("creditCardNumber");
      String  creditCardExpiration =
            req.getParameter("creditCardExpiration");
```

```
String  uname = req.getParameter("userName");
String  pwd   = req.getParameter("password");

String  pwdConfirm = req.getParameter("pwdConfirm");
String  pwdHint    = req.getParameter("pwdHint");

session.setAttribute(USERNAME_KEY, uname);
session.setAttribute(PASSWORD_KEY, pwd);

users.addUser(
    new User(firstName, lastName, address, city, state,
             country, creditCardType, creditCardNumber,
             creditCardExpiration, uname, pwd, pwdHint,
             "customer")); // customer is a role

req.setAttribute(USERNAME_KEY, uname);

return new ActionRouter("account-created-page");
    }
}
```

The new account action listed in Example 12-10.i checks to make sure that there is a collection of users present in application scope; if not, that action throws a servlet exception.

If the collection of users is present in application scope, the new account action creates a new user from the information specified in the create account form and adds that user to the collection of users in application scope. That action also stores the username and password in application scope, where they are subsequently retrieved by the login form listed in Example 12-10.k. That action then forwards to the `account-created-page`. The content for that page is listed in Example 12-10.j.

Example 12-10.j   /WEB-INF/jsp/accountCreated/content.jsp

```
<%@ page contentType='text/html; charset=UTF-8' %>
<%@ taglib uri='i18n' prefix='i18n' %>

<font size='4' color='blue'>
    <i18n:message base='app' key='accountCreated.text' />
</font>

<p><jsp:include page='../login/form.jsp' flush='true' /></p>
```

The JSP page listed in Example 12-10.j displays a message stating that a new account has been created and includes the login form JSP page. That page is listed in Example 12-10.k.

Example 12-10.k /WEB-INF/jsp/login/form.jsp

```
<%@ page contentType='text/html; charset=UTF-8' %>

<%@ taglib uri='i18n' prefix='i18n' %>
<%@ taglib uri='utilities' prefix='util' %>

<form action='<%= response.encodeURL("authenticate") %>'
      method='post'>
   <table>
      <tr>
         <td><i18n:message base='app' key='login.textfield.name'/>
         </td>
         <td><input type='text' name='userName'
            value='<util:sessionAttribute property=
               "<%= beans.app.Constants.USERNAME_KEY %>"/>'/>
         </td>
      </tr><tr>
         <td><i18n:message base='app' key='login.textfield.pwd'/>
         </td>
         <td><input type='password' name='password' size='8'
            value='<util:sessionAttribute property=
               "<%= beans.app.Constants.PASSWORD_KEY %>"/>'/>
         </td>
      </tr>
   </table>
   <br>
   <input type='submit' value=
         '<i18n:message key="login.button.submit"/>'/>
</form>
```

The login form listed in Example 12-10.k is unremarkable, except that it populates the username and password fields with information stored in session scope so the user does not have to retype them. That username and password were placed in session scope by the `new-account-action`, which is listed in Example 12-10.i.

The login form's action is `authenticate`, which is mapped in `web.xml` to `AppAuthenticateServlet`. That servlet is listed in Example 12-10.l.

Example 12-10.l /WEB-INF/classes/AppAuthenticateServlet.java

```
import javax.servlet.ServletContext;

import beans.app.Users;
import beans.app.User;

public class AppAuthenticateServlet extends AuthenticateServlet
                              implements beans.app.Constants,
                                         tags.jdbc.Constants {
```

```
public Object getUser(String username, String password) {
    ServletContext ctx = getServletContext();
    Users users = (Users)ctx.getAttribute(USERS_KEY);
    return users.getUser(username, password);
}
}
```

AppAuthenticateServlet extends the abstract AuthenticateServlet class and implements the getUser method, which returns a User object if a user exists with the specified username and password; otherwise, that method returns null. The AuthenticateServlet class is listed in Example 12-10.m.

Example 12-10.m   /WEB-INF/classes/AuthenticateServlet.java

```
import javax.servlet.ServletException;
import javax.servlet.http.HttpServlet;
import javax.servlet.http.HttpServletRequest;
import javax.servlet.http.HttpServletResponse;
import javax.servlet.http.HttpSession;
import java.io.IOException;

public abstract class AuthenticateServlet extends HttpServlet
                                 implements beans.app.Constants,
                                      tags.security.Constants {
    abstract Object getUser(String username, String pwd);

    public void service(HttpServletRequest req,
                    HttpServletResponse res)
                    throws IOException, ServletException {
        HttpSession session = req.getSession();
        String      uname   = req.getParameter("userName");
        String      pwd     = req.getParameter("password");
        Object      user    = getUser(uname, pwd);

        session.setAttribute(USERNAME_KEY, uname);
        session.setAttribute(PASSWORD_KEY, pwd);

        if(user == null) { // not authorized
            String loginPage = (String)session.
                             getAttribute(LOGIN_PAGE_KEY);
            String errorPage = (String)session.
                             getAttribute(ERROR_PAGE_KEY);
            String forwardTo = errorPage != null ? errorPage :
                                             loginPage;
            session.setAttribute(LOGIN_ERROR_KEY,
                    "Username: " + uname + " and " +
                    "Password: " + pwd + " are not valid.");
```

```
        getServletContext().getRequestDispatcher(
                    res.encodeURL(forwardTo)).forward(req,res);
    }
    else { // authorized
        String protectedPage = (String)session.
                            getAttribute(PROTECTED_PAGE_KEY);
        session.removeAttribute(LOGIN_PAGE_KEY);
        session.removeAttribute(ERROR_PAGE_KEY);
        session.removeAttribute(PROTECTED_PAGE_KEY);
        session.removeAttribute(LOGIN_ERROR_KEY);
        session.setAttribute(USER_KEY, user);

        getServletContext().getRequestDispatcher(
                    res.encodeURL(protectedPage)).forward(req,res);
    }
  }
}
```

The `AuthenticateServlet` class listed above is similar to the class of the same name discussed in "A Model 2 Framework" on page 154, except that the servlet listed in Example 12-10.m defines an abstract method for looking up a user. That servlet's `service` method stores the new user in session scope and forwards to the page that was protected in first place; in this case, that page is `/WEBINF/jsp/checkout/page.jsp`, which is listed in Example 12-10.a on page 445. Now that a `User` object exists in session scope, the entire checkout page is evaluated and the checkout region is displayed.

HTML Forms

It is vital for web applications to validate HTML forms. If a form is filled out incorrectly, web applications should redisplay that form with appropriate error messages. Those topics and more are covered in "HTML Forms" on page 60. This section discusses how the fruitstand application handles forms submissions for the create account form, which is the most complicated form in the application. That form is shown in Figure 12-16 on page 449 and is listed in its entirety in Example 12-11.a.

Example 12-11.a /WEB-INF/jsp/createAccount/content.jsp

```
<%@ page contentType='text/html; charset=UTF-8' %>

<%@ taglib uri='application' prefix='app'    %>
<%@ taglib uri='i18n'        prefix='i18n'   %>
<%@ taglib uri='tokens'      prefix='tokens' %>
<%@ taglib uri='utilities'   prefix='util'   %>
```

```
<jsp:useBean id='form' scope='request'
                    class='beans.app.forms.CreateAccountForm'/>

<font size='5' color='blue'><u>
   <i18n:message key='createAccount.header.title'/></u>
</font><p>

<% String error = (String)request.getAttribute(
                              "createAccount-form-error");
   if(error != null) { %>
      <font size='5' color='red'>
         <i18n:message key='createAccount.error.fix'/>
      </font><font size='4' color='red'>
      <%= error %></p></font>
<%     request.removeAttribute("createAccount-form-error");
   } %>

<form action='validate-account.jsp' method='post' >
   <table width='450'><tr>
      <td colspan='2'><font size='4' color='blue'>
         <i18n:message key='createAccount.header.personal'/>
      </font></td></tr><tr height='10'></tr>

      <tr><td>
         <i18n:message key='createAccount.field.firstName'/></td>
      <td><input type='text' name='firstName'
            value='<%= form.getFirstName() %>'/>
      </td></tr>

      <tr><td>
         <i18n:message key='createAccount.field.lastName'/></td>
      <td><input type='text' name='lastName'
            value='<%= form.getLastName() %>'/>
      </td></tr>

      <tr><td>
         <i18n:message key='createAccount.field.address'/></td>
      <td><input type='text' name='address' size='39'
            value='<%= form.getAddress() %>'/>
      </td></tr>

      <tr><td>
         <i18n:message key='createAccount.field.city'/></td>
      <td><input type='text' name='city'
            value='<%= form.getCity() %>'/>
      </td></tr>

      <tr><td>
```

```
   <i18n:message key='createAccount.field.state'/></td>
<td><input type='text' name='state'
          value='<%= form.getState() %>'/>
</td></tr>

<tr><td>
   <i18n:message key='createAccount.field.country'/></td>
   <td><select name='country'>

   <i18n:bean id='germany'
             key='createAccount.option.germany'/>

    <option <%=form.getCountrySelectionAttr(germany)%>/>
      <%= germany %>

   <i18n:bean id='uk'
             key='createAccount.option.unitedKingdom'/>

    <option <%=form.getCountrySelectionAttr(uk)%>/>
      <%= uk %>

   <i18n:bean id='china' key='createAccount.option.china'/>

    <option <%=form.getCountrySelectionAttr(china)%>/>
      <%= china %>

</select></td></tr>

<tr><td>
   <i18n:message key='createAccount.field.phone'/></td>
   <td><input type='text' name='phone'
           value='<%= form.getState() %>'/></td>
</tr><tr height='20'></tr>

<tr><td colspan='2'><font size='4' color='blue'>
   <i18n:message key='createAccount.header.credit'/></td>
</font></td></tr><tr height='10'></tr>

<tr><td>
   <i18n:message
             key='createAccount.field.creditCardType'/></td>
   <td><select name='creditCardType'>
      <option <%= form.getCreditCardTypeSelectionAttr(
                "Discover")%>>
         Discovery
      <option <%= form.getCreditCardTypeSelectionAttr(
                "Master Card")%>>
         Master Card
```

```
        <option <%= form.getCreditCardTypeSelectionAttr(
                    "Visa")%>>
            Visa
     </select></td></tr>

<tr><td>
   <i18n:message
          key='createAccount.field.creditCardNumber'/></td>
   <td><input type='text' name='creditCardNumber'
            value='<%= form.getCreditCardNumber() %>'/>
   </td>
</tr></tr>

<tr><td>
   <i18n:message
       key='createAccount.field.creditCardExpiration'/></td>
   <td><input type='text' name='creditCardExpiration'
            value='<%= form.getCreditCardExpiration() %>'/>
   </td>
</tr><tr height='20'></tr>

<tr><td colspan='2'><font size='4' color='blue'>
   <i18n:message
              key='createAccount.header.unameAndPwd'/></td>
</font></td></tr><tr height='10'></tr>

<tr><td>
   <i18n:message
       key='createAccount.field.username'/></td>
   <td><input type='text' name='userName'
            value='<%= form.getUserName() %>'/></td>
   </td></tr>

   <tr><td>
      <i18n:message
                  key='createAccount.field.password'/></td>
   <td><input type='password' name='password' size='8'
            value='<%= form.getPassword() %>'/></td>
   </td></tr>

   <tr><td>
      <i18n:message
                  key='createAccount.field.pwdConfirm'/></td>
   <td><input type='password' name='pwdConfirm' size='8'
            value='<%= form.getPwdConfirm() %>'/></td>

   <tr><td>
      <i18n:message key='createAccount.field.pwdHint'/></td>
```

```
      <td><input type='text' name='pwdHint'
               value='<%= form.getPwdHint() %>'/></td>
      </td>
    </tr>
  </table>
  <br>
  <input type='submit' value='create account'>
    <tokens:token/>
</form>
```

When the JSP page listed in Example 12-11.a is displayed, it accesses a CreateAccountForm bean from request scope. If the form was not previously filled out correctly, the JSP page listed in Example 12-11.a uses that bean to populate fields so the user does not have to retype them.

Next, the JSP page listed in Example 12-11.a checks to see if there is an error named createAccount-form-error in request scope; if so, that error is displayed above the form.

The action associated with the login form is a JSP page that creates the CreateAccountForm bean and initializes that bean's values according to the information that was entered into the form. That JSP page is listed in Example 12-10.g on page 450; it is relisted in Example 12-11.b for convenience.

Example 12-11.b   /validate-account.jsp

```
<jsp:useBean id='form' scope='request'
                     class='beans.app.forms.CreateAccountForm'/>

<jsp:setProperty name='form' property='*'/>

<jsp:forward page='/validate-account-action.do'/>
```

The JSP page listed in Example 12-11.c forwards to validate-account-action.do, which maps to the action class listed in Example 12-11.c.

Example 12-11.c   /WEB-INF/classes/actions/ValidateAccountAction.java

```
package actions;

import java.io.IOException;

import javax.servlet.ServletException;
import javax.servlet.http.HttpServlet;
import javax.servlet.http.HttpServletRequest;
import javax.servlet.http.HttpServletResponse;

import action.ActionBase;
```

```
import action.ActionRouter;

import beans.app.forms.CreateAccountForm;

public class ValidateAccountAction extends ActionBase
                        implements beans.app.Constants {
   public ActionRouter perform(HttpServlet servlet,
                               HttpServletRequest req,
                               HttpServletResponse res)
                               throws ServletException {
      CreateAccountForm form = (CreateAccountForm)
                                 req.getAttribute("form");
      if(form == null) {
         throw new ServletException("Can't find form");
      }

      String  errMsg;
      boolean errorDetected = false;

      if(!form.validate()) {
         errMsg = form.getValidationError();
         errorDetected = true;
         req.setAttribute("createAccount-form-error", errMsg);
      }
      return errorDetected ?
         new ActionRouter("query-account-page") :
         new ActionRouter("/new-account-action.do", true, false);
   }
}
```

The action class listed in Example 12-11.c retrieves the form from request scope and invokes its `validate` method. If that method returns `false`, meaning the form is invalid, the validate account action forwards control to the `query-account-page`, which is listed in Example 12-11.a on page 455.

The `CreateAccountForm` bean is listed in Example 12-11.d.

Example 12-11.d   /WEB-INF/classes/beans/app/forms/CreateAccountForm.java

```
package beans.app.forms;

import beans.html.NameElement;
import beans.html.OptionsElement;
import beans.html.TextElement;
import beans.html.ValidatedElement;

public class CreateAccountForm implements ValidatedElement {
   private NameElement firstName = new NameElement("First Name");
```

```java
private NameElement lastName  = new NameElement("Last Name");
private TextElement              address = new TextElement();
private TextElement                 city = new TextElement();
private TextElement                state = new TextElement();
private TextElement                phone = new TextElement();
private TextElement     creditCardNumber = new TextElement();
private TextElement  creditCardExpiration = new TextElement();
private TextElement             userName = new TextElement();
private TextElement             password = new TextElement();
private TextElement           pwdConfirm = new TextElement();
private TextElement              pwdHint = new TextElement();

private OptionsElement   creditCardType = new OptionsElement();
private OptionsElement          country = new OptionsElement();

private String error = "";

public String getFirstName()    { return firstName.getValue();}
public String getLastName()     { return lastName.getValue(); }
public String getAddress()      { return address.getValue();  }
public String getCity()         { return city.getValue();     }
public String getState()        { return state.getValue();    }
public String[] getCountry()    { return country.getValue();  }
public String getPhone()        { return phone.getValue();    }
public String[] getCreditCardType() { return creditCardType.
                                          getValue(); }
public String getCreditCardNumber() { return creditCardNumber.
                                          getValue(); }
public String getCreditCardExpiration() {
   return creditCardExpiration.getValue();
}
public String getUserName()     { return userName.getValue(); }
public String getPassword()     { return password.getValue(); }
public String getPwdConfirm()   { return pwdConfirm.getValue();}
public String getPwdHint()      { return pwdHint.getValue();}

public String getCountrySelectionAttr(String s) {
   return country.selectionAttr(s);
}
public String getCreditCardTypeSelectionAttr(String s) {
   return creditCardType.selectionAttr(s);
}

public void setFirstName(String s) { firstName.setValue(s);   }
public void setLastName(String s)  { lastName.setValue(s);    }
public void setAddress(String s)   { address.setValue(s);     }
public void setCity(String s)      { city.setValue(s);        }
public void setState(String s)     { state.setValue(s);       }
```

```
public void setCountry(String[] s) { country.setValue(s);        }
public void setPhone(String s)       { phone.setValue(s);          }
public void setCreditCardType(String[] s) { creditCardType.
                                            setValue(s); }
public void setCreditCardNumber(String s) { creditCardNumber.
                                            setValue(s); }
public void setCreditCardExpiration(String s) {
   creditCardExpiration.setValue(s);
}

public void setUserName(String s)    { userName.setValue(s);    }
public void setPassword(String s)    { password.setValue(s);    }
public void setPwdConfirm(String s) { pwdConfirm.setValue(s); }
public void setPwdHint(String s)     { pwdHint.setValue(s);      }

public boolean validate() {
   error = "";

   if(!firstName.validate()) {
      error += firstName.getValidationError();
   }
   if(!lastName.validate()) {
      if(error.length() > 0)
         error += "<br>";

      error += lastName.getValidationError();
   }
   return error == "";
}
public String getValidationError() {
   return error;
}
}
```

The bean listed in Example 12-11.d is rather lengthy because of the size of its associated form, but it's a simple class that stores form values and provides access to those values. Additionally, that bean implements a `validate` method that validates the first and last name. That `validate` method should be expanded to validate all the fields in the form, but it focuses solely on the first and last name fields for simplicity and brevity.

The bean listed in Example 12-11.d uses `NameElement` instances for the first and last name fields. The `NameElement` class is discussed in "HTML Forms" on page 60; it is relisted in Example 12-11.e for convenience.

Example 12-11.e /WEB-INF/classes/beans/html/NameElement.java

```
package beans.html;

public class NameElement extends TextElement {
   String error, fieldName;

   public NameElement(String fieldName) {
      this.fieldName = fieldName;
   }
   public boolean validate() {
      boolean valid = true;
      String value = getValue();

      error = "";

      if(value.length() == 0) {
         valid = false;
         error = fieldName + " must be filled in";
      }
      else {
         for(int i=0; i < value.length(); ++i) {
            char c = value.charAt(i);

            if(c == ' ' || (c > '0' && c < '9')) {
               valid = false;
               if(c == ' ')
                  error = fieldName + " cannot contain spaces";
               else
                  error = fieldName + " cannot contain digits";
            }
         }
      }
      return valid;
   }
   public String getValidationError() {
      return error;
   }
}
```

The NameElement class extends TextElement and overrides the validate method to disallow spaces and digits in a name field. See "HTML Forms" on page 60 for more information concerning the NameElement and TextElement classes.

Sensitive Form Resubmissions

All web applications should guard against sensitive form resubmissions, as discussed in "Event Handling and Sensitive Form Resubmissions" on page 182. This section shows how the fruitstand application guards against resubmitting the create account form listed in Example 12-11.a on page 455.

First, the `QueryAccountAction` class is designated as an action that forwards to a JSP page with sensitive forms, as you can see from the partial listing of that class below.

```
package actions;
...
public class QueryAccountAction extends ActionBase {
   public QueryAccountAction() {
      // this action forwards to a JSP page with sensitive forms
      hasSensitiveForms = true;
   }
   ...
}
```

After an action that has sensitive forms—such as `QueryAccountAction`—is performed, the Model 2 framework creates two identical tokens (strings). One of those tokens is placed in session scope and the other is placed in request scope. Subsequently, before a sensitive action is performed, the Model 2 framework checks to see that both tokens are present and identical. If that requirement is not met, the framework throws an exception; otherwise, it performs the sensitive action. That mechanism guards against resubmitting sensitive forms through a bookmark or the Back button.

The `NewAccountAction` class, which creates a new account, is designated as a sensitive action, as illustrated by the partial listing below.

```
package actions;
...
public class NewAccountAction extends ActionBase
                        implements beans.app.Constants {
   public NewAccountAction() {
      isSensitive = true; // this is a sensitive action
   }
   ...
}
```

Finally, the create account form, which is partially listed in Example 12-11.f, uses the `tokens:token` custom tag that copies the existing token in request scope to the request generated by the form submission.

Example 12-11.f /WEB-INF/jsp/createAccount/content.jsp (partial listing)

```
<%@ page contentType='text/html; charset=UTF-8' %>
...
<%@ taglib uri='tokens' prefix='tokens' %>
...
<form action='validate-account.jsp' method='post' >
   ...
   <tokens:token/>
</form>
```

SSL

In addition to guarding against sensitive form resubmissions, web applications should also use SSL when transporting confidential information, such as credit card numbers.

Two steps are involved in using SSL. First, not all servlet containers support SSL out of the box. Fortunately, it's usually a simple matter to add SSL support. For Tomcat, adding SSL support is well documented; see `$TOMCAT_HOME/doc/tomcat-ssl-howto.html` for Tomcat 3.2 final.

Second, you must specify the resources—typically, JSP pages—that require SSL. Those resources are specified in an application's `web.xml` file; for example, the fruitstand application can specify that the create account page, which transmits a credit card number, requires SSL with the following addition to `web.xml`:

```
<security-constraint>
   <web-resource-collection>
      <web-resource-name>Credit Card Page</web-resource-name>

      <url-pattern>
         /WEB-INF/jsp/createAccount/content.jsp
      </url-pattern>

   </web-resource-collection>

   <user-data-constraint>
      <transport-guarantee>CONFIDENTIAL</transport-guarantee>
   </user-data-constraint>
</security-constraint>
```

The security constraint listed above specifies that SSL should be used to access `/WEB-INF/jsp/createAccount/content.jsp`. See "Security" on page 250 for more information concerning security constraints.

Unfortunately, when this book was written neither Tomcat 3.2 final or Tomcat 4.0 implemented this feature correctly. By the time you read this, Tomcat 4.0 should work properly.

XML and DOM

It's often beneficial for web applications to handle data internally as XML, for two reasons. First, data can be stored in a Document Object Model (DOM), which is a standard data structure that is widely accepted and for which numerous tools are available. Second, XML is quickly becoming the de facto standard for transferring data from one business to another.

Using XML with JSP has already been covered extensively in "XML" on page 330. This section discusses using XML for the fruitstand's inventory.

The storefront content page is responsible for reading the fruitstand's inventory from a database, as discussed in "The Fruitstand" on page 392. Example 12-12.a lists a version of the storefront content page modified to use the DOM to store the inventory in XML format.

Example 12-12.a   /WEB-INF/jsp/storefront/content.jsp (DOM version)

```
<%@ page contentType='text/html; charset=UTF-8' %>

<%@ taglib uri='i18n' prefix='i18n' %>
<%@ taglib uri='dom'  prefix='dom'  %>
<%@ taglib uri='html' prefix='html' %>

<font size='4' color='blue'>
   <i18n:message base='app' key='storefront.form.title'/>
</font><p>

<dom:parse id='inventory' scope='application'>
   <%@ include file='inventory-to-xml.jsp' %>
</dom:parse>

<table border='1' cellPadding='3'>

<th><i18n:message base='app'
                   key='storefront.table.header.picture'/></th>
<th><i18n:message base='app'
                   key='storefront.table.header.item'/></th>
<th><i18n:message base='app'
                   key='storefront.table.header.description'/></th>
<th><i18n:message base='app'
                   key='storefront.table.header.price'/></th>
```

```
<th><i18n:message base='app'
                key='storefront.table.header.addToCart'/></th>

<% String currentItem = null, currentSku = null; %>

<dom:iterate node='<%=inventory.getDocumentElement()%>' id='item'>
   <dom:iterate node='<%= item %>' id='itemField'>

      <dom:ifNodeNameEquals node='<%= itemField %>' names='SKU'>
         <dom:elementValue id='name' element='<%= itemField %>'/>
         <% currentSku = name; %>
         <tr><td>
            <img src=
               '<%= "graphics/fruit/" + name.trim() + ".jpg" %>'/>
         </td>
      </dom:ifNodeNameEquals>

      <dom:ifNodeNameEquals node='<%= itemField %>' names='NAME'>
         <dom:elementValue id='name' element='<%= itemField %>'/>
         <% currentItem = name; %>
            <td><%= name %></td>
            <td>
                <i18n:message key='<%=name + ".description"%>'/>
            </td>
      </dom:ifNodeNameEquals>

      <dom:ifNodeNameEquals node='<%= itemField %>' names='PRICE'>
         <dom:elementValue id='price' element='<%= itemField %>'/>
         <td>$ <%= price %> /lb.</td>
         <td>
            <form action='add-selection-to-cart-action.do'>
            <html:links name='<%= currentSku + "-" +
                              currentItem + "-" + price %>'>
            <option value='0.00'>0.00</option>
            <option value='1.00'>1.00</option>
            <option value='1.50'>1.50</option>
            <option value='2.00'>2.00</option>
            <option value='2.50'>2.50</option>
            <option value='3.00'>3.00</option>
            <option value='3.50'>3.50</option>
            <option value='4.00'>4.00</option>
            <option value='4.50'>4.50</option>
            <option value='5.00'>5.00</option>
            <option value='5.50'>5.50</option>
            </html:links>
            </form>
         </td>
      </dom:ifNodeNameEquals>
```

```
    </dom:iterate>
  </dom:iterate>

  </table>
```

The JSP page listed in Example 12-12.a uses the DOM custom tags discussed in "DOM Custom Tags" on page 364 to create a DOM document representing the fruitstand's inventory. The dom:parse tag, by default, only creates that document once, so the JSP page listed in Example 12-12.a will only access the database one time.

The dom:parse tag used in Example 12-12.a interprets its body content as XML. That content is generated by inventory-to-xml.jsp, which is listed in Example 12-12.b.

Example 12-12.b   /WEB-INF/jsp/storefront/inventory-to-xml.jsp

```
<%@ taglib uri='database' prefix='database' %>

<database:query id='inventory' scope='session'>
   SELECT * FROM Inventory
</database:query>

<?xml version="1.0" encoding="ISO-8859-1"?>
<FRUITS>
   <database:rows query='inventory'>
      <ITEM>
      <database:columns query='inventory' columnName='name'
                                          columnValue='value'>
        <%= "<" + name + ">" %>
           <%= value %>
        <%= "</" + name + ">" %>
      </database:columns>
      </ITEM>
   </database:rows>
</FRUITS>

<database:release query='inventory'/>
```

The JSP file listed in Example 12-12.b uses the database tags discussed in "Databases" on page 282 to extract information from the database. That JSP file generates XML, which is used by the dom:parse tag in Example 12-12.a on page 466.

It would be a simple matter to modify the JSP file listed in Example 12-12.b to store the generated XML in a file; that modification would make that information readily available to other businesses.

Conclusion

This chapter has presented a nontrivial case study that uses the techniques discussed throughout this book; however, this chapter did not discuss all of the case study's features. To get the most benefit out of this chapter, you should download the code for this book from `www.phptr.com/advjsp` and experiment with the case study.

Appendix

SERVLET FILTERS

Note: This appendix is based on the Public Review Draft of the Servlet 2.3 Specification. That specification was scheduled for final release after this book went to press; therefore, some details in this appendix may change by the time you read this. The code for this appendix was tested with Resin1.3; see www.caucho.com *for information about Resin.*

Servlet filters, introduced in the Servlet 2.3 specification, address one of the biggest drawbacks of servlets and JSP: the inability to filter servlet output. This restriction hinders the development of many features that benefit from filtering requests, such as logging, authentication, XSLT processing, etc.

Before the Servlet 2.3 specification, the only portable way to approximate servlet filtering was with JSP custom tags; for example, you could implement a custom tag that enforces login, like this:[1]

```
<%-- At the top of a JSP Page --%>

<%@ taglib uri='/WEB-INF/tlds/security.tld'
        prefix='authenticate' %>

<authenticate:enforceLogin loginPage='login.jsp'/>
...
```

---

1. See "Programmatic Authentication" on page 271 for more discussion of the
    enforceLogin tag.

If the user has not logged in, the `enforceLogin` tag filters out the rest of the JSP page and forwards control to the login page; otherwise, the tag does nothing.

Using custom tags as filters can be cumbersome and error prone because the *JSP developer* is responsible for applying the filter (tag) to appropriate content. A servlet filter is usually a better choice for those types of tags because the *servlet container* is responsible for applying filters to content—the developer merely specifies filter mappings in the deployment descriptor. Those mappings specify one or more servlet filters, known as a filter chain, that are associated with a servlet or a URL pattern. Those filters are each given the opportunity to manipulate requests and to subsequently pass those requests to the next filter in the chain.

Servlet filters have access to their servlet's request, response, and servlet context. Filters are invoked between the servlet container and the filter's associated servlet, as shown in Figure A-1.

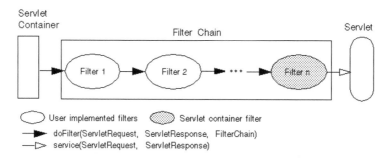

Figure A-1 How Servlet Filters Work

Without filters, a servlet container directly invokes a servlet's `service` method. With filters, the servlet container passes the request, response, and a *filter chain* to the first filter associated with a servlet. That filter handles the request as it sees fit, perhaps writing to the response, or changing headers. Subsequently, that filter can forward the request to the next filter in the chain. In this manner, the request is passed through each filter in the chain. The last filter in the chain is a special filter provided by the servlet container that invokes the servlet's `service` method.

A filter can decline to forward a request, in which case the remaining filters in the chain and the associated servlet are not invoked. In that case, it's up to the filter that terminated the request to provide an appropriate response. Filters also have access to the remaining filters in the chain, so one filter could orchestrate calls to those filters.

Using servlet filters is a simple two-step process:

1. Declare filters and filter mappings in the deployment descriptor.

2. Implement the filters.

A Servlet Filter Example

This section discusses an authentication filter that checks to see if a user is in a certain role; if so, the filter forwards the request to the next filter in the chain and the requested JSP page is subsequently displayed. If the user is not in the specified role, the filter prints an error message. Figure A-2 shows the result when the user is not in the specified role.

Figure A-2 An Authentication Filter

The first step in implementing the authentication filter used in the application shown in Figure A-2 is to specify that filter and its mappings in the application's deployment descriptor. That deployment descriptor is listed in Example A-1.

Example A-1 /WEB-INF/web.xml

```
<?xml version="1.0" encoding="ISO-8859-1"?>

<!DOCTYPE web-app
    PUBLIC "-//Sun Microsystems, Inc.//DTD Web Application 2.3//EN"
    "http://java.sun.com/j2ee/dtds/web-app_2_3.dtd">

<web-app>
    <filter>
        <filter-name>Authenticate Filter</filter-name>
```

```
      <filter-class>filters.AuthenticateFilter</filter-class>
   </filter>

   <filter-mapping>
      <filter-name>Authenticate Filter</filter-name>
      <url-pattern>*.jsp</url-pattern>
   </filter-mapping>

   <welcome-file-list>
      <welcome-file>index.jsp</welcome-file>
   </welcome-file-list>

</web-app>
```

The deployment descriptor listed in Example A-1 specifies a filter name and an associated class for the authenticate filter. That deployment descriptor also specifies a filter mapping that maps all JSP pages to the authenticate filter.

The authenticate filter referenced in Example A-1 is listed in Example A-2.

Example A-2 /WEB-INF/classes/filters/AuthenticateFilter.java

```
package filters;

import java.io.PrintWriter;
import javax.servlet.ServletRequest;
import javax.servlet.ServletResponse;
import javax.servlet.Filter;
import javax.servlet.FilterConfig;
import javax.servlet.FilterChain;

import javax.servlet.http.HttpServletRequest;

public class AuthenticateFilter implements Filter {
   private FilterConfig config;

   public void setFilterConfig(FilterConfig config) {
      this.config = config;
   }
   public FilterConfig getFilterConfig() {
      return config;
   }
```

```
public void doFilter(ServletRequest request,
                     ServletResponse response,
                     FilterChain chain)
                     throws java.io.IOException,
                            javax.servlet.ServletException {
    if(((HttpServletRequest)request).isUserInRole("resin")) {
        chain.doFilter(request, response);
    }
    else {
        response.getWriter().write("You are not authorized " +
                                   "to access this resource.");
    }
}
}
```

The authenticate filter listed in Example A-2 implements the three methods defined by the `javax.servlet.Filter` interface. The `doFilter` method checks the user's role and forwards the request by invoking `FilterChain.doFilter` if that role is resin. If the role is something other than resin, the `doFilter` method prints an appropriate error message.

Note: As this book went to press, it was expected that the Servlet 2.3 specification would be modified so that a filter's methods correspond more closely to the `Servlet` methods; for example, the `Filter` interface's `setFilterConfig` method was expected to be changed to `init`, its `getFilterConfig` method was to be removed, and a `destroy` method was to be added.

Conclusion

Servlet filters are a powerful addition to the Servlet API. Filters can be mapped to a servlet or a URL pattern, allowing you to apply one or more filters to a class of documents, such as JSP, HTML, or XML files.

Servlet filters will also change the way servlets are implemented. Instead of implementing monolithic servlets that perform many functions, you can implement servlets with a chain of preexisting filters, making servlets much more modular and therefore more extensible and maintainable.

Index

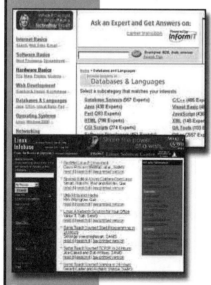

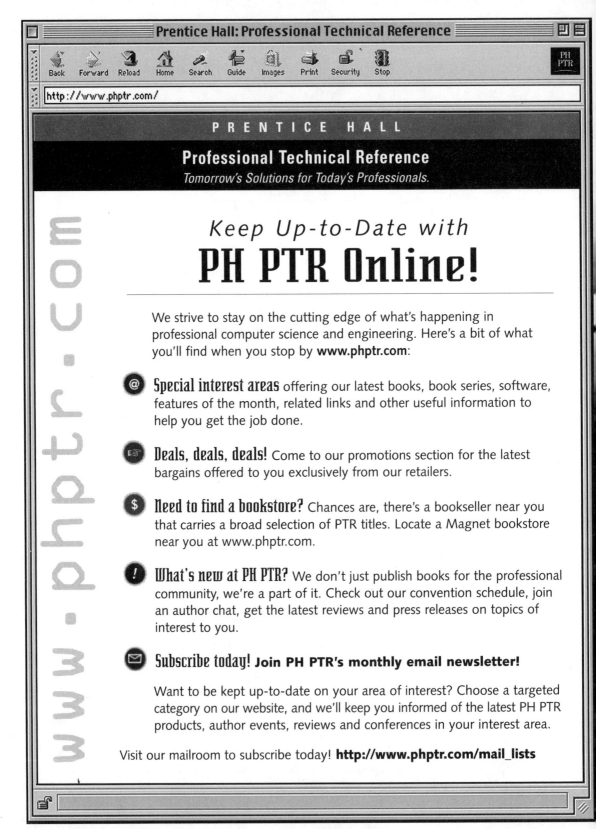